Exploring Gender at Work

Joan Marques
Editor

Exploring Gender at Work

Multiple Perspectives

Editor
Joan Marques
Woodbury University
Burbank, CA, USA

ISBN 978-3-030-64318-8   ISBN 978-3-030-64319-5   (eBook)
https://doi.org/10.1007/978-3-030-64319-5

This Palgrave Macmillan imprint is published by the registered company Springer Nature Switzerland AG
The registered company address is: Gewerbestrasse 11, 6330 Cham, Switzerland

Obsolete Program

We're programmed to compete
Against our sisters and brothers
We're programmed to get ahead
At the dreadful expense of others
We're programmed to wish
Bad luck upon our rival
We're programmed to think
That superiority equals revival

We're programmed to develop
Ego's with gigantic sizes
We're programmed to look down
On everyone who's in crisis
We're programmed to chase wealth
And achieve it at any cost
We're programmed to build walls
That help us to get others lost

We're programmed to march along
In a parade we may not even like
We're programmed to accept
That our life's a hopeless hike

We're programmed to tolerate
Hierarchies, in-groups, and strife
We're programmed to favor
A dollar over the rescue of a life

We're programmed to ignore
That we're firmly conditioned
We're programmed to believe
That we're immovably positioned
We're programmed to think
That this is all there is
We're programmed not to question
Whether anything's amiss

But if we really want
We can escape this mental penitentiary
That was a dark-aged invention
And doesn't work in the 21st century
It's time for increased awareness
To turn the tide of annihilation
And lead us onto the path
Of mutual respect and salvation

—Joan Marques

PREFACE

This collective volume was created through a wonderful collaboration of 39 authors, representing five global continents and a wide range of academic and practical disciplines. It reviews gender from the standpoints of inequality in multiple regards, such as through discrimination, stereotyping, maintaining prejudice through oftentimes longstanding, unconscious biases, industry influences, but also based on cultural, religious, political, and other boundaries. These many different gender evaluations actually affect human beings in a troublesome way in the place where they aim to perform and excel: their workplace. In order to provide a broad survey of the topic, this book consists of four parts: (I) A Historical Overview, (II) Contemporary Gender-Based Issues, (III) Gender Approaches Across the Disciplines, and (VI) Cultural Influences and Gender.

In Chapter 1, *History of Empowerment: How Far Have We Come?* Debra J. Dean and Laureen Mgrdichian review several critical movements in American culture that attempted to elevate society toward gender equality. They identify several milestones in the movement toward gender equality in America, many which have political, economic, social/cultural, and technological (PEST) roots. These authors also describe some dramatic shifts in the demographic landscape of the workplace, and subsequently discuss gender equality roles as displayed in different forms of media, thereby emphasizing the ways in which the various roles shifted in the mind of the American consumer over decades.

In Chapter 2, *Patriarchy, Religion, and Society*, Douglas Cremer takes us on a historical journey across the globe to point out the long-established binary gender identities that exist on basis of biological sex, assigning gender roles based on external sexual attributes. He clarifies that these gender identities correspond to religious, moral, and political norms in many societies, oftentimes establishing preferential leadership roles to biological males, who exhibit strong masculine traits and characteristics. This often happens with contestation from who exhibit different qualifications, such as women who demonstrate the requisite masculine traits, or biological men who do not exhibit the typical traits of paternal leadership.

In Chapter 3, *Gender-Based Inequality in the Modern American Society*, Emerald M. Archer admits that there have been significant changes in gender relationships over the course of the twentieth century, but also emphasizes that inequalities between women and men remain challenged in all spheres of life in the twenty-first century. She presents the disturbing reality of the lower pay that so many equally qualified women still receive in workplaces compared to their male colleagues, the general reality of women shouldering most of the domestic load (e.g., childcare, housework), and the persisting trend of women holding fewer executive positions in corporate America or as elected officials. Archer thereby explores theoretical perspectives from sociology, psychology, political science, and social cognition that elucidate how gender differences and hierarchies function and persist over time.

Part II of this collective work, titled Contemporary Gender-Based Issues, starts with Chapter 4, *Gender and Communication: Are There Decisive Differences?* In this chapter, Mercedes Coffman and Joan Marques examine gender communication differences in professional settings, positing that masculine rhetoric is labeled as decisive, direct, rational, authoritative, logical, aggressive, and impersonal, while feminine rhetoric is usually described as cautious, receptive, indirect, emotional, conciliatory, subjective, and polite. In highlighting myriad ways in which gender communication differences have branded men and women these authors analyze the most common stereotypical classifications of gender-related communication, provide a contemporary view on whether these classifications are myths or reality, and how they should be addressed in this third decade of the twenty-first century.

Birute Regine elaborates on gender stereotypes in Chapter 5, *The Conundrum of Gender Stereotypes*. She acknowledges that these stereotypes generally associate men with achievement, competence, ambition, and independence, and women with caring, nurturing, and concern for others. Regine stresses that these assumptions impede women's professional development, while they also impede men's emotional development, since they are forced to reject and deny any vulnerabilities. The conundrum that Regine discusses in this chapter is the fact that men need to dominate and assert their power in order to confirm gender stereotypes, while women resist and struggle to break through stereotypes. She also reveals the conundrum that emerges when we look for autocratic traits in our leaders but value a democratic work environment.

In Chapter 6, *Masculinity at Work*, Jody A. Worley first describes possible enactments of masculinity in the workplace, and subsequently explores the effects that aspects of masculinities have on the daily lives of employees in the workplace, including mismatches, tensions, and resistances such as retribution or imposter syndrome. Worley considers how these aspects of masculinity shape the organizational climate and behavioral norms in the workplace, along with the fact that implications might include behavioral, affective, or somatic responses such as anxiety and stress, aggression, adaptive or maladaptive risk-taking, avoidance of femininity and more.

An important review of the way gender stereotypes affect the marketing of the sexes is presented by Thuc-Doan Nguyen in Chapter 7, *Gender Stereotypes: The Profiling of Women in Marketing*. Nguyen provides a meta-analysis of research on gender stereotypes in advertising and content analysis of "how to market to women" in practical marketing guidelines and academic research. Pointing out the strong stereotypes of profiling women mostly as sexually attractive and young, she finds that some marketers now present more realistic female images. Nguyen accentuates that the female market is heterogeneous, and that women play multiple roles in daily life, while traditional roles are just a few among many.

Lizabeth Kay Kleintop presents us in Chapter 8, *Deciding to Be Authentic: Transgender Employees and Their Decision to Be Out at Work*, the reality of the transphobia transgender employees could experience at work when they come out, entailing exclusion from jobs, unfair work schedules, ridicule, homophobic jokes, bullying, shunning, sexual and physical harassment, job loss, and more. Kleintop asserts that transgender employees challenge norms of gender that are reinforced in interactions with others in a social process of gender authentication that may result in transphobia. She emphasizes that change agents in organizations can support transgender workers in making their decisions by understanding the role of gender in their organizations and use that understanding to create interventions, including educating co-workers, with the goal of reducing transphobia and increasing perceptions of an inclusive environment.

Entering Part III, Gender Approaches Across the Disciplines, Chapter 9, is titled, *Gender Diversity, Unconscious Bias, and Leadership for Organizational and Planetary Health.*

In this chapter, Wanda Krause and Elizabeth Hartney explain why gender diversity is beneficial for organizations and institutions. They define gender diversity in a way that goes beyond the discourse around men and women to include non-binary gender identities, cultural symbols, and archetypes, and provide a focus on the need to include those marginalized at the leadership level and at all levels of privilege and power in society. Krause and Hartney argue that the different genders come from different social contexts and experience distinctly different challenges, and thus lead in different ways. They accentuate that gender diversity is essential not only for equality but for leadership effectiveness and organizational impact, thereby enhancing psychological, societal, and planetary health.

In Chapter 10, *Working More Effectively with Non-binary Colleagues,* Wiley C. Davi and Duncan H. Spelman focus on the experiences of gender non-binary people in the workplace and provide resources to increase the effectiveness in working with non-binary colleagues. To work more successfully with gender non-conforming colleagues, Davi and Spelman emphasize the importance of understanding ourselves and how we operate within these spaces. They argue that each of us is more successful interpersonally if we first do work on ourselves intrapersonally.

Chapter 11, *Gender Equality & Gender Equity: Strategies for Bridging the Gender Gap in the Corporate World,* presents the importance of gender equity in organizations, as researched and concluded by Radha R. Sharma and Sonam Chawla. These authors particularly focus on the critical difference between gender equity and equality, and provide a variety of strategies for bridging the gender gap such as gender diversity indices, corporate governance codes, Blau and Shannon index, and gender-based legislation which have been adopted by various countries in recent years. Sharma and Chawla also discuss the importance of gender diverse boards through enforcement of non-mandatory and mandatory mechanisms like corporate governance codes and legislations.

A call for women to take a hard look at their lack of support to one another lies at the foundation of Chapter 12, *Restoring the Leadership Balance: WOMEN UNITE*. In this chapter, Joan Marques and Mercedes Coffman address the remarkable fact that women, in spite of long-term higher percentages in college graduations, and having been confirmed to lead more effectively than male leaders, only hold 21% of C-suite positions. They evaluate a series of foundational reasons for this to occur, from self-deprecation to lack of mentorship, and from excessive competition among one another to relational aggression. The chapter introduces the acronym "WOMEN UNITE" to serve as a support system for women who are eager to restore the leadership balance, and doing so in a consciously and morally responsible way.

Chapter 13, *What Hinders Me from Moving Ahead? Gender Identity's Impact on Women's Entrepreneurial Intention*, presents a compelling perspective from Eleftheria Egel, postulating that research on female innovation-driven entrepreneurialism demonstrates that the number of start-ups by women worldwide still lags that of their male counterparts. Egel asserts that this is in part due to women's lower level of entrepreneurial self-efficacy which impacts their entrepreneurial intention negatively. Using the concept of multiple identities seen from a psychodynamic perspective, Egel explores how female entrepreneurs' identity affects their entrepreneurial self-efficacy. She thereby reviews female entrepreneurs' identity as part of their multiple identities situated within their self-concept, and ultimately offers the adoption of "metaxu" as an ontological concept on how women entrepreneurs can reconcile their multiple identities and bring their best at work.

In Chapter 14, *Reviewing Representations of the Ubiquitous "Entrepreneurs Wife"*, Robert Smith and Lorraine Warren examine academic literature and media representations, and in particular gendered social constructions of the "Entrepreneurs wife" as a distinctive, entrepreneurial identity. The research these authors engaged in developed their understanding of gendered entrepreneurial identities and narratives as socially constructed. They conclude that developing a better understanding of the personal sides of entrepreneurial couples would be helpful to policymakers in understanding the entrepreneurial personality more holistically because of the financial stability that a long-term partnership brings to an entrepreneurial venture.

The title of Chapter 15 is *Strategies to Build Women Leaders Globally: Think Managers, Think Men; Think Leaders, Think Women*. In this chapter, M. S. Rao, presents an inspirational view on the skills and qualities of women, debunking myths about women leaders, and drawing a blueprint for women to fast-track their careers by equipping them with soft skills, networking skills, and negotiation skills. Dr. Rao thereby encourages women in the workplace to overcome queen bee syndrome and implores successful senior women leaders to handhold young and ambitious women leaders. He also calls upon women to smash through the glass ceiling, to refrain from shying away from responsibilities, and to stay in the game by learning and leading.

In Chapter 16, *Feminism: Legitimate, Fearful, or Feared*, Amelia F. Underwood and Debra J. Dean dive into the Bible to evaluate the role of women and the relationship between the historical context and modern-day presumptions that exist. Their review of named females in the Bible includes the likes of Bathsheba, Deborah, Mary Magdalene, and others. Underwood and Dean use their exegetical analysis to assist them in examining the modern-day role of women regarding their rights, roles, and responsibilities in society.

Entering the fourth and final part, Cultural Influences and Gender, Chapter 17 is titled, *If Iceland Is a Gender Paradise Where Are the Women CEOs of Listed Companies*. In this chapter, Ásta Dís Óladóttir, Þóra Christiansen, and Gylfi Dalmann Aðalsteinsson acknowledge that Iceland has made the greatest progress towards closing the Gender Gap, but also accentuate that no woman is CEO of a listed company on the Icelandic stock exchange in 2020. These authors find that women CEOs are more likely to lead small enterprises, and that women count for only 13% of CEOs in larger Icelandic companies. The chapter reports on the results of a survey of Icelandic women business leaders regarding their beliefs on why no woman is CEO of a listed company in Iceland and what actions they deem feasible to increase the number of women in senior positions. Responses from 189 women revealed that they feel that action must be taken, even legislative, such as enforcing gender quotas for executive positions, business cultures, and attitudes must change, women need more opportunities.

Chapter 18 takes us to Turkey. Titled, *Senior Executive Women's Views on Female Solidarity: The Role of Perceived Gender Salience*, this study, presented by Belgin Okay-Somerville and Gamze Arman, explores senior female executives' views on supporting female subordinates in managerial careers. The authors provide a distinctive approach to female managerial career development by contextualizing the study in Turkey, where several socioeconomic trends with competing influences on women's place in society are observed. Based on the findings from semi-structured interviews with 29 Turkish senior executive women, the authors posit that there is still limited evidence of support for improving women's representation in the boardroom. The findings of this study highlight the role of perceived gender salience of the context on which senior executive women anchor their views.

In Chapter 19, *Gender Quota for Workplace Inclusivity: A Mere Band-Aid?* Vartika Singh presents the case of India. She thereby focuses on the issue of gender diversity in corporate boards, with particular focus on India, and finds that women representation in the corporate boardrooms has been dismal. She stresses that this has nothing to do with merit, but concludes that gender quotas are necessary, even though they are not enough to solve the problem of workplace exclusion of women. Singh proposes solutions to make corporate workplaces more gender inclusive.

Chapter 20, *Creating Inclusion for Transwomen at Work Through Corporate Social Responsibility: The Contributions of Bandhu in Bangladesh*, presents another gender issue, captured by Enrico Fontana. He affirms that, despite their acknowledgment in 2013 as a separate gender and as they have been increasingly referred to as third gender, transwomen in Bangladesh continue to lack employment opportunities and remain among the most vulnerable segments of the population. Fontana places the spotlight on the crucial contribution of Bandhu, a human rights and non-governmental organization, to creating transwomen inclusion. In this chapter, Fontana presents an important learning tool for industry practitioners, government professionals, activists, and educators who are interested in human rights and in understanding how to better create inclusion for transwomen at work in South Asia.

Another journey is presented in Chapter 21: *Working While Homosexual in South Africa: Where Are We Now?* Prepared for this collective work by Lusanda Sekaja, Ikraam Kraft, Catherine Lötter, Nadia Daniel, M. Christina Meyers, and Byron G. Adams. These authors affirm that, while in post-democratic South Africa homosexual people are considered equal to heterosexual people, this constitutional equality does not always translate into practical equality for various reasons, in particular, religion. The authors evaluate the experiences of gay and lesbian South African employees from three empirical studies over the past five years. Results indicated that for gays and lesbians, negative experiences at work are still a reality, while religion continues to fuel stereotypes, prejudice, and discrimination.

Chapter 22, *Unfinished Business: Advancing Workplace Gender Equity Through Complex Systems Strategies Supporting Work/Family Dynamics* calls for increased balance in the lives of all genders involved in the workplace. This is where Ester R. Shapiro and Emu Kato admit that gender workplace equity remains a "stalled revolution," and suggest that work/family dynamics supporting challenges of care for the most vulnerable—children, elders, the disabled, adults experiencing ill health— need to be revisioned. They contend that gendered inequalities maintain stability through entangled forces at multiple levels, but that they can be transformed through problem-and-setting specific ecological analysis, identifying leverage points for maximum impact toward achieving valued outcomes. They thereby apply transdisciplinary cultural/developmental systems perspectives on the gendered, interdependent life-course, high- lighting shared individual, family/kin, business, and public responsibilities toward supporting work and caretaking.

Candy Williams ends this collective work on a lighter note with Chapter 23, *Men, Women, and Work-Life Balance: Then, Now and in the Future*. Williams first points out the difference between work–life balance and work–life integration. She thereby reviews married and single individ- uals, with and without children. Williams refers to the reality of a changed economy, with increases in the cost of living, and the requirements of many adults to work to support their families. She also addresses the assumed responsibility of many women to secure care of family members, which often affects their ability to advance in their careers.

On behalf of the 39 contributing authors to these chapters, repre- senting 12 nations in five global continents, I hope that this book will contribute to the dialogue of gender equity, equality, inclusion, and mutual acceptance and respect, through the multidisciplinary perspectives pertaining to gender issues and relationships at work.

Burbank, USA   Joan Marques

Contents

EDITOR AND CONTRIBUTORS

About the Editor

Joan Marques has reinvented herself from a successful media and social entrepreneur in Suriname, South America, to an innovative "edupreneur" (educational entrepreneur) in California, USA. Her entrepreneurial career spans over four decades, and includes the creation and successful management of companies in Public Relations and Advertising, Import and Export, Real Estate, Media Productions, and a Non-Profit, focused on women's advancement. In the US, she has been a co-founder of the *Business Renaissance Institute*, and the *Academy of Spirituality and Professional Excellence* (ASPEX).

Based on her impressive career and ongoing influence, Dr. Marques was awarded the highest state decoration of her home country, Suriname: *Commander (Commandeur) in the Honorary Order of the Yellow Star*, in 2015. That same year, she was also awarded the *Dr. Nelle Becker-Slaton Pathfinder Award* from the

Association of Pan-African Doctoral Scholars in Los Angeles, for her exemplary and ground-breaking professional performance. In 2019, she was awarded the *Kankantrie Life Time Achievement Award* for her accomplishments in Education from the Suriname American Network Inc. in Miami, FL. In 2016, she was granted the *Faculty Scholarly-Creative Award* as well as the *Faculty Ambassador Award*, both awarded by Woodbury University's Faculty Association.

Joan holds a Ph.D. in Social Sciences (focus: *Buddhist Psychology in Management*) from Tilburg University's Oldendorff Graduate School; and an Ed.D. in Organizational Leadership (focus: *Workplace Spirituality*) from Pepperdine University's Graduate School of Education and Psychology. She also holds an M.B.A. from Woodbury University and a B.Sc. in Business Economics from MOC, Suriname. Additionally, she has completed post-doctoral work at Tulane University's Freeman School of Business.

Dr. Marques is a frequent speaker and presenter at academic and professional venues. In 2016, she gave a TEDx-Talk at College of the Canyons in California, titled *An Ancient Path Towards a Better Future*, in which she analyzed the Noble Eightfold Path, one of the foundational Buddhist practices, within the realm of contemporary business performance. In recent years she has conducted presentations and workshops on multiple forums, such as at the Management, Spirituality, and Religion research colloquia at the Academy of Management Annual Meetings in 2018 and 2019 on *Phenomenology as a Qualitative Research Method*; a keynote address titled *Ethical Leadership: How Morals Influence Your*

Communication at the Center for Communication and Public Relations, in Paramaribo, Suriname, and an interactive workshop with thought leaders and development coaches at the Knowledge and Expertise Center Suriname, titled *On Leadership, Ethics and Social Responsibility*. In 2019 and 2020 she also represented her home country Suriname on the annual CALIFEST literary festival in Los Angeles, where she conducted workshops on successful publishing. In 2016, she presented at the Kravis Leadership Institute at Claremont McKenna College, on female leadership during the annual *Women and Leadership Alliance* (WLA) conference, resulting in the collective work, *Women's Leadership Journeys: Stories, Research and Novel Perspectives* (Routledge, 2019) in which she contributed the chapter, *Courage: Mapping the Leadership Journey*. Dr. Marques further conducts regular presentations at the Academy of Management, and at business venues in Los Angeles as well as for professional audiences in Miami and Suriname.

Joan's research interests pertain to Awakened Leadership, Buddhist Psychology in Management, and Workplace Spirituality. Her works have been widely published and cited in both academic and popular venues. She has written more than 150 scholarly articles, which were published in prestigious scholarly journals such as *The Journal of Business Ethics, Business and Society, International Journal of Organizational Analysis, Leadership & Organization Development Journal, The International Journal of Management Education, Journal of Communication Management, Journal of Management Development, Organization Development Journal,* and *Human Resource Development Quarterly.* Dr. Marques has (co)authored and (co)edited more than 30 books, among which, *New Horizons in Positive Leadership and Change* (Springer, 2020), and *Social Entrepreneurship and Corporate Social Responsibility* (Springer, 2020). *The Routledge Companion to Inclusive Leadership* (2020), *Lead with Heart in Mind* (Springer, 2019), *The Routledge Companion to Management and Workplace Spirituality, Engaged Leadership: Transforming Through Future-Oriented Design* (with Satinder Dhiman—Springer, 2018); *Ethical Leadership, Progress with a Moral Compass* (Routledge, 2017); *Leadership, Finding Balance Between Acceptance and Ambition* (Routledge, 2016); *Leadership Today: Practices for Personal and Professional Performance* (with Satinder Dhiman—Springer, 2016); *Business and Buddhism* (Routledge, 2015); and *Leadership and Mindful Behavior: Action, Wakefulness, and Business* (Palgrave Macmillan, 2014).

Joan currently serves as Dean at Woodbury University's School of Business, in Burbank, CA, where she works on infusing and nurturing the concept of *Business with a Conscience* into internal and external stakeholders. She is also a Full Professor of Management and teaches business courses related to Leadership, Ethics, Creativity, Social Entrepreneurship, and Organizational Behavior in graduate and undergraduate programs.

Dr. Marques is a member of the executive committee of the *Management, Spirituality and Religion* interest group of the Academy of Management, where she serves as the officer for Membership and Community Building. As such, she conducted workshops on qualitative research methods to global cohorts of doctoral students in 2018 and 2019.

Contributors

Gylfi Dalmann Aðalsteinsson Human Resource Management, University of Iceland, Reykjavik, Iceland

Byron G. Adams Department of Industrial Psychology and People Management, University of Johannesburg, Johannesburg, South Africa; Department of Social Psychology, Tilburg University, Tilburg, The Netherlands;
Department of Work, Organization and Society, Ghent University, Ghent, Belgium;
Department of Work and Organizational Psychology, University of Amsterdam, Amsterdam, The Netherlands

Emerald M. Archer Mount Saint Mary's University, Los Angeles, CA, USA

Gamze Arman Department of Health and Social Sciences, University of the West of England (UWE Bristol), Bristol, UK

Sonam Chawla Jindal Global Business School, O.P. Jindal Global University, Sonipat, India

Þóra H. Christiansen School of Business, University of Iceland, Reykjavik, Iceland

Mercedes Coffman Woodbury University, Burbank, CA, USA

Douglas J. Cremer Woodbury University, Burbank, CA, USA

Nadia Daniel Department of Industrial Psychology and People Management, University of Johannesburg, Johannesburg, South Africa

Wiley C. Davi Bentley University, Waltham, MA, USA

Debra J. Dean Regent University, Virginia Beach, VI, USA; Department of Business, Leadership, and Information Systems, Regent University, Virginia Beach, VA, USA

Eleftheria Egel Navigating Transformation, Female Entrepreneurship Consultancy, Muellheim, Germany

Enrico Fontana Sasin School of Management, Chulalongkorn University, Bangkok, Thailand; Mistra Centre for Sustainable Markets (MISUM), Stockholm School of Economics, Stockholm, Sweden

Elizabeth Hartney Royal Roads University, Victoria, BC, Canada

Emu Kato Department of Psychology, University of Massachusetts, Boston, MA, USA

Lizabeth Kay Kleintop Economics and Business Department, Moravian College, Bethlehem, PA, USA

Ikraam Kraft Department of Industrial Psychology and People Management, University of Johannesburg, Johannesburg, South Africa

Wanda Krause Royal Roads University, Victoria, BC, Canada

Catherine Lötter Department of Industrial Psychology and People Management, University of Johannesburg, Johannesburg, South Africa

Joan Marques Woodbury University, Burbank, CA, USA

M. Christina Meyers Department of Human Resource Studies, Tilburg University, Tilburg, The Netherlands

Laureen Mgrdichian Biola University, La Mirada, CA, USA

Thuc-Doan Nguyen School of Business, Woodbury University, Burbank, CA, USA

Belgin Okay-Somerville Adam Smith Business School, University of Glasgow, Glasgow, Scotland, UK

Ásta Dís Óladóttir Department of Business Administration, University of Iceland, Reykjavik, Iceland

M. S. Rao MSR Leadership Consultants, New Delhi, India

Birute Regine Hancock, NH, USA

Lusanda Sekaja Department of Industrial Psychology and People Management, University of Johannesburg, Johannesburg, South Africa

Ester R. Shapiro Department of Psychology, University of Massachusetts, Boston, MA, USA

Radha R. Sharma New Delhi Institute of Management, New Delhi, India

Robert Smith Aberdeen, Scotland

Duncan H. Spelman Bentley University, Waltham, MA, USA

Amelia F. Underwood School of Business and Leadership, Regent University, Virginia Beach, VA, USA

Vartika Jawaharlal Nehru University, New Delhi, India

Lorraine Warren Southhampton, UK

Candy Williams Williams Executive Leadership Development LLC, Los Angels, CA, USA

Jody A. Worley University of Oklahoma, Tulsa, OK, USA

LIST OF FIGURES

LIST OF TABLES

PART I

Gender: A Historical Overview

CHAPTER 1

History of Empowerment: How Far Have We Come?

Debra J. Dean and Laureen Mgrdichian

INTRODUCTION

Diaz (2011) wrote "gender roles were forged in colonial spaces in ways that differed greatly from those that characterized European centers since the social composition of the American territories varied dramatically from their European counterparts" (p. 207). In retrospect, one could wonder how American women evolved from the portrayal of savage indigenous creatures to the likes of June Cleaver in the 1950s and the women's empowerment movement of the twenty-first century.

Hannah Duston (born 1657) received accolades for her revenge against Native Americans. Her story is not much different than many indigenous Americans who found their family members kidnapped, abused, or murdered. The difference in Duston's story is the public

D. J. Dean (✉)
Regent University, Virginia Beach, VI, USA
e-mail: debrdea@regent.edu

L. Mgrdichian
Biola University, La Mirada, CA, USA

J. Marques (ed.), *Exploring Gender at Work*,
https://doi.org/10.1007/978-3-030-64319-5_1

perception and outcome of her choices to avenge the death of her child and her own kidnapping. Duston, a colonial Massachusetts Puritan, is now known as an American colonial heroine and American folk hero. She was honored with three statues and a mountain in northern New Hampshire. Her statue is possibly the first of a female in America. Her story was published by Puritan Minister, Cotton Mather where "he described Duston as a righteous ringleader who had every reason to convince the other captives to act" in killing ten sleeping Indians, including six children. "Mather's version of the death highlighted Indian violence to justify Duston's gruesome vengeance" (Cutter, 2018).

The following native American women have also earned their place in history. Some portrayed as vicious savages and others as peacekeepers. This small sample of history is an attempt to encourage reflection of family heritage and to seek a unified future respecting human dignity for all. Nanye-hi (born 1738) earned the name *Ghighau* (Beloved Woman) of the Cherokee. According to Kettler (2020), Nanye-hi declared at a 1781 treaty conference, "Our cry is all for peace, let it continue. This peace must last forever." Sacagawea (born 1788), a member of the Lemhi band of the Shoshone tribe, was kidnapped around age 12. She was brave and resourceful, as well as a multilingual speaker. She spoke Shoshone and Hidatsa, which proved invaluable to the expedition of Lewis and Clark. Sacagawea embarked on a long and challenging journey only two months after giving birth (Kettler, 2020). Mochi (born 1841), a Cheyenne survivor of the Sand Creek and Washita Massacres, who turned to revenge after the brutal murder of her family, was arrested in 1875 as the first Native American female prisoner. Unlike Dunston, Mochi is known as a savage, fierce, and vengeful warrior. Her accuser stated she was "a hardhearted, brutal, and cruel savage" (Richards, 2019, p. 17).

By the turn of the twentieth century, immigration and assimilation became more civil than in years past. Lerner (1975) described the typical American household in the 1920s as having marriage and traditional family values as a goal. Men worked long hours, and women cared for children and household tasks. Meleen (2006), explained "despite the image of the 1920s woman as independent and rebellious... each person within a household had male or female roles and saw the value in these tasks as a means to meet all the needs of the family as a whole."

While considering characteristics of the first women on American soil, the transformation from survivalist to domesticated leads one to wonder how it all happened. Hawn (2017) wrote "there has been a significant change in how often women are portrayed as having an existence not predicated on the home or domestic duties over time." And, just as seen with Duston and Mochi, one may wonder how many reputations have stemmed from influenced public perception instead of fact-based reasoning.

CRITICAL THEORY

Critical theory was developed in the 1920s by members of the Frankfurt Institute for Social Research (also known as the Frankfurt School). The following pioneers of critical theory drew on the work of Karl Marx and Sigmund Freud: Erich Fromm, Herbert Marcuse, Jurgen Habermas, Max Horkheimer, Theodor Adorno, and Walter Benjamin. In 1933 the Frankfurt School, located in Germany, was closed by the Nazis; however, Horkheimer reestablished the school in New York. Current day figures, including Ben Shapiro, Jordan Peterson, and Melanie Phillips, consider the theorists an intellectual group of supervillains hell-bent on undermining western culture (Nicholas, 2020). In his book, *The Devil's Pleasure Palace: The Cult of Critical Theory and the Subversion of the West*, Walsh explains that critical theory was dedicated to the destruction of western civilization, specifically faith, family, and language (2017). Walsh states that Political Correctness and Diversity & Inclusion are tools in this effort to destroy the West as we know it and calls Saul Alinsky their famous disciple. The rapid growth of such Cultural Marxism ideas on American soil points to the university curriculum, including critical theory rhetoric and their complete control of American education (Cruiser, 2015). According to Walsh, Critical Theory says, "Let's tear everything down" (ibid.).

POPULAR CULTURE AND FEMINISM

Arrow explained that popular culture was a way to brainwash women citing the 1968 "No More Miss America!" campaign and blaming soap operas for "reinforcing the image of male-dominated women" (2007, p. 214). In response, "if popular culture could perpetuate women's oppression then used in the 'right' way, it could empower women as well" (p. 214). This same argument arose after the 2020 Super Bowl halftime performance featuring Jennifer Lopez and Shakira. Brown (2020) wrote of the raunchy, sexually explicit halftime show on primetime television, watched by millions of families together. *USA Today* reported the performance as empowering, not objectifying, women, citing age and the #MeToo movement (Yasharoff, 2020). However, Franklin Graham, a Christian evangelist stated:

> I don't expect the world to act like the church, but our country has had a sense of moral decency on primetime television in order to protect children. We see that disappearing before our eyes. It was demonstrated tonight in the Pepsi Super Bowl Halftime Show—with millions of children watching. This exhibition was Pepsi showing young girls that sexual exploitation of women is okay. With the exploitation of women on the rise worldwide, instead of lowering the standard, we as a society should be raising it. I'm disappointed in Pepsi and the NFL.

BOOKS

McCabe, Fairchild, Grauerholz, Pescosolido, and Tope (2011) reviewed 5618 books spanning 101 years of American children's literature. They found an apparent disparity; whereas, "males are represented more frequently than females in titles and as central characters" (p. 207). Interestingly, the researchers found more female characters in books in the early and later years of the twentieth century; whereas, mid-century books featured more males (p. 215). The research by McCabe et al. (2011) is summed up in saying:

> Gender is a social creation; cultural representation, including that in children's literature, is a key source in reproducing and legitimating gender systems and gender inequality. The messages conveyed through representation of males and females in books contribute to children's ideas of what it means to be a boy, girl, man, or woman. The disparities we find point to the symbolic annihilation of women and girls, and particularly female animals, in 20th Century children's literature, suggesting to children that these characters are less important than their male counterparts.

According to Arrow, feminist novels "played a crucial role in the broader public acceptance of feminist ideals" (Arrow, 2007, p. 215). Cote noted the literary work of Astrid Lindgren and the 1945 introduction of Pippi Longstocking as "the most uncompromising – and uncompromised – children's heroines from the 20th Century." Cote remembers Pippi as an orphan whose mother died and father was lost at sea; therefore, nine-year-old Pippi "lives alone with a pet monkey and resists with vivacity adult's attempts to corral her into conventional childhood activities." In 1955, Beverly Cleary introduced Ramona Quimby as the American cousin of Pippi Longstocking. Cote explains the two characters were "bright beacons for little girls who have been variously told they are too much: too loud or pesky or hyperactive" (p. 40).

Many books are now available for children's literature that boldly proclaim women's liberation and female empowerment. The list includes *Born to Ride*, published in 2019 by Larissa Theule set in the 1890s warning women if they ride a bicycle, their eyes could bulge, and their jaw could clench. *How Kate Warne Saved President Lincoln*, published in 2016 by Elizabeth Van Steenwyk, refers to the investigation of an important woman who played a role in American history as she partners with the Pinkerton detective agency to uncover a plot to assassinate the president. *Rosie Revere Engineer*, published in 2013 by Chris Ferrie, is about a young girl with various inventions and a history of mockery for her imagination until her aunt arrives to encourage her.

MUSIC

Music is a powerful mechanism for influencing society. The Library of Congress notes music has served a paramount role in the women's suffrage movement. Their collection of sheet music spanned 1838–1923 and includes "rally songs and songsters written and compiled by notable composers and suffragists" (Hayden, 2020). Since the 1920s, hundreds, if not thousands, of songs were written and incorporated into the American culture to empower women to do more.

O'Connor (2017) wrote, "the logical assumption...would be to assume that the women of country music follow a similar conservative political path. However, when compared to the Women's Liberation Movement, a largely leftist political movement, we can see that ultimately this is not true" (p. ii). To expand, O'Connor notes that Kitty Wells music is an "often-contradictory understanding of the role of the housewife, as she appears prominently as a pioneer within the genre and her family's primary breadwinner" (p. ii). Tammy Wynette's music, according to O'Connor, focuses on consciousness-raising. And Loretta Lynn's lyrics "subvert what is expected of her as a Southern woman" (p. ii).

Helen Reddy's 1972 song, *I am Woman*, became the feminist anthem for the 1970s women's movement, and the one song Reddy is best known for (Arrow, 2007). Her lyrics, "I am strong, I am invincible, I am woman" contributed to her receiving the Lifetime Achievement Award for her work with the Equal Rights Amendment (ERA). Reddy's song reached women that were not part of the formalized Women's Liberation Movement. The song "was a potent, widely accessible feminist text that reached many women who might otherwise have had little awareness of the possibilities women's liberation might offer" (Arrow, 2007, p. 214).

Table 1.1 records titles of feminist anthems through the decades. With music censorship, it is astounding that such songs were allowed in the period they were released. However, this music pushed boundaries and contributed to changing American culture. Finan (2020) wrote that congress created the Federal Communications Commission (FCC) in 1934 to monitor "radio, television, wire, satellite, and cable." As examples, Finan documents a 1948 raid in Memphis where police confiscate and destroy records deemed obscene. In 1954, the Boston Catholic Youth Organization (CYO) demanded radio stations stop playing music with obscene or sexually explicit lyrics fearing the music would stir hormones. In 1955, Elvis was threatened with arrest if he continued gyrating his pelvis while performing; he was later filmed from the waist up on the 1957 Ed Sullivan Show. And, in 1955, Nat King Cole was assaulted on stage by members of the White Citizen's Council of Birmingham, Alabama. They argued such music played by black musicians was a "plot to mongrelize America by bringing out an animalism in people through the use of heavy beats in their music."

THE ROARING 20S

The 1920s is a period in American history known as the Roaring 20s due to the prosperity of the American workforce. This decade, "was the beginning of the modern era as we know it" (Amadeo, 2020). Many households obtained uncommon, even unheard-of items that most consider necessities in the twenty-first century. Such goods included automobiles, blenders, microwaves, ovens, radios, refrigerators, vacuums, and washing machines.

Along with economic success of the country, came the "first generation of independent American women" (Buccieri, 2018). Prohibition opened the door to speakeasies, which supplied the demand for music, dance,

Table 1.1 Feminist anthems through the decades

Year released	Title	Singer
1908	Take Me Out to the Ballgame	Jack Norworth and Albert Von Tizer
1910	March of the Women	Ethel Smuth and Cicely Hamilton
1923	Same Jones Blues	Bessie Smith
1924	Cell Bound Blues	Gertrude "Ma" Rainey
1924	There'll Be Some Changes Made	Marion Harris
1929	I'm the Last of the Red-Hot Mamas	Sophie Tucker
1929	I want to Be Bad	Helen Kane
1935	You Let Me Down	Billie Holiday
1952	It Wasn't God Who Made Honky Tonk Angels	Kitty Wells
1963	You Don't Own Me	Lesley Gore
1965	Paths of Victory	Odetta
1966	Four Women	Nina Simone
1967	Respect	Aretha Franklin
1967	Different Drum	Stone Poneys with Linda Ronstadt
1967	Do Right Woman, Do Right Man	Aretha Franklin
1968	Just Because I am a Woman	Dolly Parton
1968	Harper Valley PTA	Jeannie C. Riley
1972	Sisters, O Sisters	Yoko Ono
1972	I am Woman	Helen Reddy
1973	Don't Put Her Down	Hazel Dickens
1975	The Pill	Loretta Lynn
1976	Cherry Bomb	The Runaways
1978	I will Survive	Gloria Gaynor
1978	I'm Every Woman	Chaka Khan
1979	No More Tears	Donna Summer and Barbara Streisand
1980	9 to 5	Dolly Parton
1980	Bad Reputation	Joan Jett & the Blackhearts
1980	I'm Coming Out	Diana Ross
1986	Nasty	Janet Jackson
1992	Bikini Kill	Rebel Girl
1993	U.N.I.T.Y.	Queen Latifah
1993	Girls, Girls, Girls	Liz Phair
1993	Keep Ya Head Up	2Pac

(continued)

Table 1.1   (continued)

Year released	Title	Singer
1995	Just a Girl	No Doubt
1996	Guys Do It All the Time	Mindy McCready
1997	Man! I Feel Like a Woman	Shania Twain
1999	No Scrubs	TLC
2001	Independent Women	Destiny's Child
2001	I'm A Survivor	Reba McEntire
2002	Survivor	Destiny's Child
2002	I am Beautiful	Christina Aguilera
2003	This Ones for the Girls	Martina McBride
2005	Phenomenal Woman	Olivia Newton John
2005	Somebody's Hero	Jamie O'Neal
2007	Just Fine	Mary J. Blige
2007	Mother of Pearl	Nellie McKay
2007	Gunpowder and Lead	Miranda Lambert
2007	All-American Girl	Carrie Underwood
2009	She Wolf	Shakira
2011	Born this Way	Lady Gaga
2011	Run the World (Girls)	Beyonce
2012	Bad Girls	MIA
2012	Girl on Fire	Alicia Keys
2013	Q.U.E.E.N	Janelle Monae and Erykah Badu
2014	Flawless	Beyonce
2015	Wonder Woman	Lion Babe
2016	Don't Touch my Hair	Solange
2016	Tomboy	Princess Nokia
2017	Bodak Yellow	Cardi B
2017	Doves in the Wind	SZA
2017	No Man is Big Enough for my Arms	Ibeyi
2017	Quiet	Milck
2017	Woman	Kesha
2018	Girls Need Love	Summer Walker
2018	God is a Woman	Ariana Grande
2018	Nameless, Faceless	Courtney Barnett
2018	Pynk	Janelle Monae
2019	Juice	Lizzo

and alcohol. Attending those infamous, hidden party rooms were young women dressed in rakish attire. Buccieri wrote, the women "donned fashionable flapper dresses of shorter, calf-revealing lengths and lower necklines. Instead of corsets, flappers wore high heels, bras, and lingerie along with their straight and slim dress. The ladies cut their hair in short bob-style fashion and doused their faces with lipstick, mascara, and rouge."

Conservative 1950s

The 1950s was a time of cultured, sophisticated, and economically advantaged homes. Families ate dinner together and had a sense of moral family values. June Cleaver, the quintessential housewife on the *Leave it to Beaver* television show (1657–1963), was the "archetypal 1950s woman the second wave of the Women's Movement was trying to liberate" (Whiting, 2013). In one episode, Beaver says "Girls have got it lucky…They don't have to be smart. They don't have to get jobs or anything. Alls they gotta do is get married." He continues to say, "women who do not get married could do a bunch of "dumb stuff" like "become dressmakers or cut people's nails in the barber shop or take care of kids." To this, June tells her son, "Well, Beaver, today girls can be doctors and lawyers too, you know. They're just as ambitious as boys are." Hawn (2017) analyzed 1250 American television commercials spanning 1970–2016 with a specially designed test, The June Cleaver Test, to establish if June Cleaver, the perfectly dressed domesticated woman, and happy homemaker was a relevant label for today's modern women. Hawn found women were usually portrayed in domestic roles and were more likely to appear as sex objects instead of seen in occupational roles. Hawn noted, "June cleaver has not so much left the kitchen; instead, she has just updated her wardrobe" (p. ii).

Social Revolution of the 1960s

The 1960s started as a time of hope for a better future. This period is known for movements that broke barriers of preexisting social norms through media, protests, and legalities coining phrases such as *flower power* and *make love not war*. Buccieri (2010) wrote of the high expectation and confidence with President Kennedy at the helm stating the country believed they were at the dawn of the Golden Age; however, "on the contrary, by the end of the 1960s, it seemed that the nation was falling apart."

The Vietnam war spanned 1955–1975, and the United States Selective Service lotteries were held between 1969 and 1972, drafting 2.2 million American men. Approximately 7,500 women served in Vietnam. According to Veterans Affairs, 80% of the women were nurses (Aponte et al., 2015). Women were not allowed to serve in combat until 2013 (Carlisle, 2017).

Throughout the 1960s, the anti-Vietnam war movement, Civil Rights movement, student movement, and women's movement all continued to spread. In 1968, women protested outside of the Miss America Pageant, throwing items that symbolized oppression into a *Freedom Trash Can* sparking a feminist revolution (Gay, 2018). Hippies and Flower Children flocked to the 1969 Woodstock Music and Art Fair. It seemed as if most people had a cause to stand up and fight for. According to Dunn-Froebig (2006), women's liberation paralleled with the countercultural movement. In her study, she found that this period encouraged "counterculture parents with gender egalitarian values [to talk] to their children about fairness, occupations, and marriage" (p. 24).

Carlisle (2017) documented things that were off-limits to women in the 1960s. In sports, the first woman to run the Boston marathon as Kathrine Switzer in 1967. In 1972, six women were permitted to run in the New York City Marathon with the condition that they start 10 minutes before the men. In dissent, they sat down when the starting pistol sounded. While many American universities did not have sports for women, Lewis (2019) notes the first women's basketball team in America was at Smith College in 1892.

In school, women could not ask for legal help until Title IX of the Education Amendments of 1972. Women also could not go to military academies until President Ford opened training facilities in 1975. West Point Academy welcomed its first female class in 1976 (Schloesser, 2010). Ivy League schools were male-only until Yale accepted women in 1969. Because of the lack of educational opportunities, women were limited in their career options, and becoming astronauts was one role they were not eligible to fulfill until 1983 when Sally Ride became the first American woman to explore space.

Women could not sit on a jury until the 1975 case of *Taylor vs. Louisiana*. The first woman to serve on the Supreme Court was Sandra Day O'Conner in 1981. In the workplace, women were viewed as the weaker sex; they were unable to have work that needed physical exertion equal to that of a man (Carlisle, 2017). Carlisle noted that "until the 1964 Civil Rights Act, there was no legal protection for women in the workforce who were treated differently due to their gender." As such, if a working woman in the 1960s became pregnant, she was expected to become a full-time mother. This unwritten rule was not overridden until the 1978 Pregnancy Discrimination Act. A 1969 class-action lawsuit with Colgate-Palmolive and female union employees stated the women were "intentionally discriminated against by a system of job classification which deprived them of various opportunities in the plant and that they were subjected to discriminatory layoffs under a segregated plant seniority system based on the employee's sex" (Stanley, n.d.).

In most states, women could not cohabit with their boyfriend as there was a ban on unwed couples living together. Florida, Michigan, Mississippi, North Carolina, Virginia, and West Virginia still have anti-cohabitation laws (Wright, 2018). Women in the 1960s could not get a credit card of their own as most women were not financially independent from men. This unwritten rule changed with the 1974 Equal Credit Opportunity Act. Women could not breastfeed in public in the 1960s without fear of persecution. McCall (2016) explained that nursing, in general, was not an issue during the colonial era; however, once the "modern feeding bottle and nipple were invented," the act of breastfeeding declined steadily until the 1970s. A wife could also not refuse sexual relations with their husband until 1983 when most states amended their laws to account for marital rape. Legally, women could not file for divorce until 1969 when Ronald Reagan, as Governor of California, introduced the no-fault divorce bill, which was later adopted by other states.

PEST Milestones

Much change has taken place in American society on the topic of gender equality in the past 100 years. Movements have come, and some have gone, but their residue has unmistakably left an impression on the current culture. If women's rights were an industry, and some may argue that elements of it are, analytical tools would assist in understanding the marketplace and the resulting environment better. Such a mechanism could measure the impact of political, economic, social/cultural, and technological (PEST) contexts on business. These four environments are always changing, and over the past century have had a profound effect on the role of women in the workplace.

Political

Labor. Since the beginning of the twentieth century, leagues and laws have aimed at giving women equal footing in the workplace. The Women's Trade Union League (established in 1903) was founded to support women in the workplace, specifically with fair wages and to enhance working conditions. By the end of World War I (WWI) (1914–1918), women made up 20% of the manufacturing workforce (Todd-Smith, 2020). These women took on roles traditionally held by men.

Voting rights. Women gained the right to vote across the nation in 1920, with the ratification of the 19th Amendment. This same year, the Women's Bureau of the Department of Labor formed and women's causes banded together to follow their vested interests. Their approach to women's equality was not in unison; on the contrary, they became competing efforts (Blum, 1991, pp. 35–36).

Abortion rights. In the United States, it was the 1973 *Roe vs. Wade* Supreme Court case that gave women the legal right to an abortion and the opportunity to continue pursuing careers without any *unplanned* interference. The American population has never united on the abortion debate. Some view it as murder, while others view it as freedom of choice. According to Jones and Jerman (2017), abortion rates have declined since 2008, where 30% of women 45 years of age had chosen abortion at some point in their life. By 2017, this rate fell to 23.7%. It is estimated that in 2019, 42.4 million babies were aborted worldwide (Showalter, 2020).

First-wave feminism. The "first wave" of feminism spanned from 1848–1920 where women gained the right to own property, regardless if they were single or married. Women also had the right to keep their wages, sign contracts on their own, and take someone to court (Dicker, 2008, p. 6). The right to vote in 1920 was the capstone of this period.

Second-wave feminism. This "second wave" of feminism began with the release of Betty Friedan's book, *The Feminine Mystique*, in 1963. More than three million copies of the book sold in just three years. During this period the Equal Pay Act of 1963 addressed the gender pay gap, women (both married and unmarried) gained the right to reproductive choices of birth control and abortion, and Title IX improved the educational opportunities for women across the country.

Economic

War. Women reached new heights and gained significant ground in "wages, unionization, and job opportunities during the war years" (Chafe, p. 175). However, with the end of the war and the return of men, there was a shift as the role of women in the workplace was questioned, although they had proven their abilities to do the work at hand. Even Senator Harry Truman chimed in, stating that "they are entitled to the chance to earn a good living at jobs they have shown they can do" (Chafe, p. 176). Once men returned, much of the work reverted back to men so they could "provide" for their families. If a woman was working in a traditional men's role, it was thought she was taking the livelihood of another family. Many women were relegated to traditional roles in the personal service realm. Such positions included domestic service, apparel manufacturing, and telephone/telegraph communication services (Joiner & Weiner, 1942, pp. 5–6).

Recession. Throughout 1960–1999, the labor participation rate of women grew to 60 percent. Since the height of 1999, the participation rate of women in the workplace has declined. According to the U.S. Bureau of Labor Statistics, this decline is not offset with more men in the labor force. It can, consequently, be identified as a significant contributor to an overall reduction in the labor force participation rate (Toosi & Morisi, 2017, p. 2).

Social/Cultural

Unmarried women in the early 1900s worked mainly in clerical roles or as teachers. Once married, women assumed the roles of full-time wives and mothers (Barnett, 2004; Schreiner, 2017).

Sexual revolution. Birth control pills in the 1960s offered women the freedom to have sex without consequences. A shift in society's moral code was evolving. The pill reduced the fear of pregnancy, during a cultural time of "make love, not war" from the Vietnam War era, and this took a possible barrier, or excuse away to say "no" (Kotz, 2010). The 1960s launched a shift in societal views of right and wrong, morals became relative instead of absolute, and the acceptance of behavior that felt good and was not harming anyone (Drake, 1964).

Female role expectations. Debate prevails around the role and worth of women. The feminist argument is that women have equal rights on all levels in the workplace, home, and in all opportunities. The charge to ratify the Equal Rights Amendment (ERA) was born out of this philosophical soil. Schlafly (2007) proposes the amendment could accomplish the following:

> … require women to be drafted into military combat any time men were conscripted, abolish the presumption that the husband should support his wife, and take away Social Security benefits for wives and widows. It would also give federal courts and the federal government enormous new powers to reinterpret every law that makes a distinction based on gender, such as those related to marriage, divorce, and alimony.

Women of the baby-boom era have participated in a significant shift weaving together lives that include marriage, work, and parenting. It is reported that "In 1967 one-half of all women in their thirties were married mothers and full-time homemakers; by 1982 only one-fourth of women in their thirties held this traditional role" (McLaughlin et al., 1988, p. 198). This shift created a greater need for childcare and preschool options.

Women also marry and have children later. In 1960, the median age of women marrying for the first time was 20.3. This number rose to 26.6 by 2013 (Clark, 2020). According to the U.S. Census Bureau, the average age of marriage in 2018 was 29.8 for men and 27.8 for women (Jordan, 2018). And, the birth rate in American is now at the lowest point in over a century, according to Frey (2019).

TECHNOLOGICAL

Home appliances. Before the twentieth century, the bulk of a woman's day was spent doing work that modern women never consider because of technological advancements. Appliances dramatically changed lives of women globally. Automobiles, blenders, microwaves, ovens, radios, refrigerators, vacuums, washing machines, etc., have a liberating effect on women who traditionally spent the bulk of their day doing household chores. Research of Coen-Pirani, Leon, and Lugauer (2010) concludes the significant increase of women (married women, specifically) in the workplace is not tied directly to technology; however, such advances have influenced the economy and society in positive ways (p. 512). Women simply had more time available to pursue other interests.

Birth control. Advertising for birth control in the United States was prohibited in 1873 with the Comstock Act. The United States Postal Service was empowered to confiscate any such device distributed through the mail. In 1916, Margaret Sanger opened the first birth control clinic in the United States. Sanger was arrested at least eight times, charged with being a public nuisance (Larson, 1993). In 1929, Sanger's Birth Control Research Bureau was raided, and she was arrested for "giving out demoralizing information and advice" (Larson, 1993). By 1938, the Comstock Act was abolished, and diaphragms, also known as womb veils, became the favored method of birth control. In 1950, Sanger raised $150,000 to conduct research developing the first birth control pill. In 1960, the first pill was approved by the Food and Drug Administration (FDA). Thompson (2013) noted that in 1965, the Supreme Court granted permission to married couples to choose if they wanted to use birth control; however, unmarried women were not allowed the same choice since the traditional family value system encouraged virginity until marriage. In 1972, the Supreme Court announced that all citizens, regardless of marital status, were allowed to use birth control. From 1968—today, the controversy around birth control has focused on safety. Over the years, birth control devices such as the Dalkon Shield, Ortho Evra Patch, NuvaRing, and Yasmin/Yaz, have seen their fair share of lawsuits.

Computer. The rise of computers in the workplace grew dramatically in the early 1990s. By 1993 nearly fifty percent of employees were working on computers (Weinberg, 2000, p. 290). Weinberg proposes the increase in the use of computers had a restructuring effect. It diminished the emphasis on physical ability, which opened the door to higher demand for female workers (p. 305).

Demographic Landscape of the Workplace

Shifts in the Demographic Landscape of the Workplace

Much has changed in the workplace over the last century. Women in the 1950s were usually homemakers (once they married), and if they were in the workplace, they had lower-paying jobs traditionally categorized as "helper" positions (secretaries, teachers, service industries, etc.). By 2008, women were contributors to approximately 45% of their total family income (Hartmann, 2008, p. 2). According to the Center for American

Progress "64.2% of mothers were primary, sole, or co-breadwinners for their families" in 2017 (Seeberger, 2019).

Between 1940 and 1999, there was an increase in the number of women in the workforce (Toossi, 2002, p. 15). In looking at the total pool of men and women workers in 1950, women made up 34 percent of the workplace. This number grew to 46.5 percent by 2000 and is projected to increase to 47.2 by 2024 (Toosi & Morisi, 2017). Although women make up nearly half of the workforce, barriers still exist between women and executive positions (Schwanke, 2013). The number of female CEOs running America's largest companies has hit an all-time high with 37 women at the helm in the Fortune 500 (Henchliffe, 2020).

Shifts in Gender Positions of Power

Progress in women rising to positions of power has not kept up with the growing number of women in the workplace despite the fact that women have outearned men in bachelor's degrees since 1982, master's degrees since 1987, and doctorate degrees since 2006 (Perry, 2013). Although more women have achieved mid-management positions of power they are still underrepresented in executive positions. Schwanke (2013) advocates there is confusion due to media and cultural references showing far more women in executive positions than what is taking place (p. 1). Jordan (2019) proposes that the #MeToo movement could continue this stall in women achieving higher positions of power as mentoring is often a necessary component to progressing into executive positions. This movement is one that could cause reluctance for men to mentor capable women because of fear that a situation may come up within the mentorship where they are falsely accused of sexual harassment (p. 1).

Diekman and Eagly (2000) explain that social role theory recognizes stereotypes as a barometer of expectations and claim gender stereotypes are dynamic, and culture embeds new expectations for gender roles (p. 1172). The authors identified "the belief that women's personality, cognitive, and physical attributes will continue to become more like those of men should increase women's access to male-dominated roles and to socialization and training opportunities that will allow them to assume these roles" (p. 1186).

Eagly and Karau (2002) expanded on social role theory introducing role congruity theory of prejudice and evaluated how discrimination stands in the way of women acquiring exclusive executive positions (p. 573) noting the following:

- "Women were less effective than men to the extent that leadership positions were male-dominated.
- Female leaders became less effective relative to male leaders as the proportion of male subordinates increased.
- The greater the proportion of men among the raters, the less was the effectiveness of women relative to men.
- Women were substantially less effective than men in military organizations (a traditionally masculine environment) but modestly more effective than men in organizations in the domains of education, government, and social service.
- Women fared particularly well in effectiveness, relative to men, in middle-level leadership positions, as opposed to line or supervisory positions" (p. 586).

As shown throughout this chapter, powerful forces are at play with regard to the role of women in the home, at work, and in society. Reflection of how American women emerged from savage warrior, to quintessential housewife, to modern-day leader demonstrates that women are able to change. Now, the focus should be on the role(s) women desire in the future as a strategic plan is put in place to fulfill the mission. For some, it may be a return to the domesticated housewife. And, for others, it may include a seat at the head of a Fortune 500 table.

Chapter Takeaways

Critical theory demonstrates intentionality to change the future. In this case, the purpose for change was to first domesticate the savage survivalist into the modern housewife and then transform the quintessential woman into a sexual artifact. This chapter reviewed the political, economic, social/cultural, and technological (PEST) roots of the women's liberation movements. Additionally, this text examined the impact of media from a critical theory point of view with respect to the advancement of equality for women. While it is clear the movement has progressed, it is unclear if all agree on the desired outcome of feminist expectations for the future. To move forward with more intention in a purposeful movement it is recommended that we take a step back and reflect on the roles of men and women in the past to carefully craft the vision for the future.

REFERENCES

Amadeo, K. (2020). *The economy in the 1920s and what caused the great depression.* Retrieved from https://www.thebalance.com/roaring-twenties-4060511/.

Aponte, M., Balfour, F., Garin, T., Glasgow, D., Lee, T., Thomas, E., & Williams, K. (2015). *The past, present, and future of women veterans.* Retrieved from https://www.va.gov/vetdata/docs/SpecialReports/Women_Veterans_2015_Final.pdf/.

Arrow, M. (2007). It has become my personal anthem: 'I am woman', popular culture and 1970s feminism. *Australian Feminist Studies, 22*(53), 213–230. https://doi.org/10.1080/08164640701361774.

Barnett, R. C. (2004). Preface: Women and work: Where are we, where did we come from, and where are we going? *Journal of Social Issues, 60*(4), 667–674. Retrieved from https://doi-org.ezproxy.biola.edu/10.1111/j.0022-4537.2004.00378.x/.

Blum, L. M. (1991). *Between feminism and labor: The significance of the comparable worth movement.* Berkeley: University of California Press. Retrieved from http://ark.cdlib.org/ark:/13030/ft3b69n89t/.

Brown, M. (2020). *Why are we so shocked by the latest sexually charged halftime show?* Retrieved from https://www.christianpost.com/voices/why-are-we-so-shocked-by-the-latest-sexually-charged-halftime-show.html/.

Buccieri, P. (2010). *The 1960s history.* Retrieved from https://www.history.com/topics/1960s/1960s-history/.

Buccieri, P. (2018). *Flappers.* Retrieved from https://www.history.com/topics/roaring-twenties/flappers/.

Carlisle, S. (2017). *20 astonishing things that were off-limits to women in 1960.* Retrieved from https://newravel.com/uncategorized/astonishing-things-off-limits-women-1960/3/.

Chafe, W. H. (1972). *The American woman: Her changing social, economic, and political roles, 1920—1970.* New York: Oxford University Press.

Clark. (2020). Status of women in the states. *statusofwomendata.org.* Retrieved from https://statusofwomendata.org/explore-the-data/reproductive-rights/#section-4.

Coen-Pirani, D., Leon, A., & Lugauer, S. (2010). The effect of household appliances on female labor force participation: Evidence from microdata. *Labour Economics, 17*(3), 503–513. Retrieved from https://doi.org/10.1016/j.labeco.2009.04.008.

Cote, R. V. (2020). *How Ramona Quimby taught a generation of girls to embrace brashness*. Retrieved from https://lithub.com/how-ramona-quimby-taught-a-generation-of-girls-to-embrace-brashness/.

Cruiser, S. (2015). *The Frankfurt School, critical theory and how America fell victim to Europe's progressive ideas*. Retrieved from https://www.youtube.com/watch?v=A0KwdtCmvWg/.

Cutter, B. (2018). *The gruesome story of Hannah Duston, whose slaying of Indians made her an American folk "hero"*. Retrieved from https://www.smithsonianmag.com/history/gruesome-story-hannah-duston-american-col onist-whose-slaying-indians-made-her-folk-hero-180968721/.

Diaz, M. (2011). Native American women and religion in the american colonies: Textual and visual traces of an imagined community. *Legacy: A Journal of American Women Writers, 28*(2), 205–231. https://doi.org/10.5250/legacy.28.2.0205.

Dicker, R. C. (2008). *A history of U.S. feminisms*. Retrieved from https://ebo okcentral.proquest.com/lib/biola-ebooks/reader.action?docID=679800& ppg=12/.

Diekman, A. B., & Eagly, A. H. (2000). Stereotypes as dynamic constructs: Women and men of the past, present, and future. *Society for Personality and Social Psychology, 26*(10), 1171–1188.

Drake, E. (1964). The second sexual revolution. *Time Magazine, 83*(4).

Dunn-Froebig, E. (2006). *All grown up: How the counterculture affected its flower children* (Order No. EP40868). Available from ProQuest Dissertations & Theses Global (1550007181). Retrieved from http://eres.regent.edu:2048/login?url=https://search-proquest-com.ezproxy.regent.edu/docview/1550007181?accountid=13479/.

Eagly, A. H., & Karau, S. J. (2002). Role congruity theory of prejudice toward female leaders. *Psychological Review, 109*(3), 573–598.

Finan, C. (2020). *Music censorship in America*. Retrieved from https://ncac.org/resource/music-censorship-in-america-an-interactive-timeline/.

Frey, W. (2019). *With birth rates down, U.S. had slowest growth rate in a century*. Retrieved from https://www.politico.com/news/2019/12/30/with-births-down-us-had-slowest-growth-rate-in-a-century-091184.

Gay, R. (2018). *Fifty years ago, protesters took on the Miss America Pageant and electrified the feminist movement*. Retrieved from https://www.smithsoni anmag.com/history/fifty-years-ago-protestors-took-on-miss-america-pageant-electrified-feminist-movement-180967504/.

Graham, F. (2020). *Franklin Graham: February 2 Facebook post*. Retrieved from https://www.facebook.com/FranklinGraham/posts/3027376090651885/.

Hartmann, H. (2008). The impact of the current economic downturn on women: Testimony to Joint Economic Committee. *Institute for Women's Policy Research*. Retrieved from https://www.jec.senate.gov/public/_cache/files/2dbf7c2a-41d0-4502-a272-8208df674f79/hartmann-testimonyimpact ofecondownturnonwomen6608withcharts.pdf/.

Hawn, A. (2017). *Escaping June Cleaver: The domestication of women through advertising.*

Hayden, C. (2020). *Music in the women's suffrage movement: Articles and essays: Women's suffrage in sheet music: Digital Collections: Library of Congress.* Retrieved from https://www.loc.gov/collections/womens-suffrage-sheet-music/articles-and-essays/music-in-the-womens-suffrage-movement/.

Henchliffe, E. (2020). *The number of female CEOs in the Fortune 500 hits an all-time record.* Retrieved from https://fortune.com/2020/05/18/women-ceos-fortune-500-2020/.

Joiner, M. A. & Weiner, C. M. (1942). Employment of women in war production. *Social Security Bulletin.* Retrieved from https://www.ssa.gov/policy/docs/ssb/v5n7/v5n7p4.pdf/.

Jones, R. K., & Jerman, J. (2017). Population group abortion rates and lifetime incidence of abortion: United States, 2008–2014. *American Journal of Public Health, 107*(12), 1904–1909.

Jordan, J. (2018). *U.S. Census Bureau releases 2018 families and living arrangements tables.* Retrieved from https://www.census.gov/newsroom/press-rel eases/2018/families.html.

Jordan, S. (2019). #MeToo movement brings to light gender disparity in positions of power. *UWIRE Text* (p. 1). Retrieved from https://link-gale-com.ezproxy.biola.edu/apps/doc/A577566254/AONE?u=biola_main&sid=AONE&xid=eaa74a65/.

Kettler, S. (2020). *5 Powerful and influential native American women.* Retrieved from https://www.biography.com/news/famous-native-american-women-nat ive-american-heritage-month/.

Kotz, D. (2010). Birth control pill turns 50: 7 ways it changed lives. *U.S. News & World Report.* Retrieved from https://health.usnews.com/health-news/womens-health/articles/2010/05/07/birth-control-pill-turns-50-7-ways-it-changed-lives/.

Larson, J. E. (1993). "women understand so little, they call my good nature 'deceit'": A feminist rethinking of seduction. *Columbia Law Review, 93*(2), 374–472. https://doi.org/10.2307/1123051.

Lerner, W. (1975). *Historical statistics of the United States: Colonial times to 1970.* Retrieved from https://www.census.gov/history/pdf/histstats-col onial-1970.pdf/.

Lewis, J. J. (2019). *A timeline of women's basketball history 1891 to present.* Retrieved from https://www.thoughtco.com/history-of-womens-basketball-in-america-3528489/.

McCabe, J., Fairchild, E., Grauerholz, L., Pescosolido, B. A., & Tope, D. (2011). Gender in twentieth-century children's books: Patterns of disparity in titles and central characters. *Gender and Society, 25*(2), 197–226.

McCall, S. (2016). *Nursing in public: What US mothers faced from colonial times until today*. Retrieved from https://breastfeedingusa.org/content/art icle/nursing-public-what-us-mothers-faced-colonial-times-until/.

McLaughlin, S. D., Melber, B. D., Billy, J. O. G., Zimmerle, D. M., Winges, L. D., & Johnson, T. R. (1988). *The changing lives of American women*. Chapel Hill: The University of North Carolina Press.

Meleen, M. (2006). *Family life in the 1920s*. Retrieved from https://family.lov etoknow.com/about-family-values/family-life-1920s/.

Nicholas, T. (2020). *Horkheimer, Adorno and critical theory explained*. Retrieved from Horkheimer, Adorno and Critical Theory Explained.

O'Connor, F. (2017). *You ain't woman enough: Country music and the women's liberation movement*. Retrieved from https://ses.library.usyd.edu.au/bitstr eam/handle/2123/17815/FlynnO%27Connor-YouAin%27tWomanEnough-AmericanStudiesHonoursThesis.pdf?sequence3&isAllowed=y/.

Perry, M. (2013). Stunning college degree gap: Women have earned almost 10 million more college degrees than men since 1982. Retrieved December 23, 2020, from https://www.aei.org/carpe-diem/stunning-college-degree-gap-women-have-earned-almost-10-million-more-college-degrees-than-men-since-1982/.

Richards, O. G. (2019). *Native American women in non-traditional roles* (Order No. 13862014). Available from ProQuest Dissertations & Theses Global. (2242582947). Retrieved from http://eres.regent.edu:2048/login?url=://search-proquest-com.ezproxy.regent.edu/docview/2242582947?accountid=13479/.

Schlafly, P. (2007). Equal rights for women: Wrong then, wrong now. *Los Angeles Times*. Retrieved from https://www.latimes.com/la-op-schafly8apr08-story.html.

Schloesser, K. (2010). *The first women of West Point*. Retrieved from https://www.army.mil/article/47238/the_first_women_of_west_point/.

Schreiner, E. (2017). The jobs of women during the 1900s. *Career Trend*. Retrieved from https://careertrend.com/the-jobs-of-women-during-the-1900s-13654664.html.

Schwanke, D. (2013). Barriers for women to positions of power: How societal and corporate structures, perceptions of leadership and discrimination restrict women's advancement to authority. *Earth Common Journal, 3*(2). Retrieved from http://www.inquiriesjournal.com/a?id=864/.

Seeberger, C. (2019). *Nearly two-thirds of mothers continue to be family bread-winners, black mothers are far more likely to be breadwinners*. Retrieved from https://www.americanprogress.org/press/release/2019/05/10/469660/release-nearly-two-thirds-mothers-continue-family-breadwinners-black-mot hers-far-likely-breadwinners/.

Showalter, B. (2020). *42.4M babies killed by abortion in 2019; here's what's ahead for US abortion laws in 2020*. Retrieved from https://www.christianpost. com/news/424-million-babies-killed-by-abortion-2019-heres-whats-ahead-for-us-abortion-laws-in-2020.html.

Stanley, T. (n.d.). Thelma Bowe et al., Plaintiffs, Appellees, v. Colgate-Palmolive Company et al., Defendants-appellants. Thelma Bowe et al., Plaintiffs-appellants, v. Colgate-Palmolive Company et al., Defendants-appellees. Thelma Bowe et al., Plaintiffs-appellees, v. Colgate-Palmolive Company et al., Defendant-appellee, And international Chemical Workers Union, Local No. 15, Defendant-appellant. Georgianna Sellers et al., Plaintiffs-appellants, v. Colgate Palmolive Company et al., Defendants-appellees, 416 F.2d 711 (7th Cir. 1969). Retrieved from https://law.justia.com/cases/federal/appellate-courts/F2/416/711/401373/.

Thompson, K. M. J. (2013). *A brief history of birth control in the U.S.* Retrieved from https://www.ourbodiesourselves.org/book-excerpts/health-article/a-brief-history-of-birth-control/.

Todd-Smith, L. (2020). An Overview 1920–2020. Retrieved December 24, 2020, from https://www.dol.gov/agencies/wb/about/history.

Toosi, M., & Morisi, T. L. (2017). BLS spotlight on statistics: Women in the Workforce before, during, and after the great recession. *U.S. Bureau of Labor and Statistics*. https://digitalcommons.ilr.cornell.edu/cgi/viewcontent.cgi?article=2952&context=key_workplace/.

Toossi, M. (2002, May). A century of change: The U.S. labor force, 1950–2050. *Monthly Labor Review*, pp. 15–28.

Walsh, M. (2017). *The devils pleasure palace: The cult of critical theory and the subversion of the West*. New York: Encounter Books.

Weinberg, B. A. (2000). Computer use and the demand for female workers. *Industrial and Labor Relations Review, 53*(2), 290–308. Retrieved from https://doi.org/10.1177/001979390005300206/.

Whiting, S. (2013). *In defense of June Cleaver*. Retrieved from https://www.womenshistory.org/articles/defense-june-cleaver/.

Wright, S. (2018). *How does the law permit marital status discrimination in housing?* Retrieved from https://www.unmarried.org/housing/.

Yasharoff, H. (2020). *JLo and Shakira's Super Bowl halftime performance was empowering, not objectifying. Here's why*. Retrieved from https://www.usatoday.com/story/entertainment/celebrities/2020/02/03/super-bowl-halftime-why-jennifer-lopez-shakiras-performance-empowering/4643848002/.

CHAPTER 2

Patriarchy, Religion, and Society

Douglas J. Cremer

INTRODUCTION

Patriarchy is an ancient social form, arising in several areas of the world between **2500** and **5000** years ago. As defined by Gerda Lerner in *The Creation of Patriarchy*, it is "the appropriation by men of women's sexual and reproductive capacity," as well as their productive labor, occurring "prior to the formation of private property and class society" and the founding of the political state, which had an "essential interest in the maintenance of the patriarchal family" (Lerner, 1986, pp. 8–10). It is the prior social claim on some people, by virtue of being identified and classed as women, usually based on external physical differences, to provide support, material, emotional, physical, or sexual, to those identified and classed as men, again based on external physical differences. Past and current tribal organizations and clan lineages, whether in domestic agricultural domains or in nomadic pastoral regions, are almost universally marked by patriarchal and patrilineal social and gender structures, the few matriarchal or matrilineal exceptions standing out for their infrequency. Whether one looks east or west, north or south, one finds the

D. J. Cremer (✉)
Woodbury University, Burbank, CA, USA
e-mail: Douglas.Cremer@woodbury.edu

© The Author(s), under exclusive license to Springer Nature Switzerland AG 2021
J. Marques (ed.), *Exploring Gender at Work*,
https://doi.org/10.1007/978-3-030-64319-5_2

"rule of fathers" as masters of the household established before what anyone would recognize as organized, urban civilization, and definitively established by the time such civilizations arise. The primacy of fathers, of mature men (for age is one component of patriarchy) with control of wealth, whether in land or livestock, came to dominate women, as well as subordinate men, establishing hierarchical familial and political power over them, primarily harnessing and controlling women's (and often other men's) domestic production and sexual reproduction by means of social norms, law codes, and religious authority. Economic dependency, class privileges, and brute force were employed to enforce this patriarchal order for millennia. A dominant male as master of the household and father-figure, either literally or figuratively, is the focal point of the most widespread and durable form of social, political, economic, and religious organization on the planet.

One of the key characteristics of patriarchy, according to Lerner, is that these mature men establish their social and class position through control of economic and political resources. The more power they accumulate, the more patriarchal men are able to dominate subordinate men and virtually all women. These same women then owe their social and class position to their fathers, brothers, husbands, and sons. Women's access to power and security is thus mediated by their connections to the men in their lives. Those that are attached to the appropriate men are deemed respectable; those who are not so attached are therefore not respectable (Lerner, 1986, p. 10). In effect, as Simone de Beauvoir argued in *The Second Sex*, women in a patriarchal society become defined as weaker or lesser in relation to rise of masculine categories of mastery, assertion, and dominance (de Beauvoir, 1989, p. 34). Men as the masters of the households create the categories of power through which women's relative value (and the value of subordinate men) is then determined. Patriarchy is not simply the rule of men functioning as fathers; it is the rule of dominant elite males (literally, exercising the authority of fathers as patriarchy constructs it) over all others, women and men, enslaved and free, gender conforming or not, all included in a system of hegemonic values and rules crafted to perpetuate this patriarchal power.

Patriarchy enforces its codes and values through a combination of sexism, misogyny, and paternalism. Sexism, "the branch of patriarchal ideology that *justifies* and *rationalizes* a patriarchal social order," and misogyny, "the system that *polices* and *enforces*" patriarchy's "governing norms and expectations" are two closely interrelated means of perpetuating patriarchy (Manne, 2018, p. 20). Paternalism, "the interference of a state or an individual with another person, against their will, and defended or motivated by a claim that the person interfered with will be better off or protected from harm" is a closely related process wherein patriarchy is enacted (Dworkin, 2020). All three act in distinctive ways to justify, enforce, and enact patriarchal society, often with religious support and institutionalization.

Sexism, as defined by Kate Manne in *Down Girl* (2018), is the ideology and science of patriarchy, the set of values and assumptions about female–male difference that justifies patriarchy and provides the rational arguments for its implementation. Sexism elevates the social and relational value of the biological differences between women and men to seemingly natural functional and affective differences. Mildly developed, especially in religious language, as complementarianism (think mommy and daddy), or radically defended as absolute difference (think Venus and Mars), sexism posits that the differences between women and men is part of a functional duality in which the strengths of one complements the weakness of the other, all as part of a divine plan that established a human division of labor: women as communal receivers, nurturing rearers of children, harvesters of domestic production, and emotional supporters of men; men as individual agents, protectors of women and children, hunters of wild game, and rational decision-makers and planners. Some defenders of complementarianism argue that it does not necessitate hierarchical power relations, that these different roles can be seen as a balanced, mutual, and equitable sharing of responsibilities, but the very way in which the roles are structured aligns more closely to those who see a radical difference between the very natures of women and men.

Misogyny, also according to Manne, is patriarchy's enforcement mechanism and morality. Misogyny is what patriarchy does, how it attacks, belittles, and blocks women from asserting equality, power, and authority. Fundamentally, misogynistic actions threaten women who fail to fulfill the expectations of patriarchal society, who refuse to play the dutiful supportive spouse, the unassertive and supportive employee, or the deferential and receptive leader, on the rare occasion when women are allowed access to leadership roles. Misogynistic threats call out women who choose to violate the gender and behavioral norms of patriarchal society, making an effort to put them back in their proper place. Policing role norms in patriarchal society is the core function of misogyny, which may be applied indirectly, training younger men in their proper behaviors through attacking nonconforming women and subordinate men. Not all objects of misogynistic attacks, therefore, are women. Misogyny, coupled with homophobia, is often used to separate boys from their childhood, making them appropriately masculine in their objectification and derision of women and gay men (Gilligan & Richards, 2018, pp. 25–26).

Paternalism, the view that "father knows best," is the third way patriarchy justifies itself ideologically. Gerald Dworkin defines it as the underlying assumption of paternalism is that the object of paternalistic action is less than fully rational and/or capable of self-direction and decision-making (Dworkin, 2020). Paternalism denies equity and emancipation precisely because it is based on a "presumptive claim to a superior understanding of the subject's best interests than the subject may possess him- or herself" (Jackman, 1994, p. 12). The transparent assertion is that such people require the intervention of a father-figure in areas of their lives in which they do not have independent authority. This ideology aligns well with patriarchy in that women and subordinate men are consigned to these categories by their status as support personnel for dominant males in patriarchal society. Not only are gender roles reinforced by paternalist actions, so too is the hierarchical relationship between provider and receiver, stronger and weaker, more or less rational, enacted and reinforced.

Patriarchy is also rooted in the very way gender is conceived, as the polarity of masculinity and femininity; "the splitting of reason from emotion and the elevation of mind over body," elevates the "hierarchy of patriarchy, that privilege the masculine (reason and mind) over the feminine (emotion and body)," and "dims our ethical intelligence" (Gilligan & Richards, 2018, p. 3). People who are trans, nonbinary, genderqueer, or otherwise gendered are obscured from view, reduced in power and status, and often compelled to adopt an identity that is binary gender conforming in order to access resources and protections within the patriarchal system. These identities are reinforced through honor codes, shaming processes, and norms of manhood. A man's control over "his women" is a sign of his authority. Women (much like the enslaved and subordinate males) do not have honor in a patriarchal society; that is reserved only to the dominant men. Women can, however, destroy male honor through their own sexual behavior, "by engaging in nonmarital sex, i.e., by being too sexually active or aggressive ('unchaste' or 'unfaithful') before, during, or even after marriage" (Gilligan, 1997, pp. 230–231).

Aggression, "male bonding" through rituals of hazing and violence, and all group behaviors determined by codes of masculine performance, mark the ways in which patriarchy inscribes itself on men and women, on all people, alike.

Moreover, it is not just dominant elite males who perpetuate the patriarchal system. Subordinate men and women are not simply the victims of patriarchy. As Kochurani Abraham notes, they are often "active collaborators of a system that dominates them. Women become collaborators when they have internalized the hegemonic codes of a system which allots to them a subjugated status and transmits the traditions of this system uncritically." The hegemonic power of patriarchy creates women and subordinate men as sexists, misogynists, and paternalists. This social and ideological power is perpetuated through various forms of culture, controlling the system of images and ideas of a society in order to reinforce the patriarchal hierarchy of values. Enshrined in social mores and laws, patriarchy has especially relied on religion in the transmission and maintenance of these relationships: "when women assimilate religious prescriptions uncritically, believing that this is the way reality is defined, they get trapped by the hegemonic exercise of power." This creates a highly complex and ambivalent situation where women are both captive of patriarchal power, and also at times serve as uncritical perpetuators of the very same system on oppression, having internalized "the patriarchally defined 'feminine ideal' as a socioreligious system of self-surveillance," in which they are caught (Abraham, 2019, pp. 5–9). In both cases, the hegemonic power of patriarchy, initially placing them in the role of servant, cannot be lost to sight as it is the fundamental driving force of both their subjugation and service to it.

Ancient Philosophy and Religion

Ancient societies created many different ways to express and enforce these patriarchal values and rules. One of the earliest accounts is in the Hebrew Bible with the establishment of the covenant with the people of Israel, codified in writing about the time of King David of Jerusalem 3000 years ago. Five hundred years later, in ancient Greece, a society set in the values described by Homer, Aeschylus, Plato, and Aristotle further defined the "rule of fathers" in the Western tradition, while in ancient China the "rule of the gentleman" was established by Confucian philosophy. European culture was further defined by the growing influence of Roman law and its merger with the Christianity of the New Testament. Through the rise of imperialism and colonialism, Western patriarchy helped shape modern patriarchy in Latin America, Africa, and Asia, merging with indigenous patriarchies of their own.

The creation of patriarchal societies necessitated the overthrow of any previous social organization, assuming one existed, that was egalitarian or matrilineal in nature. Often symbolized through the worship of powerful fertility goddesses led by a caste of female priests, these non-patriarchal societies, according to Lerner, saw women "still play active and respected roles in mediating between humans and gods as priestesses, seers, diviners, and healers" in that their "power, especially the power to give life, is worshiped by men and women in the form of powerful goddesses" who are linked to agricultural and human fertility (Lerner, 1986, p. 10). These goddesses and their priestesses were eventually replaced by a dominant male deity, who assumed their power and authority. Lerner sees the emergence of Hebrew monotheism as an example of the attack on the widespread cults of the various fertility goddesses. In the writing of the Book of Genesis, creativity and procreativity are ascribed to an all-powerful God, whose epitaphs of "Lord" and "King" establish him as a male god. This symbolic devaluing of women in relation to the divine becomes one of the founding metaphors of Western civilization.

Genesis has in effect a rather ambivalent relationship to patriarchy, at least in terms of the creation narratives. Eve being born from the rib of Adam has been read as either a statement of equity (side by side), subordination (under his arm), or even superiority (the last made is the greatest made). The second reading has historically been the predominant one, where Eve is established as Adam's helpmeet, his fulfillment, and his complementary completion, reinforced by the curse after the fall from the garden of Eden, where God commands that Eve will suffer the pains of labor and, because of her desire for her husband, he will rule over her (Genesis 3:16). God's act of subordinating women to men, especially in the spousal relationship, is the original misogynistic act, punishing Eve for daring to eat of the tree of knowledge and for tempting her husband to do the same, making patriarchy the consequence sin that now carries the force of divine law.

This tension is especially enshrined in ancient Hebraic law, as found in the books of Exodus, Leviticus, Numbers, and Deuteronomy. Extending beyond husband–wife relationships to father–daughter roles, as Elizabeth Schüssler Fiorenza has noted, "in a patriarchal family structure, the daughter is dependent upon her father or brother and the wife becomes totally reliant on her husband. Thus, the woman remains all her life a minor. The Decalogue includes a man's wife among his possessions, along with his house and land, his male and female slaves, his ox and his ass (Exod. 20:17; Deut.5:21)" (Schüssler Fiorenza, 2013, p. 28). The divine law enshrines sexism, and the resulting androcentrism of the religious texts appears repeatedly in the stories of Abraham, the patriarch *par excellence*. The story of Sarah and Abraham in Egypt, where to save himself Abraham lies and tells the Egyptians she is his sister, so that she can be taken into a harem without them needing thereby to kill Abraham to obtain her, is both critically recounted (Genesis 12) and explained away (Genesis 20). These tensions exist throughout the Jewish (and later Christian) scriptures, where emancipatory and egalitarian readings of the text exist side by side with controlling and diminishing acts, yet the patriarchal interpretation often has the last word and becomes the standard interpretation in patriarchal society.

Ancient Greek narrative and philosophy contributed much to the contours and definitions of patriarchy. Homer's *Iliad* and *Odyssey*, composed in the seventh century BCE and centering on the archaic war against Troy and its aftermath, describe a society of warriors and wives who are clearly in a militaristic, patriarchal society (Homer, 2016, 2017). Dating from the late eighth or early seventh century BCE, the epic poems enshrined for generations the characteristics of heroic male actors: fury, rage, hubris, pride, and fame. Despite the fact that Homer often portrays these values in a critical manner, their preeminence in the texts established them, alongside the patriarchal narratives of the Bible, as the defining stories of generations of women and men in Western society and culture. Women such as Helen and Penelope are portrayed primarily as objects of male desire, whether in the rivalry between Agamemnon and Hector that causes the Trojan War itself or in the numerous suitors that occupy Odysseus' home striving for the hand of Odysseus' wife, who is assumed to be his widow. If women have any agency at all, in these classic poems, it is through the exercise of seductive charms and feminine wiles, the classic countermoves of subordinated women in patriarchal society. The texts themselves, often offered today to young men and women as part of a traditional education, inscribe the limited and acceptable means of resistance and agency for women writing patriarchy.

What happens when women overstep these acceptable boundaries becomes the substance of another epic set of stories from the Greek tradition. In Aeschylus' trilogy of plays, from the fifth century BCE, *The Oresteia*, the power and tragedy of patriarchy is on full display (Aeschylus, 2011). Agamemnon returns from his victory at Troy to find his wife Clytemnestra with his cousin Aegisthus, plotting Agamemnon's death for sacrificing his and Clytemnestra's daughter, Iphigenia, in exchange for favorable winds to Troy. A father's life and death authority over his children is challenged by the grieving mother, who conspires successfully to kill him. Their son, Orestes, with his sister Electra, in turn conspire and successfully kill their mother and her new husband, Aegisthus. The Furies, three goddesses of the underworld, pursue Orestes to seek vengeance for his murder of his mother. They bring him to trial before the gods, with Apollo, representing masculine reason, defending Orestes. Athena casts the deciding vote, freeing Orestes, and convincing the Furies to abandon their quest for vengeance. Reason triumphs over emotion, male authority to decide life or death is upheld, and peace is bought at the cost of the Furies power, not to mention the lives of Iphigenia and Clytemnestra. For Carol Gilligan and David Richards, "Athena symbolizes the power that women can wield in patriarchy: she is solely of the father, a girl completely separated from women, a daughter born out of the head of Zeus, who swallowed her mother, turning her into a fly" (Gilligan & Richards, 2008, p. 13). Female complicity in the enactment of patriarchy, as means to acquiring limited power for themselves on patriarchy's terms, is affirmed as efforts to obtain direct authority are repudiated.

The parallels in Greek philosophy of the same time are more than apparent. Plato's dialogues *Meno*, *Phaedo*, and the *Republic* reveal numerous sexist assumptions about men and women, most notable of which is the classic assignment of the public discursive sphere to men and the private domestic sphere to women. In the *Meno*, the title character sets the stage of the discussion of virtue as follows: "First, then if it's the virtue of a man you want, it's easy to say that this is the virtue of a man: to be sufficient to carry on the affairs of the city and while carrying them on to do well by his friends and harm to his enemies; and to take care that he not suffer any such thing himself. And if it's the virtue of a woman you want, that's not hard to go through, in that she needs to manage the household well, conserving what is inside and being obedient to her man" (Plato, 2004, p. 3). For Plato, the ascent of the soul by the light of reason, described in both the *Phaedo* and the *Republic*, was a possibility only for men, since the journey requires the purging of all "bodily concerns," something women would find difficult to accomplish, encumbered as women are by a womb and the resulting blood flow of menstruation (Mercer, 2019). To move beyond her body would be to move beyond what made her a woman, an irresolvable contradiction (that men are unencumbered by their own bodily nature and fluids never seems to be an issue). There may be rare exceptions for Plato, if the state provided equal education and training, and if individual women measured up to the demands of the roles they might play (as defined by men), but both would be exceptional cases. The norm in classical Greek society was that love between two men (particularly between one that is older—the teacher—and another that is younger—the student) is considered more sophisticated than love between and a man and a woman; only for matters of procreation and the construction of the patriarchal family should men and women come together. In the end, biology as destiny is given philosophical grounding in support of the patriarchal order.

The other founding metaphor is supplied by Aristotelian philosophy, one also based on the household as the model of the political state, and for which Aristotle assumes as a given that women are incomplete and damaged human beings of an entirely different order than men. He takes as obviously given that "the relation of male to female is that of what is better by nature to what is worse, and that of ruler to ruled" (Aristotle, 2017, p. 7). It follows therefore that men are better suited to political leadership, just as an elder male is more suitable than a younger one: "the male, unless he is somehow formed contrary to nature, is by nature more capable of leading than a female, and someone older and complete than someone younger and incomplete" (Aristotle, 2017, p. 18). Both of these claims are rooted in an assertion of a fundamental difference of character, where "the temperance of a man is not the same as that of a woman and a man, and neither is the courage or justice...but rather men have a ruling courage and women assistant courage, and the same holds of the other virtues" (Aristotle, 2017, p. 20). Apparent natural difference in ability and character ground the assertion of patriarchy, an assertion for which no evidence or argument is ever truly presented. It is simply assumed and obvious to all. It is with the creation of these two metaphorical constructs, which are built into the very foundations of the symbol systems of Western civilization, that the subordination of women comes to be seen as "natural," hence it becomes invisible. One of the hallmarks of patriarchy is its apparent and unquestioned assumption of female infe-riority, so deeply assumed and unconsciously acted upon that it is often not even open to question.

Western culture is not unique in making these unsupported assertions that the different natures of women and men create an unquestioned hierarchy of the latter over the former. Confucian philosophy, developed between the fifth and first centuries BCE, is also androcentric, much like the Hebrew Scriptures and Greek poetry and philosophy, a discussion between men mostly about men. The *Analects*, one of the classics of Confucian literature, barely mentions women at all, save for one passage where "the Master said, 'Women and servants are particularly hard to manage. If you are too familiar with them, they grow insolent, but if you are too distant, they grow resentful'" (Confucius, 2003, p. 211). The five hierarchal relationships of classical Confucian filial piety (ruler to ruled, father to son, elder brother to younger brother, husband to wife, and between friends) are all male to male relationships save for the one about wives being subordinate to their husbands. Even when more clearly elab-orated, as in the *Yili*, Book of Etiquette and Rites, women are defined only in relationship to men: "Before marrying, she follows her father; after marrying she follows her husband; when her husband dies, she follows her son" (Yao, 2003, p. 525). As in the Western tradition, virtually all rela-tionships are relations of inequality and power differentials, with women always occupying the inferior position.

The commentaries on the Confucian classics are even more explicit on the danger women represent in a patriarchal society. The *Zuo Commen-tary*, in particular, written sometime between the fifth and first centuries BCE, adds to the above passage and notes that women are "a force anal-ogous to alcohol that intoxicates men and leads them into immorality," especially in violating moral norms regarding proper leadership, as devious concubines and unscrupulous wives can lead men into making disastrous political decisions (Confucius, 2003, p. 211). The ideology of separate spheres, of distinctive public and private domains, warns of the dangers of intermixing these realms, of how feminine power corrupts male authority, and the distance created by the patriarchal structure of society is a defen-sive measure for the common good. Although public life models domestic arrangements, both thus falling under patriarchal authority, they are also to be kept distinct from each other. One of the other defining charac-teristics of patriarchy is the desire to have things both ways, connected yet separate, included yet subservient, necessary yet dangerous. In both its ancient Greek and Chinese manifestations, patriarchy is an incredibly flexible yet rigid ideology, bending to circumstances and situations and yet holding itself together as a coherent system of social organization.

The case is the same in ancient Rome. Roman law inscribed paternalism and patriarchy on its consideration of property rights, where "a key reason for articulating patriarchal rights over persons in terms of property was that paterfamilias was also the most common word for a property owner" (Miller, 2017, p. 8). While control of property was assured by law, others forms of control were more problematic, from the patriarchal perspective. Women were seen by men as both opportunity and danger, especially when it came to marriage and the creation of the family. Arranged marriages in Rome placed great weight on "the chastity and fidelity of women, for only such limitations on women's sexuality could assure their husbands that a woman's children were his" (Gilligan & Richards, 2008, p. 27). As in many patriarchal societies, fathers decided whom their children, especially their daughters, would marry, almost always to further the political and/or economic status of the family. In marriage, even when women were trusted advisors and confidants to their husbands, it was always behind the scenes. The messaging to women was clear: be attractive, but not too attractive; be helpful, but do not be seen as being helpful. Roman mothers, as women in many patriarchal societies have experienced, had to witness their sons being separated from them and at an early age trained for war, their daughters are taken from them at adolescence and married away for the fortunes of the family. These are just a pair of the ways that patriarchy in the ancient world, and in many ways to this day, ruptured "intimate relationships… [splitting] mind and body, thought and emotion, self and relationships" (Gilligan & Richards, 2008, p. 266). Patriarchy is not merely oppressive; it is, as many have noted, traumatizing in its effects.

Early Christianity was no exception to these patriarchal norms, although as in the Hebrew Scriptures, ambivalence exists, only to be overwhelmed by androcentric prescriptions and interpretations. As with the founders of other religions, one dimension of the humanity of the historical Jesus is his gender; he was incarnated as a male human being. This historical fact has been used throughout the Christian tradition as one of the ways to deny the full humanity of women, despite the fact that women were included among the early disciples, witnessed his execution, and were the first to proclaim his resurrection. The New Testament often downplays their contributions, relegating them to silence and anonymity.

In the "so-called household code texts of the later Pauline literature," patriarchy is upheld and demands "the subordination of the wife to the husband… [using] rules of conduct for women, children, and slaves [that] are not specifically Christian, but are a part of the Jewish and Greco-Roman culture of the time" (Schüssler Fiorenza, 2013, p. 35). What had existed initially as a radical movement founded on egalitarian inclusion, property sharing, and the "assertion that 'there is neither male nor female' (Gal 3:28)… was replaced by traditional patriarchy" of defined subordinate roles for women (Rakoczy, 2008, p. 140).

The ascendancy of Late Roman patriarchy within Christianity is captured by the work of Augustine of Hippo in the fourth century CE. In a manner similar to the Confucian suspicion of women, he wrote to his friend Laetus that he ought to "watch out that she does not twist and turn you for the worse. What difference does it make whether it is in a wife or in a mother, provided we nonetheless avoid Eve in any woman?" (Augustine, 2005, p. 168). Women are generally a source of temptation for Augustine, well-known as he is for his struggles with concupiscence or sexual desire. The original woman, Eve, and her role in the story of Genesis was also much on his mind. Augustine could not comprehend even how Eve was to be a helper for Adam, unless it was through procreation: "If woman is not given to man for help in bearing children, for what help could she be? To till the earth together? If help were needed for that, man would have been a better help for man" (Augustine, 1982, p. 75). One might be tempted to excuse these comments as the typical prejudice of the age, yet Augustine remains one of the most influential of early Christian writers. In effect, he found little useful in women, arguing that they could provide small "comfort in solitude. How much more pleasure is it for life and conversation when two friends live together than when a man and a woman cohabitate?" (Augustine, 1982, p. 75). The diminution of women in the patriarchy of late antiquity to a role only in procreation, and otherwise either useless or a danger, has had serious consequences for the construction of patriarchy into modernity.

The overall tradition set by these sources provided all that was necessary to define, justify, enforce, and act upon patriarchy. The divine male God of the Judeo-Christian tradition, whether as lord or father, had created a world in which the natural order of things was characterized by dependent women and dominant men. Fathers ruled over their households, and thus by extension over the state, ideally in a manner that cared for those dependent persons entrusted to their rule, but in actuality often in a ruthless and exploitative way. Men are leaders, heroes, adventures, statesmen, prophets, and kings. Women are not. Women are instead subject to their fathers, then their husbands, and finally their sons. She is one of his possessions, subject to his control, a diminished, dangerous, and dependent person. Her utility is defined by her ability to provide children to her husband and manage the affairs of his household. When she oversteps these bounds, refuses to accept her subordinate role, she is subject to punishment, even to the point of death. The extent to which these norms and conditions remain true in the contemporary world is both highly variable and frustratingly persistent.

Modern Patriarchy

Up through the eighteenth century CE, patriarchal ideology held powerful sway over the imaginations and actions of men and women, creating "a powerful discursive tradition that affected the way relations between them were thought about, debated, contested and reinvented, by both the rulers and the ruled" (Miller, 2017, p. 12). Classical education in the West, Confucian education in the East, both converged in the effort to sustain and reinforce the patriarchal hierarchy of society, establishing norms for behavior, rules of law, and forces for compulsion. Patriarchal readings of the Bible, Greek literature, and the Confucian classics served as respective proof-texts for patriarchal ideology. Nevertheless, late in the century, voices arose that began to challenge this ideology on the basis of both new conceptions of human equality that confronted patriarchy directly as well as new arguments for women's equality on the basis of a maternalist ideology that claimed equal status to paternalism and indirectly challenged the dominance of patriarchal structures.

Patriarchy varied by location: in rural communities, among aristocratic families, and in the new urban economies. For rural women, their position was most traditional; their positions as a new daughter-in-law, as a surviving widow, or as the reigning wife and mother were all dependent upon the status of their husband within the family. They had begun to assert some control over the courting rituals and marriage of their children, and were responsible exclusively for the realm of childbirth, but their power, such as it was, was clearly circumscribed to the domestic sphere. Aristocratic patriarchy had become stronger, and women's reproductive, as opposed to their productive, roles were even more emphasized and exaggerated. Marriage was a political and dynastic act, and childbirth was the aristocratic women's chief occupation. Noblewomen hired wet-nurses, attended to restricted forms of hierarchy, and indulged in various physical pleasures, all of which served to differentiate their position in society from that of the villager. Lastly, urban women were an interesting combination of these two: freer than the rural women, yet just as important to the family's economic well-being. They worked a trade with their husbands, used nursemaids, or even practiced their own trades: weaving, lacemaking, etc. Yet they were most often semi-skilled and less trained than males, unable to obtain apprenticeships or guild memberships, and many urban women were either servants in aristocratic households or laborers in the newly emerging factory economy (Smith, 1988).

One of the first women to challenge directly the patriarchal order was Mary Wollstonecraft in her *Vindication of the Rights of Woman*, written in 1791. Published during the French Revolution, Wollstonecraft attacked first of all what she saw patriarchy had done to aristocratic and urban women: imprisoned on the throne of beauty, solicited by men for their inferiority, enervated by male standards, made dependent, weak, and frivolous. The consequences of patriarchy for women were that their virtues were socially defined solely as patience, docility, good humor, and flexibility, all of which rendered women apparently inferior only because they had been raised to see themselves as such. Fully embracing the values of the revolutionary age: reason, virtue, temperance, knowledge, and a belief in the laws of society, Wollstonecraft demanded that men consider women as human beings first, born with equal reason, encumbered only by the restrictions patriarchal society placed upon them, and subjugated to male authority only through the threat of force. She uncovered the brute reality behind patriarchy, a dependency on a morality based on "might makes right": men may by nature be stronger, but that does not make them by reason any more virtuous.

For Wollstonecraft, marriage ought to be a partnership, where sexual distinctions are only motivated by love, not convention or social mores. Women ought to be their husband's friend and companion, rather than his dependent. Merely because women have been subjugated, she argued, is no proof of their inferiority. In fact, such equality, based on "rational fellowship," would make of women "more observant daughters, more affectionate sisters, more faithful wives, more reasonable mothers–in a word, better citizens" (Wollstonecraft, 1999, p. 240). In effect, she sought to rewrite the terms of the set of relationships women and men naturally found themselves in, to reestablish them on a basis of reason, virtue, equality, and partnership. Her chief means of reform was through education. Women were to be educated in serious subjects, and "sexual virtue," that is gendered virtue, which men or women were to partake of to the exclusion of the other, were to be abolished. The difficulty with her at the time of radical reforms was that it would only be possible for women of the aristocratic or urban classes to benefit from them; working-class and rural women would still need to fulfill many of the domestic responsibilities they had previously shouldered so that other women could be free from patriarchy. Wollstonecraft laid the foundation for modern Western feminism in making these claims against patriarchy, revealing both the pernicious power that patriarchy represented as well as the class privileges that the overthrow of patriarchy alone could not erase. The tension in Wollstonecraft's analysis and program between revolutionary change on the basis of sex and/or on the basis of class would persist well into the next two hundred years.

An alternative to patriarchy that sought to preserve, rather than over-throw, some of the gendered virtues Wollstonecraft decried, was the development of an ideology of maternalism. Coming in the nineteenth century, on a wave of resistance both to the established patriarchy and to rational, liberal efforts to make women and men equals in the public sphere (in effect abolishing the distinction of separate spheres), mater-nalism was a religiously inspired alternative to paternalism, arguing that women were more than capable of caring for themselves and their fami-lies if given the opportunity. Arguing more for equality of responsibility and choice within a traditional ideology of separate spheres, maternalist women argued for real autonomy and authority within the domestic realm, still leaving public affairs to men. Driven by the intersection of working-class, religious, and anti-paternalist concerns, they advanced a claim, based on their roles as wives and mothers, for freedom to focus on their domestic roles, to be freed from the double burden of working to manage the household and working to earn income for the family. From their class perspective, what was most hypocritical of existing patri-archy was that it consigned women to the domestic sphere in theory while compelling lower-class and rural women to work doubly hard at earning income outside the home in a factory or shop, or at least outside their role by taking in income-generating piece work they could do from home.

By the early twentieth century, this idea had crystallized in a movement among religious working women in Europe. Elisabeth Gnauck-Kühne, who was instrumental in the organization of German Catholic working-women, "openly rejected the idea that the 'women's question' would be solved if only women could return to their homes" (Cremer, 2001, p. 428). The old paternalist slogan "everything for–but nothing *through* the worker," she provocatively replaced with an emancipatory one: "We do not want your soup; give us our rights, and then we will eat meat!" She would not tolerate any suggestion that a woman's double burden of labor inside and outside the home was not a reality that had to be addressed: "The saying, that [women] 'belong in the house' regretfully does not meet with reality any more. In fact, it has become a bitter irony" (Gnauck-Kühne, 1906). To many of her contemporaries, a Catholic middle-class woman speaking of working women organizing for themselves, of working women's "rights," and of the "bitter irony" of working women's double burden seemed oddly out of place, yet she got to the heart of one of the contradictions of patriarchy: expecting women to fulfill contradictory and conflicting expectations. Her solution was empowering women to make a choice between domestic labor (which has unrecognized and unaccounted value in and of itself) and remunerative labor (whether inside her home our outside of it). The point was to give women the right to make decisions for themselves, without also requiring the total revolution of the system itself. Class intersections with patriarchy, as well as the tension between revolution, rights, and reform, dominated women's efforts to change, if not end, the system of patriarchal oppression until the late twentieth century.

By then, questions of gender and race, or more precisely the constructions of gender and race, complicated the understanding and analysis of patriarchy and different women's positions within the patriarchal order. It was increasingly understood that the long-established binary gender identities based on biological sex were not primarily claims about biology but rather claims about power. Examining law, literature, institutions, and politics, as we have done here, reveals what is constitutive of the social construction of gender, drawing attention to the ways in which these sources explain the different behaviors and unequal conditions of women and men. Gender differences, often invoked in order to establish not truths about sexual difference, more powerfully offer legitimization for patriarchal policies, practices, and power, which in turn rest on assuming the acceptance of gendered relationships (Scott, 1986). The very way we think concerning gender and sex, the way gender is acted upon and performed, creates an invisible and self-referential system (Butler, 1988).

Successfully breaking into patriarchy and undoing it becomes all the more difficult, requiring the investigation of religious, social, literary, legal, and political domains to get to the root of patriarchal power.

The integration of the question of race into this dynamic complicates the analysis and possible alternative strategies to overcoming patriarchy even further. It also helps explain why the overcoming of patriarchy has been such a difficult and lengthy process. Given that all human actors are not only members of identifiable groups, they are also all particular and specific. No one type of human being represents universal humanity. Gender and the multiple and contradictory meanings we attribute to sexual difference, as well as race and the multiple and contradictory meanings we attribute to physical appearance in terms of skin colors, facial features, and hair textures, are both contemporary aspects of social organization. The basic biological sexual differences of female and male, and the assumptions about this difference patriarchy makes, are subject to multiple complications when we take into account how the constructions of race and gender intersect with sexual difference, showing the interconnections between patriarchal power and racism. Focusing on "the concept of intersectionality to denote the various ways in which race and gender interact" (Crenshaw, 1994, p. 94), one can see the complex set of forces patriarchy draws upon to sustain itself. The power of racism to erase some women from visibility, to make their particular struggles and violence they suffer indiscernible. The multiple ways patriarchy, in alliance with racism and through its own sexism, misogyny, and paternalism, segregate, violate, and render invisible the oppression of many women, has become a constituent part of modern patriarchy, which cannot be fully understood without this kind of intersectional analysis.

CONCLUSION

"For if patriarchy is anything here and now… I believe it consists largely (though by no means exclusively) in this uneven, gendered economy of giving *and taking* moral-cum-social goods and services" (Manne, 2018, p. 107). One final way to think about patriarchy is entitlement: the view that men are entitled by their nature and status simply as men to take certain valuable goods from women (affection, obedience, sex, deference, etc.), who in turn are obligated to give, by their nature and status, these same goods. The sexist ideology that justifies this, that women are naturally weaker, inferior, and dependent, the misogynist enforcement that punishes women through threats and violence those who refuse to deliver these goods, and the paternalist practice that defines how men exercise patriarchal control over women, all are part of this patriarchal economy. Religious belief has justified the kinds of moral goods women are expected to give, primary among them domestic subservience and children. Society's norms have determined the kinds of social goods women are expected to give, primary among them economic support and deference. Both religious and social beliefs define what men are legitimately able to take from women and justify the kinds of violence men may exercise when women refuse to comply. Class, gender, and racial status affect and complicate this fundamental relationship, adding enhanced entitlements and expanded dimensions of expected giving and demanded taking to the patriarchal economy.

Overcoming patriarchy will take combined, concerted, and long-term effort. A system thousands of years in the making cannot be overturned in a few decades or even a few generations. Attention to the diverse ways patriarchy justifies, enforces, and extends its authority over the diverse lives of more than a few billion women obviously takes the time and effort of many different people. Contributions from multiple perspectives and experiences are constantly required to keep up with the shifting ways patriarchy perpetuates itself. Reforms, even revolutions, in educational methods, domestic arrangements, and workplace expectations, coupled with leadership development, political progress, and racial equity will be required. Patriarchy touches all aspects of our contemporary life, and its influences are felt in every avenue of the contemporary world. If the "rule of fathers" is to come to an end, women and men will have to join together in a consistent effort to remove patriarchal expectations and entitlement from religious belief, social organization, literature, and law in multiple cultures across the planet. Knowing that patriarchy is a constructed ideology, designed to the benefit of the few over the many, to perpetuate a specific form of oppressive power, and not an immutable natural or divine law inextricably embedded in absolute sexual difference, is the beginning of that end.

CHAPTER TAKEAWAYS

1. Patriarchy is an ancient and pervasive form of social organization rooted in an ideology concerning human sexuality and gender. It

forms a persistent, pervasive, and unavoidable problem throughout the contemporary world.

2. Patriarchy is the way older and dominant men acquire and hold power over all women and younger, subordinate men. It has taken different and diverse forms throughout time and space that complicate the analysis of patriarchal power and place for its overcoming.

3. It is composed of a combination of sexism (its justification), misogyny (its enforcement), and paternalism (its practice).

4. Its roots are deeply embedded in Western and Eastern literary, religious, and philosophical traditions.

5. Modern patriarchy is complicated and enhanced by class, gender, and racial hierarchies that reinforce patriarchal power.

6. The struggle to overcome patriarchy has been and will be a long and protracted effort by many people over many generations.

References

Abraham, K. (2019). *Persisting patriarchy: Intersectionalities, negotiations, subversions*. New York: Palgrave Macmillan.

Aeschylus. (2011). *The complete Aeschylus: Volume one: The Oresteia* (A. Shapiro, Trans.). Oxford: Oxford University Press.

Aristotle. (2017). *Politics* (C. D. C. Reeve, Trans.). Indianapolis: Hackett.

Augustine. (1982). *The literal meaning of genesis* (Vol. 2). Mahwah, NJ: Paulist Press.

Augustine. (2005). *The works of Saint Augustine: A new translation for the 21st century: Letters, 211–270* (R. Teske, Trans.). Hyde Park, NY: New City Press.

Butler, J. (1988). Performative acts and gender constitution: An essay in phenomenology and feminist theory. *Theatre Journal, 40*(4), 519–531.

Confucius. (2003). *Analects* (E. Slingerland, Trans.). Indianapolis: Hackett.

Cremer, D. (2001). The limits of maternalism: Gender ideology and the south German Catholic workingwomen's associations, 1904–1918. *The Catholic Historical Review, 87*(3), 428–451.

Crenshaw, K. (1994). Mapping the margins: Intersectionality, identity politics, and violence against women of color. In M. Fineman & R. Mykitiuk (Eds.), *The public nature of private violence* (pp. 93–118). New York: Routledge.

De Beauvoir, S. (1989). *The second sex*. New York: Vintage.

Dialeti, A. (2018, July). Patriarchy as a category of historical analysis and the dynamics of power: The example of early modern Italy. *Gender & History, 30*(2), 331–342.

Dworkin, G. (2020) Paternalism. In E. N. Zalta (Ed.), *The Stanford encyclopedia of philosophy.* https://plato.stanford.edu/archives/sum2020/entries/paternalism/.

Gilligan, J. (1997). *Violence: Reflections on a national epidemic.* New York: Vintage.

Gilligan, C., & Richards, D. (2008). *The deepening darkness: Patriarchy, resistance and democracy's future.* Cambridge: Cambridge University Press.

Gilligan, C., & Richards, D. (2018). *Darkness now visible: Patriarchy's resurgence and feminist resistance.* Cambridge: Cambridge University Press.

Gnauck-Kühne, E. (1906). *Einführung in die Arbeiterinnenfrage.* Mönchengladbach: Volksverein für das katholische Deutschlands.

Homer. (2016). *The Iliad* (C. Alexander, Trans.). New York: Ecco.

Homer. (2017). *The Odyssey* (E. Wilson, Trans.). New York: Norton.

Jackman, M. (1994). *The velvet glove: Paternalism and conflict in gender, class, and race relations.* Berkeley: University of California Press.

Lerner, G. (1986). *The creation of patriarchy.* New York: Oxford University Press.

Manne, K. (2018). *Down girl: The logic of misogyny.* New York: Oxford University Press.

Mercer, C. (2019, July 1). The philosophical origins of patriarchy. *The Nation.* https://www.thenation.com/article/archive/patriarchy-sexism-philosophy-reproductive-rights/.

Miller, P. (2017). *Patriarchy.* Taylor & Francis.

Plato. (2004). *Plato's Meno* (G. Anastaplo & L. Berns, Trans.). Newburyport, MA: Focus Publishing.

Rakoczy, S. (2008). The theological vision of Elizabeth A Johnson. *Scriptura, 98,* 137–155.

Schüssler Fiorenza, E. (2013). *Interpreting patriarchal traditions.* Minneapolis: Augsburg Fortress.

Scott, J. (1986). Gender: A useful category of historical analysis. *American Historical Review, 91*(5), 1053–1075.

Smith, B. (1988). *Changing lives: Women in European history since 1700.* New York: D. C. Heath.

Wollstonecraft, M. (1999). *Vindication of the rights of woman.* New York: Oxford University Press.

Yao, X. (Ed.). (2003). *RoutledgeCurzon encyclopedia of confucianism* (Vol. 2). New York: Routledge.

CHAPTER 3

Gender-Based Inequality in the Modern American Society

Emerald M. Archer

INTRODUCTION

American discourse on gender has changed dramatically over the course of the twentieth century and inequalities between women and men are continually challenged in all spheres of life in the twenty-first century. Yet, gender gaps and inequalities persist: full-time working women make only 85 cents for every dollar that their male counterparts earn, women shoulder the majority of the domestic load (e.g., childcare, housework) in their partnerships, and they are less likely to hold executive positions in corporate America or represent large constituencies as elected officials. How do these gaps persist in an advanced industrialized country that has enjoyed social and economic transformation in the modern era? Enduring gender stereotypes are largely responsible for these stubborn inequities that frame how women and men interact with one another and inform our beliefs about the roles each is permitted to inhabit. Negotiations among individuals are continuously influenced by gender

E. M. Archer (✉)
Mount Saint Mary's University, Los Angeles, CA, USA
e-mail: emarcher@msmu.edu

© The Author(s), under exclusive license to Springer Nature Switzerland AG 2021
J. Marques (ed.), *Exploring Gender at Work*,
https://doi.org/10.1007/978-3-030-64319-5_3

45

stereotypes, which results in antiquated thinking about men and women and their relationships with one another that are carried forward and reproduced unconsciously. This chapter explores theoretical perspectives from different disciplines that elucidate how gender differences and hierarchies function and persist over time. Cumulative disadvantage is utilized as a case study to illustrate the ways in which gender stereotypes produce inequities across a woman's career. Until men and women can break free from unconscious bias and reliance on gender stereotypes, inequities like the gender wage gap and underrepresentation in key economic sectors will continue to be the norm rather than the exception.

Gender-Based Inequality in the United States

Evidence for progress made in the name of gender equity over the last century is ample in the United States. Over the last one hundred years, women won the vote, enjoyed the pursuit of degrees in higher education, entered the paid labor force, lead Fortune 500 companies, and served in elected offices at the local, state, and national levels. Despite women's undisputed progress and clear gains, progress has stagnated and gaps remain.

The share of women participating in the labor force has grown over the last several decades and recently leveled off (Horowitz, Parker, & Stepler, 2017). Over half (57%) of women (aged 16 and older) were either employed or looking for work in 2017, which is slightly more than were in the 1980 labor force (51%) but less than the 1999 labor force (60%). Mothers entering the labor force have been a primary driver of the increased share of women participating, holding steady at 73% since 2000.

Women's progress in the American workforce is, in part, a result of gains made in educational attainment. Women aged 25–64 are more likely than their male counterparts to have a bachelor's degree; specifically, "38% of these women and 33% of men had a bachelor's degree" (Geiger & Parker, 2018). A greater share of women than men are attaining postgraduate degrees: "In 2017, 14% of women ages 25 to 64 had an advanced degree, compared with 12% of men. In 1992, a higher share of men (9%) than women (6%) in this age group had an advanced degree" (ibid.). While this is good news, there is no parity when it comes to particular Science, Technology, Engineering, and Mathematics (STEM) training.

For example, women receive only 18% of bachelor's degrees in engineering and computer science; these fields remain sex segregated, which makes it harder for women to both enter and stay in a male dominated workforce (National Science Board, 2018).

Occupational sex segregation, or the high concentration of women and men in different occupations, continues despite women's educational attainment and training. Occupations such as "health care support, administrative assistance, early childhood care and education, and food preparation and services are composed of more than 60 percent women" (Washington Center for Equitable Growth, 2017). The segregation in today's workforce is, in part, a result of gender stereotypes about men and women's work; that is, care taking and administrative work aligns with expectations Americans have for "women's work," while executive and leadership roles are associated with men's work. As such, leadership is one domain where women are still underrepresented. Few women occupy the C-suite in Fortune 500 companies; women make up only seven percent of CEOs for these companies and hold 25% of board seats (Connley, 2019). One-hundred and twenty-seven women (24%) occupy seats in the 2020 U.S. Congress and 90 (29%) hold statewide elective executive offices across the country (Center for American Women in Politics, 2020).

Even though women have flooded the labor force in the twentieth century, the gender wage and wealth gap persists. Women continue to make and save less than their male counterparts, all things being equal. In 2018, women earned 85 cents for every dollar men earned nationally and the estimated 15 cent gap today has narrowed substantially from 36 cents in 1980 (Graf, Brown, & Patten, 2019). Where parents are concerned, research had found that mothers in the workforce make less annually (the motherhood penalty) and fathers get a pay raise (the fatherhood bonus) (Budig, 2014). However, these penalties and rewards are not felt across the board: "high-income men get the biggest pay bump for having children, and low-income women pay the biggest price" (Miller, 2014). The wealth gap is another powerful predictor of economic agency among women. Women across the nation have accrued wealth (assets like property and homeownership, investments, and financial savings) that is 32% that of men (McCulloch, 2017). Overall, the narrowing of the wage and wealth gap is attributable to increased educational attainment and work experience, and the loosening of occupational sex segregation.

It is worth noting that a general review of gender-based inequities masks real differences among women. It becomes apparent that some women are more disadvantaged than others when the data are disaggregated by race and ethnicity. Compared to white women, the effect of gender-based inequities are amplified for women of color. Women of color experience occupational sex segregation at all educational levels, as they are segregated into lower-wage jobs more than their white peers of similar skill levels (Washington Center for Equitable Growth, 2017). The wage gap is also more pronounced for women of color (Hegewisch & Hartmann, 2019). Compared to white men who have the highest earnings, Asian American women make 90 cents, African-American women make 62 cents, Native American women make 57 cents, and Latinas make 54 cents for every dollar their white male counterpart earns (National Partnership for Women & Families, 2020). If women of color are paid less annually, it follows that they will save less over time: for example, "where the median single white man has accumulated almost $30,000 in wealth, single [African American] women have a median wealth of only $200" (Phillips, 2020). Inequities experienced by women of color are exacerbated by intersecting systems of oppression.

Due to the stark inequities already discussed, American women are more likely than men to state that they have faced gender discrimination at work. Women are twice as likely to say they have experienced at least one specific form of gender discrimination on the job. Geiger and Parker (2018) elaborate:

> One-in-four working women (25%) say they have earned less than a man who was doing the same job, compared with just 5% of men who say they've earned less than a female peer. Women are also about four times as likely as men to say they have been treated as if they were not competent because of their gender (23% of women vs. 6% of men), and they are about three times as likely to say they have experienced repeated small slights at work because of their gender (16% versus 5%).

Beyond the labor force, the home can be a site for gender inequality as well. Women do the bulk of unpaid labor, the kind that labor economists define as "time spent doing routine housework, shopping for necessary household goods, child care, tending to the elderly…and other activities related to the household maintenance" (Wezerek & Ghodsee, 2020). In the United States, women perform almost double the work—or an average of four hours compared to men's two and a half hours weekly (ibid.). Working mothers are also more likely to miss work when their children are sick or childcare falls through than working fathers (Maume, 2008).

Caregiving responsibilities, whether it is for children or aging family members, is a concern that sheds light on structural inequality as it appears in American law and the corporate sector. Paid family leave policies are designed to help workers balance work and family obligations by compensating employees while taking time off to care for family members. However, the United States has no national paid family leave policy and "only 17 percent of U.S. private-sector workers have access to paid family leave through their employers" (Rossin-Slater & Stearns, 2020). Low income workers often have no access to this benefit, while high-income earners have greater access to this opportunity. Rossin-Slater and Stearns (2020) explain that "federal law requires 12 weeks of job-protected *unpaid* leave under the 1993 Family and Medical Leave Act, but stringent eligibility requirements mean that less than two-thirds of the U.S. workforce is eligible." Out of necessity, women take far more time than husbands when it comes to caring for a new child. Ninety percent of fathers take some time off in this period, but the majority of them take fewer than 10 days of leave (US Department of Labor, 2017). Organizations that normalize and actively promote the idea that mothers should take more leave than fathers preserve gendered stereotypes that ultimately prevent greater equality in the workforce. Because women and men are not seen as equal when it comes to caregiving by federal law or organizational policy, the responsibility of caregiving will continue to fall to women, inhibiting their professional and career growth by extending their time away from work (Levs, 2019).

Theoretical Frameworks for Understanding Gender-Based Inequality

Early explanations of the inequities experienced by men and women in the workforce and the domestic sphere were described by a functionalist approach that emphasized sex roles as complementary, and therefore, uniquely different. Specifically, women bore the responsibility of childbearing, and by extension, rearing, while men where unencumbered such that they could pursue industrial era employment (Murdock, 1949). It was not until decades later—in the 1960s and 1970s—that feminist scholars critiqued the functionalist approach and pointed to a system of stratification that separated men from women (Lopata & Thorne,

1978). Rather than a biological difference claimed in the functionalist approach, feminists argued that specific behaviors encode gendered meanings, these gendered stereotypes then determine the division of labor, and finally social structures and institutions incorporate gendered values within them (Ferree, 1990). Social science disciplines, particularly sociology and psychology, offer many theories to explain the mechanisms involved in producing and reproducing gender inequity. These theories are often organized within three theoretical frameworks: (1) individual level theories, (2) interactional theories, and (3) organizational theories.[1]

Individual Level Theories

Theories situated in this first level of analysis typically focus on how our gendered selves come to be. Said another way, these theories elucidate how people come to identify with (and are conditioned to conform to) typically masculine or feminine characteristics. Socialization and cultural influence have been invoked to describe gender inequities across disciplines.

Socialization—how boys and girls are raised and internalize their gendered selves—is one mechanism that can explain differences between men and women. Parents are the first to influence socialization, but boys and girls are socialized in gendered ways from preschool forward. Chodorow (1978) claimed that the relationships mothers have with their daughters and sons develop antithetical personalities in boys and girls. For example, the intimate relationships mothers have with their daughters aid in the development of interpersonal attachment and nurturing characteristics while the more distant relationship between mothers and sons emphasizes independence and agency. In preschool settings, Martin (1998) identifies different way teachers interact with boys and girls. Preschool teachers are more likely to encourage relaxed behavior (e.g., movement in the classroom) among boys and formal behaviors among girls (e.g., raising a hand before speaking), and disciplinary action for girls and boys may come in the form of asking them to be quiet or involve restraining action, respectively. This kind of socialization goes on throughout a child's adolescence and as older children acquire these

---

[1] This chapter provides a brief snapshot of possible theoretical explanations of gender inequity and is not exhaustive. For a more robust description of theoretical approaches to gender inequity, see Scarborough and Risman (2018), Kroska (2014), and Kirby (1999).

gender-differentiated ways of operating, "they contribute to the social-ization process by providing models for younger, same-sex children to follow" (Kroska, 2014, p. 487).

The influence of culture on how boys and girls are socialized has been well documented. Bem's (1993) enculturated lens theory emphasizes the influence of culture on differentiated development. Bem's psycho-analytic theory argues "that culture provides individuals with a set of principles about acceptable thought and behavior, called lenses, which are embedded in society's values, social structures, and people's minds" (Corrado, 2009, p. 358). A variety of lenses exist in any given society and these lenses—or implicit norms, values, and beliefs—allow soci-eties to reproduce themselves over generations. Bem focuses on three particular lenses that are central to gender differentiation in the United States: gender polarization, androcentrism, and biological essentialism. The gender polarization lens offers the idea that men and women are situated in opposition to one another, underlying the organization of society. The lens of androcentrism focuses on the concept that men are superior to women and, as a consequence, the male experience is the universalized norm against which women are judged. The biological essentialism lens "both minimizes and justifies gender polarization and androcentrism by interpreting these lenses as biologically ordained; men's presumed superiority, using men as the default category, and unequal power relations between men and women in society are viewed as the result of natural, unavoidable differences, rather than socially constructed differences, between males and females" (ibid., p. 358).

Overall, these lenses work in concert to influence individuals to think and act in gendered ways that are supported by a particular culture. In the United States, androcentric cultural norms may be reinforced by practices as benign as men holding doors open for women, which perpetuates the notion that women are frail and dependent on the aid of men. Cultural beliefs about gender can also impact the way individuals evaluate their own talents. Gendered stereotypes applicable to math aptitude—specif-ically, that men are better at math than women—can result in women assessing their math competence as lower than that of men even when test scores and grades are the same (Correll, 2001). People have a tendency to feel more competent in tasks that are congruent with gender stereotypes and less competent in tasks that contradict gender role expectations.

Interactional Level Theories

Gender inequality also emerges due to the way gender influences interpersonal interactions. The way people *perform* gender can reinforce difference and inequality; interactions between men and women often rely upon gender stereotypes which leads to cognitive bias. The "doing gender" perspective, along with "expectation states theory," is useful to understand how gender inequality persists.

West and Zimmerman (1987) introduced the term "doing gender" in response to the view that gender is an individual trait and focused on the way gender is reproduced through the behavior of individuals. This perspective is predicated on the notions that gender is a social construction and that gender is achieved through daily interactions with others (Butler, 1988; Corrado, 2009). West and Zimmerman argued that a person's gender performance is judged against their sex category (the sex assigned at birth by observation of genitalia). A person's behavior is judged as acceptable if their gender performance aligns with society's expectations of their sex category. If a person's gender performance and sex category are incongruous, s/he may be punished and deemed deviant or abnormal. By "doing gender" and behaving in ways that align with normative expectations of men and women, people reinforce difference in society that sustains inequality among men and women. This concept has been widely used in sociological literature.

The varying degrees by which men and women perform masculinity and femininity is a good example. In general, men and masculinity are typically associated with "agentic" traits like assertiveness and decisiveness, whereas women and femininity are associated with "communal" traits like trustworthiness and benevolence. Some women and men conform closely to feminine and masculine standards, respectively, others merge masculine and feminine behaviors to produce a more androgynous gender performance, and still others tend toward behaviors associated with the opposite gender. Scholars who study men and masculinity have posited that the behavior and identity of men are often held to an ideological ideal, to a hegemonic masculinity. Connell and Messerschmidt (2005) state that hegemonic masculinity operates such that the dominant position of men and the subordinate position of women is reinforced. In the American context, hegemonic masculinity emphasizes "…(hetero)sexual conquest, violence, control over women, and the denigration of homosexuality" (Scarborough & Risman, 2018, p. 344). While no man can actually meet the demands of the ideal, they are judged against it and often try to behave in ways that confirm it. Overall, this extreme form of masculinity maintains unequal gender structures in society because it requires the subjugation of women.

The power of stereotypes to create cognitive bias that inform our behaviors is another reason why gender disparities remain so prominent in American society. Ridgeway (2011) argues that gender inequality "operates as a diffuse status characteristic in the background of social relations, subtly conditioning the way people interpret and evaluate the actions of others in ways that systematically disadvantage women" (ibid.). Ridgeway uses what is referred to as "expectation states theory" to show how interactions between men and women are fraught with gender stereotypes. Expectation states theory explains how expected competence forms the foundation for status hierarchies in small groups. Moreover, specific pieces of social information (e.g., apparent gender, racial category, perceived ability) plays a role in organizing these hierarchies (Berger, Conner, & Fisek, 1974). With respect to gender, people subconsciously organize interactions based on what they may expect men or women to do when limited information about an actor is available. This is problematic as men benefit from positive associations like competence and agency and women are disadvantaged by the association with empathy and dependence. These diffuse status characteristics may privilege men in the context of management and women in the context of childcare because these contexts align with gender role stereotypes.

Organizational Level Theories

Organizational level theories of gender inequality focus on the way systems, institutions and organizations put women in a disadvantageous position relative to men. These macro-level theories show how structural attributes of workplaces can undermine the advancement of women. Rehel (2014) investigated how family leave policies shape the opportunities for men and women in ways that perpetuate gender inequality. When mothers are given extended periods with their newborns and fathers are given a few days, the gender difference is reinforced and more equitable sharing of childcare is minimized.

One of the first studies of gender inequities and organizational structures was undertaken by Kanter (1977) who argued that women's lack of career success resulted from the fact that women were forced to behave in ways described as "bossy" or "controlling" because the organizational structure hindered their progress. Three obstacles were enumerated by Kanter that undermined women at the time: lack of opportunity, limited access to power and resources, and their token status in the workplace.

Acker's (1990) theory of gendered organizations builds on Kanter's work and argues that gender inequality is persistent because it is baked into the structure of organizations. Employers have an implicit preference for male workers because they stereotypically have fewer distractions outside of work and, as a consequence, are viewed as more loyal to an organization. Thus, many employers see men as the *ideal worker* (Williams, 2001). This preference places women at a disadvantage since they are likely to be the primary caregiver for family members. Acker went further to identify five processes that reproduce gender in organizations: the division of labor, cultural symbols, workplace interactions, individual identities, and organizational logic. While all processes are important, organizational logic is distinctive because it "draws attention to how hierarches are rationalized and legitimized in organizations. It encompasses the logical systems of work rules, job descriptions, pay scales, and job evaluations that govern bureaucratic organizations" (Williams, Muller, & Kilanski, 2012). Acker conceived of organizational logic as the taken-for-granted policies used by managers to exert control in the workplace that *appear* gender neutral. Williams, Muller, and Kilanski (2012) illustrate Acker's point:

> ...Organizations supposedly use logical principles to develop job descriptions and determine pay rates. But Acker argues that managers often draw on gender stereotypes when undertaking these tasks, privileging qualities associated with men and masculinity that then become reified in organizational hierarchies. Through organizational logic, therefore, gender discourses are embedded in organizations, and gender inequality at work results. (p. 550)

It is important to note that organizational logics applied to bureaucratic workplace policies can be racialized in the same way that they are gendered, putting people of color at a disadvantage. For example, Harvey-Wingfield (2009) investigates how racialization and gendering intersect to shape the experiences of African-American male nurses working in a feminized field. She shows that the advancement of these male nurses in the profession was thwarted by the hostility from their female colleagues and that negative stereotypes were applied to them by doctors and their patients. Namely, they were "misidentified as maintenance workers or janitors, but never as doctors or hospital administrators" (Scarborough & Risman, 2018, p. 347).

Synthesizing the Theoretical Frameworks

While not exhaustive, this section attempts to illustrate the various ways one can understand the origins of gender inequality. It is critical to recognize that no one level of analysis alone can explain the complexity of gender inequity, but that each theoretical approach allows one to understand a particular part of a multidimensional and complex social problem. Risman (2004) argues that theories that locate gender only at the individual, interactional, or organizational level are at risk of oversimplifying the complexities of gender. In response, she developed her *theory of gender as a social structure* and synthesized the existing scholarship into a multilevel framework to better understand how the aforementioned approaches interlock.

Risman employed the same dimensions outlined above (individual, interactionist, and organizational) in the theory, noting that material and cultural processes operate to create gender difference in each dimension. Scarborough and Risman (2018) explain:

> Material processes are based upon physical bodies, laws, or geographical locations and how these impact social lives. Cultural processes are ideological or socially constructed notions that orientate people's perspectives and worldviews. Each component of the gender structure is mutually constitutive and reflexive, such that the material forces in the interactional-level influence and are influenced by the cultural forces in the interactional-level. Similarly, each dimension, the individual, interactional, and macro [organizational], is interconnected with the other dimensions. A change in one dimension reverberates across other dimensions to alter the gender structure of the whole. (p. 347)

An example that illustrates the interlocking nature of the dimensions that produce inequality are innovations in STEM training opportunities for women. At the macro-level, educational initiatives are developed by non-profits that encourage young women to learn science and math skills that can ultimately influence the individual preferences of young women who later might pursue employment in STEM fields. However, "the potential for change inspired by such macro and individual processes could ultimately be stunted by interactional processes — as women who study or work in STEM fields often face discrimination and alienation by their colleagues, increasing the chance that they will leave the field for one that is less hostile toward women" (Risman, 2018). One can begin to understand the dynamic patterns of change—both toward gender equity and resisting it—when gender is conceptualized in a multidimensional framework.

CASE STUDY: CUMULATIVE DISADVANTAGE AT WORK

The mechanisms of perpetuating gender inequality discussed in the previous section apply to every domain of American life, from navigating male dominated industries to negotiating gender equity in the home. Gender roles and stereotypes that we are brought up with (socialization) inform our beliefs about the characteristics women and men possess and the positions for which they are best suited, which leads to bias. Biases, or errors in decision-making that are based on stereotypes, contribute to the inequities in the workplace. More specifically, implicit biases about gender can affect each stage of a woman's career and is the case study used here to illustrate the power of gender stereotypes in producing inequities between men and women. The process of cumulative disadvantage is one way to explain why women consistently, across industries, are passed over for promotion and why the gender wage gap is so stubborn.

Inequalities in the workplace are often a product of social processes rather than a natural difference between men and women. The theory of cumulative disadvantage illustrates that inequalities like the gender wage and wealth gap are attributed to a series of small setbacks that unfold over the course of one's career. Tower and Latimer (2016) suggest that "early career disadvantages can compound over time, resulting in important disparities in career advancement, compensation, and opportunities." Unconscious bias and stereotypes about women and their capabilities are responsible for these setbacks as these biases can creep in and influence critical workplace decisions about who gets promoted, who collects a bonus, and who gets assigned a top project. Recall that men are usually associated with "agentic" traits like ambition and control, whereas women are associated with "communal" traits (helpful and supportive). Communal traits are seen as antithetical to good leadership and will inform our conscious and unconscious assumptions about people. Implicit bias informs choices made at the interview stage, in team interactions and performance assessments, whether someone receives a prestigious assignment, and ultimately, compensation.

At the interviewing and hiring stage, what researchers find is not only are women held to a higher standard than men but even when the standards are higher, occupational segregation starts. Women will make it through the hiring process in the technology industry, for example, and then "can find themselves steered out of technical roles and into careers such as marketing, human resources and project management, which often pay less and may not have the same potential for advancement" (Bianco, 2017). Marketing and project management roles track more closely to cultural stereotypes about women's work whereas engineering and technology are consistent with what we might expect among the skillset of men. In this instance, technology companies place women on a certain track at the point of entry; this is the gender segregation of labor that also results in more women in lower paying jobs in many organizations.

After being hired, individuals engage in team interactions where women can contribute their ideas, knowledge and expertise to influence the choices that are made and improve processes.

Research shows that women have a much harder time getting credit for their work and ideas in team interactions than their male peers (Haynes & Heilman, 2013; Heilman, 2016). These moments of inequality affect how individuals are perceived for their contributions and expertise in the workplace and if they will be promoted over time. Likewise, in the performance assessment and promotion phase, women were significantly more likely to be in the middle of the performance range when managers evaluated their team members (Cecchi-Dimeglio, 2017). Men were more likely to be placed at the top rung of performance as compared to women. Correll and Simard (2016) also found "women are systematically less likely to receive specific feedback tied to outcomes, both when they receive praise and when the feedback is developmental." In other words, men are offered more specific guidance of what is needed to improve and get to the next level. If women are more likely to be perceived as middling when it comes to performance and given vague feedback for which it is impossible to respond, they are unlikely to be rewarded with special assignments or bonuses.

Another factor in cumulative disadvantage lies in the kind of work women are assigned. Due to gender role expectations, women have an extra burden because they are expected to be collaborative and warm. Women often get tasked with a specific assignment that is important to the well-being of the organization but does not lead to promotion. In the domain of academia, Misra, Lundquist, Holmes, and Agiomavritis (2011) find that female faculty members spent on average eight hours more a week on service activities (e.g., mentoring, teaching, committee work) than their male counterparts. As a consequence, female faculty spent less time on research, which is the criterion that was most determinant of a promotion.

The cumulative disadvantage terminal point for women is compensation—what they are paid for their work annually. All of the pervious points of contact affect compensation. If female applicants are channeled into lower paying positions by human resource offices, they will never have the earning power of their male colleagues. If they are not credited for their ideas or seen as influential on teams, it is unlikely that they will receive lucrative assignments. And it follows that if evaluators do not give female employees concrete feedback from which to respond, their ascent up the proverbial ladder will be slower. In order to further narrow the wage gap, organizations must do better about thinking through all of the points where bias introduces itself that affects the difference in compensation between men and women over the course of a career.

Conclusion

This chapter has illustrated that gender-based inequality is alive and well in modern American society. In almost every industry and sphere, women are at a disadvantage compared to men. The disadvantages felt by women—lower salaries and savings, more hours spent on maintaining the home, and biases that thwart their ascent to leadership positions—are predicated on gender stereotypes that are embedded in the society and structures in which we live and operate. Similar to racial categories, gender is a categorical form of inequality that is founded on an individual's membership in a group (i.e., men and women) and these "categorical inequalities in a society are created and sustained by embedding [categorical] membership…in systems of control over material resources and power" (Ridgeway, 2011). Theoretical approaches from sociology and social psychology illustrate how these inequities are created (socialization) and sustained over time (theory of gender as social structure). In the context of male-dominated industries like STEM, men generally control most stages of career development in their organizations—from finding talent through their own networks, to assigning employees to teams where they can contribute, and deciding at what point women are promoted if their performance warrants such a reward—which may result in fewer wages, rewards, and advancement at each step when compared to their male peers. This cumulative disadvantage makes entry and career satisfaction harder for women in these fields, potentially pushing women out of these industries and sustaining low representation among women. The solutions to gender-based inequities are complex and require a multi-faceted approach. Beliefs and norms about what behaviors are appropriate for men and women will need to loosen and evidence suggests that this systemic change is very slow (Haines, Deaux, & Lofaro, 2016). Organizations will also have to make policy changes that put men and women on a more equal footing—for example, paid family leave policies that give men and women the same time home with a new family member will normalize equal caretaking responsibilities among parents. Culture change and shifts in societal expectations around gender roles are slow moving, but gender equity is possible if individuals are cognizant of their biases and how they might impact their beliefs about and evaluations of women in the workplace.

CHAPTER TAKEAWAYS

The five key ideas for this chapter are:

1. While gender-based inequality has improved over the last century, it persists across multiple institutions (education, employment, family, politics, and law).
2. Theories explaining the mechanisms of gender inequality are organized into three categories: (1) individual, (2) interactional, and (3) structural.
3. Theories that locate gender only at the individual, interactional, or organizational level are at risk of oversimplifying the complexities of gender. Risman's theory of gender as a social structure shows how the 3 approaches interlock to create a multilevel framework of gender.
4. Intersecting systems of oppression (e.g., racial, socio-economic status, and gender) can exacerbate inequalities for women.

5. Implicit biases that are informed by gender stereotypes create cumulative disadvantage that women experience over their careers and contributes to the gender wage gap.

Three major conclusions can be drawn from this chapter:

1. Gender stereotypes that are used to describe men and women's behavior, and the unconscious application of gendered stereotypes in decision-making has real consequences for women.
2. Theories drawn from sociology and social psychology provide a vocabulary and explanatory framework for how gender-based inequities persist over time.
3. Combatting unconscious bias in American society is difficult, but possible. Men and women can more intentionally understand their biases as they relate to gender and other socially constructed categories (e.g., race, sexuality) so they are able to resist the traps of stereotypes.

References

Acker, J. (1990). Hierarchies, jobs, bodies: A theory of gendered organizations. *Gender & Society, 4*, 139–158.

Bem, S. (1993). *The lenses of gender: Transforming the debate on sexual inequality.* New Haven, CN: Yale University Press.

Berger, J., Conner, T., & Fisek, H. (1974). *Expectation states theory: A theoretical research program.* Cambridge: Winthrop.

Bianco, M. (2017). *Finding solutions to the gender pay gap in tech.* The Clayman Institute of Gender Research, Stanford University. https://gender.stanford.edu/news-publications/gender-news/finding-solutions-gender-pay-gap-tech.

Budig, M. (2014). The fatherhood bonus & the motherhood penalty: Parenthood and the gender gap in pay. *The Third Way.* https://www.west-info.eu/children-boost-fathers-career-but-damage-mothers/next_-_fatherhood_motherhood/.

Butler, J. (1988). Performative acts and gender constitution: An essay in phenomenology and feminist theory. *Theater Journal, 40*(4), 519–531.

Cecchi-Dimeglio, P. (2017). How gender bias corrupts performance reviews, and what to do about it. *Harvard Business Review.* https://hbr.org/2017/04/how-gender-bias-corrupts-performance-reviews-and-what-to-do-about-it.

Center for American Women in Politics. (2020). *Women in statewide elective executive office 2020 factsheet*. Rutgers, the State University of New Jersey. https://cawp.rutgers.edu/women-statewide-elective-executive-office-2020.

Chodorow, N. (1978). *The reproduction of mothering: Psychoanalysis and the sociology of gender*. Berkeley: University of California Press.

Connell, R., & Messerschmidt, J. (2005). Hegemonic masculinity: Rethinking the concept. *Gender and Society, 19*, 829–859.

Connley, C. (2019, May 16). The number of women running Fortune 500 companies is at a record high. *CNBC*. https://www.cnbc.com/2019/05/16/the-number-of-women-running-fortune-500-companies-is-at-a-record-high.html.

Corrado, C. (2009). Gender identities and socialization. In J. O'Brien (Ed.), *Encyclopedia of gender and society* (Vol. 1, pp. 356–363). New York: Sage.

Correll, S. (2001). Gender and the career choice process: The role of biased self-assessments. *American Journal of Sociology, 106*(6), 1691–1730.

Correll, S., & Simard, C. (2016, April 29). Research: Vague feedback is holding women back. *Harvard Business Review*. https://hbr.org/2016/04/research-vague-feedback-is-holding-women-back.

Ferree, M. (1990). Beyond separate spheres: Feminism and family research. *Journal of Marriage and Family, 52*(4), 866–884.

Geiger, A., & Parker, K. (2018, March 15). For women's history month, a look at gender gains – and gaps – in the U.S. *Pew Research Center*. https://www.pewresearch.org/fact-tank/2018/03/15/for-womens-history-month-a-look-at-gender-gains-and-gaps-in-the-u-s/.

Graf, N., Brown, A., & Patten, E. (2019). The narrowing, but persistent, gender gap in pay. *Pew Research Center*. https://www.pewresearch.org/fact-tank/2019/03/22/gender-pay-gap-facts/.

Haines, E. L., Deaux, K., & Lofaro, N. (2016). The times they are a-changing … or are they not? A comparison of gender stereotypes, 1983–2014. *Psychology of Women Quarterly, 40*(3), 353–363.

Harvey-Wingfield, A. (2009). Racializing the glass escalator: Reconsidering men's experiences with women's work. *Gender & Society, 23*(1), 5–26.

Haynes, M. C., & Heilman, M. E. (2013). It had to be you (not me)!: Women's attributional rationalization of their contribution to successful joint work outcomes. *Personality and Social Psychology Bulletin, 39*(7), 956–969.

Hegewisch, A., & Hartmann, H. (2019, March 7). The gender wage gap: 2018 Earnings differences by race and ethnicity. *Institute for Women's Policy Research*. https://iwpr.org/publications/gender-wage-gap-2018/.

Heilman, M. E. (2016, March 14). What working women can do when they don't get Credit for collaboration. *Quartz*. https://qz.com/638286/the-practical-steps-working-women-can-take-to-get-credit-when-its-due/.

Horowitz, J., Parker, K., & Stepler, R. (2017, October 18). Wide partisan gaps in U.S. over how far the country has come on gender equality. *Pew Research Center*. https://www.pewresearch.org/fact-tank/2018/03/15/for-womens-history-month-a-look-at-gender-gains-and-gaps-in-the-u-s/.

Kanter, R. (1977). *Men and women of the corporation*. New York: Basic Books.

Kirby, M. (1999) Theories of gender inequality (Chapter 7). In *Stratification and differentiation. Skills-based sociology*. London: Palgrave.

Kroska, A. (2014) The social psychology of gender inequality. In J. McLeod, E. Lawler, & M. Schwalbe (Eds.), *Handbook of the social psychology of inequality*. Handbooks of Sociology and Social Research. Dordrecht: Springer.

Levs, J. (2019, March 11). Why paternity leave is needed to promote gender equality. *Strategy & Business*. https://www.strategy-business.com/article/Why-paternity-leave-is-needed-to-promote-gender-equality?gko=ab6b8.

Lopata, H., & Thorne, B. (1978). One the term "sex roles". *Signs, 3*(3), 718–721.

Martin, K. (1998). Becoming a gendered body: Practices in preschools. *American Sociological Review, 63*(4), 494–511.

Maume, D. (2008). Gender differences in providing urgent childcare Among dual-earner parents. *Social Forces, 87*(1), 273–297.

McCulloch, H. (2017). *Closing the women's wealth gap: What it is. Why it matters, and what can be done about it*. https://womenswealthgap.org/wp-content/uploads/2017/06/Closing-the-Womens-Wealth-Gap-Report-Jan 2017.pdf.

Miller, C. (2014, September 6). The motherhood penalty vs. the fatherhood bonus. *The New York Times*. https://www.nytimes.com/2014/09/07/upshot/a-child-helps-your-career-if-youre-a-man.html.

Misra, J., Lundquist, J., Holmes, E., & Agiomavritis, S. (2011). The ivory ceiling of service work. *American Association of University Professors*. https://www.aaup.org/article/ivory-ceiling-service-work?wbc_purpose=basic&WBCMODE=presentationunpublished#.XrHnMZNKjFw.

Murdock, G. P. (1949). *Social structure*. New York: The Free Press.

National Partnership for Women & Families. (2020). *Quantifying America's gender wage gap by race/ethnicity*. https://www.nationalpartnership.org/our-work/resources/economic-justice/fair-pay/quantifying-americas-gender-wage-gap.pdf.

National Science Board. (2018, January). Chapter 2: Higher education in science and engineering. In *Science & engineering indicators*. https://nsf.gov/statistics/2018/nsb20181/report/sections/higher-education-in-science-and-engineering/undergraduate-education-enrollment-and-degrees-in-the-united-states.

Phillips, C. (2020, March 8). To close the wealth gap for women of color, business can take the lead. *The Boston Globe*. https://www.bostonglobe.com/2020/03/08/opinion/close-wealth-gap-women-color-business-can-take-lead/.

Rehel, E. (2014). When dad stays home too: Paternity leave, gender, and parenting. *Gender & Society, 28*(1), 110–132.

Ridgeway, C. (2011). *Framed by gender: How gender inequality persists in the modern world*. New York: Oxford University Press.

Risman, B. (2004). Gender as a social structure: Theory wrestling with activism. *Gender & Society, 18*, 429–450.

Risman, B. (2018). Gender matters: Bringing in a gender structure analysis. A comment on "paternal and maternal gatekeeping? Choreographing care-giving in families" by Tina Miller and "rethinking family socialization to gender through the lens of multi-local, post-separation families" by Laura Merla. *Sociologica, 12*(3), 67–74.

Rossin-Slater, M., & Stearns, J. (2020, February 18). The economic imperative of enacting paid family leave across the United States. *Washington Center of Equitable Justice*. https://equitablegrowth.org/the-economic-imperative-of-enacting-paid-family-leave-across-the-united-states/.

Scarborough, W., & Risman, B. (2018). Gender Inequality. In A. Treviño (Ed.), *The Cambridge handbook of social problems* (pp. 339–362). Cambridge: Cambridge University Press.

Tower, L. E., & Latimer, M. (2016). Cumulative disadvantage: Effects of early career childcare issues on faculty research travel. *Affilia, 31*(3), 317–330.

U.S. Department of Labor. (2017). *Paternity leave: Why parental leave for fathers is so important for Working families*. https://www.dol.gov/sites/dol gov/files/OASP/legacy/files/PaternityBrief.pdf.

Washington Center for Equitable Growth. (2017). *Occupational segregation in the United States*. https://equitablegrowth.org/wp-content/uploads/2017/09/092717-occupational-seg.pdf.

West, C., & Zimmerman, D. (1987). Doing gender. *Gender & Society, 1*(2), 125–151.

Wezerek, G., & Ghodsee, K. (2020, March 5). Women's unpaid labor is worth $10,900,000,000,000. *The New York Times*. https://www.nytimes.com/interactive/2020/03/04/opinion/women-unpaid-labor.html.

Williams, C. L., Muller, C., & Kilanski, K. (2012). Gendered organizations in the new economy. *Gender & Society, 26*(4), 549–573.

Williams, J. (2001). *Unbending gender: Why family and work conflict and what to do about it*. New York: Oxford University Press.

PART II

Contemporary Gender-Based Issues

CHAPTER 4

Gender and Communication: Are There Decisive Differences?

Mercedes Coffman and Joan Marques

INTRODUCTION

Communication can be defined in a few words, but comprises a gamut of nuances that are hard to capture in one mere sentence. To start with a generic definition, communication is "a process by which information is exchanged between individuals through a common system of symbols, signs, or behavior" (Communication, 2020). Petkeviciute and Streimikiene (2017) point out that, aside from a process of information exchange in multiple environments and through myriad means, communication should also be considered from the perspectives of both, the sender and the receiver. For each of the constituents, the process requires several sequential processes such as encoding and decoding, which brings along the process of interpretation. In addition, communication can be manifested through multiple modes, such as linear, cyclic, triangular, or spiral.

M. Coffman · J. Marques (✉)
Woodbury University, Burbank, CA, USA
e-mail: Joan.Marques@woodbury.edu

J. Marques (ed.), *Exploring Gender at Work*,
https://doi.org/10.1007/978-3-030-64319-5_4

In their analysis on the origins of sex differences in human behavior, Eagly and Wood (1999) associate men with characteristics of power, success, achievement, leadership and control, while they link women with emotions, relationships, and communication. Interestingly, communication is generally considered to be a core aspect in leadership, even though the connection between communication and leadership is not always explicit (Cunningham, Hazel, & Hayes, 2020). While some sources may describe communication as a transactional process in leadership behavior—where leaders use communication to accomplish their goals—it is becoming more apparent that communication also works transformational, as it can serve communal goals, and address as well as resolve social challenges such as "political discourse, political unrest, persistent social inequalities, and uncertainty brought on by new realities such as climate change" (Cunningham et al., 2020, p. 23).

The mere way communication is perceived, and the weight it gets assigned, differs based on professions. Bloksgaard, Fekjær, and Møberg (2020) for instance, find that, while many police recruits in Scandinavia don't agree on stereotypes of men being more competent at handling violence and women being better with care and communication, there is still a decent percentage that believes the stereotypes have merit.

COMMUNICATION AND GENDER

The next section of this chapter will discuss some gender-influenced communication modes and a number of perceived stereotypes, as explained by multiple scholars over the past decades. A stereotype is a representation of a social group that accentuates a characteristic or a set of characteristics, which may give rise to a uniform impression of that group (Moriarty, Mitchell, & Wells, 2009). Stereotypes entail simplified symbols, accepted by large parts of a community, influencing the way members of social groups are perceived (Gauntlett, 2002). As for gender stereotypes, Browne (1998) describes these as general beliefs about specific qualities and roles attributed to psychological characteristics and behaviors of men and women. Kotzaivazoglou, Hatzithomas, and Tsichla (2018) add a caveat that we should be mindful about the concept and context of gender, as this is an organic process. In other words, with the changing implementations of masculinity and femininity, gender roles may shift.

When considering communication within the scope of gender, we find that there have been differences registered in the way men and women process information, apply emotional intelligence, display leadership traits, use skills, and interpret communication (Jones et al., 2018). Pearson (1981) presented the terms masculine rhetoric versus feminine rhetoric, with the first one being decisive, direct, rational, authoritative, logical, aggressive, and impersonal, and the second being cautious, receptive, indirect, emotional, conciliatory, subjective, and polite (Baker, 1991). Several other resources (Leaper, 1991; Maltz & Borker, 1982; Wood, 2009) have confirmed that women are more prone to use communication as a relationship instrument with other people, while men focus their communication more on dominance and power exertion, and outcome expectations. Augustahealth.com (2017) discussed gender differences pertaining to verbal centers and memory. It states that "female brains have verbal centers in both hemispheres with more connections between words, memories, and feelings, while male brains tend to only have verbal centers in the left hemisphere with fewer connections between words, memories, and feelings." Although this may lead to the assumptions that women use more words than men, it could also offer insights into the lack of confidence and competitiveness women may exhibit in the workplace. Since women have more connections between memory, feelings, and words, they may be more inhibited due to more vivid memories of past failures, consideration of potential failures, and over analysis and calculation of risks. Based on their research, Jones et al. (2018) observed that women seem to be more detailed and apologetic, while men get to the point more directly; women use communication to develop relationships and focus on the needs of others, while men are more geared toward giving rise to an impression of confidence.

The following two interesting side notes on gender communication styles may provide some insights in how these styles translate in professional success.

1. Juodvalkis, Grefe, Hogue, Svyantek, and DeLamarter (2003) found that men with dominate communication styles were more likely to be hired over comparable female applicants. The cause for this to happen may have its foundation in the very structure of job interviews, where problem-solving skills are high on the priority list, thus skewing the balance in favor of the direct and authoritarian communication styles of men.

2. Lammers and Gast (2017) found that today's era, promoting "soft skills" as most desirable and effective, and with that, a more feministic communication style, still does not propel more women into leadership positions. At the same time that female, people-centered leadership skills, such as empathy, communication, and emotional intelligence, are encouraged in corporate suites, there seems to be an undermining campaign toward affirmative action which includes hiring more women at the C-level. Several studies have found that the expected increase of women in leadership positions due to harboring the right skills has created renewed efforts to sustain gender inequality, indicating that even positive stereotypes confirming that women are particularly well qualified for leadership can hurt them in their ascent to top positions (Lammers & Gast, 2017).

Gender and Virtual Communication

Jones et al. (2018) noted that communication styles don't significantly change through communication platforms. In online communication, these authors have noted the stereotypical divergence, with women frequently coming across as politer and more appreciative than men, and being more concerned about care-related issues, while men seem to be more focused on bring about change. An interesting, related finding came from Baruh, Chisik, Bisson, and Şenova (2014), who discovered that greater online information disclosure from males was perceived in a more positive light, and led to greater connectivity desires, while this was the other way around with females: the more information they disclosed about themselves, the less attractive they seemed to come across. Baruh et al. presented the potential explanation that conventional gender perspectives may be foundational here, with males being considered the action oriented ones, taking more initiatives, while females are considered to be more reserved and discreet.

Gender and Nonverbal Communication

Gender influences are also registered in nonverbal communication. In several societies, males are depicted as aggressive, controlling, and having a take-charge attitude, while females are perceived as sensitive, emotional, and passive (Phutela, 2015).

Women are more expressive when they use non-verbal communication; they tend to smile more than men and use their hands more. Men are less likely to make eye contact like women. Men also come off as more relaxed, while women seem tenser. Men are more comfortable with close proximity to females, but women are more comfortable with close proximity with other females. In terms of interpreting non-verbal signals, women are better than men. (Phutela, 2015, pp. 46–47)

Crowley and Knowles (2014) largely concur with the above by affirming that there are lower expectations for women to regulate their emotions in social settings as there are for man, because women are often trained from an early age to avoid conflict and communicate in an overtly pleasant and agreeable manner. These authors also agree that smiling is more expected from women than from men, pointing out that a smile is sometimes perceived as a token of appeasement from those with less power. Conversely, Crowley and Knowles (2014) underscore that there is a higher expectation for men to show aggressive behavior, such as anger and contempt, since society seems to consider these negative emotions more appropriate for men Bringing these behavioral cues within the realm of mental health, Crowley and Knowles posit that men more often express negative emotions but also experience higher levels of violent behavior, while women more often suppress negative emotions yet experience higher levels of passive-aggressive behavior.

Gender and Information Processing

In regard to the processing of information, Chua and Murray (2015) highlight some differences that can be useful in optimizing the effectiveness of intra-organizational communications. The research of these scholars yielded that men appear to respond best to messages that are thematic, containing attribute-based features that emphasize the distinctive characteristics of a product, while women appear to prefer advertisements that are detailed, descriptive and have a tendency to compare products. Goldman (2017) states that a woman's hippocampus, critical to learning and memorization, is larger than a man's and works differently. This may offer insights into why women prefer more detailed communication styles as it is more easily stores into learning and memory parts of the brain. Men, as stated by Goldman tend to have a larger amygdala, which is associated with the experiencing of emotions and the recollection of such experiences. This may also offer insights into why men take more risks than women. In work environments this could lead to the recommendation that women may prefer leaders that are highly detailed in their communication, while men may prefer short communications that highlight the areas of importance and how the information concerns them.

It seems, however, that the aging process mellows many of the gender-based communication discrepancies. In a study comprising 153 men and 151 women over the age of 40 focusing on sex differences in the communication values of mature adults and what the possible influence of psychological gender (masculinity versus femininity) was therein, MacGeorge, Feng, and Butler (2003) found that older men and women value affective and instrumental communication skills to a very similar degree. The main significance in divergence that these scholars found was that women placed somewhat more value than men on conflict management and comforting skill, while men placed somewhat more value than women on persuasive skill.

Considering Gender Communication Differences

In the sections above, a range of gender-based communication perspectives were shared, including differences. The general consensus seems to be that the following are some of the most frequently mentioned differences in gender communication: (1) women are more vocal than men; (2) women are more verbally skilled than men; (3) men are more action oriented in their use of language, while women are more relationship oriented; (4) Men are more competitive in their language use, while women are more cooperative; and (5) the above differences lead to regular communication frictions between men and women (Cameron, 2007). Some other communication differences often highlighted are, that men mainly communicate to support their prominence, while women do so to build relationships; men smile less than women, women use more paralanguage (nonverbal indicators of listening and understanding) than men do; men will use communicative touching more to confirm their dominance (pat on the back or shoulder), while women will touch for connection (arm-touching or offering a hug), and women use more eye contact than men (Admin/Public Relations ..., 2017).

It needs to be underscored here that stereotypes are not always congruent with reality, as there will be many members from each gender who cannot identify with the stereotypes their group has been ascribed to. Additionally, as pointed out earlier in this chapter, gender expectations and implementations change over time, meaning that even stereotypes have a dynamic nature and change over time. Let us now review the above-listed stereotypes and reflect on their legitimacy in modern society.

Are Women More Vocal Than Men?

Taking the persistent claim that women talk more than men into consideration, Hammond (2013) reviewed multiple sources over time on this subject, and found that there is no consistency in findings, and that the allegation is therefore not validated. Referring to a long-standing and often repeated allegation that women express an average of 20,000 words a day, while men only utter about 7,000, Hammond discussed a wide range of studies made of children (boys versus girls) and adults (men versus women) and reported that, while in some studies the female cohort did express some more words than the male cohort, the differences were fairly insignificant. Yet, she also presented a series of findings in which men were the bigger talkers. Aponte (2019) draws a similar conclusion and warns for falling prey to holding on to stereotypes that may turn out to be unsubstantiated and harmful to some. Roeder (2014) specifies that women may speak more when in larger groups, but in general the talk volume is determined by contexts, and can therefore not explicitly be attributed to men or women.

Are Women More Verbally Skilled Than Men?

Swaminathan (2008) took a deeper look into this stereotypical assertion, and found that it is factual. There is also a scientifically proven reason for this to be, since girls seem to display greater brain activity when tapping into their linguistic skills than boys. Boys seem to need more illustrative assistance in learning language than girls, while girls have a greater ability to spell and determine the meaning of words, resulting in greater language accuracy.

While the verdict is not completely out, there have been scientific conversations about testosterone being a potential instigator of poorer verbal skills in men. Tests with transgender men have shown that their verbal skills diminished during the testosterone intake process, but this finding has so far been refuted as unsubstantial. While neuroscientists and psychiatrists are still debating whether there is a difference between male brains and female brains, with some confirming and others discounting it, Barclay (2015) concludes that more studies will be needed to solidify this assertion. In an article debunking several gender stereotypes, Fulbright (2011) admits that a wide range of studies show a moderate advantage of women over men in this regard, but also asserts that there has been very little difference found in reading comprehension, vocabulary, and verbal reasoning between the genders.

Are Men More Action-Oriented and Women More Relationship-Oriented in Their Language Use?

In a study among Iranian graduate students (male and female), Pakza-dian and Tootkaboni (2018) found that women showed more acceptance and facilitation in conversations, while men demonstrated a more assertive mode, and used different strategies such as interruption, topical changes, criticizing, and engaging conflict to establish or maintain their conversa-tional dominance. One may take into consideration the cultural influences in a male domineering society that may have skewed the findings of this study. In a 2005 study University of California, Irvine, gathered findings that "men have approximately 6.5 times the amount of gray matter, while women have nearly 10 times the amount of white matter." Gray matter allows for more task-focused actions, while white matter allows for easier multitasking. These finding may explain while men are more drawn to business-oriented fields with a compartmentalized focus, while women tend to operate from a broader focus when considering choices and behavioral actions (*Intelligence in Men and Women...*, 2005). In a senior thesis at Claremont Colleges, Merchant (2012) cites several authors to support her statement, "[o]verall, women are expected to use commu-nication to enhance social connections and relationships, while men use language to enhance social dominance" (p. 17). Women have utilized the "tend and befriend" communication style for centuries. Women commu-nicate to strengthen relationship bonds, while men communicate to solve problems. To balance out this stereotype, Ni (2020) points out that masculine and feminine communication styles are not gender-specific, and that there are both men and women adhering to masculine and feminine styles. Ni stresses that regardless of one's gender it is best to be comfortable with both, feminine and masculine styles of communication. Upon clarifying this important side note, Ni (2020) lists the masculine communication style as power-oriented, self-geared, verbally dominant, action, goal and issue focused, and the feminine style as relation and human-connection oriented, inquisitive and focused on others, affirming, mindful toward others' emotions, and humane. Addressing some weaknesses of each style, Ni (2020) emphasizes that the masculine style may be considered destructive to relationships, cause separation and isolation, may seem narcissistic, and disconnected from genuine emotions, while the feminine style could be seen as self-sacrificing, repressive of own wants, needs and feelings, subject to becoming dominated, and losing a sense of true self.

Are Men More Competitive and Women More Cooperative in Their Language Use?

The Harvard Women and Public Policy Program created an online Gender Action Portal, in which it confirmed study findings that men are more competitive than women. The portal posits that, while gender-based behavioral differences are factual in childhood, puberty, and adulthood, the stereotypes are perpetuated in the professional realm through a mix of discrimination and job preferences among women, based on requirements. This, then, may be the foundational factor behind why there are only 2.5% of the highest paid US executives being women. The Portal further explains that women may turn away from the long hours that executive jobs require, while they may also be turned off by the high degree of competition needed to succeed in such positions. (Harvard Kennedy School, 2019). Sharing the study findings, the Portal highlights that, while women hold the ability to be equally competitive as men, they often deliberately turn away from competitive choices.

The above perspective is verified by Niederle and Vesterlund (2011), who also found that women, while equally capable, often differ in willingness to compete. Niederle and Vesterlund add that part of this trend may be attributed to the fact that, aside from a greater passion for competition, men tend to have more confidence in their abilities than women. The above affirmation does not clarify whether the lesser degree of willingness could be related to childrearing, and gender role stereotypes and whether the assertion also applies to unmarried, childless women.

Is There a Difference in Communication Philosophy Between Men and Women?

In an insightful article, Kinsey Goman (2016) reiterates several of the earlier made points about gender related ways of communicating. She considers verbal and nonverbal communication cues, and highlights strengths and weaknesses of each. Females, she asserts, focus their communication on reading body language, listening, and displaying empathy, while men have a more commanding physical presence, are more to the point, and know how to display power. Referring to the weaknesses in their communication, Kinsey Goman (2016) warns that women may come across as overly emotional, not getting to the point, and unauthoritative, while men risk the chance of making an overly blunt, insensitive, and too self-assured impression. Also similar to earlier cited authors, Mohindra and Azhar (2012) link gender communication differences to the ways the sexes are generally raised, with girls often being taught to "use their manners, play quietly, and be ladylike," and boys being allowed to "use rough language, play loudly, and be rambunctious" (p. 18). In line with other authors, Kinsey Goman alerts us that in work environments we need an appropriate balance of the masculine and feminine style to be considered positively. The trick is, that there is no recipe for this balance, as it will be determined by circumstances, needs, and audiences.

Do Women Smile More Than Men?

In a 2017 article, McDuff et al. stated that women are known to exaggerate their facial expressions more, resulting in them laughing more often. McDuff et al. found, from a study with 708 males and 863 females, that a higher percentage of the participating women smiled more and often longer than the male participants.

Do Men and Women Touch in Communication for Different Reasons?

Touching is a form of nonverbal communication that varies based on individuals' aggression, comfort, sympathy, and love. At best, this way of communicating can be called ambiguous, as it varies, even between the genders (Major, 1981). DiBiase and Gunnoe (2004) add culture and age to the parameters that determine the degree and application of communicative touching. When considering human interactions, it becomes apparent that touching is more widely accepted when initiated by a person with a higher status toward one with lower rank, such as manager with employee, doctor with nurse or customer with waitress (Major, 1981). Henley (1977) posits that nonreciprocal touch is associated with power, may represent the balance of power in a relationship, and can serve as a cue symbolic of power. Since most C-level positions, till date, are held by males, this type of touching, represented by pats on the back or touching shoulders, have been predominantly assigned to men, leading to the general impression that men professionally touch to confirm their dominance, while women, often in less powerful positions, and attributed with greater expressiveness of emotions such as empathy and interest, touch for connection. Henley (1973) confirms the above by stating that the frequently occurring status difference (in work settings), gives men a touching privilege, which, in turn, contributes to their domination of women. DiBiase and Gunnoe (2004) add that men are more prone to touch with their hands, while women touch more with other body parts. These authors also caution that touching patterns should not be generalized without caution, as male and female touching patterns are not universal, so they are unlikely to be the result of biological predispositions only (Fig. 4.1).

Addressing Gender Communication Patterns in Contemporary Times

As several authors cited in this chapter have indicated, gender stereotyping is complicated due to the ever-changing nature of humans and the ways they behave within and perceive genders. As social dynamics change, and certain professions and behaviors become more accepted across genders, stereotyping may increasingly gain the reputation of a slippery slope. Other important contributors to the fading stereotypes may be the changing ways boys and girls are raised, with deliberately less emphasis on their gender, while cultural aspects may also become diluted in our increasingly interconnected world with growing exposure through social and other media.

As has also been mentioned in this chapter, there is still debate among various streams of scientists about the issue of brain differences between males and females, with some sources claiming that there is no such thing as a male or a female brain, and others vehemently defending the

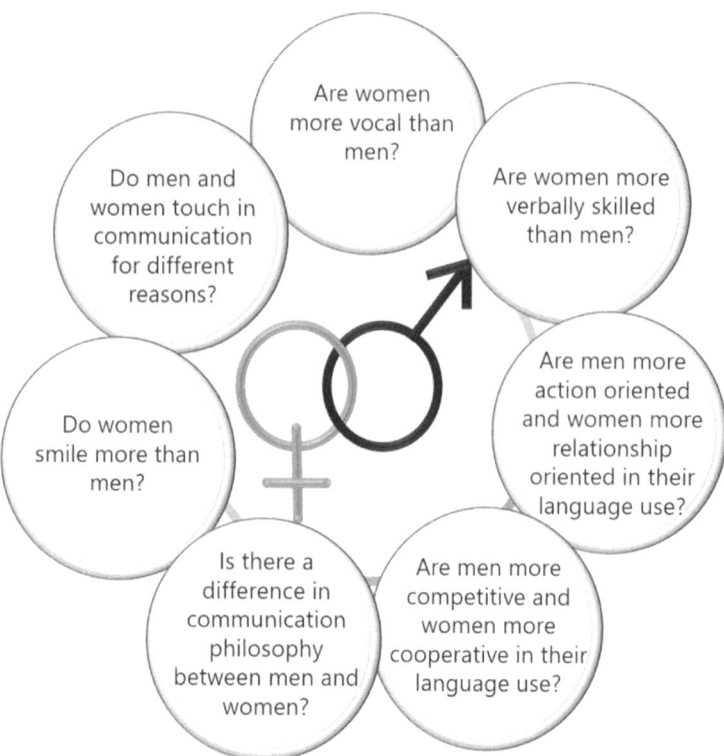

Fig. 4.1 Overview of the gender communication differences discussed

divergences in, for instance, the uses of language skills, and sensitivity awareness.

It is, indeed, not an easy task to discern where certain communication trends originate from, and the most acceptable answer to this question may be that we will learn more as cultural, social, and professional dynamics shift.

We may consider ourselves fortunate that contemporary times dilute many of the gender stereotypes, thus reducing the opportunity to nurture biases toward behaviors of men and women. That said, it is critical to end this chapter with the cautionary statement that the magnitude of "typical" gender assigned behaviors remain at the individual level, and will continue to be applied or defied as such.

Chapter Takeaways

- Several sources relate males with characteristics of power, success, achievement, leadership and control, and females with emotions, relationships, and communication.
- The way communication modes are accepted among male and female counterparts is often influenced by factors such as upbringing, culture, and work environments.
- We should be mindful about the concept and context of gender, as this is an organic process. With the changing implementations of masculinity and femininity, gender roles are shifting.
- Several resources have confirmed that women are more prone to use communication as a relationship instrument with other people, while men focus their communication more on dominance and power exertion, and outcome expectations.
- Communication styles don't significantly change through communication platforms. In online communication, women frequently coming across as politer and more appreciative, while men seem to be more focused on bring about change.
- Gender influences are also registered in nonverbal communication. In several societies, males are depicted as aggressive, controlling, and having a take-charge attitude, while females are perceived as sensitive, emotional, and passive.
- In regard to the processing of information, women may prefer leaders that are highly detailed in their communication, while men may prefer short communications that highlight the areas of importance and how the information concerns them.
- Addressing some commonly listed differences in gender communication:
  - *Are women more vocal than men?* There is no clear evidence that such is the case. Much of the talk volume is determined by contexts, and can therefore not explicitly be attributed to men or women.
  - *Are women more verbally skilled than men?* While the verdict is not completely out, a wide range of studies show a moderate advantage of women over men in this regard, but also asserts that there has been very little difference found in reading comprehension, vocabulary, and verbal reasoning between the genders.

- *Are men more action-oriented and women more relationship-oriented in their language use?* Masculine and feminine communication styles are not gender-specific. There are both men and women adhering to masculine and feminine styles. Regardless of one's gender it is best to be comfortable with both, feminine and masculine styles of communication.
- *Are men more competitive and women more cooperative in their language use?* Studies have found that men are more competitive than women. The stereotypes infused in the raising process are often perpetuated in the professional realm through a mix of discrimination and job preferences among women, based on requirements. While women hold the ability to be equally competitive as men, they often deliberately turn away from competitive choices.
- *Is there a difference in communication philosophy between men and women?* Females generally focus their communication on reading body language, listening, and displaying empathy, while men have a more commanding physical presence, are more to the point, and know how to display power. In work environments we need an appropriate balance of the masculine and feminine style to be considered positively. There is no recipe for this balance. It will be determined by circumstances, needs, and audiences.
- *Do women smile more than men?* Studies found that a higher percentage of women smile more and often longer than their male participants.
- *Do men and women touch in communication for different reasons?* Touching is more widely accepted when initiated by a person with a higher status toward one with lower rank. Since most C-level positions, till date, are held by males, this type of touching, represented by pats on the back or touching shoulders, have been predominantly assigned to men, leading to the general impression that men professionally touch to confirm their dominance, while women, often in less powerful positions, and attributed with greater expressiveness of emotions such as empathy and interest, touch for connection. However, touching patterns should not be generalized without caution, as male and female touching patterns are not universal, so they are unlikely to be the result of biological predispositions only.

- Gender stereotyping is complicated due to the ever-changing nature of humans and the ways they behave within and perceive genders. As social dynamics change, and certain professions and behaviors become more accepted across genders, stereotyping may increasingly gain the reputation of a slippery slope.

References

Admin/Public Relations & Advertising. (2017, December 12). *Gender differences in communication styles.* Retrieved from https://online.pointpark.edu/public-relations-and-advertising/gender-differences-communication-styles/.

Aponte, C. (2019, October 10). Do women really talk more than men? What's the evidence? *Psychology Today.* Retrieved from https://www.psychologytoday.com/us/blog/marriage-equals/201910/do-women-really-talk-more-men.

AugustaHealth.com. (2017, September 19). *Battle of the sexes: Male vs. female brains.* HealthFocused: Educational health information to improve your well-being. Retrieved from https://www.augustahealth.com/health-focused/battle-of-the-sexes-male-vs-female-brains.

Baker, M. A. (1991). Gender and verbal communication in professional settings: A review of research. *Management Communication Quarterly, 5*(1), 36.

Barclay, R. S. (September 11, 2015). *Is testosterone the reason women have better verbal skills than men?* Healthline. Retrieved from https://www.healthline.com/health-news/is-testosterone-the-reason-woman-have-better-verbal-skills-than-men-090315#1.

Baruh, L., Chisik, Y., Bisson, C., & Şenova, B. (2014). When sharing less means more: How gender moderates the impact of quantity of information shared in a social network profile on profile viewers' intentions about socialization. *Communication Research Reports, 31*(3), 244–251.

Bloksgaard, L., Fekjær, S. B., & Møberg, R. J. (2020). Conceptions of gender and competencies among police recruits in Scandinavia 1. *Nordic Journal of Working Life Studies, 10*(2), 43–59.

Browne, B. A. (1998). Gender stereotypes in advertising on children's television in the 1990s: A cross-national analysis. *Journal of Advertising, 27*(1), 83–96.

Cameron, D. (2007, October 1). What language barrier? *The Guardian.* Retrieved from https://www.theguardian.com/world/2007/oct/01/gender.books.

Chua, S. M. Y., & Murray, D. W. (2015). How toxic leaders are perceived: Gender and information-processing. *Leadership & Organization Development Journal, 36*(3), 292–307.

Communication. (2020). Definition of communication. *Merriam-Webster Online*. Retrieved from https://www.merriam-webster.com/dictionary/communication.

Crowley, J., & Knowles, J. (2014). Gender differences in perceived happiness and well-being of individuals who engage in contemptuous communication. *Communication Reports, 27*(1), 27–38.

Cunningham, C. M., Hazel, M., & Hayes, T. J. (2020). Communication and leadership 2020: Intersectional, mindful, and digital. *Communication Research Trends, 39*(1), 4–31.

DiBiase, R., & Gunnoe, J. (2004). Gender and culture differences in touching behavior. *The Journal of Social Psychology, 144*(1), 49–62.

Eagly, A. H., & Wood, W. (1999). The origins of sex differences in human behavior: Evolved dispositions versus social roles. *American Psychologist, 54*(6), 408–423.

Fulbright, Y. K. (2011, November 17). Male-female communication: Debunking the Mars-Venus myth. *Huffington Post*. Retrieved from https://www.huffpost.com/entry/male-female-communication_b_813095.

Gauntlett, D. (2002). *Media, gender and identity: An introduction*. London and New York: Routledge.

Goldman, B. (2017). Two minds: The cognitive differences between men and women. *Stanford medicine: Sex, gender and medicine*. Retrieved from https://stanmed.stanford.edu/2017spring/how-mens-and-womens-brains-are-different.html.

Hammond, C. (2013, November 11). Prattle of the sexes: Do women talk more than men? *BBC − Future*. Retrieved from https://www.bbc.com/future/article/20131112-do-women-talk-more-than-men.

Harvard Kennedy School. (2019). Do women shy away from competition? Do men compete too much? *Gender Action Portal*. Retrieved from https://gap.hks.harvard.edu/do-women-shy-away-competition-do-men-compete-too-much.

Henley, N. M. (1973). Status and sex: Some touching observations. *Bulletin of the Psychonomic Society, 2*, 91–93.

Henley, N. M. (1977). *Body politics: Power, sex, and nonverbal communication*. Englewood Cliffs, NJ: Prentice-Hall.

Intelligence in Men and Women is a Gray and White Matter. (2005, January 22). ScienceDaily, University of California, Irvine. Retrieved from https://www.sciencedaily.com/releases/2005/01/050121100142.htm.

Jones, J. S., Tapp, S. R., Murray, S. R., Palumbo, R. J., Strange, A. T., & Ritschel-Trifilo, P. (2018). Gender differences in online communication and the impact of faculty gender. *Academy of Business Research Journal, 1*, 20–40.

Juodvalkis, J. L., Grefe, B. A., Hogue, M., Svyantek, D. J., & DeLamarter, W. (2003). The effects of job stereotype, applicant gender, and communication style on ratings in screening interviews. *International Journal of Organizational Analysis, 11*(1), 67–84.

Kinsey Goman, C. (2016, March 31). Is your communication style dictated by your gender? *Forbes.* Retrieved from https://www.forbes.com/sites/carolkins eygoman/2016/03/31/is-your-communication-style-dictated-by-your-gen der/#675cab9eb9d3.

Kotzaivazoglou, I., Hatzithomas, L., & Tsichla, E. (2018). Gender stereotypes in advertisements for male politicians: Longitudinal evidence from greece. *International Review on Public and Non - Profit Marketing, 15*(3), 333–352.

Lammers, J., & Gast, A. (2017). Stressing the advantages of female leadership can place women at a disadvantage. *Social Psychology, 48*(1), 28–39.

Leaper, C. (1991). Influence and involvement in children's discourse: Age, gender, and partner effects. *Child Development, 62*(4), 797–811.

MacGeorge, E. L., Feng, B., & Butler, G. L. (2003). Gender difference in communication values of mature adults. *Communication Research Reports, 20*(3), 191–199.

Major, B. (1981). Gender patterns in touching behavior. In C. Mayo, et al. (Eds.), *Gender and nonverbal behavior.* New York, NY: Springer-Verlag.

Maltz, D. N., & Borker, R. A. (1982). A cultural approach to male-female miscommunication. In J. J. Gumperz (Ed.), *Languages and social identity* (pp. 196–216). Cambridge: Cambridge University Press.

McDuff, D., Kodra, E., el Kaliouby, R., & LaFrance, M. (2017, April 19). A large-scale analysis of sex differences in facial expressions. *Plos One Journal* [Open Access]. Retrieved from https://journals.plos.org/plosone/article?id= 10.1371/journal.pone.0173942.

Merchant, K. (2012). How men and women differ: Gender differences in communication styles, influence tactics, and leadership styles. *CMC Senior Theses.* Retrieved from https://scholarship.claremont.edu/cgi/viewcontent. cgi?article=1521&context=cmc_theses.

Mohindra, V., & Azhar, S. (2012). Gender communication: A comparative analysis of communicational approaches of men and women at workplaces. *IOSR Journal of Humanities and Social Science, 2*(1), 18–27.

Moriarty, S., Mitchell, N., & Wells, W. (2009). *Advertising: Principles & practice* (8th ed.). Upper Saddle River, NJ: Pearson Prentice Hall.

Ni, P. (2020, February 9). How to be an effective, well-rounded communicator. *Psychology Today.* Retrieved from https://www.psychologytoday.com/us/ blog/communication-success/202002/how-be-effective-well-rounded-com municator.

Niederle, M., & Vesterlund, L. (2011). Gender and competition. *The Annual Review of Economics*. Retrieved from https://web.stanford.edu/~niederle/NV.AnnualReview.Print.pdf.

Pakzadian, M., & Tootkaboni, A. A. (2018). The role of gender in conversational dominance: A study of EFL learners. *Cogent Education, 5*(1), 1560602. Retrieved from https://doi.org/10.1080/2331186X.2018.1560602.

Pearson, S. S. (1981). Rhetoric and organizational change: New applications of feminine style. In B. L. Forisha & B. H. Goldman (Eds.), *Outsiders on the inside* (pp. 55–74). Englewood Cliffs, NJ: Prentice-Hall.

Petkeviciute, N., & Streimikiene, D. (2017). Gender and sustainable negotiation. *Economics & Sociology, 10*(2), 279–295.

Phutela, D. (2015). The importance of non-verbal communication. *IUP Journal of Soft Skills, 9*(4), 43–49.

Roeder, A. (2014, July 23). Do women talk more than men? *Harvard School of Public Health*. Retrieved from https://www.hsph.harvard.edu/news/features/do-women-talk-more-than-men/.

Swaminathan, N. (March 5, 2008). Girl talk: Are women really Better at language? New research shows that young girls may learn language more completely than their male peers. *Scientific American*. Retrieved from https://www.scientificamerican.com/article/are-women-really-better-with-language/.

Wood, J. (2009). *Feminist standpoint theory. Encyclopedia of communication theory* (pp. 397–399). Thousand Oaks, CA: Sage.

CHAPTER 5

The Conundrum of Gender Stereotypes

Birute Regine

INTRODUCTION

On September 20, 1973, during the second wave of the women's liberation movement, Billie Jean King accepted Bobby Riggs' challenge to a $100,000 winner-takes-all tennis match. Riggs had dubbed King the "leading women's libber of tennis." King had ignored an earlier challenge from Riggs offer to a match, but she felt compelled to play him after he beat Australian tennis star Margaret Court, a leading money-maker on the women's professional tour. The 55-year-old Bobby Riggs, a tennis champion from the late 1930s and 40, was notoriously and openly skeptical of women's talents on the tennis court, belittling women players. A blatant male chauvinist (his associates insisted it was an act) he claimed women's game was inferior to men's, and that women "don't have the emotional stability to win…women belong in the bedroom and kitchen,

B. Regine (✉)
Hancock, NH, USA
e-mail: biruteregine@comcast.net

in that order."[1] Riggs, who was a self-described hustler, had coined the match "the battle of the sexes."

Dubbed by some "the libber vs. the lobber," the match took place in front of a sold-out Houston Astrodome crowd. About 90 million people watched on TV, the most watched tennis match of all time. The 29-year-old King felt enormous pressure to win, fearing that a loss would set back the women's movement by fifty years. Riggs, ever the provocateur, came wearing a warm-up jacket emblazoned with "Sugar Daddy" on it. In spite of all the drama and histrionics, King prevailed, 6-4, 6-3, 6-3. At a news conference after the match, Riggs admitted that King was too good, too fast. She returned all his passing shots and made great plays off them. He had seriously underestimated his rival.

King had a significant role in developing greater respect and recognition for women athletes and inspired a generation of women to enter sports. She advocated for gender equality and equal pay. After Riggs' death at age 77 in 1995, King complimented her former rival and his, probably accidental, contribution to the advancement of gender equality.

Although the match had been coined the battle of the sexes, it had ultimately been a struggle between maintaining gender stereotypes (Riggs' goal) and shattering them (King's goal). Male chauvinism, where men disparaged or denigrated women, believing that they were inferior to men and thus deserving of less than equal treatment, was still pretty blatant back in the 1970s in spite of the women's movement. But here in the twenty-first century surely, we must be beyond that. But are we?

In March 2020, US Soccer claimed it wouldn't pay women and men players equally because, it argued, the men's game required a higher level of skill. Male players, they asserted, have more responsibility, an argument it used in a 2019 gender discrimination lawsuit filed by the US Women's National Soccer team. This argument flies in the face of the fact that these women players who, compared to their male counterparts were denied equal pay, training, travel conditions, equal promotion, support, and development of their games, had more successes than the men's team. The women's team won four World Cups and four Olympic Gold Medals. The furthest the men's team advanced in the World Cup was the quarterfinals in 2002. You can hear clear echoes of the themes of gender

---

[1] "The Battle of the Sexes," on-line Encyclopedia Brittanica.

stereotyping (and of Riggs' earlier assertions of male superiority in US Soccer's statements) here.

Gender stereotypes associate men with achievement, competence, ambition, and independence, and women with being more concerned with others, caring, and nurturing. It also assumes that the attributes associated with men cannot apply to women and vice versa. For men to be caring and nurturing or anything associated with the feminine are disparaged as weak, wimps, and mama's boy. Women who embrace their ambition and independence are attacked and smeared as unwomanly, ruthless, and cold. When qualities such as caring and ambition become gendered both women and men are denied the reality that these are *human* traits. I will argue here that gender stereotyping limits both men and women's life experiences and denies them dimensions of their shared humanity. Neither men nor women get to be a whole person.

Gender Stereotypes Impede Women's Professional Growth

Gender bias against women has largely been associated with women being held back from advancing in their careers. Take for instance, Marsha Firestone who wanted to be a lawyer. After she had graduated from college in 60s, she applied to law school. During an interview, the dean of admissions said to her, "You have a boyfriend, don't you." She said, "Yes, I do." He said, "Why should I give this spot to you when I can give it to some guy who can support his family? You're just going to get married and have babies anyway." Marsha was a straight A student and involved in lots of leadership activities at school. Despite that, she didn't get in. Had she been a man, there's little doubt that his admission would have been a breeze.

Although the dean stopped Marsha from becoming a lawyer, it didn't stop her from becoming successful. She went on to get a doctorate in communications and in 1997 became the founder and president of Women's Presidents Organization, a global organization with the goal of the acceptance and advancement of women entrepreneurs in all industries.

Many ambitious baby boomer women encountered such gender barricades. It was bad enough then, but is it still going on now?

More and more women are entering male-dominated fields today, which most are, and are facing a high level of competition. They worry about finding a job in traditionally male fields once they graduate from college. A friend recently told me about the different experiences of her daughter, "Mary," and her roommate who were pursuing an internship at a Wall Street firm. Both young women were very capable, both were at the top of their class. But these admirable qualities were not sufficient by themselves to ensure success.

After several interview rounds, Mary's roommate finally met with the top honcho of the firm. He said, "I have two questions for you. First question. Do you have a boyfriend?" The roommate said she didn't. "The second question: Do you want to have children?" She said no. She was hired. Mary, on the other hand, did have a boyfriend and did want to have children. She was not hired.

Fifty years separated Marsha Firestone's experience and that of Mary and her roommate, and yet the same gender biased questions persist. Young women today don't often encounter the blatant gender bias the way baby boomers did, basically being told to stay home and be a wife and mother. Mary's roommate didn't really see anything unusual in this "two-question interview." She just wanted to get the job; that's all that mattered to her.

There is something to be said for learning to play the game, as this young woman was eager and willing to do. But when do we change the game of two question interview and get beyond the gender bias embedded in those questions?

The Maternal Wall Bias

What did these questions really ask of this young woman? You can have the job if you deny being a woman? If you deny having a life outside work? If you hang out as a boy? If you don't have children? Gender discrimination impedes women's career growth on the sheer fact that they are women. What does this portend for women's careers who want or have children?

These two interviews illustrate the obstacles women face as potential mothers and mothers in advancing their careers, what is called the "maternal wall bias. This bias perceives mothers or pregnant women as less competent or at least less committed to their job, which is a major problem for women's career advancement. Women with children are often excluded from challenging assignments or promotions because of their assumed lack of time or desire. Sometimes they are told flat out they should be home with their children. This gender bias relegates women to low paying clerical and administrative work, while men are set on a career path.

At Cornell University, Shelley Correll, Stephen Bernard, and In Paik reported on their research survey results in "Getting a Job: Is there a Motherhood Penalty" in 2007. They found that mothers suffered a substantial wage penalty. The participants in the study evaluated the application materials of equally qualified same gendered job candidates, some with children, and others without. The researchers found that women with children were 79% less likely to be hired. If she was hired, she would be offered an average of $11,000 less in salary. Mothers were penalized on a host of measures, from salary recommendations to perceived competence. Men were not penalized and sometimes benefited from being a parent.

The bias that mothers can't be both good workers and good parents is pervasive and potentially corrosive. Beliefs such as children and family suffer if women work often impede women's ability to advance, as the above study illustrates. And women with children who do manage to advance in their careers often internalize these beliefs, and as a result find themselves guilt-ridden about their children and never feel good enough in their job. The traditional male role assumes a men's job is to be the breadwinner, spending long hours at work, which denies them opportunities to develop their nurturing tendency with their family. On the other hand, women's traditional role is caretaker, caregiver, and often one who forgoes her own desires for others and looks after the home and family. These role definitions are long-standing manifestations of gender stereotypes that again limit their human potential.

Actions
- *What are your assumptions when you see a pregnant woman at work?*
- *What assumptions do you bring to the table when working with women who have children?*

A Battle Women Don't Even Know They Are fighting: Unconscious Bias

Limiting women's career growth based on their anatomy and maternal function is very concrete form of bias. There is another form of bias that is much more insidious, made so by the fact that it is largely unconscious.

For example, here's a situation a majority of women have experienced, leaving many perplexed. In the middle of the meeting on a controversial financial proposal, "Jane" had a flash of insight into the problem at hand, and she explained her ideas to the group. She looked at the men and women around the table as she enthusiastically elaborated on what she believed to be an important point that could bridge their conversation. After she finished speaking, she waited to hear responses to her comments. No one responded. No one picked up on the idea. It was as if they didn't even hear what she had said.

Jane felt confused and frustrated. Self-doubt began to creep in. She thought she was bringing a lot to the table, but then why wasn't she getting any reinforcement or even acknowledgement? Maybe her observation wasn't really as worthwhile a contribution as she thought? Maybe she just didn't have the leadership abilities needed?

Fifteen minutes later one of the men in the group describes "his" solution to the problem, one that is essentially exactly what Jane had said, but worded slightly differently. It is heard loud and clear. People declared his idea to be "brilliant!" What is going on? Virginia Valian, Professor of Psychology and Linguistics at Hunter College, New York, has an explanation.

In her 1997 book *Why so Slow? The Advancement of Women*, Valian explored why women's advancement has advanced at such a snail's pace. Along the way she uncovered the world of culturally bound assumptions about men and women that are unconscious. She called these unconscious assumptions "gender schemas."

The key insight here is that women are first assumed incompetent until proven otherwise. It's the opposite for men. It works like this: If a woman is successful, it's assumed it is because she's a hard worker, or was lucky; if she fails it's because she's incompetent. If a man succeeds, the assumption is that it's because he's competent; if he fails it's because of bad luck. This insidious landscape of assumed male versus female competence in the workplace shapes who is better equipped to be successful leaders in the workplace. So right from the start women are not perceived as leaders.

Consequently, cultural biases consistently *overrate* men and *underrate* women. Self-assessment studies consistently show that men and women apply the same assumptions to themselves. On a scale of one to ten, women tend to evaluate themselves two points lower than an objective measure, while men will evaluate themselves two points higher.[2]

Assumed incompetence puts women on the defensive and rattles their self-confidence. As a result, their struggle to prove themselves keeps them on a never-ending treadmill. If you as a woman have felt held to a higher standard, it's not your imagination; you have been. It's the Fred Astaire/Ginger Rogers syndrome: Ginger has to do everything Fred does, except in high heels and backwards. Some will take on the challenge, yet others will leave, not seeing the value in putting themselves through the grist mill. A loss to the woman and to her field.

It's not just men assuming women are incompetent; women also fall prey to assuming incompetence in women. A woman may feel that she's competent, but she likely won't assume that of other women. In one global experiment called the "Goldberg paradigm" researchers asked men and women in one group to evaluate a particular article or speech supposedly written by a man. Then they asked a similar group to judge the same material, this time supposedly authored by a woman. In countries all over the world, participants rated the very same words higher when putatively coming from a man than from a woman.

The fact that women often assume other women are incompetent may, in part, explain why women traditionally haven't been so great at helping each other up the ladder. That's changing however, with the plethora of organizations and initiatives dedicated to women supporting women, such as the Women's Presidents Organization I mentioned earlier. Others include Catalyst, Lean In, American Association of University Women, and Financial Women's Association. A revolution, perhaps an evolution, is underway, with a new level of collaboration developing among women.

When I talk with younger women about gender schemas, some say they don't experience this assumption. And may they never! It's a pretty level playing field when entering the work force. After all, 46% of employees in Fortune 500 are women. The good news is the number of Fortune 500 companies with greater than 40% diversity has more than doubled from 69 to 145 since 2012, according to the "Missing Pieces Report: The 2018 Board Diversity Census of Women and Minorities on Fortune 500 Boards," a multiyear study published by the Alliance for Board Diversity (ABD), in collaboration with Deloitte. Women and minorities now

[2] J. Zenger, "The Confidence Gap in Men and Women: Why It Matters and How to Overcome It," *Forbes*, April 8, 2018.

comprise an all-time high of 34% of Fortune 500 board seats, up from 30.8% in 2016. Studies have consistently demonstrated that businesses that have more women on their boards are more successful in traditional bottom line measures. Fortune 100 companies do even better than Fortune 500 companies in terms of female and minority representation on boards: 38.6% compared with 34%.

The higher you go up the career ladder, however, the wider the gap. The playing field is not so equal. While Caucasian white men hold 66% of all Fortune 500 board seats, they hold 91.1% of chairmanships. Of the CEOs who lead the companies that make up the 2018 Fortune 500 list, just 24 are women. That number is down 25% from the previous year's record-breaking 32 female CEOs, the highest share of women since the Fortune's first 500 list in 1955. While women were at the helm of 6.4% of the companies on 2017s list, that number is now down to 4.8%.

Some women use the negative gender schemas against them to their advantage. These women play along as if they don't know what's going on when in reality, they are five steps ahead of the guys. As Mae West put it, "Brains are an asset, if you hide them." Being underestimated can work to a woman's advantage when she is covertly outsmarting men, but that's a short-term benefit. In the end, feigning ignorance only helps perpetuate a misperception. What you permit, you promote.

Make the Unconscious Conscious

It is important to point out these unconscious assumptions, but it is even more important to actively make them conscious. If you are heading a group, be more observant. If a woman is not being heard, go out of your way to ask her opinion and then value what you hear. If a woman says something that is out of your framework of thinking, don't jump to reject it but take time to understand that alternative. This is how you create conditions for an open and diverse discussion.

If you, as a woman, feel overlooked, don't assume you have nothing to contribute or are not a leader. Rather consider an unconscious assumption has kicked in. If you agree with what a woman coworker might be offering to the discussion, don't wait to tell her at the water cooler. Speak up and stand beside her in a project meeting and give her credit. Be an ally and find allies.

If someone takes your idea and claims it as their own, don't let them stick you in the margins. Do what I heard a woman cancer researcher did when faced with someone taking credit for her idea: Tell that person, "Thanks, I'm so glad you love my idea!"

Even when women have achieved a certain level of stature, they still have to deal with gender bias. Take Janiece Webb. She achieved an impressive level of status, by becoming a Senior Vice President at Motorola, in a predominantly male environment, by the time she was 47. Early in her career she was in charge of developing a missile's most crucial component, the guidance system. When she was to give an important presentation to three hundred military top brass, she found herself a bit intimidated by the experience, even though she had worked with men her whole career. She chided herself as she had many times before, "I can do this," and walked up on the stage. An admiral, assuming she had come to set up the audiovisual equipment, said, "Honey, I think we're all set there. You can get down now." Janiece told him that she was the program manager and head of the project. Taken aback, the admiral shouted, "What the hell is the world coming to that Motorola would send some broad to talk to me about my ordnance!" He turned his back to her, laughing out loud, with three hundred men joining in.

Resisting feelings of humiliation as she stood there alone, Janiece had to think fast on her feet and figure out how to dig herself out of this man-made hole. After a brief pause, she spoke firmly, "Excuse me, admiral," she said. "I'm here to report on the status of the MK 45 target-detection-device engineering program. Sir, I will do my best to earn your respect. If you give me a chance, you will find I can do this job, and if not, you can fire me." He turned around and said, "That's pretty gutsy. Let's hear what you have to say."

Today it may not be so overt, but how we perceive competence nevertheless continues in more subtle ways, that ultimately affect promotions, salaries, and opportunities.

As I noted earlier, women are often as guilty as men in embracing gender schemas of female incompetence, which can undermine women's self-confidence. Instead of limitations being imposed, women may self-impose limitations. Women often feel compelled to go to extremes to compensate for these perceived inadequacies, over preparing for a job or assignment, gaining more experience than they really need to do it well, and demanding impossible perfection in themselves. Men, on the other hand, feel free to learn on the way and expect that someone will help them along; and if they fail, they get help to pick themselves up and dust themselves off.

Actions
- *Take stock of your own assumptions.*
- *Do you first assume a woman isn't competent until proven otherwise? If so, it's a way to keep good ideas out of the discussion.*
- *Do you feel you are never good enough?*
- *Are you imposing an unnecessary limitation on yourself, or are you perhaps reacting to someone's bias?*
- *When you walk into a mixed meeting of men and women, who do you assume the leader of the group to be?*

Male Stereotypes Impede Men's Emotional Growth

Gender bias generally refers to preferential treatment of men, specifically white, heterosexual men. However, men face their own restrictions. Why, for instance, is it necessary for a man to go to great lengths to demonstrate and defend his masculinity, often putting himself at unnecessary risk in the process? Why does a man have to suck it up? Why is it okay for men to have angry outbursts but not okay to cry or demonstrate other emotions? Why do they have to pretend they are tough and always have the answers? In other words, why do men have to seem invincible in order to be regarded as strong and manly?

A gender bias on men is a taboo on revealing their vulnerability. Vulnerability, perhaps the most human of traits, is gender-coded as feminine and therefore shameful for men. No one likes to feel vulnerable, but if men must constantly feign invulnerability, or always battle to control his environment in order to avoid vulnerable feelings, then he leaves whole dimensions of himself unknown as well as emotionally stifling others along the way. By avoiding vulnerability, its emotional pain, its potential for personal growth and connection, men end up limiting their humanity and their emotional development.

Gender bias arises as an unconscious expectation that men should physically, emotionally, and mentally camouflage their needs and dependencies with the mask of invincibility. He must struggle to deny and mask weakness—fear, uncertainty, ambivalence, dependency—in order to be regarded as a real man. Perhaps the truth lies closer to what Henry David Thoreau observed, "The mass of men leads lives of quiet desperation."

Because of this bias for men to be tough, they are ill prepared to deal with their more delicate and tender feelings. They can swing in the other direction and engage in hubris, bullying, elitism, behaviors that are counterproductive in the workplace. I call this denial of vulnerability, manifested as bullying, the "gladiator defense."

Unwilling or unable to admit their vulnerabilities, gladiators fend off and avoid these feelings by externalizing them and projecting them onto others. They exercise power by humiliating, shaming, avenging, and hurting—all vulnerable feelings they themselves have, but cannot or will not deal with. Instead they force these feelings of weakness on others and proceed to attack the very thing in another that they despise in themselves. In sport speak, "The best defense is a good offense." When a gladiator attacks, he is actually attacking a hidden part of himself. The attack is not an exercise of self-assertion. Instead, the gladiator is attempting to destroy what he does not want to see in himself or feels ill-equipped to deal with.

Regarded primarily as a weakness rather than as a powerful source of connection to themselves and others, vulnerability is derided as an anathema to manhood and boys learn this at an early age. Boys learn that they have to feign a sense of invincibility. Sports is a wonderful source for learning teamwork but can also be a path to this indoctrination of manhood: toughing it out through injury, destroying the opposition, dominating the game, and so on. Boys are also taught to be femiphobic, to deny and fear all the feminine aspects of themselves because, generally, to embrace the feminine means being demeaned as powerless, soft, inferior, and shunted.

Tethering men to an unrealistic male identity of invincibility that demands they disconnect from their vulnerability is not only inhumane, but also impedes their willingness to be truly courageous and negatively impacts the organization itself. Just as assuming women's incompetence keeps out good ideas in an organization, so does bullying through intimidation. Unlike women who suffer from consequences due to gender bias, men who bully are not generally held accountable for their behavior. In fact, they are often rewarded with promotions and viewed as strong. As a consequence, men generally do not feel able to admit to failures, mistakes, wrongdoings, or lack of knowledge without it being a threat to their manliness. This is detrimental to the health and business success of organizations because a willingness to admit mistakes and failures can be a rich source of learning, creativity, and progress in the organization. It takes courage to admit mistakes and failures, and when this practice is part of an organization's culture, everyone benefits.

The Hidden Battle of Gender Stereotypes

How do these gender biases play out in the workplace? A common pattern is that men often assert their dominance in order to fulfill their gender stereotype of being strong, competent, in charge, whereas women struggle to break out of theirs, where they are assumed incompetent, weak, submissive, and therefore unequal. Here are a couple of examples of this power struggle and its resolution playing out in the workplace.

Ricky and Alan

Before Ricky Burges became CEO of the Western Australia Local Government Association, she worked at an organization as the sole female director among all male directors, a distinction that subjected her to her fair share of injustice, from fighting for a company car that the other directors automatically received to arguing for equal pay. But the biggest challenge occurred with one director who was hell-bent on sabotaging her success.

This one director, "Alan," tried to prevent Ricky from recommending creative initiatives by insisting she stay strictly within the limits of her role. His lies and dishonest behaviors surrounded her, which created barriers to Ricky's effectiveness. In some cases, Alan withheld information from Ricky, which prevented her from doing her job. In other cases, he deliberately swamped her with information, which overwhelmed her and made it impossible for her to determine what she really needed to know. Alan didn't even bother to conceal his effort to block her and throw obstacles in her path. Some of the other directors found the spectacle amusing and, like spectators at a sporting event, sat in the stands, idly watching to see how it would all end. This pattern of emotional abuse continued for several years. Ricky was exhausted from the whole thing, thinking, "What can I do?"

What Ricky finally did about it came impulsively and as a complete surprise to her. One day, as she headed for a project meeting with the other directors, she knew from experience that one way or another Alan would exert the usual emotional abuse. She went into the kitchen and there was this huge carving knife on the counter. She picked it up. She saw a box of tissues and picked that up too. She had no idea why she did that; she just did it instinctively. Ricky went into the meeting and put the tissues and the knife on the table. "I'm sick of this," she said. "If I have to use these [she held up the box of tissues], then I'm surely going to have to use this [she flourished the knife]." She didn't know where she got this idea. Shocked by Ricky's statement, Alan rose from his seat and walked out of the room.

The next day Alan approached Ricky and insisted on a private conversation. This guy who had been bullying her for three years shut the door, sat in the chair and just about cried. "I don't understand why you hate me so," he blurted. Ricky and Alan then had a great heart-to-heart conversation about their difficult history and in part what drove Alan's behavior, feeling intimidated by Ricky's competence. That day changed their relationship and they began to work well together.

In her showdown with the director, Ricky stripped away gender roles, in which Alan routinely established his masculinity by dominating and demeaning Ricky. In other words, he was forcing her into a position of inadequacy, and fulfilling the unconscious expectation that women are less competent. By admitting her vulnerability, the tissues, and saying she would take no more abuse, the knife, she stepped out of the victim, good girl role and claimed her authority. By calling Alan on his game and unmasking him as a bully, Ricky forced Alan to expose the vulnerability he had so ardently tried to deflect and hide. With Ricky free of the cloak of vulnerability that had been cast upon her, she connected to her strength. With his mask of invulnerability lifted, Alan could connect to his true emotions.

You can see, then, that when Ricky and Alan were ultimately able to connect to genuine places in themselves, they could honestly engage with each other and develop a real relationship, beyond stereotypes.

Action
Be brave and take the problem head on.

- Be open to unexpected outcomes.
- Ask yourself, is this my vulnerability or someone casting theirs on me?

Celeste and David

Celeste wasn't so much looking for a job but rather was ready to take the next step in developing her career. She applied for a position that seemed a perfect fit on that path. When she learned that the job was as a director, she said that was below her level of experience and skills. She let it be known that she wasn't interested in anything lower than a VP position. Despite Celeste's clear statement of her requirements, the company repeatedly tried to slot her into the directorship level. And Celeste repeatedly declined. The hiring committee encouraged Celeste to go through the interview process anyway, which she agreed to. Although Celeste wanted a VP position as a career step for herself, she also felt it was right for the company because the role needed to be interacting with the executive team. She made this absolutely clear during the interview.

When the offer letter arrived, it was for a director position. Instead of getting upset about the letter, Celeste met with the HR person. Again she reiterated that she had made it very clear from the very beginning of the interviews that she wasn't interested in a director level position, only a VP position.

The executives argued that a title wasn't important, but it was important to Celeste. She persisted and insisted. Ultimately, the hiring committee recognized she was the right person for the job. By the end of day, Celeste had the offer letter corrected to VP of sales.

Celeste learned another person, "David," had just been hired at a director level in marketing. David, who was confident and competent, assumed, incorrectly, that he would control the entire sales and marketing area. He immediately saw there was a problem: Celeste. Because she was in charge of sales and in a higher management position, Celeste threatened his sense of authority.

David immediately started to assert what he assumed was his rightful level of authority "He was so obvious. It was a big barbaric run for power. He was befriending the male executives and diminishing the work of the female executives. He would introduce some concepts and act like everyone was just going to go along with what he wanted to do. I didn't agree with his strategy and told him so very directly. He looked at me like, 'How dare you!' In a couple of meetings, I made it very clear he wasn't going to dominate me."

The men quickly aligned in support of David. At the same time, the women felt threatened by Celeste, and left her to fend for herself. Celeste wondered how different it might have been for her had the executive women rallied with her.

When Celeste refused to play David's game, he changed his tactics and started looking for insecurities and vulnerabilities in Celeste that might give him an advantage over her. His fishing around turned up nothing.

After several weeks it became clear to David that his efforts to elevate his position by attacking Celeste had failed, and he was very upset about it. Celeste held her ground against his aggression, but she also praised him for his work. People would ask her what she thought of David and she consistently said she thought he did a great job at what he did, because she genuinely thought that.

Celeste was able to separate David's aggressive behavior from his considerable abilities. She focused on his good qualities rather than getting caught up in office politics, posturing, and one-upmanship. In other words, she refused to play his game. She drew a line in the sand, but she was kind to him as well. At one point, the company was going through a reorganization and David was to report to Celeste. Celeste told her boss that David wasn't going to be happy reporting to her, given their history; it wouldn't be a good dynamic for either of them. If it made him feel more comfortable and productive reporting to someone else, she said she would be fine with that.

> It's very powerful to walk through the day knowing you are confident in your ability. You don't have to engage in that destructive behavior. I've told people that I am not participating in that toxic behavior. They all admit that it's toxic and they are exhausted by it; it takes a lot of energy.

At the end of the day, David and Celeste had more of a friendship with each other than with anyone else in the organization. A budding collaborative work relationship developed. Celeste feels good that she could "be friends with someone who was so clearly trying to dominate me. I didn't allow that domination and at the same time I was able to be supportive of his work; that's an accomplishment. I saw his aggressive strategy as more a reflection of his socialization and how he was expected to behave rather than who he really is. The domination game is all David knew, the only game he knew how to play. I know he has a tremendous amount of respect for me now because he's seen me say no and he also learned he was supposed to report to me and I diverted it."

Celeste switched the traditional game by not playing along with it. She trusted her competence rather than question it; she maintained her authority rather than cede it. Celeste recognized that David was fulfilling a stereotype of the dominant alpha male, the traditional role in the business environment, but instead of reacting to it she spoke to the competent man behind it. By shattering gender stereotypes of a dominant man and incompetent woman, Celeste and David were able to develop a genuine relationship with each other as two human beings doing their best.

The battle of the sexes isn't about a battle between men and women but rather a struggle to get beyond these gender stereotypes that impede real connection between people. Getting beyond these stereotypes benefits the organization as a whole because it opens the door to true collaboration and an inclusive and open work environment.

And it can be contagious. Celeste had four young women come to her, asking if they could work for her because they saw a different way of working, and they wanted it.

"Younger women really want the more collaborative model; they are starving to see it. Although I don't agree with the other executive women trying to dominate and micromanage me, I have no animosity towards them. I know they are very smart women and I know they will be relieved if we can all work together. I just think they're acting out a model they have seen over and over again and just accepted it as normal."

Actions
- *Change the game by not playing the game.*
- *If you are clear as to what you bring to the table then be insistent and persistent.*
- *See the gladiator defense for what it is, fulfilling an unconscious assumption about what it is to be a man. Take the bully by the horns and call him/her on their game without engaging in it.*
- *Speak to what is best in a person, rather than the stereotype, while still holding your ground.*
- *Focus on how everyone can succeed.*
- *Know you are modeling behavior for others.*

THE CONUNDRUM

Decades of research shows that women are more likely than men to be democratic and less autocratic, as we could see in how Celeste and Ricky dealt with a difficult situation. Women tend to emphasize collaboration and cooperation, perhaps in part because of the gender stereotypes that have limited their access to bastions of power. If you don't have the power, you invite people to participate, you lead through motivation, rather than incentives, and you engage shared interests. These strategies proved to be a more effective style of leadership than one based on power over others and domination. Studies show that not only is this style of leadership more effective in traditional bottom line numbers, but also that people prefer this style of leadership because it generates a more positive work environment. For instance, employees like an environment where there is a sense of a shared humanity, a feeling of community, and a shared purpose. Yet, when people are asked to identify the leadership traits they prefer, they describe traits associated with men and a more autocratic style—in control, in charge, competitive. Here lies the conundrum. The qualities we expect in leaders are not the qualities that would produce the desired environment we want at work. Having said that, there is a cultural shift happening where companies see the value of collaboration and espouse it. However, they may not pursue creating such an environment in earnest because of the conundrum created by this subterranean struggle of gender stereotypes that remain unconscious.

Ultimately the small steps and choices we take in making the unconscious conscious can have a big effect and create meaningful change in our organizations. Moving beyond gender stereotypes holds the promise of genuine and authentic human connection that can enrich all our lives.

CHAPTER TAKEAWAYS

- Gender stereotypes associate men with achievement, competence, ambition, and independence, and women with being more concerned with others, caring, and nurturing. It also assumes that the attributes associated with men cannot apply to women and vice versa.
- Gender bias against women has largely been associated with women being held back from advancing in their careers.

- The bias that mothers can't be both good workers and good parents is pervasive and potentially corrosive. Beliefs such as children and family suffer if women work often impede women's ability to advance.
- Limiting women's career growth based on their anatomy and maternal function is very concrete form of bias. There is another form of bias that is much more insidious, made so by the fact that it is largely unconscious.
- Even when women have achieved a certain level of stature, they still have to deal with gender bias.
- Gender bias generally refers to preferential treatment of men, specifically white, heterosexual men. However, men face their own restrictions.
- Gender bias arises as an unconscious expectation that men should physically, emotionally, and mentally camouflage their needs and dependencies with the mask of invincibility.
- Gender biases are manifested in the workplace by men often asserting their dominance in order to fulfill their gender stereotype of being strong, competent, in charge, and women struggling to break out of theirs, where they are assumed incompetent, weak, submissive and therefore unequal.
- Women are more likely than men to be democratic and less autocratic. Women tend to emphasize collaboration and cooperation.

CHAPTER 6

Masculinity at Work

Jody A. Worley

MASCULINITY AND GENDER EQUALITY

There is a broad range of ideologies and varieties of masculinity. In many ways, masculinity is a valued social identity (Maass, Cadinu, Guarnieri, & Grasselli, 2003) and, for some, masculinity is understood as an achieved status that is not assumed on the basis of physical or biological development but is earned through ongoing demonstrations of manhood (Vandello & Bosson, 2013; Vandello, Bosson, Cohen, Burnaford, & Weaver, 2008). However, a dynamic personal understanding combined with a heavy external cultural influences makes masculinity a concept that is not easily defined (Thompson & Bennett, 2015). In any event, aspects of masculinity have implications for organizational dynamics and human relations in the context of gender at work. Those aspects include: relational styles, ways of caring, self-reliance, a worker/provider tradition, risk-taking, group orientation, use of humor, and (in some instances) heroism. A description of possible enactments of these aspects of masculinity in the workplace will be presented later. Unfortunately, some

J. A. Worley (✉)
University of Oklahoma, Tulsa, OK, USA
e-mail: jworley@ou.edu

© The Author(s), under exclusive license to Springer Nature
Switzerland AG 2021
J. Marques (ed.), *Exploring Gender at Work*,
https://doi.org/10.1007/978-3-030-64319-5_6

103

dominant forms of masculinity, hegemonic masculinity for example, reinforces gender inequality relative to more equality masculinities (Messerschmidt, 2012).

Berdahl, Cooper, Glick, Livingston, and Williams (2018) argue that much of what often appears to be (or is proclaimed to be) a level playing field of opportunities and demands for doing what it takes *for anyone* to get ahead at work is more accurately understood as counterproductive work behavior aimed at proving masculinity on the job. While there is evidence to suggest that men and women alike must play the game to win, or survive as the case may be, studies show that women of all races report higher workloads that include "office housework" compared with White men, and women and nonwhites report less access to glamor work (Berdahl & Min, 2012; Brescoll & Uhlmann, 2008; Rudman, 1998). Studies of corporate settings have identified successful managers as being those who are decisive, instrumental, and willing to take risks (Collinson & Hearn, 1994; Kerfoot & Knights, 1993; Messerschmidt, 1995; Pfeffer, 2010). These are reasonable characteristics attributable to people across gender identity group affiliations. Indeed, one recent report indicates that 29% of senior management roles in 2019 were held by women globally, and 87% of global businesses have at least one woman in a senior management role (Grant Thornton, 2019, p. 5).

Research on gender stereotypes across cultures in the 1980s confirmed a consistent belief in male agency and action, with people from 30 nations universally rating men as more adventurous, dominant, forceful, and independent than women (Williams & Best, 1990). Although these characteristics might be attributable to anyone, these aspects of masculinity are sometimes enacted by men as a response to a perceived threat to masculinity. Masculinity threat will be discussed in more detail in the next section but has implications for observed and experienced gender equality. For example, Heilman and Okimoto (2007) observed that penalties for women's success in stereotypical, male-dominated manager roles may result from the perceived violation of gender-stereotypic prescriptions. However, they also demonstrated that bolstering woman's feminine credentials (e.g., motherhood status) reduces penalties for success in a stereotype incongruent role.

Masculinity threat is also associated with physical aggression (Bosson, Vandello, Burnaford, Weaver, & Wasti, 2009), victim-blaming (Munsch & Willer, 2012), and sexist and homophobic attitudes (Weaver & Vescio, 2015; Willer, Rogalin, Conlon, & Wojnowicz, 2013). These studies provide evidence of various compensatory responses to perceived masculinity threat by men, and these responses are directed at people who are viewed as the source of that threat. Taking a slightly different focus, Munsch and Gruys (2018) also provide insight into understanding young adult men's reported experiences of masculinity threat as it relates to women/femininity and as it relates to other men/masculinity.

Benevolent sexism (BS), for example, includes paternalistic behaviors reflecting the extent to which people believe women deserve to be provided for and protected; implying that women cannot adequately or sufficiently provide and care for themselves. When men endorse BS, they communicate that men's power over women is justified by women's need for men for guidance and protection. *Hostile sexism* (HS) reflects general antipathy toward women, but also the idea that women fail to acknowledge men's legitimate power over them. Examples of hostile sexism include behaviors such as disproportionately interrupting or talking over women in meetings; or believing that women seek to gain power by getting control over men. These enactments of masculinity have implications for interpersonal relationship quality and organizational dynamics in the workplace climate.

In general, most people are woefully inadequate at predicting affective (emotional) impact of future events (Wilson, Centerbar, Kermer, & Gilbert, 2005; Wilson & Gilbert, 2005; Wilson, Wheatley, Meyers, Gilbert, & Axsom, 2000). People also overestimate the hurtfulness of *hostile sexism* due to the dramatic nature of that type of incident. Likewise, there is a tendency to underestimate the impact of *benevolent sexism*. Consequently, a common assumption is that hostile sexism relative to benevolent sexism tends to produce more extreme negative emotions in the short run and requires longer recovery (Bosson, Pinel, & Vandello, 2010). There is evidence of an intensity bias in predictions about initial reactions of anger and disgust from women who experienced benevolent or hostile sexism (Bosson et al., 2010). Although women who experienced either type of sexism reported equal levels of fear and depression, bystanders overestimate depression and fear responses to hostile sexism, and underestimate those emotional responses to benevolent sexism relative to experiences of hostile sexism. This intensity bias was present among bystanders in general, but the estimates of impact were also biased among people who had themselves experienced sexism of the same type in the past.

Despite these less admirable enactments of masculinity there is encouraging evidence to suggest that the dynamics of gender relations in the workplace are changing in positive ways. Although most research on the topic focuses on how gender is done (enacted) and gender inequality is perpetuated through men's actions, there are studies that explore how the enactments of masculinity by men are supporting or challenging the existing gender system. That is, how they are doing and undoing gender in the workplace (Cf. Eagly, 2009; Ely & Meyerson, 2010; Kelan, 2018; Ollilainen & Calasanti, 2007). Ely and Meyerson (2010) wrote about an organizational approach to undoing gender in a case study of workers at offshore oil platforms. Kelan (2018) also addressed the issue of men doing (and undoing) gender at work. Ollilainen and Calasanti (2007) stretch the boundaries of beliefs and knowing when it comes to gender roles by exploring metaphors at work for maintaining the salience of gender in self-managed teams. This chapter aims to contribute to this conversation by exploring how different aspects of masculinity intersects with the daily lives of all employees in the workplace and then discussing some possible implications for equity and inclusion.

MASCULINITY ENACTMENTS IN THE WORKPLACE

Prosocial behavior is any voluntary action intended to benefit or help someone including sharing, comforting, guiding, and perhaps defending. Prosocial engagement among women and men is common, but the expression is unique. Women and men emphasize unique types of prosocial behaviors. Women are more communal and relational, whereas men are more agentic and oriented toward prosocial behaviors that are more collective, or group focused. It was Bakan (1966) who introduced and summarized two-dimensional concepts that distinguish women as more relational and communal (connected with others), and men as more agentic, or reliant on individual agency, self-assertive, dominant, and competitive (Newport, 2001). This predominance of communal and agentic orientation in social exchange is pervasive across world cultures (Williams & Best, 1990) and likely contributes to variations in the enacted prosocial behaviors of women and men. These sex differences in social exchange behaviors also match widely shared beliefs about gender roles.

Origins of gender role beliefs lie outside of organizations in which we work, yet they spillover into the workplace context and undoubtedly influence the division of labor. For example, consider who schedules the meetings or office parties (and procures the party supplies) versus who runs the meetings (or cleans up after the party). The point is that there is a biosocial interaction between physical attributes and social structure when it comes to gender relations in the workplace.

The effects of the beliefs about gender roles are mediated by hormonal processes, social expectations, and individual dispositions; None of which are easily defined because they are not fixed or even stable. Individual dispositions, like hormones and social expectations, change over time and across specific situational contexts. Interested readers may want to review empirical evidence and details on how gender stereotypes have changed over time from 1946 to 2018 (Cf. Eagly, Nater, Miller, Kaufmann, & Sczesny, 2019).

Observations and everyday lived experiences suggest there are many dimensions that comprise the system of influences on individual choices, social exchanges, and public institutions. Prosocial behaviors are only one domain of human behavior. Beliefs about prosocial helping behavior as kindness and showing concern are often associated with stereotypes of women (Diekman & Goodfriend, 2006). Yet, men in many occupational roles also take enormous risks on behalf of others (e.g., law enforcement officers or soldiers who protect communities and nations from attack). A first step toward understanding the role of masculinity in the enactments of prosocial behavior involves examination of gender roles.

Gender role beliefs are descriptive and prescriptive in that they provide distinction between what men and women usually do and expectations for behavior (what they *should* do). Descriptive aspects of gender role beliefs, including stereotypes, inform people about typical behaviors. Stereotypes and sex-typical behaviors are most often relied upon (intentionally or implicitly) when situations are ambiguous or confusing. The prescriptive aspect of gender role beliefs informs people about what is desirable or admirable for gaining social approval in the social or situational context.

Culturally shared beliefs provide a general framework for understanding why prosocial behavior can be enacted differently by women and men depending on the specific situational context. Gender role beliefs and stereotypes dictate/predispose different prosocial behaviors for women and men. To understand the relevance of the stereotype beliefs about communion and agency for prosocial behavior in general, and in workplace settings in particular, it is helpful to consider the implications of these beliefs for the types of social relationship bonds that people form.

Social bonds take a relational (communal) form by linking people together in close personal relationships. Alternatively, social bonding may take a collective form by linking people together in groups and organizations (Brewer & Gardner, 1996). By ascribing ambitious and competitive qualities to men, gender role beliefs imply a social context in which people differ in status and men strive to improve their hierarchical position (Baumeister & Sommer, 1997; Cross & Madson, 1997; Fiske, Cuddly, Glick, & Xu, 2002). In general, superior social status is conveyed by the agentic status ascribed to men (e.g., being dominant and assertive), but these attributes are not evaluated as favorably as the communal attributes ascribed to women (Langford & MacKinnon, 2000). Therefore, a gender role analysis (Eagly, 2009; Wood & Eagly, 2002) suggests that prosocial behaviors are more common in women to the extent that the behaviors have a relationship focus that provides supporting and caring for individuals; whereas, prosocial behaviors are more common in men to the extent that the behaviors have an agentic focus where collective emphasis facilitates gaining status, or implies higher status.

This is not to say that differences between gender roles are exclusive to one or the other sex (e.g., that all men act one way, or that all women act another way), or that only men (or women) would be expected to behave a certain way in specific situations. However, the intersection of gender roles with other individual factors do influence the enactment of prosocial behaviors. Gender roles influence behavior in combination with many other roles, including roles associated with group memberships other than gender (e.g., religion, race, ethnicity, age) and roles that are associated with specific obligations (e.g., occupational role; family responsibility; caregiver for a family member).

The point is that despite the diverse range of possible influences on social behaviors, gender roles are a contributing factor and they function to influence behavioral interactions partly through social norms and the expectations that others have in certain situations or contexts. Gender roles also function through personal identification with one's gender and are tied to hormonal processes that influence behaviors interpreted as either feminine or masculine (Cf. Wood & Eagly, 2009).

Trends in classification of agentic and communal prosocial behaviors are evident across social contexts (interactions with strangers, interactions in close relationships, interactions in workplace setting; other social settings) using multiple methods of observation reported in a variety of studies including meta-analyses, archival data, field observations, and laboratory experiments (Becker & Eagly, 2004; Eagly & Crowley, 1986; Eagly, Nater, Miller, Kaufmann, & Sczensny, 2019; Huston, Ruggiero, Conner, & Geis, 1981; Johnson et al., 1989; Lyons, 2005; Organ & Ryan, 1995).

In the workplace context, prosocial behaviors are sometimes operationalized as *organizational citizenship behaviors* (Organ & Ryan, 1995) that might include voluntarily helping a colleague with excessive workload or other discretionary behaviors not explicitly recognized or formally rewarded, but that promote organizational functioning. On the surface, there are not significant differences between women and men engaging in prosocial behaviors in the workplace. This is not surprising given that formal job descriptions apply equally to men and women having the same job. That is, it is reasonable to expect that there would be fewer sex differences in behaviors bound by the requirements of the job. However, there are clear differences between men and women within the domain of extra-role behaviors that go beyond required expectations and that may lead to personal gains in status or reward (e.g., attending meetings that are not mandatory; volunteering for extra-role behaviors that offer little or no immediate reward or compensation). Women appear to engage in relational prosocial behaviors more than men (Farrell & Finkelstein, 2007; Heilman & Chen, 2005; Kidder, 2002). In a Canadian sample, women, regardless of job status, reported more communal behaviors than men (friendly, unselfish act) especially when interacting with other women (Moskowitz, Suh, & Desaulniers, 1994). Moreover, in a meta-analysis of findings from across multiple studies, female managers offer attention to individual needs and personal consideration that focuses on mentoring and developing employees who report to them (Eagly, Johannesen-Schmidt, & van Engen, 2003). By contrast, men, more than women, appear to engage in behaviors that focus on the organization itself (Farrell & Finkelstein, 2007; Heilman & Chen, 2005; Kidder, 2002).

Given the differences in how prosocial behaviors are enacted between women and men, attention is sometimes drawn to helpful and harmful manifestations of these behaviors. Attempts to gain insight and understanding or explanation are warranted when social exchanges and organizational dynamics appear to favor one group over another. This is particularly the case when the people who seem to have the most to gain (or lose) are associated with a particular identity group affiliation. Recent work to better understand the dynamics of gender relations in the work-place has identified and directed a focus on the role of masculinity identity threat as a potential explanatory factor.

MASCULINITY IDENTITY THREAT

The notion of masculinity threat is based on the idea that masculinity is precarious when it is believed to be a function of hierarchy and status (Vandello et al., 2008). When this is the case, masculinity identities are easily threatened (Bosson & Vandello, 2011). In fact, Vandello et al. (2008) argue that manhood is threatened more easily than womanhood and through a wider range of transgressions. An alternative perspective, of course, might be that perhaps women have more flexible interpretations of femininity and womanhood, and/or a broader range of acceptable criteria for womanhood. In any event, the main thesis for Vandello et al. (2008) is that manhood status is not a developmental certainty, and that even once achieved it is vulnerable and can be lost. Furthermore, "because of the precarious nature of manhood, anything that makes salient its precariousness, or calls one's masculinity into question, should be especially anxiety provoking," (Vandello et al., 2008, p. 1326). Rather than conceptualizing manhood as a developmental certainty, many gender role theorists have instead argued that achieving manhood (i.e., agency, instrumentality and achievement) are central to most psychological definitions of masculinity (Ashmore, Del Boca, & Wohlers, 1986).

Research has also demonstrated that affective and reparative responses to threatened masculinity are not uncommon. *Affective responses* to masculinity threat stem from concerns about what others might think when masculinity is threatened publicly. In the face of adversity and perceived threat to masculinity, men experience negative affect and concern about the perceptions they believe others have of them (Dahl, Vescio, & Weaver, 2015). This notion is supported with evidence of increases in negative thoughts (Vandello et al., 2008) and reported concerns that others may assign negative labels (Rudman & Fairchild, 2004), but also with increases in reported anger (Dahl et al., 2015). The increase in anger has been shown to predict social dominance orientation over women and benevolent sexism (Dahl et al., 2015). *Reparative responses* are behaviors that are an attempt to reestablish one's masculinity in the eyes of others. Men (but not women) respond to gender threats with attempt to repair tarnished social identities (Vandello et al., 2008).

One example of reparative responses to perceived masculinity threat is often observed in financial negotiations between men and women in the workplace.

Netchaeva, Kouchaki, and Sheppard (2015) conducted three studies based on precarious manhood theory to investigate the reaction of men to women who are in supervisor roles. In their experiment on negotiation strategies between women and men, where participants were negotiating with either a male or female supervisor, several interesting findings were reported. First, males negotiated higher counteroffers than female participants regardless of the gender of the manager. Second, among male participants, those who negotiated with a female manager presented significantly higher counteroffers relative to counteroffers when negotiating with male managers. Third, males negotiating with female managers made significantly higher counteroffers than females who made counteroffers to female managers. In fact, although the amount of the counteroffer (a measure of assertiveness in the study) was clearly associated with gender of the manager for male participant, manager's gender did not affect female negotiators; there was no significant difference between counteroffers made by female participants when they negotiated with a female versus male manager.

Netchaeva et al. (2015) interpreted these findings as evidence that a female manager elicits a threat to masculinity of male participants resulting in more assertive behavior (higher counteroffers in negotiation) from her male subordinates. In an attempt to buffer the presumed threat, these researchers conducted a follow-up study to compare the elicited threat behavior (assertiveness in negotiation) in a different sample of men who were negotiating with a female team leader displaying either administrative (communal; soft) versus ambitious (agentic; assertive) negotiating style. In this follow-up study, male and female participants negotiated higher amounts with team leaders who displayed more ambitious leadership regardless of the team leader's gender. Males, compared with other males, negotiated higher with ambitious female leaders than with ambitious male leaders. However, when confronted with administrative female leaders (less ambitious), there was no significant difference in the negotiated amount. In other words, female leaders with administrative rather than ambitious approach stood to lose less with male negotiators. Female participants did not differentiate between ambitious female or ambitious male leaders. Female participants negotiated higher with ambitious leaders, relative to administrative leaders, but gender of leader was not a factor in the negotiated amount, only the ambitious style of the leader. Female participants did not differentiate between gender of leader when negotiating with administrative leaders. For these researchers, the higher counteroffer (assertiveness) by men when negotiating with females who have a higher status role is viewed as evidence of an enacted behavioral attempt to restore perceived threat to masculine identity. Next, we will see how perceived threats to masculine identity may also lead to increased anxiety and stress, increased risk-taking, aggression, and avoidance of any activity that might be perceived as feminine.

Common themes across the vast literature on male gender roles and masculinity from across multiple disciplines and perspectives suggest that manhood is elusive and tenuous, and that manhood requires social demonstration as proof. In other words, "real men" are made, not born. Vandello et al. (2008) note that they are not suggesting that manhood *is* more precarious than womanhood as a social construction of a gendered reality, but that people in many cultures define, perceive, react, and operate *as if* this were true. If this is true, there are important implications of this way of operating for interpersonal relations in the workplace context (Cf. Brescoll, Uhlmann, Moss-Racusin, & Sarnell, 2012). Certainly, it is possible that beliefs about relative precariousness of manhood versus womanhood no longer prevail within contemporary, industrialized societies.

Anxiety and Stress. Studies on masculinity conducted in the 1980s provided evidence that was interpreted to mean that gender role anxiety is central to several theories of masculinity (Eisler & Skidmore, 1987; Eisler, Skidmore, & Ward, 1988; O'Neil, Helms, Gable, David, & Wrightsman, 1986). More recent studies have also demonstrated an association between threatened gender identity and anxiety and stress-related responses that are stronger for men than for women (Caswell, Bossom, Vandello, & Sellers, 2014; Michniewicz, Vandello, & Bossom, 2014; Vandello et al., 2008). For example, Vandello et al. (2008) hypothesized that reminders of precariousness and uncertainty of manhood activate anxiety-related and aggression-related cognitions for men. They interpret their results as support for the hypothesis that feedback perceived as gender threatening arouses stronger feelings of anxiety and related emotions (e.g., threat and shame) among men than among women, a pattern that is consistent with the notion that manhood is a more tenuous, precarious state than womanhood. This finding and interpretation might have implications for social and interpersonal interactions in workplace settings to the extent that situations or conditions are viewed as a gender threat (masculinity threat) for men in the workplace.

Aggression. Threats to masculinity, unlike threats to femininity for women, seems to prime aggressive behaviors for some men (Dahl et al., 2015) or assertive behaviors when aggression is inappropriate (Netchaeva et al., 2015) that are intended to reestablish power associated with masculinity and maintain the traditional gender-based status quo. In the Vandello et al. (2008) study, threats to one's gender identity increased the likelihood for priming aggressive thoughts more strongly for men than for women.

In seeking to understand the structure, rather than the content of gender roles, Bosson and Vandello (2011) offer insight on the use of physical aggression and active responses to gender identity threats among men. They found support for their hypothesis that situational and cultural factors that increase the precariousness of manhood and the tenuous nature of a man's view and beliefs about his manhood also increase the likelihood of aggressive behavioral displays in response to those factors. Viewing gender status as vulnerable has implications for attitudes and behaviors across several life domains including health, interpersonal relationship, and perhaps workplace behaviors. Men define their own gender status in terms of the active things they *do* more so than their ways of *being* and who they are as a person (Bosson & Vandello, 2011). This may help to explain why some men take greater physical risks than women (Byrnes, Miller, & Schafer, 1999; Munsch & Gruys, 2018). Bosson and Vandello (2011) propose that men and women are different in the ways they view, interpret, and use physical aggression and action behaviors. They suggest that men are more likely than women to believe that action and aggression are tools for demonstrating one's masculinity to others in social and cultural context. Their findings suggest that men do associate manhood with behavior and that they perceive aggression and aggressive displays as an effective way to restore manhood when being threatened.

Men in situations where there is masculinity threat have also been found to engage in aggressive behaviors other than physical aggression. Other aggressive behaviors associated with power and dominance believed to compensate or "repair" perceived threats to masculinity (Babl, 1979) might include sexual aggression (Maass et al., 2003). As mentioned earlier, hostile sexism and benevolent sexism are distinct enactments and elicit different responses (Bosson, Pinel, & Vandello, 2010; Dahl et al., 2015; Glick & Fiske, 1996).

Risky Behaviors. Studies have focused on two general types of risky behaviors in the context of response to masculinity threat: aggression and financial risk. When induced to perform a public and stereotypic feminine task, gender threats were linked to physical aggression more readily among men than among women, whether in terms of cognitive accessibility or interpretations of others' actions (Bosson et al., 2009). Several studies have also shown that men take greater financial risks than women and that merely priming masculinity increases financial risk-taking behaviors among men (Bernasek & Shwiff, 2001; Meier-Pasti & Goetze, 2006; Sunden & Surette, 1998; Weaver, Vandello, & Bosson, 2012).

Avoidance of femininity. Men and women alike must negotiate work and nonwork demands. In response, many organizations around the world have shown increased willingness to accommodate work-life balance with flexible work arrangements and other related initiatives. However, these initiatives are often underutilized by men (Allen, 2001; Hill, Hawkins, Martinson, & Ferris, 2003; Kossek, Lautsch, & Eaton, 2006). This may reflect men's resistance to work arrangements that prioritize stereotypically feminine concerns such as childcare and family (Vandello, Hettinger, Bosson, & Siddiqi, 2013).

Masculinity Contest Culture in Organizations

The chapter concludes with a consideration for how these aspects of masculinity shape organizational workplace climate and behavioral norms in the workplace (i.e., masculinity contest culture). Berdahl et al. (2018) outline a theoretical framework for considering the workplace as a masculinity contest culture (MCC) such that men experience ongoing pressure to continually demonstrate behavioral displays as evidential support for their manhood. In any event, the masculinity contest concept focuses on how behaviors believed to signify masculinity in the workplace evolve to define the structure of the organizational cultural norms. In that sense, then, MCC is the organizational manifestation of precarious manhood (Bosson & Vandello, 2011). Organizational culture is shaped by traditional masculinity norms and masculinity contest culture (Berdahl, 2007b; Berdahl et al., 2018). MCC norms apply to men and women (Ely & Kimmel, 2018), and most probably have important and largely unexplored implications for social exchanges among people who are transgender and non-binary. High MCC is associated with sexist norms and zero-sum thinking such that men in masculinity contest work cultures may be inclined to view any power gains by women as a threat or potential for loss in status or power of men (Kuchynka, Bosson, Vandello, & Puryear, 2018).

The consequences for organizations with high MCC include toxic leadership, higher incidences of harassment and bullying, along with low employee outcomes on several hygiene factors such as work engagement, dedication, and well-being at work. Toxic masculinity "involves the need to aggressively compete and dominate others" (Kuppers, 2005, p. 713). However, not all masculinity is toxic and not all workplaces that employ men, whether the workforce is predominately male or female, are a masculinity contest culture. Work becomes a masculinity contest when enacted organizational values are more reflective of masculinity norms than the espoused organizational mission. Examples of masculinity culture might include, but are certainly not limited to competitive displays of workload (Williams, 2013), sexual harassment (Berdahl, 2007a, 2007b), physical aggression (Bosson et al., 2009), risk-taking (Iacuone, 2005).

Chapter Takeaways

Gender inclusion and work-life integration are key factors that promote flexible workplace practices and progress by interrupting cycles of gender bias (Bailyn, 2011; Dutton, Ashford, Lawrence, & Miner-Rubio, 2002). Gender inclusion consists of organizational awareness of and support for equal gender representation at senior organizational levels and intolerance for "Good old boy" networks in which small groups of men control the workplace and offer an occasional "sweetheart deal" for women employees.

If competitive us-versus-them perspectives elicit hostile or aggressive behaviors among men in response to success of women in the workplace, then one key to creating more gender equity and inclusion in the workplace may involve finding ways to diffuse this type of zero-sum thinking. Organizations that have more gender diversity enjoy significant concrete rewards including enhanced innovation and decision-making (Galinsky et al., 2015). Organizational leadership can intentionally modify practices and wording in policies that appear to benefit or privilege any group at the expense of another. Adopting organizational strategies that appear to benefit or single out any particular group or class of employee may be counterproductive and create backlash. For example, implementing diversity training, equity and inclusion workshops, or initiatives for work-life integration into organizations that have high masculinity contest cultures are not likely going to result in meaningful change (Williams, 2013). Although intuitively appealing, these types of organizational practices often have the unintended consequences of increasing resentment.

Initiatives that promote work-life integration allow and encourage all workers to control when and where they work while advancing creative flexible solutions. Work-life norms counterbalance the masculinity contest culture norms that value devotion to the centrality of work in life. Policies and practices that seek to benefit or celebrate specific groups very likely activate a competitive or protective mindset among high-status group members. Organizations seeking to reduce zero-sum thinking might benefit from the intentional framing of gender fair policies with wording that support *all* workers. Subtle changes in wording such as replacing "maternal leave" with "parental leave" communicates support for *all* parents regardless of gender identity.

Giving and taking is what reciprocity and social exchange (power exchange currencies) are all about. Perceptions of gender and gender roles certainly influence the interpersonal exchanges that occur in a workplace setting. This chapter has focused on the specific role that masculinity plays at the intersections of gender relations in the workplace between and among the multidimensional aspects of gender identity.

REFERENCES

Allen, T. (2001). Family-supportive work environments: The role of organizational perceptions. *Journal of Vocational Behavior, 58,* 414–435.

Ashmore, R. D., Del Boca, F. K., & Wohlers, A. J. (1986). Gender stereotypes. In R. D. Ashmore & F. KDel Boca (Eds.), *The social psychology of female-male relations* (pp. 69–119). Orlando, FL: Academic Press.

Babl, J. D. (1979). Compensatory masculine responding as a function of sex role. *Journal of Consulting and Clinical Psychology, 47,* 252–257.

Bailyn, L. (2011). Redesigning work for gender equity and work-personal life integration. *Community, Work & Family, 14,* 97–112.

Bakan, D. (1966). *The duality of human existence: Isolation and communion in Western man.* Boston: Beacon Press.

Baumeister, R. F., & Sommer, K. L. (1997). What do men want? Gender differences and two spheres of belongingness: Comment on Cross and Madson (1997). *Psychological Bulletin, 122,* 38–44.

Becker, S. W., & Eagly, A. H. (2004). The heroism of women and men. *American Psychologist, 59,* 163–178.

Berdahl, J. L. (2007a). Harassment based on sex: Protecting social status in the context of gender hierarchy. *Academy of Management Review, 32*, 641–658.

Berdahl, J. L. (2007b). The sexual harassment of uppity women. *Journal of Applied Psychology, 92*, 425–437.

Berdahl, J. L., Cooper, M., Glick, P., Livingston, R. W., & Williams, J. C. (2018). Work as masculinity contest. *Journal of Social Issues, 74*, 422–448.

Berdahl, J. L., & Min, J. A. (2012). Prescriptive stereotypes and workplace consequences for East Asians in North America. *Cultural Diversity and Ethnic Minority Psychology, 18*, 141–152.

Bernasek, A., & Shwiff, S. (2001). Gender, risk, and retirement. *Journal of Economic Issues, 35*, 345–356.

Bosson, J. K., Pinel, E. C., & Vandello, J. A. (2010). The emotional impact of ambivalent sexism: Forecasts versus real experiences. *Sex Roles, 62*, 520–531.

Bosson, J. K., & Vandello, J. A. (2011). Precarious manhood and its links to action and aggression. *Current Directions in Psychological Science, 20*, 82–86.

Bosson, J. K., Vandello, J. A., Burnaford, R., Weaver, J., & Wasti, A. (2009). The links between precarious manhood and physical aggression. *Personality and Social Psychology Bulletin, 35*, 623–634.

Brescoll, V. L., & Uhlmann, E. L. (2008). Can an angry woman get ahead? Status conferral, gender, and expression of emotion in the workplace. *Psychological Science, 19*, 268–275.

Brescoll, V. L., Uhlmann, E. L., Moss-Racusin, C., & Sarnell, L. (2012). Masculinity, status, and subordination: Why working for a gender stereotype violator causes men to lose status. *Journal of Experimental Social Psychology, 48*, 354–357.

Brewer, M. B., & Gardner, W. (1996). Who is this "we"? Levels of collective identity and self-representations. *Journal of Personality and Social Psychology, 71*, 83–93.

Byrnes, J. P., Miller, D. C., & Schafer, W. C. (1999). Gender and risk-taking: A meta-analysis. *Psychological Bulletin, 125*, 367–383.

Caswell, T. A., Bossom, J. K., Vandello, J. A., & Sellers, J. G. (2014). Testosterone and men's stress responses to gender threats. *Psychology of Men and Masculinity, 15*, 4–11.

Collinson, D. L., & Hearn, J. (1994). Naming men as men: Implications for work, organization and management. *Gender, Work and Organization, 1*, 2–22.

Cross, S. E., & Madson, L. (1997). Models of the self: Self-construals and gender. *Psychological Bulletin, 122*, 5–37.

Dahl, J., Vescio, T., & Weaver, K. (2015). How threats to masculinity sequentially cause public discomfort, anger, and ideological dominance over women. *Social Psychology, 46*, 242–254.

Diekman, A. B., & Goodfriend, W. (2006). Rolling with the changes: A role congruity perspective on gender norms. *Psychology of Women Quarterly, 30,* 369–383.

Dutton, J. E., Ashford, S. J., Lawrence, K. A., & Miner-Rubio, K. (2002). Red light, green light: Making sense of the organizational context for issue selling. *Organizational Science, 13,* 355–369.

Eagly, A. H. (2009). The his and hers of prosocial behavior: An examination of the social psychology of gender. *American Psychologist, 64,* 644–658. https://doi.org/10.1037/0003-066X.64.8.644.

Eagly, A. H., & Crowley, M. (1986). Gender and helping behavior: A meta-analytic review of the social psychological literature. *Psychological Bulletin, 100,* 283–308.

Eagly, A. H., Johannesen-Schmidt, M. C., & van Engen, M. (2003). Transformational, transactional, and laissez-faire leadership styles: A meta-analysis comparing women and men. *Psychological Bulletin, 129,* 569–591.

Eagly, A. H., Nater, C., Miller, D. I., Kaufmann, M., & Sczesny, S. (2019). Gender stereotypes have changed: A cross-temporal meta-analysis of U. S. public opinion polls from 1946 to 2018. *American Psychologist, 75,* 301–315. https://doi.org/10.1037/amp0000494.

Eisler, R. M., & Skidmore, J. R. (1987). Masculine gender role stress: Scale development and component factors in the appraisal of stressful situations. *Behavior Modification, 11,* 123–136.

Eisler, R. M., Skidmore, J. R., & Ward, C. H. (1988). Masculine gender-rose stress: Predictor of anger anxiety, and health risk behaviors. *Journal of Personality Assessment, 52,* 133–141.

Ely, R. J., & Kimmel, M. (2018). Thoughts on the workplace as a masculinity contest. *Journal of Social Issues, 74,* 628–634.

Ely, R. J., & Meyerson, D. E. (2010). An organizational approach to undoing gender: The unlikely case of offshore oil platforms. *Research in Organizational Behavior, 30,* 3–34.

Farrell, S. K., & Finkelstein, L. M. (2007). Organizational citizenship behavior and gender: Expectations and attributions for performance. *North American Journal of Psychology, 9,* 81–95.

Fiske, S. T., Cuddy, A. J. C., Glick, P., & Xu, J. (2002). A model of (often mixed) stereotype content: Competence and warmth respectively follow from perceived status and competition. *Journal of Personality and Social Psychology, 82,* 878–902.

Galinsky, A. D., Todd, A. R., Homan, A. C., Phillips, K. W., Apfelbaum, E. P., Sasaki, S. J., et al. (2015). Maximizing the gains and minimizing the pains of diversity: A policy perspective. *Perspectives on Psychological Science, 10,* 742–748.

Glick, P., & Fiske, S. T. (1996). The ambivalent sexism inventory: Differentiating hostile and benevolent sexism. *Journal of Personality and Social Psychology, 70,* 491–512.

Grant Thornton. (2019, March). *Women in business: Building a blueprint for action.* Grant Thorton International, Ltd. Retrieved at: https://www.grantt hornton.global/globalassets/global-insights—do-not-edit/2019/women-in-business/gtil-wib-report_grant-thornton-spreads-low-res.pdf.

Heilman, M. E., & Chen, J. J. (2005). Same behavior, different consequences: Reactions to men's and women's altruistic citizenship behavior. *Journal of Applied Psychology, 90,* 431–441.

Heilman, M. E., & Okimoto, T. G. (2007). Why are women penalized for success at male tasks?: The implied communality deficit. *Journal of Applied Psychology, 92,* 81–92.

Hill, E. J., Hawkins, A. J., Martinson, V., & Ferris, M. (2003). Studying "working fathers": Comparing fathers' and mothers' work-family conflict, fit, and adaptive strategies in a global high-tech company. *Fathering, 1,* 239–261.

Huston, T. L., Ruggiero, M., Conner, R., & Geis, G. (1981). Bystander intervention into crime: A study based on naturally occurring episodes. *Social Psychology Quarterly, 44,* 14–23.

Iacuone, D. (2005). "Real men are tough guys": Hegemonic masculinity and safety in the construction industry. *The Journal of Men's Studies, 13,* 247–266.

Johnson, R. C., Danko, G. P., Darvill, T. J., Bochner, S., Bowers, J. K., Huang, Y.-H., et al. (1989). Cross-cultural assessment of altruism and its correlates. *Personality and Individual Differences, 10,* 855–868.

Kelan, E. K. (2018). Men doing and undoing gender at work: A review and research agenda. *International Journal of Management Reviews, 20,* 544–558.

Kerfoot, D., & Knights, D. (1993). Management, masculinity and manipulation: From paternalism to corporate strategy in financial services in Britain. *Journal of Management Studies, 30,* 659–678.

Kidder, D. L. (2002). The influence of gender on the performance of organizational citizenship behavior. *Journal of Management, 28,* 629–648.

Kossek, E. E., Lautsch, B. A., & Eaton, S. C. (2006). Telecommuting, control, and boundary management: Correlates of policy use and practice, job control, and work-family effectiveness. *Journal of Vocational Behavior, 68,* 347–367.

Kuchynka, S. L., Bosson, J. K., Vandello, J. A., & Puryear, C. (2018). Zero-sum thinking and the masculinity contest: Perceived intergroup competition and workplace gender bias. *Journal of Social Issues, 74,* 529–550.

Kuppers, K. A. (2005). Toxic masculinity as a barrier to mental health treatment in prison. *Journal of Clinical Psychology, 61,* 713–724.

Langford, T., & MacKinnon, N. J. (2000). The affective bases for the gendering of traits: Comparing the United States and Canada. *Social Psychology Quarterly, 63,* 34–48.

Lyons, M. T. (2005). Who are the heroes? Characteristics of people who rescue others. *Journal of Cultural and Evolutionary Psychology, 3,* 245–254.

Maass, A., Cadinu, M., Guarnieri, G., & Grasselli, A. (2003). Sexual harassment under social identity threat: The computer harassment paradigm. *Journal of Personality and Social Psychology, 85,* 853–870.

Meier-Pasti, K., & Goetze, E. (2006). Masculinity and femininity as predictors of financial risk-taking: Evidence from a priming study on gender salience. *European Advances in Consumer Research, 7,* 45–46.

Messerschmidt, J. W. (1995). Managing to kill: Masculinities and the space shuttle challenger explosion. *Masculinities, 3,* 1–22.

Messerschmidt, J. W. (2012). Engendering gendered knowledge: Assessing the academic appropriation of hegemonic masculinity. *Men and Masculinities, 15*(1), 56–76.

Michniewicz, K., Vandello, J. A., & Bossom, J. K. (2014). Men's (mis)perceptions of the stigma of unemployment. *Sex Roles, 70,* 88–97.

Moskowitz, D. S., Suh, E. J., & Desaulniers, J. (1994). Situational influences on gender differences in agency and communion. *Journal of Personality and Social Psychology, 66,* 753–761.

Munsch, C. L., & Gruys, K. (2018). What threatens, defines: Tracing the symbolic boundaries of contemporary masculinity. *Sex Roles, 79,* 375–392.

Munsch, C. L., & Willer, R. (2012). The role of gender identity threat in perceptions of date rape and sexual coercion. *Violence Against Women, 18,* 1125–1146.

Netchaeva, E., Kouchaki, M., & Sheppard, L. D. (2015). A man's (precarious) place: Men's experienced threat and self-assertive reactions to female superiors. *Personality and Social Psychology Bulletin, 41,* 1247–1259.

Newport, F. (2001, February 21). *Americans see women as emotional and affectionate, men as more aggressive: Gender specific stereotypes persist in recent Gallup poll.* Retrieved April 16, 2020, from, https://news.gallup.com/poll/1978/americans-see-women-emotional-affectionate-men-more-aggressive.aspx.

Ollilainen, M., & Calasanti, T. (2007). Metaphors at work: Maintaining the salience of gender in self-managing teams. *Gender & Society, 21,* 5–27.

O'Neil, J. M., Helms, B., Gable, R., David, L., & Wrightsman, L. (1986). Gender role conflict scale: College men's fear of femininity. *Sex Roles, 14,* 335–350.

Organ, D. W., & Ryan, K. (1995). A meta-analytic review of attitudinal and dispositional predictors of organizational citizenship behavior. *Personnel Psychology, 48,* 775–802.

Pfeffer, J. (2010). *Power: Why some people have it and others don't.* New York: Harper Business.

Rudman, L. A. (1998). Self-promotion as a risk factor for women: The costs and benefits of counter-stereotypical impression management. *Journal of Personality and Social Psychology, 74,* 629–645.

Rudman, L. A., & Fairchild, K. (2004). Reactions to counter-stereotype behavior: The role of backlash in cultural stereotype maintenance. *Journal of Personality and Social Psychology, 87,* 157–176.

Sunden, A. E., & Surette, B. J. (1998). Gender differences in the allocation of assets in retirement savings plans. *American Economic Review, 88,* 207–211.

Thompson, E. H., Jr., & Bennett, K. M. (2015). Measurement of masculinity ideologies: A (critical) review. *Psychology of Men & Masculinity, 16*(2), 115.

Vandello, J. A., & Bosson, J. K. (2013). Hard won and easily lost: A review and synthesis of theory and research on precarious manhood. *Psychology of Men & Masculinity, 14*(2), 101.

Vandello, J. A., Bosson, J. K., Cohen, D., Burnaford, R. M., & Weaver, J. R. (2008). Precarious manhood. *Journal of Personality and Social Psychology, 95,* 1325–1339.

Vandello, J. A., Hettinger, V. E., Bosson, J. K., & Siddiqi, J. (2013). When equal really isn't equal: The masculine dilemma of seeking work flexibility. *Journal of Social Issues, 69,* 303–321.

Weaver, K. S., & Vescio, T. K. (2015). The justification of social inequality in response to masculinity threats. *Sex Roles, 72,* 521–535.

Weaver, K. S., Vandello, J. A., & Bosson, J. K. (2012). Intrepid, imprudent, or impetuous? The effects of gender threats on men's financial decisions. *Psychology of Men and Masculinity, 14,* 184–191.

Willer, R., Rogalin, C., Conlon, B., & Wojnowicz, M. T. (2013). Overdoing gender: A test of the masculine overcompensation thesis. *American Journal of Sociology, 118,* 980–1022.

Williams, J. C. (2013, May 29). Why men work so many hours. *Harvard Business Review*. Retrieved April 20, 2020 from, https://hbr.org/2013/05/why-men-work-so-many-hours.

Williams, J. E., & Best, D. L. (1990). *Measuring sex stereotypes: A multination study* (rev ed.). Newbury Park, CA: Sage.

Wilson, T. D., Centerbar, D. B., Kermer, D. A., & Gilbert, D. T. (2005). The pleasures of uncertainty: Prolonging positive moods in ways people do not anticipate. *Journal of Personality and Social Psychology, 88,* 5–21.

Wilson, T. D., & Gilbert, D. T. (2005). Affective forecasting: Knowing what to want. *Current Directions in Psychological Science, 3,* 131–134.

Wilson, T. D., Wheatley, T. P., Meyers, J. M., Gilbert, D. T., & Axsom, D. (2000). Focalism: A source of durability bias in affective forecasting. *Journal of Personality and Social Psychology, 78,* 821–836.

Wood, W., & Eagly, A. H. (2002). A cross-cultural analysis of the behavior of women and men: Implications for the origins of sex differences. *Psychological Bulletin, 128,* 699–727.

Wood, W., & Eagly, A. H. (2009). Gender identity. In M. R. Leary & R. H. Hoyle (Eds.), *Handbook of individual differences in social behavior* (pp. 109–125). New York: Guilford Press.

CHAPTER 7

Gender Stereotypes: The Profiling of Women in Marketing

Thuc-Doan Nguyen

INTRODUCTION

Stereotyping in advertising can be considered both "mirror" and "mold", reflecting and shaping the values of its target audience. However, research shows a large gap between portrayals of women in advertising and the changing roles of women in society. Although the financial, social, and educational status of women has evolved significantly over the decades, one research stream shows that there have been few changes in female portrayals in advertising, and stereotyping has in fact become worse (Ganahl, Prinsen, & Netzley, 2003; Milner & Higgs, 2004; Plakoyian-naki & Zotos, 2009; Tsichla & Zotos, 2013). On the other hand, another research stream shows improvement in female portrayals in keeping with female status improvement in society (Furnham & Mak, 1999; Wolin, 2003).

Gender stereotypes in advertising have also been used to promote products (Courtney & Whipple, 1983; Furnham & Mak, 1999).

T.-D. Nguyen (✉)
School of Business, Woodbury University, Burbank, CA, USA
e-mail: Thuc.Nguyen@woodbury.edu

© The Author(s), under exclusive license to Springer Nature Switzerland AG 2021
J. Marques (ed.), *Exploring Gender at Work*,
https://doi.org/10.1007/978-3-030-64319-5_7

123

However, a study shows that 91% of female consumers feel that advertisers do not understand them. Furthermore, 7 in 10 women say they feel alienated by advertising (*The Guardian*). According to the study, 59% of women feel misunderstood by food marketers; 66% feel misunderstood by health care marketers; and 74% feel misunderstood by investment marketers. A survey conducted by SheKnows found that 52% of female respondents said they purchased a product because they liked how a brand and its ads portrayed women. However, female portrayals in advertising seem disconnected from female roles in society as well as the interests of female audiences. The study of female portrayals in advertising has attracted scholarly interest for the past 60 years. However, the connection between stereotyping of women in advertising and marketers' profiling of women has not yet been explored. To address the issue, this study provides meta-analysis of research on gender stereotypes in advertising and content analysis of "how to market to women" in practical marketing guidelines and academic research. The stereotype of women in contemporary advertising will be linked to the marketer's perception of female consumer profiles.

LITERATURE REVIEW

Gender Stereotypes

Gender stereotypes are beliefs that a set of attributes differentiates women from men (Ashmore & Del Boca, 1981). Deaux and Lewis (1984) suggest four independent dimensions of gender stereotypes: trait descriptors (e.g., self-assertion, concern for others), physical characteristics (e.g., hair length, body height), role behaviors (e.g., leader, taking care of children), and occupational status (e.g., truck driver, housewife). Each dimension has masculine and feminine versions, which are strongly related to gender types. For example, the masculine role includes the notions of authority, leader, and decision-maker while the feminine role includes traditional and decorative roles such as caretakers and subordinates.

Gender stereotypes might lead to expectations and judgments that restrict life opportunities for one gender. For example, stereotyping physical characteristics of women such as weight and skin color can lead to body dissatisfaction and reduced self-confidence. Stereotyping role behaviors of women as supportive and caring might lead to harm-promotion opportunities for women. Gender stereotyping provides a dichotomous model, which thinks and speaks of women in comparison to men (Tuchman, 1979).

The "Mold" versus "Mirror" Debate

Scholars have long discussed the interaction between advertising and society. There are two opposite points of view: the "mold" and the "mirror" (Holbrook, 1987). The "mirror" camp suggests that advertising reflects dominant values in a culture. The underlying rationale is that there are environmental factors that shape the value system in a society. Advertising is a representation of the existing value system; it has no significant impact on that value system (Holbrook, 1987). Thus, female portrayals in advertising are shaped by dominant beliefs about gender roles in society (Zotos & Tsichla, 2014b).

In contrast, the "mold" argument states that advertising has a significant impact on the values held by its target audience (Pollay, 1986, 1987). People learn from media. Gender stereotypes in advertising create, shape, and reinforce the audience's perceptions about society. Gradually, advertising changes people's attitude and behavior (Ganahl et al., 2003). Gender stereotypes in advertising are incorporated into people beliefs about gender. Advertising creates gender identity, the stereotyped iconography of masculinity and femininity (Schroeder & Zwick, 2004). Female portrayals in advertising model lifestyles and forms of self-representation that female consumers use to define their gender roles (Plakoyiannaki et al., 2008).

Scholars speculate that the truth lies in the continuum between the "mirror" and "mold" arguments (Graua & Zotos, 2016; Zotos & Tsichla, 2014a). Advertising both reflects and shapes the value system in society (Hall, 1980; Albers-Miller & Gelb, 1996).

Female Portrayals in Advertising Review

Scholarly interest in female portrayals in advertising dates back six decades. Content analysis has been widely used to study whether gender stereotypes exist, identify specific types of stereotypes, track whether the degree of stereotyping changes when gender roles in society advance, and identify factors that moderate stereotypes. This interest started in America, but recently scholars have also studied female portrayals in advertising in cultural contexts around the world (Nam, Lee, & Hwang,

2011; Milner, 2005; Morris & Nicholas, 2013). Studies have also spread across media types, including print advertising, radio commercials, television commercials, and online advertising. Research also found that the stereotyping of female images in advertising varies with the advertised product categories (Frith, Cheng, & Shaw, 2004). Furthermore, the audience toward whom the advertising is directed also determines how women are represented in that advertising (Nam et al., 2011).

Content analysis studies have used coding categories based on Goffman's scale. Goffman (1979) explains how advertising frames social reality. Advertising selects and highlights certain aspects of social ideals. Goffman (1979) investigated gender stereotype through the hands, eyes, postures, and movements of advertising models. He classified gender stereotypes into six categories:

- Relative Size: women are exaggeratedly shown as smaller and shorter than men
- Feminine Touch: Women are shown caressing objects or touching themselves as delicate and precious objects.
- Function Ranking: women have the subordinate role when cooperating with men.
- Family Scenes—Women are depicted as mothers and caretakers while men are portrayed as protectors of the family
- Ritualization of Subordination: Women are more likely to be shown lying down, often in flirtatious or childish poses, even when it is not appropriate.
- Licensed Withdrawal: Women remove themselves physically or psychologically from the situation at hand. They are distracted or not involved in their surroundings.

Kang (1997) added two categories to Goffman's original scale (1) Body Display: women are shown in revealing clothes and (2) Independence/Self-assurance: the overall impression of independence and/or self-assurance by showing a poker face, a straight and confident gaze and a space-occupying posture.

Another research stream focuses on female role stereotypes. Female role stereotypes are classified under four themes: (1) women in decorative roles, where they are portrayed as sex objects in pursuit of beauty and physical attractiveness; (2) women in traditional roles, where they are depicted as dependent on a male's protection, as good wives, and as belonging at home; (3) women in non-traditional roles, where they are career-oriented or engaging in activities outside the home (e.g., sport); and (4) women portrayed as equal to men (Belkaoui & Belkaoui, 1976; Lysonski, 1985; Mitchell & Taylor, 1990; Zotos & Lysonski, 1994).

Both "mirror" and "mold" arguments claim that female portrayals in advertising are connected to gender-related development. Several studies have examined whether the degree of stereotyping has varied given social changes and transformation. All research found that gender stereotypes still exist in advertising. However, some studies claim that the degree of stereotyping has slightly decreased (Wolin, 2003). Women are shown less in traditional roles and settings and more in modern roles as well as outside settings (Furnham & Mak, 1999). In contrast, several studies stress that female images in advertising have gotten worse. Recent studies found that women are more frequently portrayed in traditional roles in recent years, compared with results from studies in the nineteenth century (Ganahl et al., 2003; Milner & Higgs, 2004). What makes it worse is the fact that with contemporary social changes promoting women's roles in our society, increasing gender stereotyping in advertising widens the gap between female portrayal in advertising and women's experiences in uplifting their social, financial, and educational status.

Spear and Amos (2014) found that traditional female images in advertising portraying women as housewives, nurturers, and comforters are relatively consistent over time. During times of societal distress and crisis, the prevalence of these traditional female images intensifies. Advertisers choose to stick with popular viewpoints about females during crisis periods. In prosperous and peaceful times, advertisers try to choose riskier, emerging ideas. Modern and emergent female roles are shown more in boom times. Their study explains the contradictory results of research on trends and the direction of female portrayals in advertising.

Methodology

Meta-Analysis

To answer the first research question, a qualitative meta-analysis named the *thematic synthesis* (Thomas & Harden, 2008) is used. Qualitative meta-analysis consists of a secondary analysis of the primary, original, studies addressing the same research questions (Timulak, 2014). In this study, the topic of the qualitative meta-analysis is how females are portrayed in advertising.

The search for studies for inclusion in thematic synthesis is purposive, not exhaustive. It is not necessary to identify all available primary studies. Studies are selected depending on their contexts, concepts, and divergence. The sampling process ends when data is saturated—that is, when there is no new theme emerging from new data (Thomas & Harden, 2008).

I searched extensively for studies focusing on female images in advertising. The first step was to use a simple electronic search of a database. Next, I spend a considerable amount of time screening titles and abstracts. I was searching for variety in terms of advertising media from magazines and radio to websites. I also considered variety in terms of product categories and cultures. At last, references in the chosen articles were searched and screened as above. This study is interested in female portrayals in advertising since 2000. Only studies that collect advertisements published in and after the year 2000 were selected. This results in 26 studies included in the pool.

Content Analysis

A content analysis of "how to market to women" is used to explore the female consumer profiles created by marketers. Qualitative content analysis is a method for systematically assigning the meaning of qualitative data (Schreier, 2014). This method reduces data related to the research question through coding, categorizing, and abstracting to find emerging themes.

Collecting Materials

Keyword searches for "marketing to women", "targeting," "female consumers," and "advertising to women" were used on a number of databases and internet search engines (e.g., Factiva, Google, EBSCO) to finds articles from industry related to the topic "how to market to women." Only materials dated since 2010 are selected. The sampling process was purposive, not exhaustive. The sampling process ended when data was saturated. There were 50 articles included in the pool.

FINDINGS

Female Portrayals in Advertising Since 2000

There still exist gender stereotypes in advertising. Gender stereotypes exist in all cultures from Asia, Africa, Australia, Eastern and Western Europe as well as in the Americas. However, the degree of gender stereotypes varies across cultures.

Age. Female central characters are more likely portrayed as young while male central characters are in the middle age and older age segments (Prieler, Ivanov, & Hagiwara, 2015). Women are also shown as unmarried while men are more likely to be portrayed as married. Young and unmarried women are perceived as attractive. The stereotype emphasizes the physical attractiveness of female youth. Seniority, by contrast, is associated with knowledge and power. The lack of aging women shows that women are valued primarily because of their youth and attractiveness, not for their knowledge and power (Prieler et al., 2015; Kim & Lowry, 2005; Gerbner, 1998). Asian women are shown as younger than Western women (Nam et al., 2011).

Sexism. Significant gender differences in the degree of dress and strong associations between gender and type of dress were found in many studies (Eisend, 2010; Kim & Lowry, 2005). Males are more likely to be fully dressed than females while women are often seen partially dressed or nude. Female central characters are also portrayed with a more feminine touch. They are shown as childlike, pouting, or cute and smiling (Nam et al., 2011). All these portrayals create ideal images of females as sex objects, triggers for seduction and desire, and displays of physical attractiveness. Western women are shown as more sexually provocative than Asian women (#4). They are more likely to show body shape and nudity than their Asian counterparts. Women are more often portrayed as sexually attractive in ads targeting male audiences.

Roles. Women are significantly portrayed in decorative roles and traditional roles. Women are seen as beauty objects or sex objects in their decorative roles. They are using products to obtain beauty and attractiveness when the ads target a female audience. However, when the ads target a male audience, the images of beautiful and attractive women are used as the reward for buying products. Male consumers are portrayed as using products to obtain attractive women (Baker, 2005).

Women are also popular in traditional roles such as housewife, nurturer, and comforter. They are shown cooking, cleaning, and doing other housework or relaxing at home (Nam et al., 2011; Plakoyiannaki & Zotos, 2009). Women are often shown in dependent roles, not having any "voice of authority," but rather asking or listening to advice. Although this portrayal varies depending on social condition (whether the society that produced the advertisement is in crisis or prosperous), women are rarely portrayed in non-traditional roles (Spear & Amos, 2014) as professional, authorities, experts. Women are more likely to be seen as central characters in advertising of cosmetics/toiletries, household goods, and simple or unimportant products. Men, however, are more often seen in advertising for technical products such as cars or high-tech devices (Valls-Fernández & Martínez-Vicente, 2007; Kim & Lowry, 2005). Women are less likely to be seen as professionals, executives, and high-level workers. They are seen as homemakers, or as unpaid or low-paid workers. They are often seen nurturing children and doing household chores (Milner & Higgs, 2004).

Female Consumer Profiles

While the advertising industry relies heavily on gender stereotyping to promote products, marketers have recognized its pitfalls. Plenty of "how to" guides on marketing to women point out the mistake of stereotyping female consumers. Overly simplistic or stereotypical characterizations do not do much for brand loyalty and can actually damage brand reputation (Zbooker, 2019). Content analysis of materials from industry provides the following themes related to female consumer profiles.

Heterogeneity. One of the main themes emerging from the data is that the female market is very diverse. It includes multiple segments of different life stages, various lifestyles, diverse values, and commitment to several causes. Thus, it is no surprise that 45% of respondents participating in Kantar's "Getting Gender Right" survey report that advertising is based on stereotypes and that women are portrayed in outdated ways. Stereotyping treats women as if they are all the same, which risks insulting a marketer's target audience.

Multiple Roles. It is undeniable that women often serve as primary caregivers, as stereotyped in advertising. However, caregiver is only one of their roles. Globally, women are in the labor force more now than ever before. They account for about 39% of the workforce globally, and about 46% in the US (Catalyst). In fact, although the ratio remains small, women have already joined the C-suite. About 7% of Fortune

500 companies' CEOs are women. Women account for nearly a third of senior managers. Women even earn more higher-education degrees than men do. Women get married at older ages. Japanese women are increasingly opting out of marriage entirely. More women are choosing not to have children. These demographic trends drive the world's female populations into multiple roles not only at home but also in public. At different life stages, certain roles emerge as dominant ones that shape female consumers' decisions.

A study by Insight Marketing reveals that 91% of female respondents do not feel that marketers effectively target them. Female consumers want to tell their stories, which are related to women's own situations, with a female voice. Gender stereotyping in advertising cannot connect to female consumers.

Causes and Values. Ernst and Young's Groundbreakers report revealed that women reinvest 90% of their income into their families and communities. Women hold on and commit to their values, whether those involve the environment, equity, inclusion, health, or spiritual life. They want companies to be good corporate citizens. They want to see companies contributing to and taking substantial action toward social causes that matter to them and their community.

Feeling Empowered and Becoming More Active. In a recent survey conducted by the website SheKnows, 71% of female respondents said that brands should promote positive attitudes to women and girls. Nike, Adidas, Gatorade, Under Armour, and Twitter are among the few pioneering brands who promote images of female athletes, active women, and powerful female leaders in their ads. Gender stereotypes of subordinate and decorative female roles are wildly outdated images that are no longer connected with female consumers. Recently, movies such as *Hidden Figures, Wonder Woman,* and *Moana* have authentically and massively connected with female audiences. It is evident that women want to be seen as strong, assertive, and active, not passive.

DISCUSSION AND CONCLUSION

This study shows that gender stereotypes are still prevalent in advertising. Women are portrayed in traditional roles as homemaker and decorative objects. Women are shown to be younger than men are. They are also seen as sexually provocative. Meanwhile, some marketers present more realistic female images. The female market is heterogeneous. Women play multiple roles in daily life, and traditional roles are just a few among many. Female consumers are strong, assertive, and active. They join the labor force and gain higher social, financial, and educational status. They support social causes that matter to their communities and the societies in which they live.

A possible explanation for outdated gender stereotypes in advertising is the gender imbalance in the field. Advertising, as a creative industry, is male-dominated (Gulas, McKeage, & Weinberger, 2010). Advertising is structured around White, male norms. Thus, female images in advertising are created from one point of view: the view of the White male.

Today, women are raising their voices about diversity. They are trans women, women of color, Black women, and LGBT women. They are single moms, traditional stay-at-home moms, athletes, and CEOs. Gender stereotypes in advertising disconnect brands from their target audience. A survey conducted by the website SheKnows found that 52% of female respondents purchased a product because they liked how a brand and its ads portrayed women. Negative, gender-biased depictions of women in advertising may have adverse effects on the reputations of the companies that use those advertisements. Studies have found that women are critical of advertising using female images that are not consistent with their gender orientation (Ford et al., 1997).

Beyond potential damage to companies' bottom lines, advertising has a powerful impact on the value system of society (Zayer & Coleman, 2015). Gender stereotypes in advertising can affect women's self-esteem and feelings of inadequacy (Gulas & McKeage, 2000; Zayer & Otnes, 2012). The focus on female roles as traditional homemakers, the emphasis on their contributions to unpaid work, undermines women's aspiration to join the labor force. The images of women in subordinate roles may prevent them from aiming for higher positions. Focus on physical beauty can lead to eating disorders and unsafe use of cosmetic surgery. Furthermore, the rigid dichotomy between male and female excludes other segments—notably, LGBT consumers.

CHAPTER TAKEAWAYS

- Research shows a large gap between portrayals of women in advertising and the changing roles of women in society.

- Gender stereotypes are beliefs that a set of attributes differentiates women from men. Four independent dimensions of gender stereotypes are, (1) trait descriptors, (2) physical characteristics, (3) role behaviors, and (4) occupational status. Each dimension has masculine and feminine versions, which are strongly related to gender types.
- When considering the interaction between advertising and society, there are two opposite points of view: the "mold" and the "mirror". The "mirror" camp suggests that advertising reflects dominant values in a culture. The "mold" argument states that advertising has a significant impact on the values held by its target audience.

  - Both "mirror" and "mold" arguments claim that female portrayals in advertising are connected to gender-related development.

- There still exist gender stereotypes in advertising. Gender stereotypes exist in all cultures from Asia, Africa, Australia, Eastern, and Western Europe as well as in the Americas. However, the degree of gender stereotypes varies across cultures.
- While the advertising industry relies heavily on gender stereotyping to promote products, marketers have recognized its pitfalls. Content analysis of materials from industry provides a variety of themes related to female consumer profiles, including heterogeneity, multiple roles, causes and values, feeling empowered and becoming more active.
- Today, women are raising their voices about diversity. They are trans women, women of color, Black women, and LGBT women. They are single moms, traditional stay-at-home moms, athletes, and CEOs. Gender stereotypes in advertising disconnect brands from their target audience.
- Gender stereotypes in advertising can affect women's self-esteem and feelings of inadequacy. The focus on female roles as traditional homemakers, the emphasis on their contributions to unpaid work, undermines women's aspiration to join the labor force.

REFERENCES

Albers-Miller, N. D., & Gelb, B. D. (1996). Business advertising appeals as a mirror of cultural dimensions: A study of eleven countries. *Journal of Advertising, 25,* 57–70.

Ashmore, R. D., & Del Boca, F. K. (1981). Conceptual approaches to stereotypes and stereotyping. In D. L. Hamilton (Ed.), *Cognitive approaches in stereotyping and intergroup behaviour* (pp. 1–35). Hillsdale: Lawrence Erlbaum Associates.

Baker, C. (2005). Images of women's sexuality in advertisements: A content analysis of black- and white-oriented women's and men's magazines. *Sex Roles, 52*(1), 13–27.

Belkaoui, A., & Belkaoui, J. M. (1976). A comparative analysis of the roles played by women in print advertisements: 1958, 1970, 1972. *Journal of Marketing Research, 8*(2), 168–172.

Courtney, A. E., & Whipple, T. W. (1983). *Sex stereotyping in advertising.* Lexington, MA: Lexington Books.

Deaux, K., & Lewis, L. L. (1984). Structure of gender stereotypes: Interrelationships among components and gender label. *Journal of Personality and Social Phychology, 46,* 991–1004.

Eisend, M. (2010). A meta-analysis of gender roles in advertising. *Journal of the Academy of Marketing Science, 38,* 418–440.

Ford, J. B., LaTour, M., & Honeycutt, E. D. (1997). An examination of cross-cultural female response to offensive sex role portrayals in advertising. *International Marketing Review, 14*(6), 409–423.

Frith, K. T., Cheng, H., & Shaw, P. (2004). Race and beauty: A comparison of Asian and Western models in women's magazine advertisements. *Sex Roles: A Journal of Research, 50*(1–2), 53–61.

Furnham, A., & Paltzer, S. (2010). The portrayal of men and women in television advertisements: An updated review of 30 studies published since 2000. *Scandinavian Journal of Psychology, 51*(3), 216–236. https://doi.org/10.1111/j.1467-9450.2009.00772.x.

Furnham, A., & Mak, T. (1999). Sex-role stereotyping in television commercials: A review and comparison of fourteen studies done on five continents over 25 Years. *Sex Roles, 41,* 413–437.

Ganahl, D. J., Prinsen, T. J., & Netzley, S. B. (2003). A content analysis of prime time commercials: A contextual framework of gender representation. *Sex Roles, 49,* 545–551.

Gerbner, G. (1998). Cultivation analysis: An overview. *Mass Communication & Society, 1*(3/4), 35–58.

Goffman, E. (1979). *Gender advertisements.* Cambridge, MA: Harvard University Press.

Graua, S. L., & Zotos, Y. C. (2016). Gender stereotypes in advertising: A review of current research. *International Journal of Advertising, 35*(5), 761–770.

Gulas, C. S., & McKeage, K. (2000). Extending social comparison: An examination of the unintended consequences of idealized advertising imagery. *Journal of Advertising, 29*(2), 17–28.

Gulas, C. S., McKeage, K., & Weinberger, M. (2010). It's just a joke: Violence against males in humorous advertising. *Journal of Advertising, 39*(4), 109–120.

Hall, S. (1980). Encoding/decoding. In S. Hall, D. Hobson, A. Lowe, & P. Willis (Eds.), *Culture, media, language*. London: Hutchison.

Holbrook, M. B. (1987). Mirror, mirror, on the wall, what's unfair in the reflections on advertising? *Journal of Marketing, 51*, 95–103.

How advertising industry fails women. (*The Guardian*). Retrieved from https://www.theguardian.com/women-in-leadership/2016/feb/03/how-advertising-industry-fails-women#:~:text=Women%20are%20the%20most%20p owerful,85%25%20of%20all%20purchasing%20decisions.&text=Unsurpris ingly%2C%20according%20to%20research%2C%2091,feel%20%E2%80%9Calie nated%E2%80%9D%20by%20advertising.

Kang, M. (1997). The portrayal of women's images in magazine advertisements: Goffman's gender analysis revisited. *Sex Roles, 37*, 979–996.

Kim, K., & Lowry, D. T. (2005). Television commercials as a lagging social indicator: Gender role stereotypes in Korean television advertising. *Sex Roles, 53*(11/12), 901–910. https://doi.org/10.1007/s11199-005-8307-1.

Lysonski, S. (1985). Role portrayals in British magazine advertisements. *European Journal of Marketing Science, 38*(4), 418–440. https://doi.org/10.1007/s11747-009-0181-x.

Milner, L. (2005). Sex-role portrayals in African television advertising: A preliminary examination with implications for the use of Hofstede's research. *Journal of International Consumer Marketing, 17*(2/3), 73–91.

Milner, L. M., & Higgs, B. (2004). Gender sex-role portrayals in international television advertising over time: The Australian experience. *Journal of Current Issues and Research in Advertising, 26*, 81–95.

Mitchell, P. C. N., & Taylor, W. (1990). Polarising trends in female role portrayal in UK Advertising. *European Journal of Marketing, 24*(5), 41–49.

Morris, P. K., & Nicholas, K. (2013). Conceptualizing beauty: A content analysis of U.S. and French women's fashion magazine advertisements. *Online Journal of Communication and Media Technologies, 3*(1), 49–74.

Nam, K., Lee, G., & Hwang, J. S. (2011). Gender stereotypes depicted by western and Korean advertising models in Korean adolescent girls' magazines. *Sex Roles, 64*, 223–237.

Plakoyiannaki, E., & Zotos, Y. (2009). Female role stereotypes in print advertising: Identifying associations with magazine and product categories. *European Journal of Marketing, 43,* 1411–1434.

Plakoyiannaki, E., Mathioudaki, K., Dimitratos, P., & Zotos, Y. (2008). Images of women in online advertisements of global products: Does sexism exist? *Journal of Business Ethics, 83,* 101–112.

Pollay, R. W. (1986). The distorted mirror: Reflections on the unintended consequences of advertising. *Journal of Marketing, 50*(2), 18–36.

Pollay, R. W. (1987). On the value of reflections on the values in 'The distorted mirror.' *Journal of Marketing, 51*(3), 104–109.

Prieler, M., Ivanov, A., & Hagiwara, S. (2015). Gender representations in East Asian advertising: Hong Kong, Japan, and South Korea. *Communication & Society, 28*(1), 27–41.

Schreier, M. (2014). Qualitative content analysis. In Uwe Flick (Ed.), *The sage handbook of qualitative data analysis* (pp. 170–183). London: Sage.

Schroeder, J. E., & Zwick, D. (2004). Mirrors of masculinity: Representation and identity in advertising images. *Consumption, Markets and Culture, 7,* 21–52.

Spears, N., & Amos, C. (2014). Twentieth century female ad images: Cultural interconnections, social learning, and the dialectical logic of advertising. *Journal of Business Research, 67,* 441–448.

Thomas, J., & Harden, A. (2008). Methods for the thematic synthesis of qualitative research in systematic reviews. *BMC Medical Research Methodology, 8*(45). https://doi.org/10.1186/1471-2288-8-45.

Timulak, L. (2014). Qualitative meta-analysis. In U. Flick (Ed.), *The sage handbook of qualitative data analysis* (pp. 481–495). London: Sage.

Tsichla, E., & Zotos, Y. C. (2013). Gender stereotypes in Cypriot magazine advertisements: A comparison of single and relationship portrayals. Paper presented at the 18th International Conference on Corporate and Marketing Communication, April 11–12, Salerno, Italy.

Tuchman, G. (1979). The symbolic annihilation of women by the mass media. In G. Tuchman, A. K. Daniels, & J. W. Benet (Eds.), *Hearth and home: Images of women in the mass media* (pp. 3–38). New York: Oxford.

Valls-Fernández, F., & Martínez-Vicente, J. M. (2007). Gender stereotypes in Spanish television commercials. *Sex Roles: A Journal of Research, 56*(9–10), 691–699.

Wolin, L. D. (2003). Gender issues in advertising—An oversight of research: 1970–2002. *Journal of Advertising Research, 43,* 111–129.

Zayer, L. T., & Coleman, C. A. (2015). Advertising professionals' perceptions of the impact of gender portrayals on men and women: A question of ethics? *Journal of Advertising, 44*(3), 1–12. https://doi.org/10.1080/00913367.2014.975878.

Zayer, L., & Otnes, C. (2012). Climbing the ladder or chasing a dream: Men's responses to idealized portrayals of masculinity in advertising. In C. Otnes & L. Zayer (Eds.), *Gender, culture, and consumer behavior* (pp. 87–110). New York, NY: Routledge.

Zbooker, A. (2019). How to Target female consumers. Retrieved June 19, 2020, from, https://medium.com/@namegenderpro/how-to-target-female-consumers-4-effective-case-studies-9e39839add0e.

Zotos, Y. C., & Tsichla, E. (2014a). Female stereotypes in print Advertising: A retrospective analysis. *Procedia—Social and Behavioral Sciences, 148,* 446–454.

Zotos, Y. C., & Tsichla, E. (2014b). Snapshots of men and women in interaction: An investigation of stereotypes in print advertisement relationship portrayals. *Journal of Euromarketing, 23*(3), 35–58.

Zotos, Y. C., & Lysonski, S. (1994). Gender representations: the case of Greek magazine advertisements. *Journal of Euromarketing, 3*(2), 27–47.

CHAPTER 8

Deciding to Be Authentic: Transgender Employees and Their Decision to Be Out at Work

Lizabeth Kay Kleintop

INTRODUCTION

For employees who are transgender and not yet out to their peers, supervisors, leadership, or Human Resources at work, coming out can be a fearful event. Over half of transgender employees in the U.S. not out at work feared coming out would negatively affect their chance of future promotions according to one survey (Johnson, 2015). As many as 67% of respondents to the 2015 U.S. Transgender Survey who applied for a job in the year previous to the survey reported not being hired, denied a promotion, and/or being fired or forced to resign because they were out as a transgender person (James, Herman, Rankin, Keisling, Mottet, & Anafi, 2016). The fear of coming out is more than just fear of losing jobs or job opportunities though those are significant fears. The fear of

L. K. Kleintop (✉)
Economics and Business Department, Moravian College, Bethlehem, PA, USA
e-mail: kleintopl@moravian.edu

coming out also results from concerns over the responses and behaviors of co-workers to the presence of a transgender person in their workspaces.

Coming out at work reduces the stress of hiding one's identity, increases productivity at work while developing closer, more genuine relationships with colleagues, customers, and clients, and builds self-esteem from being known for who one really is (Human Rights Campaign [HRC], 2015). These are benefits for employers as well as transgender employees. Employers benefit from successful transitions as they show the inclusiveness of the organization, demonstrating the extent to which the "organization values and integrates diversity and supports it through fair employment practices" (Singh, Winkel, & Selvarajan, 2013). Successful transitions assist employers in attracting and retaining the people most qualified for jobs while enhancing productivity, innovation, and creativity of their workforce (Society for Human Resource Management [SHRM], 2017). An employer's focus on judging people by their abilities provides evidence of their meeting diversity and inclusion initiative goals, as well as demonstrating compliance with employment laws.

Coming out as transgender is a momentous and challenging decision. The workplace can be a fearful place for transgender employees, yet coming out can have both personal and career benefits. The equation which a transgender employee evaluates about coming out is a balance between being true to oneself and the perceived safety of their workplace. Transgender employees look at costs and benefits of coming out at a personal level which is influenced by their work environment including policies, processes, and co-workers. They judge how safe they will be when coming out at work against the fears of stigmatization they perceive in their work environment and whether that level of safety, physical and psychological, is sufficient for them to come out and be their true selves.

This chapter examines how employers can reduce barriers to transgender employees coming out at work by examining the role played by stigmatization and bias associated with transgender employees bending societal expectations of gender. Overcoming these barriers allows employers to create a psychologically safe workplace that will allow transgender employees to be themselves at work to their and their employers' benefit.

CHALLENGES TO TRANSGENDER
EMPLOYEES COMING OUT AT WORK

Transgender people have experienced a wide range of discriminatory behaviors in workplaces including exclusion from jobs based on bona fide occupational qualifications, physical assault, verbal harassment and abuse, destruction of their property, ridicule, homophobic jokes, unfair work schedules, workplace sabotage, restrictions to their career, resentment by others for their perceived "special treatment," religious intolerance, "deadnaming" or the use of former names or pronouns, bullying, ignoring, shunning, avoidance, sexual assault, coercive social and cultural domination, name-calling, and job loss (Budge, Tebbe, & Howard, 2010; Hill, 2009; Kirk & Belovics, 2008). Fears about coming out at work also include the fear of having to talk about being transgender and being forced to explain what it means (Johanna [spacegirl_j], 2020).

Employers also have a stake in ensuring a safe workplace for transgender employees. Employers want to demonstrate inclusiveness which they expect to lead to productive, innovative, and creative workforces (SHRM, 2017). Safe workplaces demonstrate that employers value and support diversity with equitable employment practices (Singh, et al. 2013). Safe workplaces support the recruitment and retention of individuals in organizations with the competencies needed to achieve the employers' strategic goals.

The Human Rights Campaign (2015), Out & Equal Workplace Advocates (2014), and the Society for Human Resource Management (SHRM, 2016, 2017) and others have provided directions to employers for creating a workplace that is safe for transgender employees to transition as have many authors (Sawyer & Thoroughgood, 2017; Stirba, Goldstein, Gentili, Reynolds, Hill-Meyer, & Scarborough, 2014; Walworth, 2003; Weiss, 2007). These recommendations often are incorporated into transition plans for transgender employees, plans to guide the transition process to ensure legal compliance by preventing discrimination and establishing a talent environment maximizing the value of people regardless of who they are (Cadrain, 2009). Even so, transitions by transgender employees do not always result in successful outcomes.

The 2015 US Transgender Survey shows the discriminatory behaviors transgender employees can experience in the workplace. Forty-one percent of respondents to that survey who reported being fired, forced to resign, or denied a promotion believed it was due to discrimination because of their transgender status (James et al., 2016). Other mistreatment at work was shown including respondents reporting one or more experiences of information being shared about them that should not have been shared, negative job reviews, being forced to resign, being forced to use a restroom not consistent with their gender identity or not being able to work out an acceptable restroom situation, being required to present in the wrong gender, removal from direct contact with clients, customers, or patients, or being forced to transfer to another department (James et al., 2016).

The targeting of transgender employees by others at work suggests failures in transition planning. These failures directly impact transgender employees and negatively impact the employment brand of their organizations. Transition plans focus on changing the behaviors of employees but not the attitudes that employees bring with them into the workplace. Leaders demonstrating inclusivity by using their preferred pronouns in their email signatures and allowing employees to self-identify their gender on survey forms are good tactics for meeting legal requirements (Bennett & Reed, 2020). On their own, however, those tactics may not go far enough to ensure a workplace that transgender employees feel will be safe for them when they come out. To create such a workplace, employers need to consider the social norms employees bring with them to the workplace about gender that may lead to stigmatization of transgender employees and biased behaviors enacted towards them by co-workers.

Transitioning and the Stigmatization of Transgender People

Transitioning is living one's true gender identity in one's personal and work lives. Not all transgender people transition, but those who choose to transition do so to live in a manner consistent with their gender identity (Out & Equal Workplace Advocate, 2014). Individuals transitioning their gender in the workplace desire to be their authentic self, to be who they really are. They are usually interested in keeping their jobs along with the compensation that comes with that. Most of all, they want to contribute all of themselves to the work they do while being true to themselves.

Regardless of their goal to be themselves in their lives, transgender people experience some level of apprehension around their coming out at work if not outright fear of the outcomes of such behavior. They would have assessed the tradeoff between coming out and staying in the closet at work even if they are out in their home and social environment.

Those disclosing their transgender status must determine to whom to disclose their transgender status, the best time and place to disclose, the right amount of information to share, and the appropriate words to use in their disclosure (Chaudoir & Fisher, 2010). Reaching out to a supervisor or to the human resources office to initiate a workplace transition, however, is not an easy decision to make for most people. Fear of rejection and anticipated stigmatization can lead to decisions not to disclose their identity (Chaudoir & Fisher, 2010).

Stigmatization is the result of labeling, stereotyping, separation, status loss, and discrimination occurring together in a social situation (Link & Phelan, 2001, p. 377). Ragins (2008) notes that individuals who are stigmatized are often seen by others to be undesirable, deviant, or to have repulsive characteristics. In the workplace, co-workers can apply the attitudes of the broader society about transgender people, separate transgender people as the "them" in comparison to the "us," and use their workplace relationships to create conflict and barriers for their transgender co-workers, particularly when supervisors and other authorities support such behaviors. Once the label of stigma is applied to transgender employees by co-workers stigmatization can lead to status loss, discrimination that may lead to differentiated treatment by peers and supervisors, and coping behaviors that may have negative consequences for the transgender employee as well as co-workers and employers (Link & Phelan, 2001).

White Hughto, Reisner, and Pachankis (2015) identified the stigma experienced by transgender people at structural, interpersonal, and individual levels. *Structural* stigma refers to the societal norms and institutional policies that constrain access to resources, while *interpersonal* stigma refers to direct or enacted forms of stigma such as verbal harassment, physical violence, and sexual assault due to one's gender identity or expression.

At the *individual* level, stigma includes the feelings people hold about themselves or the beliefs they perceive others to hold about them that may shape future behavior such as the anticipation and avoidance of discrimination (White Hughto et al., 2015). Structural and interpersonal stigma can lead to individual stigma for transgender people. Individual stigma is highly prevalent in the experiences of transgender people and have been linked to adverse health outcomes including depression, anxiety, suicidality, substance abuse, and HIV (White Hughto et al, 2015).

As stated earlier, transgender people transition to reduce the stress of hiding their identity, be more productive at work, develop closer, more genuine relationships with colleagues, customers, and clients, build self-esteem from being known for who they really are, and become role models for others (HRC, 2015). Stigmatization, however, threatens their perceptions of psychological safety at work which leads them to be reluctant to transition and gain the benefits of being out at work.

Kahn (1990, p. 705) defined psychological safety as the "sense of being able to show and employ self without fear of negative consequences to self-image, status, or career. When an organization creates a psychologically safe environment, employees feel more "safe in taking risks of self-expression and engaging the process of change" (Kahn 1990, p. 708). Singh, Winkel, and Selvarajan (2013) in a study of racially diverse work settings found that in a supportive diversity climate employees felt psychologically safe expressing their identities. They further linked positive perceptions of psychological safety to employee performance. Psychological safety is created within interpersonal relations, group dynamics, management style and processes, and organizational norms (Kahn, 1990).

Structural and interpersonal level stigmatization are barriers in organizations to transitions because of the fear they create for transgender employees about coming out. These fears are real for transgender people as expressed in a tweet by Johanna [spacegirl_j] (2020):

> I am still in the closet: Fear of talking about it and explaining. Fear of rejection, judgment, harassment, violence… Fear of change. Fear of dysphoria not getting better. Fear of all the new problems. And most of that is because of society and I can't change any of that.

Stigmatization becomes internalized, individual level stigma for transgender people. Individual level stigma shapes how transgender people see themselves and others, as well as the environment in which they work. Individual level stigma may lead transgender people to expect rejection, act to avoid stigma or conceal it when it happens, and reduce self-efficacy as a way to cope with stigma-related stressors (White Hughto et al., 2015)

The response to individual level stigma by many transgender employees is not to come out at work. Fifty-three percent of respondents to the 2015 US Transgender Survey reported chosing not to disclose their gender identity at work and 29% delayed their gender transition (James et al., 2016). In a more extreme action, 25% of the respondents reported that in the last year they hid that they already transitioned their gender when they were at work.

Change agents can affect perceptions of psychological safety by creating an environment that reduces individual level stigma for transitioning employees by working to remove structural and interpersonal stigma in the workplace. Structural and interpersonal level stigma contribute to the individual level stigma experienced by transgender employees who are deciding to transition at work. By examining structural and interpersonal level stigma in the workplace, change agents can advocate for changes to policies and organizational culture, as well as work toward changing employee behaviors to reduce individual level stigma and increase the perceived safety of coming out for transgender employees. Transition plans can be the vehicle for eliminating those barriers to transgender employees coming out at work.

Transition Plans for Creating Psychological Safety

The purpose of a transition plan is to guide the transition process for an individual within an organization to ensure legal compliance by preventing discrimination and establishing a talent environment maximizing the value of people regardless of who they are (Cadrain, 2009). Transition plans are created for transitioning employees to allow the organization to maintain predictability and have control over the process of transitioning. This control benefits both the transitioning employee and the organization by minimizing risks for both.

Failure of transition plans can create significant risks for employers. Those risks include decreased productivity of transitioning employees as they deal with harassment and mistreatment while remaining in the workplace, resignations of knowledgeable employees who do not want to continue to work in unsupportive environments creating a loss of competencies for the employer and costs for recruiting, hiring, and training new talent, and risks of legal actions by employees, former employees, and/or governmental organizations.

Understanding structural and interpersonal level stigma and their relationship to perceptions of psychological safety can lead to improved transition plans for transgender employees that are less likely to result in failed transitions. Examining and eliminating sources of structural level stigma and anticipating interpersonal level stigma can reduce individual level stigma experienced by transgender employees and lead to perceptions of psychological safety thus reducing barriers that result in failed transitions.

Structural Level Stigma and Workplace Transition Plans

Structural stigma is promulgated through laws and policies, cultural norms and institutional policies that constrain opportunities, resources, and the wellbeing of stigmatized groups (Hatzenbuehler, 2017). State laws banning transgender athletes from competing with those based on their espoused gender are examples of societal-level stigmatization of transgender people (Deese, 2020). Arguments before the United States Supreme Court recently highlighted the discrimination experienced by transgender people and the lack of explicit bans on such discrimination in national law and policy (Howe, 2019). Only 22 of 50 states in the U.S. have laws that explicitly bar employment discrimination against transgender people (Movement Advance Project [MAP], 2020b). The Trump Administration has moved to pull back Federal regulations governing the Affordable Care Act that protect transgender people from discrimination in the provision of healthcare services (Diamond, 2020). Conversion therapy, an effort to change a transgender person's gender identity using shaming, emotional trauma, and sometimes physical pain, has been linked to adverse mental health outcomes for adults, including suicide attempts (Turban, Beckwith, Reisner, & Keuroghlian, 2020); only 20 of 60 states ban conversion therapy for transgender youth (MAP, 2020a). These laws and policies, or lack of them, express structural stigma toward transgender people in the U.S.

In the 2015 US Transgender Survey, 30% of the respondents indicated that they were fired from at least one job in their lifetime because of their transgender status (James et al., 2016). Over the year prior to the survey, 27% of the respondents indicated that they were not hired for a job they applied for, were denied a promotion, or were fired because of their transgender status (James et al., 2016). Having no access to an appropriate restroom at work because of their transgender status was reported by 14% of the respondents (James et al., 2016). The lack of a safe and convenient restroom to use can lead to health issues such as dehydration and urinary tract and kidney infections (Collins, McFadden, Rocco, & Mathis, 2015).

These reported workplace experiences are indicative of workplace policies that create structural stigmatization of transgender employees.

Structural level stigma is the target of most diversity and inclusion efforts and transition plans that are implemented by employers. Incorporating gender-affirming choices in healthcare insurance policies, such as coverage for psychological services, hormone treatments, and surgeries, adding preferred pronouns to business cards, and designating gender-neutral restrooms are examples of removing institutional barriers that could have resulted in structural stigma to transgender people. Transition plans that address restroom designation, dress codes, personal identification and records, health insurance, use of appropriate pronouns, as well as the roles and responsibilities of the transitioning employee, the employee's manager, and human resources as recommended by Cadrain (2009) and Taylor, Burke, Wheatley, & Sompayrac (2011) address structural stigma within an organization.

Training often included in transition plans is also a tool for overcoming structural level stigma. Training can inform co-workers of the employer's expectations for the transition process. The focus of transition training, according to the Society for Human Resource Management (2016), needs to be on employees understanding "the organization's expectations when a transgender employee is joining their ranks or when a current employee is in gender transition." This training may not address interpersonal stigma, however.

The goal of training for co-workers of the transgender employee as part of a transition as expressed by Ms. Connie Summers, Cultural Diversity and Inclusion Manager at Boeing is not to change employees' minds "but we do ask them to change their behaviors" (Cadrain, 2009, p. 62). There needs, however, to be congruency between the espoused policies of the employer and the actual behaviors of employees to create a supportive organizational climate for transgender employees to reduce or eliminate their perceptions of the likelihood of their being mistreated or discriminated against because of their disclosure (Follmer, Sabat, & Siuta, 2019). Supportive behaviors of co-workers, supervisors, peers, and subordinates bolster transgender employees' perceived psychological safety. Lack of supportive behaviors is evidence of interpersonal stigma that lead to bias incidents against the person transitioning.

Transition plans that only address structural level stigma are insufficient for increasing transgender employees' perceptions of psychological safety. Change agents also need to consider interpersonal level stigma in the creation of transition plans.

Interpersonal Level Stigma and Workplace Transition Plans

Interpersonal level stigma takes the form of verbal harassment, physical violence, and sexual assault due to one's gender identity or expression. There is substantial evidence that transgender people experience interpersonal level stigma in the workplace. The 2015 US Transgender Survey showed that 15% of respondents experienced verbal harassment, physical attacks, and/or sexual assaults at work because of their transgender status (James et al., 2016). Sixteen percent of respondents reported that a boss or co-worker shared personal information about them that should not have been shared, 6% reported that they received a negative performance review because they were transgender, and 4% were told to present in the wrong gender in order to keep their job (James et al., 2016, p. 153). Physical assault, verbal harassment and abuse, destruction of property, ridicule, homophobic jokes, unfair work schedules, workplace sabotage, barriers to pursuing career goals, resentment from peers for perceptions of special treatment, religious intolerance, the use of former names or pronouns, bullying, ignoring, shunning, avoidance, sexual assault, coercive social and cultural domination and name-calling have frequently been the experience of transgender people at work (Budge et al., 2010; Hill, 2009; Kirk & Belovics, 2008).

Transgender people, particularly transgender women, create a particular challenge for organizations when they transition because they do not conform to usual expectations of gender in society. Their gender nonconformity challenges deeply held societal norms of a binary gender system that is reinforced by a multitude of social and regulatory processes (Rudin, Ruane, Ross, Farro, & Billing, 2014). Employees may hold community-level biases around gender nonconformity which may be explicit (known to them and within their control) or implicit (automatically activated, often subconscious biases for which people have limited control) (White Hughto et al., 2015). Information about transgender people that does not fit their co-workers' conceptions of expected gender behaviors may create a gap between what they see happening in a transition, the experiences of transgender people, and their own experiences of life. These gaps challenge understanding and create anxiety among co-workers and may lead to bias and unconscious or conscious discrimination, harassment, misgendering, microaggressions, and bullying (Robinson, van Esch, & Bilimoria, 2017; Schilt & Connell, 2007).

This anxiety resulting from the gap in experiences may lead to gender policing by co-workers of transitioning employees. Gender policing refers to gender-related stigma communicated to transgender people verbally or nonverbally about expected gender behaviors, including a dress code, work roles, and restroom and locker room use (Mizock, Riley, Yuen, Woodrum, Sotilleo, & Ormerod, 2017). Gender policing can result in active harassment, including verbal and physical abuse, ridicule, transphobic jokes, exclusion from jobs based on bona fide occupational qualifications, dead naming, and other actions from co-workers and managers that are meant to pressure transgender people to conform to their expectations of gender roles (Budge et al., 2010; Hill, 2009; Kirk & Belovics, 2008; Mizock, et al., 2017). The 2015 US National Transgender Survey reported many incidents of such behaviors in the workplace (James et al., 2016).

Co-workers' anxiety can also lead to resentment for what they perceive as special treatment for transitioning employees, open criticism of diversity policies, or more frequently, passive resistance with marginal cooperation, a lack of involvement, and excuse making with respect to diversity policies (Hill, 2009). The transitioning employee may also come to be the subject of microaggressions, commonplace, interpersonally communicated othering messages related to a person's perceived marginalized status (Nordmarken, 2014; Robinson et al., 2017). Backlash may be more overt and expressed as bullying, ignoring, shunning, avoidance, and acts of violence, physical and symbolic, in the workplace (Hill, 2009). Resistance and backlash may create an environment that puts not only the safety and well being of the transitioning employee at risk but also puts the organization at risk for legal action.

The behaviors discussed above are incidents of interpersonal level stigma. Consideration of this level of stigma is not always included in the development of transition plans or, if included, is not successful in changing co-workers' behaviors. Employee training is usually the instrument for addressing interpersonal level stigma.

Training programs for co-workers of transitioning employees have been identified as important parts of transition plans (Taranowski, 2008; Sawyer & Thoroughgood, 2017; SHRM, 2016). This training focuses employees on understanding "the organization's expectations when a transgender employee is joining their ranks or when a current employee is in gender transition" (SHRM, 2016). This form of training is an educational approach to transitions (Tompkins, Shields, Hillman, & White, 2015). The focus of this training is to create supportive group dynamics that lead to perceived psychological safety through lessening of all employees' conscious and unconscious anxieties about the transition (Kahn, 1990).

Evidence about the efficacy of traditional diversity training programs, however, suggests that such programs do not have a positive impact on bias in the workplace. Dobbin and Kalev (2016) in summarizing the findings of the diversity training literature and their research stated that the value of such training rarely lasts beyond one or two days and might activate bias rather than eliminate it as well as spark backlash against minority group members. Negative effects of diversity training are seen in organizations because the training is often mandatory and focuses on negative effects of discrimination, such as lawsuits. These are perceived to be threats to the trainees and threats "don't win converts" (Dobbins & Kalev, 2016, p. 54). Efforts to force compliance result in backlash against diversity efforts because of the threat to people's authority in the workplace, especially in the case of managers.

The choice of training approaches enacted as part of the transition process is an important variable in eliminating interpersonal level stigma. Tompkins et al. (2015) found that the approach that humanizes transgender people with first person narratives and perspective-taking tasks versus an educational approach involving a slide show and a video talk by an expert about gender identity disorder led to different outcomes. Subjects participating in the humanizing condition were much more likely to demonstrate more favorable attitudes than those who participated in the educational approach; those in the educational approach endorsed greater levels of transphobia after the intervention than before (Tompkins et al., 2015). McCullough, Dispenza, Chang, & Zeligman (2019) found that previous contacts between cisgender, heterosexual individuals, and gay and lesbian people resulted in lower levels of anti-transgender prejudice. They suggested that those dialogues led to lower anti-transgender prejudice through greater understanding. Moss-Racusin and Rabasco (2018) found that humanizing a newly hired transgender employee to co-workers resulted in increased perceived hireability of the transgender employee, self-other overlap, and perspective taking, looking at a situation from a viewpoint that is different from one's usual viewpoint

(American Psychological Association, 2018). The levels of hireability, self-other overlap, and perspective taking were found to be at a level similar to those of a newly hired cisgender co-worker, although the transgender target was still viewed as less likable than the cisgender target. These findings also suggest the effort to humanize transgender people will have positive outcomes for the workplace. These findings on humanizing transgender people in the eyes of their co-workers as part of diversity training is consistent with Dobbins & Kalev's (2016) findings that getting people involved and engaged with minorities will result in diversity and inclusion gains in the workplace.

SUMMARY AND RECOMMENDATIONS

Structural level stigma in society and the workplace and interpersonal level stigma coming from the behaviors of co-workers and managers create individual level stigma, an internalization of the attitudes and behaviors others express toward those who are transgender. Transgender employees enact individual level stigma when they anticipate negative behaviors toward them from co-workers and others at work and act to avoid discrimination at work. They will assess the levels of stigmatization they face and use that assessment in determining whether to come out at work, or not.

Transgender employees weigh the benefits of coming out at work, including reduced stress and increased job satisfaction, against the costs of coming out associated with their understanding of their safety at work, both physical and psychological safety. When the balance of that equation is negative, transgender employees will remain in the closet at work and continue to live with the uncertainty, stress, and fear that is part of being transgender in many societies. That choice has negative consequences for employers as the transgender employee's work engagement and job satisfaction will not be optimal and that person may leave and cause the loss of valuable competencies, as well as the loss associated with replacement costs. Furthermore, a decision by a transgender employee to not come out at work suggests the diversity and inclusion climate of the organization is not such as will attract other underrepresented persons to the organization.

Change agents have the opportunity to assist organizations reach their diversity and inclusion goals by understanding the challenges facing transgender employees who want to transition their gender identity at work.

Understanding that structural and interpersonal barriers heighten transgender employees' concerns about their psychological safety provides the start for diagnosing the barriers caused by stigmatization in the organization followed by the creation of intervention plans that can result in successful transitions and the attainment of diversity and inclusion goals for the employer.

Transition plans are valuable tools for ensuring a successful transition that demonstrates inclusiveness and supports not only the transgender employee but also the organization's brand as an inclusive, productive, and innovative employer. Change agents can support achieving these outcomes by reviewing the organization's policies for structural level stigma that create barriers to successful transitions starting with the organization's non-discrimination statement. Other structural level stigma-related barriers to look for include gender specific dress codes for some or all roles and gendered spaces including restrooms, locker rooms, and break areas. Forms used in human resources and other functional areas should be examined to ensure that the forms are written with gender inclusive language. Removing structural level stigma barriers sends the message to all employees of leadership's goal to be an inclusive organization.

Interpersonal stigma barriers also need to be addressed by change agents. Change agents need to understand the diversity climate of their organizations including the behaviors of employees related to gender role expectations. Visiting and talking with employees in their teams and work units is valuable for understanding the diversity climate. In addition to the leadership expressing and showing support for a transition, further suggestions for interventions to decrease interpersonal stigma barriers include diversity efforts such as those espoused by Dobbin and Kalev (2016, p. 59). Those authors suggested that diversity programs can benefit from voluntary programs that do not force people to participate. To support diversity they proposed involving employees, particularly managers, with

- self-managed teams involving different groups of people across functional areas of the organization to increase the level of diversity they experience,
- cross-training opportunities to expose them to different groups of people,

- mentoring programs, particularly with underrepresented people, including transgender people, shown to turn mentors into advocates for underrepresented employees, and
- diversity task forces or employee resource groups that promote social accountability as ideas come back to work groups and are implemented.

These examples from Dobbin and Kalev are longer-term interventions needing implementation before a transition plan is executed. They should be implemented as part of a broader diversity program. For a specific transition plan, though, a program of training that humanizes transgender people as shown by Thompkins et al. (2015) to reduce transphobia should be used in the workplace, particularly in the immediate work group in which the transgender employee is transitioning. And, it is vital that the leadership of the organization express their support for the transition process. That expression of support will set expectations for employees of what standards they will be held to as the transition unfolds. Finally, following-up with the transgender employee, their manager, and their workgroup is an important step the change agent needs to enact. Regular check-ins to see how the transition is unfolding will provide a mechanism to surface problems as well as giving the employee who is transitioning an opportunity to provide feedback on the process and what else may be needed for their support.

Accounting for the sources of stigma that create barriers for transgender employees who want to come out at work is important for a successful outcome for the employee and the organization. Such an accounting will bring an understanding of the workplace culture and diversity climate and surface information a change agent can use to create a transition climate that will reduce, if not fully remove, the concerns the transitioning employee has about their psychological safety. When transitioning employees feel safe in coming out they will do so and create positive outcomes for themselves and their employer.

CHAPTER TAKEAWAYS

- For employees who are transgender and not yet out to their peers, supervisors, leadership, or Human Resources at work, coming out can be a fearful event.

- Coming out as transgender is a momentous and challenging decision. The workplace can be a fearful place for transgender employees, yet coming out can have both personal and career benefits.
- Transgender people have experienced a wide range of discriminatory behaviors in workplaces. Fears about coming out at work also include the fear of having to talk about being transgender and being forced to explain what it means.
- The targeting of transgender employees by others at work suggests failures in transition planning. These failures directly impact transgender employees and negatively impact the employment brand of their organizations.
- Regardless of their goal to be themselves in their lives, transgender people experience some level of apprehension around their coming out at work if not outright fear of the outcomes of such behavior. Those disclosing their transgender status must determine to whom to disclose their transgender status, the best time and place to disclose, the right amount of information to share, and the appropriate words to use in their disclosure.
- Transition plans are created for transitioning employees to allow the organization to maintain predictability and have control over the process of transitioning. Failure of transition plans can create significant risks for employers.
- Transgender people, particularly transgender women, create a particular challenge for organizations when they transition because they do not conform to usual expectations of gender in society.
- Training programs for co-workers of transitioning employees have been identified as important parts of transition plans. The focus of this training is to create supportive group dynamics that lead to perceived psychological safety through lessening of all employees' conscious and unconscious anxieties about the transition.

References

American Psychological Association. (2018). *Perspective taking*. Retrieved from https://dictionary.apa.org/perspective-taking.

Bennett, S., & Reed, L. (2020, April). INSIGHT: Employer tips for accommodating non-binary workers. *Bloomberg Law*. Retrieved from https://news.bloomberglaw.com/health-law-and-business/insight-emp loyer-tips-for-accommodating-non-binary-workers.

Budge, S. L., Tebbe, E. N., & Howard, K. A. S. (2010). The work experiences of transgender individuals: Negotiating the transition and career decision-making processes. *Journal of Counseling Psychology, 57*, 377–393.

Cadrain, D. (2009, October). Accommodating sex transformations. *HR Magazine*, 59–62.

Chaudoir, S. R., & Fisher, J. D. (2010). The disclosure processes model: Understanding disclosure decision making and post-disclosure outcomes among people living with a concealable stigmatized identity. *Psychological Bulletin, 136*(2), 236–256. https://doi.org/10.1037/a0018193.

Collins, J. C., McFadden, C., Rocco, T. S., & Mathis, M. K. (2015). The problem of transgender marginalization and exclusion: Critical actions for human resource development. *Human Resource Development Review, 14*(2), 205–226. https://doi.org/10.1177/1534484315581755.

Deese. K. (2020, March 31). Idaho governor signs two bills aimed at limiting transgender individuals. *The Hill.* Retrieved from https://thehill.com/ homenews/state-watch/490338-idaho-governor-signs-two-bills-aimed-at-lim iting-transgender-individuals.

Diamond, D. (2020, April 24). Trump team moves to scrap protections for LGBTQ patients. *Politico.* Retrieved from https://www.politico.com/news/ 2020/04/24/trump-team-moves-to-scrap-protections-for-lgbtq-patients-206398.

Dobbin, F., & Kalev, A. (2016). Why diversity programs fail. *Harvard Business Review, 94*(7/8), 52–60.

Follmer, K. B., Sabat, I. E., & Siuta, R. L. (2019). Disclosure of stigmatized identities at work: An interdisciplinary review and agenda for future research. *Journal of Organizational Behavior, 41*, 169–184. https://doi.org/10.1002/ job.2402.

Hatzenbuehler, M. L. (2017). Advancing research on structural stigma and sexual orientation disparities in mental health among youth. *Journal of Clinical Child and Adolescent Psychology, 46*(3), 463–475. https://doi.org/10. 1080/15374416.2016.1247360.

Hill, R. J. (2009). Incorporating Queers: Blowback, backlash, and other forms of resistance to workplace diversity initiatives that support sexual minorities. *Advances in Developing Human Resources, 11*(1), 37–53.

Howe, A. (2019, October). Argument analysis: Justices divided on federal protections for LGBT employees (UPDATED), *SCOTUSblog.* Retrieved from https://www.scotusblog.com/2019/10/argument-analysis-justices-div ided-on-federal-protections-for-lgbt-employees/.

The Human Rights Campaign. (2015). *Coming out in the workplace as trans-gender*. Retrieved from http://www.hrc.org/resources/coming-out-in-the-workplace-as-transgender.

James, S. E., Herman, J. L., Rankin, S., Keisling, M., Mottet, L., & Anafi, M. (2016). *The report of the 2015 U.S. transgender survey*. Washington, DC: National Center for Transgender Equality.

Johanna [spacegirl_j]. (2020, April 2). *I am still in the closet: Fear of talking about it and explaining. Fear of rejection, judgment, harassment, violence… Fear of change. Fear of dysphoria not getting better. Fear of all the new problems. And most of that is because of society and I can't change any of that.* [Tweet]. Retrieved from https://twitter.com/spacegirl_j/status/124559705 6602746880.

Johnson, I. (2015, December). *LGBT diversity: Show me the business case*. Utrecht, The Netherlands: Out Now.

Kahn, W. A. (1990). Psychological conditions of personal engagement and disengagement at work. *Academy of Management Journal, 33*(4), 692–724.

Kirk, J., & Belovics, R. (2008). Understanding and counseling transgender clients. *Journal of Employment Counseling, 45,* 29–43.

Link, B. G., & Phelan, J.C. (2001). Conceptualizing stigma. *Annual Review of Sociology, 27*(1), 363–385. https://doi.org/10.1146/annurev.soc.27.1.363.

McCullough, R., Dispenza, F., Chang, C. Y., & Zeligman, M. R. (2019). *Correlates and predictors of anti-transgender prejudice*. Psychology of Sexual Orientation and Gender Diversity: Advance online publication. https://doi.org/10.1037/sgd0000334.

Mizock, L., Riley, J., Yuen, N., Woodrum, T. D., Sotilleo, E. A., & Ormerod, A. J. (2017). Transphobia in the workplace: A qualitative study of employment stigma. *Stigma and Health, 3,* 275–282.

Moss-Racusin, C. A. & Rabasco, H. (2018). Reducing gender identity bias through imagined intergroup contact. *Journal of Applied Psychology, 48,* 457–474. https://doi.org/10.1111/jasp.12525.

Movement Advance Project. (2020a, April). *Conversion "therapy" laws*. Retrieved from https://www.lgbtmap.org/equality-maps/conversion_therapy.

Movement Advance Project. (2020b, April). *Nondiscrimination laws*. Retrieved from https://www.lgbtmap.org/equality-maps/non_discrimination_laws.

Nordmarken, S. (2014). Microaggressions. *Transgender Studies Quarterly, 1,* 129–134.

Out & Equal Workplace Advocates. (2014). *Workplace gender identity and transition guidelines*. Retrieved from http://outandequal.org/app/uploads/2016/09/Transition-Guidelines-Full-Edition.pdf.

Ragins, B. R. (2008). Disclosure disconnects: Antecedents and consequences of disclosing invisible stigmas across life domains. *Academy of Management Review, 33*(1), 194–215. https://doi.org/10.5465/AMR.2008.27752724.

Robinson, M. J., van Esch, C., & Bilimoria, D. (2017). Bringing transgender issues into management education: A call to action. *Academy of Management Learning & Education, 16*, 300–313.

Rudin, J., Ruane, S., Ross, L., Farro, A., & Billing, T. (2014). Hostile territory: Employers' unwillingness to accommodate transgender employees. *Equality, Diversity and Inclusion: an International Journal, 33*, 721–734.

Sawyer, K., & Thoroughgood, C. (2017). Gender non-conformity and the modern workplace: New frontiers in understanding and promoting gender identity expression at work. *Organizational Dynamics, 46*, 1–8.

Schilt, K., & Connell, C. (2007). Do workplace gender transitions make gender trouble? *Gender, Work and Organization, 14*, 596–618.

Singh, B., Winkel, D. E., & Selvarajan, T. T. (2013). Managing diversity at work: Does psychological safety hold the key to racial differences in employee performance? *Journal of Occupational and Organizational Psychology, 86*, 242–263.

Society for Human Resource Management. (2016, September). *Employing transgender workers*. Retrieved from http://www.shrm.org/templatestools/toolkits/pages/employingtransgenderworkers.aspx.

Society for Human Resource Management. (2017, June). *Managing gender transition in the workplace*. Retrieved from https://www.shrm.org/resourcesandtools/tools-and-samples/toolkits/pages/managinggendertransitioninthewporkplace.aspx.

Stirba, J. L., Goldstein, Z. G., Gentili, C., Reynolds, H. M., Hill-Meyer, T., & Scarborough, D. (2014). Employment. In L. Ericson-Schroth (Ed.), *Trans bodies, trans selves: A resource for the transgender community* (pp. 155–173). New York: Oxford University Press.

Taylor, S., Burke, L. A., Wheatley, K., & Sompayrac, J. (2011). Effectively facilitating gender transition in the workplace. *Employee Responsibilities and Rights Journal, 23*, 101–116. https://doi.org/10.1007/s10672-010-9164-9.

Taranowski, C. J. (2008). Transsexual employees in the workplace. *Journal of Workplace Behavioral Health, 23*, 467–477.

Tompkins, T. L., Shields, C. N., Hillman, K. M., & White, K. (2015). Reducing stigma toward the transgender community: An evaluation of a humanizing and perspective-taking intervention. *Psychology of Sexual Orientation and Gender Diversity, 2*, 34–42.

Turban, J. L., Beckwith, N., Reisner, S. L, & Keuroghlian, A. S. (2020). Association between recalled exposure to gender identity conversion efforts and psychological distress and suicide attempts among transgender adults. [Abstract]. *JAMA Psychiatry, 77*(1), 68–76. https://doi.org/10.1001/jamapsychiatry.2019.2285.

Walworth, J. (2003). *Transsexual workers: An employer's guide*. Bellingham, WA: Center for Gender Sanity.

Weiss, J. T. (2007). *Transgender workplace diversity: Policy tools, training issues and communication strategies for HR and legal professionals.* North Charleston, SC: BookSurge Publishing.

White Hughto, J. M., Reisner, S. L., & Pachankis, J. E. (2015). Transgender stigma and health: A critical review of stigma determinants, mechanisms, and interventions. *Social Science and Medicine, 147,* 222–231. https://doi.org/10.1016/j.socscimed.2015.11.010.

PART III

Gender Approaches Across the Disciplines

Gender Diversity, Unconscious Bias, and Leadership for Organizational and Planetary Health

Wanda Krause and Elizabeth Hartney

INTRODUCTION

Gender diversity is beneficial for companies. The current over-representation of the dominant (unhealthy male) gender in leadership roles negates the perspectives of over half of the population in decisions that impact society. Furthermore, leadership discourses which are grounded in outdated notions of male privilege and superiority, control through force, and the negation of leadership ideals grounded in stereotypically feminine characteristics, are the underlying basis of our current hierarchical system. This is based on thousands of years of male dominance throughout history personified through archetypes of unhealthy and abusive males. This is most notably illustrated by the Western image of God as an all-powerful male—which has been found to have a direct

W. Krause (✉) · E. Hartney
Royal Roads University, Victoria, BC, Canada
e-mail: Wanda.1krause@royalroads.ca

influence on the degree to which white men are perceived as fit for leadership (Roberts et al., 2020). It is only in recent decades that women have, for the most part, held leadership roles. They have done so only through taking on the mantle of stereotypically male characteristics. To be clear, the gender characteristics we are discussing are social constructs, not inherent and inflexible traits attached to male or female biological sex. Rather, we argue that in order to shift the discourse of leadership to better represent the totality of society, leadership needs to be exercised by people with a variety of lived experience. Leadership then has the potential to meet the needs of people across society, not just the needs of economically privileged men, as has been the case almost exclusively throughout history (until recently). Considering the current state of the planet, there is an overwhelming need for this shift in discourse, and concurrent shift in societal values to recognize the need to heal the planet and its peoples, who have been, and continue to be oppressed and exploited by the stereotypical values of power, privilege, and profit at any cost.

What Is Gender Diversity?

Gender diversity is most commonly defined as the equal ratio of men and women. One will frequently read stories or research about gender diversity in corporate boardrooms and other areas traditionally dominated by men. While this focus has brought some insight, it is superficial and, in fact, misrepresents and even marginalizes gender issues. This framing of gender diversity ignores the intersectional experience of gender discrimination and bias. Furthermore, while understanding the gaps between men and women is certainly important, much research fails to include the process toward the disparities that involve many variables. Recognizing and identifying the biases, practices, behaviors, cultures, structures, and systems that have created inequality between genders is key. The gender disparities cannot be addressed without first a discussion around the multiple ways in which people are marginalized. Gender diversity goes beyond the discussion around men and women and to those with non-binary gender identities.

Gender diversity as a starting point considers the ratio of men to women but is furthermore about respecting that there are multiple ways to identify beyond the male and female binary. While perceived gender is what people believe one's gender to be, and while gender roles is what one's society deems is appropriate to men or women, the way in which one identifies as true is internal to that particular person. Gender inclusion is a higher value in that while diversity is merely acknowledging the different genders, inclusion is taking further action to create opportunities for all to be and feel part of the larger whole, be that the organization or a community. To be effectively gender inclusive, however, requires an awareness of bias not only in regard to gender but the various other identities that lead to bias against a person.

Planetary Health and Toxic Leadership

How might greater gender diversity help us achieve planetary health? In brief, planetary health is defined as "the health of human civilisation and the state of the natural systems on which it depends" (Horton & Lo, 2015, p. 1921). As noted above, this is not simply a superficial exercise in meeting gender quotas with no consideration of the characteristics of the people taking on the role of leader. Biological sex, while influential, is not a true indication of values or behaviors. Indeed, power-seeking women strive to compete with men on men's terms, and often abandon the very characteristics which are stereotypically feminine, and which might enable them to make a significant contribution to leadership for planetary health, in order to achieve the power they crave. These women recreate themselves in the image of the unhealthy, abusive male—choosing competitiveness, greed, ambition, violence, and oppression of their peers over caring, compassion, nurturance, healing, cooperation, forgiveness, and inclusion. Such toxic women leaders have focused on individual and selfish gain over the wellbeing of the community and have been absorbed by a system that is creating ever greater inequalities throughout the world rather than reefined it.

Yet not all women leaders have simply mimicked the most oppressive and unethical values and behaviors of male leaders. Some have taken on leadership roles that are changing the system in the ways that ideally reflect a greater diversity of perspectives. Research has indicated that firms with women CEOs or gender diverse boards have stronger business and equity practices, and gender diverse leadership teams demonstrate stronger business and equity outcomes than teams characterized by gender homophily (Cook & Glass, 2018). Similarly, there are many examples of male leadership and followership that reflect stereotypically feminine values of compassion and liberation.

These findings take us beyond superficial feminist arguments, and demonstrate that diversity is distinctly superior to homophily, regardless of gender. In this vein, research shows that just as male dominance is unhealthy, predominantly female teams can be detrimental, resulting in greater conservatism, and similar negative effects as homophily on male-dominated teams: lack of dissent, lower levels of team learning, and reduced innovation (Cook & Glass, 2018). Conversely, gender diversity at leadership and followership levels appear to be consistent with promoting the values of learning organizations (Senge, 1990).

Tokenism

It follows then, that it is naïve to assume that simply placing women in traditionally male leadership roles without addressing the underlying power dynamics and values of individuals and organizations will automatically result in improvements. Research indicates that in spite of improving organizational integrity, employing greater numbers of female employees can be detrimental to organizations, particularly when the most senior leader is a woman, for example, by increasing the number of sexual harassment and sexual violence incidents (Choi et al., 2018), and promoting lateral violence (Sheridan-Leos, 2008). Female-dominated workplaces increase the risk of workplace bullying for both women and under-represented men (Salin, 2015). Furthermore, representation of women in top corporate leadership may create a false sense of having addressed the problem of gender diversity, through creating an inaccurate view of women's equality and decreasing concern with gender inequality in other domains (Georgeac & Rattan, 2019). The woman leader may be little more than a token, without true change in terms of representation of women or the values that people of different genders could contribute to organizations, and ultimately, to planetary health.

The importance of greater diversity of genders, however, is not only related to the value of inclusion as part and parcel of decolonizing our organizations and workplaces, but also supports endeavors to take steps toward, for example, Truth and Reconciliation, a process as part of an overall holistic and comprehensive response to the Indian Residential School legacy in Canada, with Indigenous peoples, whose marginalized are foremost women. Recognizing and identifying the biases, practices, behaviors, cultures, structures, and systems that have created inequality between genders is key. The gender disparities cannot be addressed without first a discussion around the multiple ways in which people are marginalized.

This work adds to a growing number of studies that recognize the significance of gender diversity in organizations by investigating the link between the gender diversity of organizations and performance, well-being, and consequently, beyond the organization to bringing awareness to planetary health. We argue that diversity enhances innovation and the ability of the organization to thrive. We suggest that the impact of a thriving organization is important, not just to the organization as a whole or an entity but as a building block for a thriving civilization. Consequently, the chapter provides recommendations for companies and organizations to uncover unconscious bias as a first step to recognizing the multiple ways in which diversity is not enacted, and how to take the appropriate steps to enhance gender diversity, equality and inclusion, which includes shifting one's organizational culture for the health of the organization and ultimately planetary health.

Hence, our definition of gender diversity goes beyond the discussion around sex and socially prescribed gender roles; it provides a focus on the need to include those marginalized at the leadership levels and within organizations through inclusive leadership. It illustrates awareness of the unconscious bias of decision makers to facilitating diversity (Perry et al., 2015) as a key barrier to achieving gender diversity. Clearly, socialization processes have created different ways of leading according to gender identity, which bring therefore different leadership styles, lenses, and approaches to policy and to how people work and engage with one another. Finally, we identify the steps to enhancing gender diversity and inclusion for organizational and planetary health.

This work makes a number of contributions to the literature. First, it adds to diverse perspectives on the topic. Second, an increased role for women in organizations has been the subject for a number of years but without a recognition for diversity of gender, meaning the lines of demarcation are not only subject to sex difference, although it is of importance to discuss increasing women's participation into the workforce and the various forms of organization. Third, while the gender gap debate has been advocated for in view of the value of equality, other ethical reasons to redress such imbalance adds value to the discussions around racial diversity and more importantly, as a result of bias enacted by the same gender, inclusion of women by women, as part and parcel of a wider discussion around gender bias. Fourth, what is perceived to be an underrepresentation of women in organizations must be viewed as an ethical issue around marginalization along gender lines, race, religion, color, and identities. Fifth, this discussion is of significance to not only organizational health but planetary health.

The Role of Unconscious Bias

Unconscious bias is defined as "a particular tendency or inclination, especially one that prevents unprejudiced consideration of a question" (Fre eDictionary.com). Unconscious (or sometimes referred to as implicit) bias occurs during rapid and automatic judgments and assumptions of people and situations, without conscious awareness of the mental processes making such quick and automatic assessments and conclusions. Our quick judgments arise from a variety of sources. These arise from our upbringing, the educational, social, political, or economic environment that shaped our formative years, our past and current cultural environments, individual experiences, our internal states, such as fear or openness to those experiences, which are also shaped by observing our parents' reactions to such or similar stimuli, level of exposure to different peoples and perspectives, and arguably also level of particular competencies and traits, such as, trust-building, empathy, intercultural communication, inquiry, humility, curiosity, resilience, and adaptability. This latter category influencing unconscious bias, thus, comprises capabilities that one might learn to help one peel back the many layers of unconscious bias that we all have. After all, every one of us has bias.

Unconscious bias happens favorably and unfavorably when we make judgments regarding promotions between genders in the workplace, choose which person to offer more training, decide on who is ready to lead a particular group or project, and who is of lesser competence. It is important, however, to understand that we can also make judgments with awareness that we are being biased toward or against a person or group. It may not be so uncommon to many to have heard a co-worker disparage a particular ethnic group or make dismissive statements in private about a particular gender only then in front of a larger audience or the boss to utter praises of or engage appreciatively with the same mentioned group or gender. People conceal their true biases to be politically correct or say or do what is expected by those present, because of fear of personal consequences.

Unconscious bias intensifies under conditions perceived as threatening and is more likely when we are rushed or have cognitive overload. That is because we reach into the unconscious mind to fill in gaps. When we are in a rush, we resort to bias. People are grouped not just according to gender, race, and ethnicity but age, religion, class, sexuality, and disability, among other things. Hence, discrimination against a particular gender may be compounded for that gender if they are perceived to have other identities that involve unfavorable bias. Women can also internalize misogyny and cultural conditioning and have been shown to be biased against other women (Agrawal, 2018). According to the "queen bee syndrome," as defined by Staines, Tavris, and Jayaratne (1973), women who are individually successful in male-dominated environments and attain positions of high status are more likely to endorse gender stereotypes. According to this view, women they supervise are viewed as competitors and, as a result, the queen bee expresses negative attitudes toward them and, thus, tends to discriminate against these female subordinates (Blau & Devaro, 2007, p. 13). This phenomenon has been documented by several studies where women are seen to be bullied more by their female counterparts and managers (Agrawal, 2018).

In a United States survey, conducted by the Pew Research Center with a nationally representative sample of 4,914 adults, gender bias was found to have numerous negative consequences. About four in ten working women (42%) in the United States say they have faced discrimination on the job because of their gender (Parker & Funk, 2017). This research found that women are about three times as likely as men to have experienced sexual harassment at work. However, gender bias cannot be fully understood without grasping the confounding variables that lead to bias as well as the intersectional variables that can increase bias. For example, about three in ten women with a postgraduate degree (29%) say they have experienced repeated small slights at work because of their gender, as compared with 18% of women with a bachelor's degree and 12% of women with less education (ibid). Black women stand apart in their reporting of having been passed over for the most important assignments due to their gender with 22% of employed black women saying this has happened to them, as compared with 8% of white women and 9% of Hispanic women (ibid.).

Gender Diversity for Planetary Health

In the final report of The Rockefeller Foundation–Lancet Commission on Planetary Health, planetary health is defined as "the achievement of the highest attainable standard of health, wellbeing, and equity worldwide through judicious attention to the human systems—political, economic, and social—that shape the future of humanity and the Earth's natural systems that define the safe environmental limits within which humanity can flourish" (Horton & Lo 2015, p. 1921). In other words, it concerns the health of human civilization and the state of the natural systems on which our civilization depends and can thrive. What does gender diversity mean for planetary health? There are two key dimensions that working toward gender diversity and inclusion has for supporting and advancing planetary health.

First, working toward gender diversity and inclusion situates the health of organizations, as a form of human systems, and the health of societies, as a form of human organization, as integral to the health of the planet—the system upon which we all rely. Any form of chaos or imbalance within the smaller system creates chaos and imbalance within the overall health and wellbeing of our world. This is a systems perspective that sees all parts supporting the whole. Hence, we do not see planetary health as only concerning the natural systems but the system within which we exist. Therefore, "[t]he threats that our species faces are not abstract physical risks … The risks we face lie within ourselves and the societies we have created" (Horton & Lo, 2015, p. 2021), and as a result human cultures contain both the threat and opportunity for human flourishing.

Horton and Lo (2015, p. 2022) argued that we underestimate the intricate interplay of environmental, political, and sociocultural resilience, and quoted Butzer's argument to focus on "leaders, elites, and ideology" as a way of creating planetary health. Our concern with gender diversity within organizations is not disconnected, but rather part of a larger concern for human and civilizational flourishing, here viewed as of significance to planetary health. From this wider systems perspective, gender diversity is not merely viewed as a rights issue for marginalized genders. Planetary health is a global health issue (Demaio & Rockström, 2015, p. 36). The final report of The Rockefeller Foundation–Lancet Commission on Planetary Health emphasizes the need to work toward the UN's Sustainable Development Goals (SDGs), among several key goals, for planetary health. The special event on Women Leaders for Planetary Health at the UN Climate Summit (COP25) in Madrid in 2019 was a new initiative of the Institute for Advanced Sustainability Studies (IASS) focused on women's empowerment as prerequisite for addressing our current climate crisis and effectively implementing the UN Sustainable Development Goals (SDGs). However, to date, very little has been contributed from civil society research, research on organizational well-being and particularly gender, although SDG 5 specifically relates to gender. Hence, in way of bridging the link between gender in organizations and planetary health, we seek to support a better understanding of gender imbalance in organizations to offer concrete recommendations about the kind of leadership needed for organizational and planetary health.

Second, working toward gender diversity and inclusion through inclusive leadership offers us greater understanding around the concept of harmony. The dominant perspective on gender disparity and inequality offers a binary view based on sex, excluding and marginalizing the deeper and holistic understanding or worldview of planetary health and harmony through the balancing of genders along the feminine and masculine. It also excludes the different ways of looking at and interpreting equality and equity, as well, dignity, harmony, and balance. The complex issue of balance between opposing forces can also be expressed in terms of the principle: "balance between feminine and masculine energy" (Arahmaiani & Campbell, 2019, p. 204). These authors argue that every culture can make valuable contributions and valuing difference and supporting equality make for a bright and sustainable future (p. 208).

The feminine and masculine principles are also important. Unhealthy masculinity is not just harmful to men and society as a whole—it's also harmful to the planet (Brough, 2017). While this specific study focused on men, we would argue two important points. One, the unhealthy masculinity or masculine is toxic and not confined to one sex. This unhealthy masculinity that is fearful of the healthy feminine can reside in women too. For example, women in the "queen-bee" theory or women who feel they have had to fight so hard to get to their positions of power and take action to ensure their female subordinates experience just as much difficulty breaking through the "glass-ceiling" are also uncomfortable with supporting feminine expression among female and male employees. Consequently, this fear, or even hate, of feminine power, then, requires a mindset change around the essences that are of value to the harmony, balance, and health of the organization. Equally, fear, and hate, of healthy masculine power requires a mindset change. Feminist approaches that bash men and throw all men into a category of those to be wary of and fight to get equal rights is not just harmful to women and society as a whole—it is also harmful to the planet.

This imbalance requires healing. However, Western mindsets focused on binaries is resistant to a holistic approach to transformation. A holistic approach or framework, however, is reliant upon the principle of healing as the way forward to health, harmony, and sustainability. A yin-yang approach, that appreciates the healthy interplay of supports between the masculine and feminine, or, in taking an Indigenous approach, through what Atleo (2011) refers to as *hahuulism* which "can be defined by the struggle for balance and harmony" and which requires what he refers to as "protocols of Tsawalk," which are agreements "to move competitive relationships away from conflict and towards harmony" (p. 156) provide examples of inclusion in orientation. We require a framework that recognizes inclusive approaches, including primarily holistic approaches, and those which enables a healthy masculinity and healthy femininity to shine and co-create in their multiple forms, and to engender transformation for organizational and planetary health.

Leadership for Organizational and Planetary Health

Inclusive leadership is concerned first and foremost with inclusion, both in its processes and the ends for which it strives (Ryan, 2006, p. 3). Inclusive leadership focuses on relationships that promote mutual benefit (Hollander, 2008, p. 3). Here, inclusive leadership will be defined as leadership that enables individuals and collectives to be recognized, respected, dignified, whole and well, and their interconnections enhanced for mutual benefit. Key principles of inclusive leadership are working "with" others who are different, exercising the opposite of homophily, which is the essence of inclusion. They include actively involving others in decision-making, which is the essence of self-determination; strengthening and valuing relationships and connections, social justice, plurality, fairness and welfare, which form the essence of civil society. It is, therefore, imperative to understand the kind of leadership that is generative and enabling of diversity and inclusion for organizational and planetary health.

A discussion around what both diversity and inclusion constitute must take place around how to address power imbalance. This includes conflict, exclusion, marginalization, colonization, imperialism, imbalance of "haves and have nots," and the underlying power and economic and organizational structures that continue to create barriers to a healthy life for all. These anti-inclusive forces may be echoed at an organizational level, through nepotism, favoritism, cliques, and workplace bullying, which may be implicitly rewarded through practices which encourage competition over collaboration. Individual health and flourishing is about personal happiness; however, personal happiness or feeling good also relates to or is influenced by the degree to which an individual feels they are equal, have equal rights, equal access, such as to promotion, have means for equity, feel dignified, feel respected, have the means, capacity and context for living and working purposefully, have choices, opportunities, and enjoy safety and security, among myriad factors that contribute to how an individual defines their wellbeing.

The prescriptive advantage of inclusive leadership is, that being inclusive, it does not place the burden on individuals to take care of themselves, but emphasizes instead the relational and structural nature shaping a healthy whole (Ryan, 2006, p. 6). The subject of individual and organizational health is a collective one. One's health isn't merely a personal goal that could be achieved passively; it is the responsibility of the organization (People Diagnostics, 2019, p. 3). When people are excluded, they often do not have the resources, tools, or skills to create their own wellness, or the means to acquire them. Purposeful inclusion, then, requires that the system change (Ryan, 2006, p. 6).

For an environment to be inclusive, people must believe that they are treated fairly, valued for who they are, and included in core decision-making (Gottfredson, 2019). Whether organizational participation and leadership or larger systems participation and governance, leadership that is inclusive means that leaders acknowledge power structures and that particular contexts and environments influence how well one feels. Hence, the prerogative of an inclusive leader is also acknowledging context that shapes wellbeing and health. This includes others who are marginalized from power structures of inequality, and means taking a step beyond mere inclusion into a hierarchy of power relations but toward plurality. Inclusion requires the transformation of the environment of imbalance and inequity for inclusion to shift into plurality; that is, plurality of individual and collective participation and contribution for meaningful co-creation.

It must be recognized that employee mental health can be impacted at work from both the design of work (e.g., workload, co-worker and supervisor support, autonomy), and individual factors (e.g., practicing self-care, nurturing positive relationships, savoring positive experiences). The development of relationships with particular people can be influenced by not only bias against a particular gender but that gender in addition to other intersectional identities outside one's usual in-group. Psychological health and cultural safety at work is a shared responsibility (People Diagnostics, 2019, p. 3). In connecting the benefit of individual health to the organization as a whole, and to planetary health, the subject of health becomes a concern and imperative for leaders within organizations, within the state, region—and despite these seemingly neat divisions, categories and borders, health considers a global view of leadership and followership for mutual benefit and wellbeing.

Participation is not apolitical. It should entail leadership that seeks to recognize, respect, dignify, and make whole and healthy. It should be inclusive and aim to be transformative and purposeful. Embracing the ethic of human flourishing and planetary health and the constituent parts will be one of the greatest challenges for the inclusive leader, but gives promise of a future that is sustainable and hopeful of possibilities. It is, therefore, of significance to leadership research and work to understand how best to support individual and planetary health and collaboratively create change on the individual, collective, and planetary levels. The concept of inclusive leadership enables us to better secure health for the benefit of individuals, the whole, and so for the common good. We assert that by extension these principles entail a broader sense of health—individual, communal, and planetary.

A Roadmap for Greater Inclusion of Gender Diversity

Protocols, or a roadmap, "are hammered out of apparent contradictions over an appropriate period of time" (Atleo, 2011, p. 156). For greater inclusion of gender diversity, we suggest a framework based on an integral model and leadership that is inclusive. We adapt the integral model, originally developed by Wilber (1997), to understand and work with key dimensions of reality. "Integral" means comprehensive, balanced, and inclusive (Wilber, Patten, Leonard, & Morelli, 2008, p. 27). This model has four areas or quadrants to illustrate at least four key perspectives: (1) the individual subjective (including bias, worldviews, masculine and feminine health, as well mental and spiritual health), (2) the individual behaviors we can observe, (3) collective norms and culture (as #1, less easy to observe), and (4) larger macro systems (such as planetary health). We can plan an inclusive leader's steps within and across each area or quadrant that entail a systematic, linear, circular, and emergent process. With this framework, we can work with an overview of health that helps us see how, depending on which area we are focusing, we can map overlap, connections, and interdependencies. This framework, thus, enables us a process for change that is inclusive of the different dimensions of wellbeing and health and supports evolution in each dimension that is interdependent. It rests on the individual and collective approach and worldview to see ourselves as interconnected, interdependent, and, at our best, co-developing with each other (Schieffer & Lessem, 2016, p. 15). The following presents steps for an inclusive leader's strategic plan for enhancing gender equality and one that would recognize the intricacies of bias from an intersectional lens, as would be focused on an organization.

Step 1: Begin developing inclusive leadership competencies first. Before leading others you must begin to lead yourself. The process of leading change often omits the idea that transforming leaders is part of the overall transformation process (Metcalf, 2013, p. 11). Develop greater awareness around who you are, which involves peeling back your unconscious bias. These are the particular biases we all have and with which we interpret and make meaning of the world. How you reason and the logic you use depend on the values you aspire to and currently live. An insecure leader may feel threatened by their subordinates, whether, for example, based on their being male or female, or gender fluid, or additionally connected with further identities, and, thus, the leader may consciously or unconsciously undermine their progress, in an effort to retain superiority. As mentioned above, according to the "queen bee syndrome" women who are individually successful in male-dominated environments and attain positions of high status are more likely to endorse gender stereotypes. Hence, awareness of actions that lead to inclusion and exclusion are not related to men in particular.

Thus, an inclusive leader continually aspires to develop their intelligence and consciousness "with a sufficient altitude that they gain the widest lenses and new capacities" (Hamilton, 2008, p. 115). An inclusive leader is one who embodies the values and competencies of an inclusive and planetary citizen and steward, and continually works on expanding into capacity to hold greater perspectives. These are leaders who speak about matters that impact the whole planet, can catalyze interconnectedness, and improve the flow of products, profits, people, priorities, energy, security, and resources for all (ibid. pp. 116–118). One might consider reflecting on the values one actually does embody and set a vision for oneself of who one wants to become and the values they want to espouse with goals for evolving into embodying these and presencing these in one's life, work and sphere of influence. How one evaluates and co-creates human flourishing and health with others will hugely depends on this first step.

Step 2: Evaluate the state of affairs. There are multiple methods an inclusive leader can use to evaluate where an individual, team, organization, and/or community is at on a scale measuring, for example, health. This stage involves collecting the information one needs to set direction for greater health of the organization. The process involves mapping a starting point from within the organization for creating and enhancing human and planetary flourishing and health and which entails mapping that starting point at (1) the individual and subjective area, (2) the behavioral and competency area, (3) the culture and communal area, and (4) the systems or planetary.

Actions in this second area aim to uncover behaviors, practices, habits, or techniques used, etc., that are supporting gender diversity or undermining diversity, thus, the health of the organization. For creative, exploratory and positive momentum, one would want to lead inquiry into what is working for enhancing gender diversity and healthy states and behavior. However, appreciation for what is working cannot run the risk of minimizing what is not working and posing barriers to greater health. Inquiry does need to uncover what and where needs to shift in behavior, actions, techniques, and practice. Thus, inquiry in the third area would work toward understanding and learning what collective needs for health exist. Here the "collective" might mean different groups with different understandings of what the groups need to feel healthy, culturally safe, respected, balanced, be included, dignified, and work productively without fear of discrimination. These need to be explored. Inquiry in the fourth area involves exploring the systems factors that relate to unequal relationships, processes of colonization and decolonization, and, thus, the structures that oppress some and privilege others, and policies, laws, and regulations that are similarly differentially disabling and enabling. It is important, if not more important, to be attentive to informal practices, protocol, or "unwritten laws" that are not necessarily part of official policy, laws, or governance structures.

Step 3: Prioritize and plan. Prioritizing and planning, for the inclusive leader, involves co-decision-making with others and setting direction together. Such processes entail that the leader is in service of the vision and mission of the organization and its people and puts health front and center. To prioritize, the inclusive leader uses data collection methods that rely on collaboration and engagement to come to prioritization and planning. Examples are world café or focus group methods. These are good examples because of the collaborative objective as process. How the groups are divided depends on the gaps and issues identified around diversity and inclusion, particularly paying close attention with an intersectional lens to gender discrimination, and whether the diverse groups wish to form around those gaps and issues or whether they see utility in forming groups representing of diversity in different or newer and evolving ways.

Changing organizational culture is one of the hardest tasks for any leader. But when we have a shared understanding of what individual and planetary health means to us as individuals and as a collective in an organization, and have critical social supports in place, we can be well placed to keep disciplined in reaching and maintaining health and inclusion as values. All cultures are based on value systems and to create change in any value system takes a common framework, support and discipline until health, enhanced gender diversity, and inclusion are intrinsic values. There will be times ahead in an increasingly turbulent world, more immediately as a consequence of COVID-19, when the market share sees even greater competition, but that is when we will need to rely on individual health and engaged individuals to make it through. Individual health and gender diversity is the new model for economic growth leading organizations and planetary health.

Step 4: Create supports. The ability to set direction and make any headway will be contingent upon the inclusive leader's active support. Inclusive leaders will communicate to the wider community the objective to put health front and center as a value and practice. As a result, leadership will be responsible for including health as an objective in communications, priorities, espoused values, policies, and programs. What health among all groups and individuals will look like would be under development and co-lead with a committee; however, to get traction involves putting the goal of health on the radar and providing structural supports. Creating time to work on a plan for individual spiritual, mental, and emotional health demonstrates seriousness. Creating a budget shows commitment and capacity. Ensuring processes for health that are officially recognized will be significant too; for example, risk, injury, promotion, or bullying mitigation steps or policies.

Putting wellbeing on the radar means the leader is attuned to the culture of individual and organizational health in the organization as identified in *Step 2*. This is where incremental shifting needs to take place simultaneously in the communications and work with the committee, individuals at all levels of an organization—those who are impacted by policy and programs and those who have influence and power by virtue of their positional roles in the organization, as well as key stakeholders, and those who are in a position to and are willing to champion the action plan for wellbeing.

Creating supports holistically means being attuned to and responsive to behaviors, as they show up, that support or pose barriers to health, diversity, and inclusion. This means being aware of multiple collectives and their perhaps different if not conflicting needs or goals, to that of the collective, within and outside the organization. For the latter, the inclusive leader is mindful that actions, choices, and behaviors can potentially contribute to in-group (i.e., the organization one leads) interests that exclude and may even harm those considered as outside the group. The inclusive leader seeks to build and expand on what is working to extend extraterritorial (inter-organizational) collaborations and networking for the strengthening of relationships and support for addressing broader planetary issues. Creating supports means leading health, diversity, and inclusion by example and being aware of individual needs also to ensure equity.

Step 5: Create the organizational and planetary health plan of action. The plan of action is dreaming big about what the planet would look like in a healthy, harmonious state, and designing an appropriate learning and change strategy. What this plan looks like is co-created and emergent with the criteria of health developed into higher levels and betterment considering all four areas or perspectives listed above. It will continue to be iterated and developed through tracking and evaluating transformation within the organization. The strategy to embed health will entail that the steps, strategies, and process are sustainable and reinforced by mapping those supports across the four areas. The plan of action can look different depending on the organization. Hence, no plan created can be plugged into a new setting and expected to work. Further, the agreed upon priorities, plan, and strategy to embed wellbeing will require ongoing commitment, conversation, refining, and repeating these five steps. This takes time and commitment to the process and vision for ensuring diversity and inclusion.

Chapter Takeaways

The takeaways from this chapter that we hope to offer is for greater awareness of the need for gender diversity within organizations.

- Enhanced gender diversity is critical not merely for the sake of gender rights or a feminist objective to decrease the gender gap between the sexes in organizations.
- This chapter offered a deeper understanding of the interrelatedness between individual and collective health within organizations as aligned to the impact that human flourishing has on the outside world, in particularly what concerns planetary health.
- Recognizing and identifying the biases, practices, behaviors, cultures, structures, and systems that have created inequality between genders is key.
- Planetary health cannot be addressed without first a discussion around the multiple ways that chaos, disorder, and disharmony is entrenched.
- The gender disparities cannot be addressed without first a discussion around the multiple ways in which people are marginalized.
- This chapter offered an inclusive framework to map how to create transformation toward greater diversity, inclusion and individual and collective health within the organization. Such transformation puts the organization and those within the organization in a position of being a healthy pillar for supporting and evolving a trajectory of mindful inclusion of all for a better world, a world that can sustain all those living upon it. We hope that a planetary ethic can evolve through the conscious and deliberate shifts in thinking, behavior, collective action, and structures within the organization as one major and essential step.

REFERENCES

Agrawal. (2018, December). Here is how unconscious bias holds women back. *Forbes.* https://www.forbes.com/sites/pragyaagarwaleurope/2018/12/17/here-is-how-unconscious-bias-holds-women-back/#2832148e2d4f.

Atleo, R. (Umeek). (2011). *Tsawalk: A Nuu-chah-nulth worldview.* Vancouver: UBC Press.

Arahmaiani, & Campbell, S. (2019). Balancing feminine and masculine energy. *Southeast of Now: Directions in Contemporary and Modern Art in Asia, 3*(1), 201–213. https://doi.org/10.1353/sen.2019.0015.

Blau, F., & Davero, J. (2007). New evidence on gender differences in promotion rates: An empirical analysis of a sample of new hires. *Industrial Relations—A Journal of Economy and Society, 46*(3), 511–550.

Brough, A. (2017, December). Men resist green behaviour as unmanly. *Scientific American.* https://www.scientificamerican.com/article/men-resist-green-behavior-as-unmanly/

Demaio, A. R., & Rockström, J. (2015). Human and planetary health: Towards a common language. *Lancet, 386*(10007), 36–37.

Choi, H., Hong, S., & Lee, J. W. (2018). Does increasing gender representativeness and diversity improve organizational integrity? *Public Personnel Management, 47*(1), 73–92.

Georgeac, O., & Rattan, A. (2019). Progress in women's representation in top leadership weakens people's disturbance with gender inequality in other domains. *Journal of Experimental Psychology: General, 148*(8), 1435–1453.

Glass, C., & Cook, A. (2018). Do women leaders promote positive change? Analyzing the effect of gender on business practices and diversity initiatives. *Human Resource Management, 57*(4), 823–837.

Gottfredson, R. (2019). *Understanding different leadership types and styles.* Retrieved from https://www.ryangottfredson.com/blog/2019/1/21/what-is-inclusive-leadership-amp-why-is-it-important

Hamilton, M. (2008). *Integral city: Evolutionary intelligences for the human hive.* Gabriola Island, BC: New Society Publishers.

Hollander, E. P. (2008). *Inclusive leadership: The essential leader-follower relationship.* London: Taylor & Francis.

Horton, R., & Lo, S. (2015). Planetary health: A new science for exceptional action. *Lancet, 386*(10007), 1921–1922.

Perry, S. P., Murphy, M. C., & Dovidio, J. F. (2015). Modern prejudice: Subtle, but unconscious? The role of bias awareness in Whites' perceptions of personal and others' biases. *Journal of Experimental Social Psychology, 61,* 64–78.

Parker, K., & Funk, C. (2017). *Gender discrimination comes in many forms for today's working women.* Pew Research Center. https://www.pewresearch.org/fact-tank/2017/12/14/gender-discrimination-comes-in-many-forms-for-todays-working-women/.

People Diagnostics. (2019). *Flourishdx: A comprehensive approach to workplace psychological health, safety, and wellbeing. An implementation guide*. Retrieved from PwC Report.

Roberts, S. O., Weisman, K., Lane, J. D., Williams, A., Camp, N. P., Wang, M., Robison, M., Sanchez, K., & Griffiths, C. (2020). God as a White man: A psychological barrier to conceptualizing Black people and women as leadership worthy. *Journal of Personality and Social Psychology*. https://doi-org.ezproxy.royalroads.ca/10.1037/pspi0000233.supp.

Ryan, J. (2006). Leadership and policy in schools. *Taylor & Francis Group, 5*, 3–17. https://doi.org/10.1080/15700760500483995.

Salin, D. (2015). Risk factors of workplace bullying for men and women: The role of the psychosocial and physical work environment. *Scandinavian Journal of Psychology, 56*, 69–77.

Schieffer, A., & Lessem, R. (2016). *Integral development: Realising the transformative potential of individuals, organisations and societies*. London: Routledge.

Senge, P. (1990). *The fifth discipline: The art and practice of the learning organization*. Doubleday.

Sheridan-Leos, N. (2008). Understanding lateral violence in nursing. *Clinical Journal of Oncology Nursing, 12*(3), 399–403.

Staines, G., Tavris, C., & Jayaratne, T. E. (1973). The Queen Bee Syndrome. In C. Tavris (Ed.), *The female experience*. Del Mar, CA: CRM Books.

Steffen, S. L., & Rezmovits, J. (2019). Introduction. In S. L. Steffen, J. Rezmovits, S. Trevenna, & S. Rappaport (Eds.), *Evolving leadership for collective wellbeing*. Bingley, UK: Emerald Publishing.

Wilber, K. (1997). An integral theory of consciousness. *Journal of Consciousness Studies, 4*(1), 71–92.

Women Leaders for Planetary Health. https://www.womenleadersforplanetaryhealth.org/.

Wilber, K., Patten, T., Leonard, A., & Morelli, M. (2008). *Integral life practice: A 21st century blueprint for physical healthy, emotional balance, mental clarity, and spiritual awakening*. Boston: Integral Books.

CHAPTER 10

Working More Effectively with Non-binary Colleagues

Wiley C. Davi and Duncan H. Spelman

INTRODUCTION

For a year now, you have been working in the cubicle adjacent to Kevin's. While most of your interactions focus on helping each other learn the ins and outs of the new prototyping software recently acquired by your company, you have also gotten to know a bit about him personally. When at home, he spends most of his free time playing video games. He has been with his girlfriend Nyla, who he refers to often as "the wife," for 10 years. Whenever your team goes out to lunch, he orders the same sandwich: a turkey and avocado on ciabatta.

This chapter draws from our book *Leading with Uncommon Sense: Slowing down, looking inward, taking action.* Springer Nature (2020)

W. C. Davi (✉)
Bentley University, Waltham, MA, USA
e-mail: WDAVI@bentley.edu

D. H. Spelman
Bentley University, Waltham, MA, USA

© The Author(s), under exclusive license to Springer Nature Switzerland AG 2021
J. Marques (ed.), *Exploring Gender at Work*,
https://doi.org/10.1007/978-3-030-64319-5_10

181

One day, you get an email from Kevin that he has sent to the entire company. It reads, "With the support of Human Resources and my boss Charlene, I am writing to let you know that while I have been going by the pronouns "he, him, and his," I have recently decided to be more authentic at work, so I will be going by the gender-neutral pronouns they/them/theirs to better reflect my genderqueer identity. I appreciate your support." As you finish reading Kevin's email, you realize that he— you catch yourself and replace the pronoun—*they* are hard at work in their cubicle right next to you.

Moments like this are occurring in the workplace with greater frequency, and companies are taking notice (Noguchi, 2019; Sawyer & Thoroughgood, 2017). Much is being written on the experiences of transgender people at work (Dietert, & Dentice, 2009; Sheridan, 2009). More recently, scholarship is emerging on a specific subcategory of the transgender community—gender non-binary employees (Boncori, Sicca, & Bizjak, 2019). Gender non-binary refers to individuals who do not identify simply as a man or as a woman. Gender non-binary people may identify entirely outside of these categories, or they may see themselves as a bit of both or even somewhere in between. The number of individuals who identify as gender non-binary is increasing, and companies are recognizing the need to create more inclusive workspaces (Flores, Herman, Gates, & Brown, 2017).

TRANSGENDER 101

Before going much further, we'd like to take a moment to talk about terminology. First, it's important for all of us to keep in mind that while we can do a Google search for a definition of a term, when we are discussing terms pertaining to our identities, these terms are personal and individual to each of us. For example, one person's use of the term genderqueer may be somewhat different from someone else's (and, we know terms will undoubtedly evolve). Thus, here we will define terms as we currently understand them but encourage you to engage in dialogue with colleagues whenever possible to avoid assuming people are using terms the same way you are. While there is an extensive list of key terms pertaining to gender identity, we are limiting our explanations to terms we use in this chapter. We encourage you to consult other sources as needed.

The terms "gender" and "sex," while often used interchangeably, are distinct. "Sex" refers to biological differences between males and females, such as sex chromosomes and sex organs. "Gender," or more aptly "gender identity," pertains to how individuals perceive themselves. Gender attribution refers to the identities we ascribe to people, and much of this is based on an individual's gender expression, which includes their physical appearance, mannerisms, behaviors, and other observable external attributes (Speer, 2005). Historically, most societies have operated from a gender binary—man and woman. Fortunately, in some cultures we have moved beyond the binary, and people can identify as men, women, neither, both, and more.

The term "transgender" serves as an umbrella term to refer to both people whose gender identity (that is, how they self-identify) is different from the sex they were assigned at birth, and people whose gender identity does not fit the traditional man or woman binary. We will be focusing in this chapter on the gender identities that go beyond the binary. Individuals with such identities may use the terms gender non-conforming, gender non-binary, genderqueer, or gender fluid (or some other term that they choose) to describe themselves.

The term "cisgender" refers to individuals whose gender identity aligns with the sex they were assigned at birth. For example, Duncan identifies as a man and was assigned male at birth; he is a cisgender man. Wiley, however, was assigned female at birth but does not identify as a woman. Rather, Wiley identifies as genderqueer. For them, neither category—man or woman—feels quite right, so the term genderqueer establishes a space outside of those categories. The term also reflects their willingness to be seen by some as a man and by others as a woman. What is most important to keep in mind here is that while Duncan, Wiley, and any of us was assigned a sex, we each choose, discover and/or determine our own gender identity.

OUR PURPOSE

In this chapter, our primary goal is to shine a light on the experiences of non-binary people in the workplace and offer some resources that could increase your comfort and effectiveness working with non-binary colleagues, whether you fit easily into the gender binary or are non-binary yourself. We recognize that every person's gender identity is unique, so we encourage you to tailor our suggestions accordingly.

To create more inclusive workplaces for gender non-conforming colleagues, a familiar approach is to think about their needs and make any corresponding adjustments in the work environment. For example, a recent *Harvard Business Review* article, "Creating a Trans-Inclusive Workplace," details a variety of approaches that organizations can use to improve the environment for transgender employees (Thoroughgood, Sawyer, & Webster, 2020). Organizations have altered the language in HR policies, created gender-neutral bathrooms, or altered the options for self-identification on forms. While we commend these and similar approaches and understand their benefits, we wish to emphasize the importance of understanding ourselves and how we operate within these spaces. In other words, paying attention to our environments is important, but we must also pay attention to ourselves.

Similarly, resources designed to improve the experiences of trans-gender, genderqueer, or other marginalized people often emphasize developing a deep understanding of those individuals' experiences. While it is certainly important to know about the people with whom you work as fully and deeply as possible, understanding yourself is an essential first step to being a good coworker. Quite often, for example, when we find ourselves in a situation like the one with your coworker Kevin that opens this chapter, the impulse may be to try to think of the correct thing to say or how to respond appropriately to our colleague. However, we propose that before taking any action, you first pause to examine what is happening in *you*.

By understanding ourselves, we suggest, we are better able to understand and interact with others. In hopes of helping you increase your effectiveness with non-binary colleagues, we begin with the suggestion that each of us is more successful interpersonally if we first do work on ourselves *intrapersonally* (Davi & Spelman, 2020). To do this work of understanding ourselves, we suggest a two-step approach (Davi & Spelman, 2020). The first step is to pause. Pausing allows us to step back and take a deeper look at ourselves. When we pause, we give ourselves the time to engage in the second step—introspect. Introspecting allows us to ask questions of ourselves to examine such things as what is out of our awareness, how our emotions are influencing us, how social identities are in play, and how we may be seeing things through a desire for certainty.

Pause

When we pause, we allow ourselves time to choose where we focus our attention; it's paying attention with purpose. It often requires that we interrupt the flow of events to jump off the proverbial merry-go-round in order to give ourselves time to look more closely.

Sometimes we may need to pause in the moment as something is unfolding before us. At those times, we recommend something as simple as taking a breath. Returning to our opening scenario, after reading Kevin's email and before sliding your chair over to their cubicle, you might take a deep breath. This one act has a calming effect on the brain and essentially signals that everything is fine (Kozub, 2017). Another option is to move around a bit. Again, using our opening example, consider closing your email and taking a short walk. By doing this, you shift the focus and give yourself time to engage in deeper reflection and introspect, which we discuss more in depth further on. While these suggestions may seem obvious at first glance, pausing requires a conscious choice, and it often makes a significant difference in our ability to respond.

Sometimes we don't have our wits about us enough to pause in the moment, and we can come away feeling dissatisfied or unsettled. That gnawing feeling is also a signal that it's a good time to pause. In those moments, find a few minutes to slow down and carve out a space to look inwards. When it comes to experiencing these feelings in the workplace, it's worth reminding ourselves that we almost always have the option to go back and revisit something, especially if it is an exchange with someone with whom we have an ongoing relationship. We can pause, think things through, and then go back and address it again.

We can also be proactive about pausing by building it into our daily routine. One useful way of doing this is to develop a meditation practice. There are a wide variety of approaches to meditation, but they all involve consciously slowing down and interrupting the flow of daily events—pausing (Valcour, 2015). Another proactive approach is to schedule time to pause; for example, you might use the recurring function in your electronic calendar to schedule pauses at the beginning of each day, week, month, or year (although we highly advocate pausing much more often than once a year!). For those of us with the ability to go further, we can build in personal retreats for longer periods of pausing. Finally, getting a good night's sleep is a way in which we can pause daily. Sleep is an essential way to refresh or reset our brains (Walker, 2017). It helps us make sense of our experiences and it allows us to moderate our emotions. "Sleeping on it" really does work.

By pausing, we give ourselves a chance to pay closer attention to ourselves, which, ultimately helps us to be more effective with our colleagues. More importantly, pausing allows you a moment to do what we call introspect—to look at what is going on inside you.

INTROSPECT

Imagine that you are participating in a divisional meeting. The company's new CMO has been invited to speak to the division to provide an update on the recent rebranding campaign. During the Q&A, a colleague poses a question to the CMO by stating, "Sir, you have provided a clear outline of our recent efforts…" After the CMO responds, another colleague follows up with a statement addressed to all of you and in the comment refers to the CMO as "*she*." You immediately notice people stealing less than furtive glances at each other.

For people who are gender non-conforming, this scenario is quite common. For those of us who are cisgender, the impulse may be to focus on what is happening in the moment for the non-conforming individual. While we appreciate any feelings of care or concern for a colleague, we advocate looking first at what is happening in you.

When introspecting, we suggest using the following four reminders to help you explore what is happening internally: be humble, be emotional, be "impolite," be uncertain. We will also offer a question to ask yourself that accompanies each reminder.

Be humble. While it can be unsettling to admit, research has proven that there is much that goes on outside of our conscious awareness (Wilson, 2004). To keep that in mind, we offer the reminder to be humble. To be humble, ask yourself, **"What is out of my awareness?"** For example, what assumptions may have been out of your awareness when you were listening to the CMO? Most basically, did you assume you knew the CMO's gender? How might your internalization of the gender binary have prevented you from considering that both terms could be accurate? Might it have been unconsciously upsetting to you to imagine the CMO as gender non-conforming?

Or imagine this scenario: You reluctantly decide to attend your company's annual summer barbeque. While there, your colleague Joanna introduces you to a person whose feminine gender expression leads you to say, "Hi, nice to meet you. You must be Joanna's sister." Joanna turns to you and says, "They aren't my sister; they're my spouse."

The impulse to attribute a gender to people often happens so automatically that we don't even have time to notice that it happens. Think, for example, of the times someone has welcomed you into a restaurant or store with the words, "Hello, sir" or "Welcome, ma'am." In a split second, they somehow decided what your gender was. Because the gender binary is so deeply internalized in most of us, we rarely think beyond the two categories. For example, our brains rarely go to "genderqueer."

As an aside, it's also interesting to consider why "you" in the barbeque example decided that Joanna's genderqueer spouse must be her sister rather than her spouse. Were you embedded in not only the gender binary but also in the assumption that Joanna's spouse must be a man?

The reminder to be humble helps us to pay attention to what is out of our awareness and to be mindful that unconscious forces may be influencing conscious thoughts, words, and actions. Psychologist Jonathan Haidt uses the wonderful image of a rider on the back of an elephant to illustrate how our conscious and unconscious operate (Haidt, 2006). What often unsettles people is that the conscious mind is merely the rider.

Having unconscious forces operating out of our awareness in and of itself is not a problem. In fact, those operations in our brain play important roles in our everyday actions. For example, unconscious processes include procedural memory and automatic processing. Every time you tie your shoes, for example, you likely give it no thought. When you find yourself suddenly driving in a rainstorm, you turn on the windshield wipers thanks to unconscious processes (those same processes likely influence you to also turn down the radio).

Our need to be humble, then, is less about paying attention to those helpful automatic responses and more about investigating other unconscious processes, such as how our perceptions are formed, how our memories operate, and how we make decisions.

One unconscious process worthy of our attention is bias, which operates largely out of our awareness. Unconscious biases are those associations, prejudices, or stereotypes that linger out of our awareness and influence our thoughts and actions. Unconscious bias around gender non-conforming identity can play out in any number of ways and on a continuum that ranges from benign to brutal.

This unconscious bias operates in members of the LGBTQ community, as well. Wiley recalls a day when they and their spouse Michele were driving along, and Wiley, after seeing someone walking on the sidewalk, asked, "Is that a man or a woman?" Michele turned to Wiley and said, "You of all people are asking the question that way?" Wiley's unconscious bias influenced them to see only the two options.

To be humble, we highly recommend continually asking ourselves, "What is out of my awareness?"

Be emotional. A second introspect reminder focuses on our feelings. Our emotions provide us with valuable information, but we often fail to pay attention to them. To be emotional, ask yourself, **"What are my emotions telling me?"** In the annual summer barbeque scenario mentioned earlier, consider what emotional reaction you may have had. What might you have felt when you misidentified (and, perhaps, misgendered) Joanna's spouse? What might your emotional reaction have been had this been the first time you were speaking with someone who identifies as genderqueer?

Similarly, while you may have never been in a situation like the one at the company barbeque, you can also pay attention to your emotions as *a reader* of that scenario. Did you have any emotional reaction as you were reading that exchange of someone misgendering someone? Did it call to mind and bring up an emotional reaction you may have had in a similar situation where you misidentified someone?

Historically, reason and emotion have been perceived as two separate aspects of who we are, often with reason being valued over emotion. More recently, studies have proven that the two are in collaboration with each other (Haidt, 2006). For example, neuroscientist Antonio Damasio's study (1994) of people with damage to the part of brain that generates emotional responses revealed that they were unable to make decisions, including simple decisions such as what to eat.

Emotions are important data that can help you recognize which option is more important to you, which you care about more. Your emotions help you make sense of your experiences, help you decide how to act, and help you determine what to believe (Davi & Spelman, 2020). By introspecting, we can pay attention to what those emotions are telling us.

People who identify as genderqueer report having witnessed both strangers and colleagues having strong emotional reactions to their fluid gender identity (Nadal, Whitman, Davis, Erazo, & Davidoff, 2016). Wiley has had numerous experiences where individuals have expressed outright anger toward them because of their gender nonconformity. They had an experience traveling through London with a group of students in which a stranger yelled to the students about Wiley, "Get away from the one that looks like a man but is a woman; it will lead you to hell" (Davi, 2006). Emotions can run high when we confront the unfamiliar.

Another example of emotional reactions relates to the use of the third-person pronoun "they" that has been adopted by many (by no means all) people who identify as genderqueer because it is a gender-neutral pronoun. In 2019, Merriam Webster Dictionary included the single-person version into its list of words. However, there has been backlash among people who find it frustrating to make the switch, who have an emotional attachment to words as they have come to know and use them, or those who report feeling "weird" when they use "they" to refer to an individual (Steinmetz, 2019).

In fact, we ourselves admit to having struggled with the term when it first came to our awareness and recall having conversations about ways in which it triggered emotional responses in us because of our training in traditional grammar. Through our exploration of our feelings, we recognized that for both of us, we were uncomfortable with the loss of control stemming from new rules that flew in the face of that to which we were accustomed.

When interacting with someone who introduces themselves to you and who states they go by they/theirs/them, pause and ask yourself if you are having an emotional reaction. Consider what those emotions might be telling you.

To be emotional, ask yourself, "What are my emotions telling me?"

Be "impolite." Our third reminder to guide your introspection is to be "impolite." To be impolite, ask yourself, **"Am I neglecting identity differences?"** We bracket impolite with quotation marks to signal our ironic intention. Many of us were taught that it is not polite to mention someone's race, religion, or other identities. Think of the instruction that many of us (especially white people) received to be "colorblind." This approach advocates *not* seeing differences for fear of that awareness leading to discrimination. With this reminder, we suggest being *impolite*. We argue that it is important to notice social identity differences, to notice our reactions to social identity differences, and to pay attention to how our own social identities influence our perceptions, thoughts, and actions.

Additionally, it is important to recognize that we are a mix of social identities and that the ways in which those identities intersect make our lived experiences even more complex (Crenshaw, 1990). For example, the intersectional challenges of a white genderqueer person may be wholly different from those of an African American, genderqueer person. Imagine how the complexity increases with the overlay of one's socio-economic status, religious affiliation, or other identity differences.

Our social identities influence how we fit into society, how we see others, and how we see ourselves (Davi & Spelman, 2020). Certain social identities, for example, may provide us with access to opportunities not available to people with other social identities. Our social identities give us more or less power. For example, men have historically had greater access to influence, possibilities, and promotions within organizations than women have had. Consider, then, what the implications for genderqueer employees might be based on their gender identity vis-a-vis professional advancement. Gender non-conforming employees have experienced discrimination in the workplace, such as being fired or denied promotion because of their gender identity (Grant et al., 2011).

In addition to how we fit into society and how others see us, our identities influence *how we see others*. The communities within which we grow up and live implicitly and explicitly assign positive and negative connotations to a wide range of identities. We are taught to consider others' identities whether we are consciously aware of them or not. Stereotypes get assigned to certain social identities. For example, older employees report being treated as if they are not capable or willing to learn or adapt to new approaches in the organization (Chiesa, Zaniboni, Guglielmi, & Vignoli, 2019). What, then, might be the ways in which genderqueer employees are treated based on how others see them? Gender non-conforming employees report having been made to present in the wrong gender to keep their job, and many have been removed from direct contact with clients (Grant et al., 2011).

Our identities also influence how we see ourselves. Our self-perceptions are powerfully influenced by how we feel about our various identities and how social identity dynamics play out in different situations. For example, being genderqueer while participating in an LGBTQ parade versus being the only genderqueer individual in a company-wide meeting undoubtedly influences how one perceives oneself.

The powerful effects of social identities on how we are seen by others, how we see others, and how we see ourselves suggest that ignoring social identities is an unwise approach to dealing with our coworkers. Instead, we should pay attention to their social identities and to our own as they affect our interactions at work.

To be impolite, ask, "Am I neglecting identity differences?"

Be uncertain. Finally, the fourth reminder is to be uncertain, which helps us resist a human tendency toward certainty that usually leads us to oversimplify. To be uncertain, ask, **"Am I too sure?"** Our brains want predictability and, therefore, see patterns and clarity even if they don't exist. To protect us from the anxiety of uncertainty, our brains produce a "feeling of knowing," which kicks in involuntarily even when we don't have adequate evidence to support feeling certain (Burton, 2009, p. 3). At times when we have formulated a conclusion or belief, we seek sources that reinforce rather than challenge that belief (Burton, 2009). Our brains discern patterns based on bits of information that influence us to see what we anticipate seeing or even want to see (Balcetis & Dunning, 2006).

For many of us, uncertainty leads to feeling anxious. Psychiatrist Christopher Andre (2011) argues that all forms of anxiety reflect an intolerance for uncertainty. Consider the feelings of anxiety that are likely to emerge in us if we can't "figure out" someone's gender. When we experience those feelings, we would be wise to resist the comforting tug toward certainty. For example, if you are unsure of a colleague's gender, sit with the feeling of uneasiness. Pay attention to ways in which you may be trying to fit that person into a particular gender identity in order to feel more certain and less anxious with your not knowing.

To more fully understand our tug toward certainty, it's helpful to understand how our brains operate. "The Ladder of Inference" describes how quickly we move from observations to assumptions and beliefs and ultimately to actions, building our feelings of certainty with each step (Argyris, 1982). We often rely on past experiences to reinforce our certainty regarding our interpretations and assumptions.

For example, imagine you are giving a presentation, and you notice that your colleague Susan yawns. One immediate response might be, "Susan is bored by me." If you have noticed Susan yawning in prior presentations you have given, you might start moving up the ladder rather quickly, thinking, "She's often disengaged when I present. She doesn't value what I have to say." Imagine, several months later, that you are making a decision about a promotion within your division and Susan is a candidate. Without even being conscious of it, you might find yourself not very impressed by Susan's application. Consciously, you may not even be aware of how these earlier small observations of Susan are now influencing your decision not to promote her.

Consider how quickly we run up the ladder of inference in the context of gender identity. Since the gender binary is so powerful, most of us are not even aware that we are drawing conclusions about someone's gender. We don't notice that we've climbed the rungs of the ladder. Again, consider how often servers in restaurants or cashiers in grocery stores welcome customers with the salutation "Hello, sir," or "Hello, ma'am." Such quick thinking laden with hidden assumptions and biases can have powerful impacts in the workplace. Often, out of our awareness, we develop beliefs about who is right for a certain job, who you want to have on a team project, and who you turn to for professional advice.

In addition, as you examine your resistance to uncertainty, consider whether or not as you read this chapter you find yourself wanting more concrete rules. For example, we find when we facilitate LGBTQ awareness workshops, attendees want to know exactly how to behave. They want to know what they should say or how they should act in order to be an effective ally. That mindset reflects the impulse toward certainty that we encourage you to identify and resist. The recommendation is to notice when our brains are seeking certainty and operating with too much certainty. We suggest that these are the moments when we are more apt to get into trouble.

Instead, we suggest that you resist certainty by holding off on drawing conclusions too quickly. We suggest that you recognize and then question your initial thoughts and assumptions. We also encourage you to embrace ambiguity and welcome complexity. When you find yourself asking, "But what is the best response?" we encourage you to notice that question as your brain's tug toward certainty.

For example, Wiley is often asked by colleagues and new acquaintances which pronoun they prefer. The question is a respectful one, but for our purposes here, consider how it signals a need for certainty. Similarly, Wiley's response, "I'm comfortable with any pronoun – he, she, they..." usually elicits the following response, "No, but really, which one do you prefer?" Again, rather than seek a clear answer, another approach might be to instead respond to Wiley by saying, "I'm not accustomed to a response like that, but I hear you and am glad we talked." Another option would be to ask if there was more time to have a conversation so you could learn more about such an openness to pronouns. Rather than seeking *the* answer, sit with the complexity.

Here, you might ask yourself whether the use of different gendered terms in reference to the CMO did unsettle you because it left you with a question about the CMO's answer. In other words, do you find yourself distracted in the meeting because you just don't know? By engaging with *yourself* in this moment, by introspecting, you will be better prepared to engage with your colleagues and with the CMO. Starting with ourselves positions us to create environments where people can work more effectively across differences. Consider, for example, what your reaction may have been had we decided to use different pronouns when we referred to Wiley (she, he, and they). Might that have confused you or unsettled you?

To resist certainty, ask yourself, **"Am I too sure?"**

Conclusion

We would be remiss if we encouraged you to pause and to engage in paying attention to yourself but failed to say anything about what comes next, about taking action. While pausing to introspect is crucial, we also want to caution against falling into analysis paralysis. Understanding yourself more deeply but failing to act is incomplete. You can never have all the information you want, and the best course of action will seldom be completely clear. Taking action often means taking risks and it requires courage. Some failure is inevitable. But more productive relationships with your genderqueer colleagues depend on taking the plunge. Better to err on the side of action than to do nothing and maintain the status quo.

Let's return to Kevin in our opening example. When you realize Kevin is in the cubicle next to you, what are you going to do after you have paused and introspected? Will you report your self-introspection? Will you roll your chair over and explain your thinking? Will you spend some time thinking about your investment in the gender binary and ways in which it may have manifested itself in your earlier exchanges with Kevin? Will you acknowledge receiving the email and explain that you value your working relationship and want to proceed humbly and with greater awareness of the dynamics that might make life more challenging for Kevin?

You'll notice that the previous paragraph is a series of questions rather than rules to follow. The work of diversity and inclusion is messy. As an ally, you may get it "wrong;" as someone who identifies as genderqueer, you may get it "wrong." By putting the word wrong in quotations, we want to signal that there may be times when you paused, introspected, and acted, but that things didn't go as smoothly as you intended, and that's okay. In fact, it is to be expected. One of the benefits of doing this kind of work within a community such as a workplace is that you often get opportunities to go back and try again. We want to encourage you to see those moments when things didn't go as you hoped as moments when you can pause again, introspect again, and act again. With each attempt, you will develop your intrapersonal capabilities as well as your interpersonal capabilities, and you will, thereby, become more effective working with your gender non-conforming colleagues as well as others.

Chapter Takeaways

- Gender non-conforming people are becoming a more visible part of the workplace.
- Companies are recognizing the need to create more inclusive workspaces for gender non-conforming employees.
- To work more successfully with gender non-conforming colleagues, it is essential to understand ourselves and how we operate within our places of employment. That is, to be effective interpersonally, we must first be effective intrapersonally.
- Pausing is the first step that allows us to stop and look inward. Pausing allows us to interrupt the flow of events to take a closer look at ourselves, more specifically, to introspect.
- While introspecting, we recommend the following four reminders and accompanying questions:

  - Be humble by asking, "What is out of my awareness?"
  - Be emotional by asking, "What are my emotions telling me?"
  - Be "impolite" by asking, "Am I neglecting identity differences?"
  - Be uncertain by asking, "Am I too sure?"

References

André, C. (2011). *Looking at mindfulness*. New York: Blue Rider Press.

Argyris, C. (1982). *Reasoning, learning, and action: Individual and organizational*. San Francisco: Jossey-Bass.

Balcetis, E., & Dunning, D. (2006). See what you want to see: Motivational influences on visual perception. *Journal of Personality and Social Psychology, 91*(4), 612–625.

Boncori, I., Sicca, L. M., & Bizjak, D. (2019). Transgender and gender non-conforming people in the workplace: Direct and invisible discrimination. *Inequality and organizational practice* (pp. 141–160). Cham: Palgrave Macmillan.

Burton, R. A. (2009). *On being certain: Believing you are right even when you're not*. New York: Macmillan.

Chiesa, R., Zaniboni, S., Guglielmi, D., & Vignoli, M. (2019). Coping with negative stereotypes toward older workers: Organizational and work-related outcomes. *Frontiers in Psychology, 10*, 649. Retrieved from https://www.ncbi.nlm.nih.gov/pmc/articles/PMC6439334/.

Crenshaw, K. (1990). Mapping the margins: Intersectionality, identity politics, and violence against women of color. *Stanford Law Review, 43*, 1241.

Damasio, A. R. (1994). *Decartes' error: Error, reason, and the human brain*. New York: Grosset/Putnam.

Davi, A. (2006). Reflections of a transgender medievalist. *Radical Teacher, 77*, 40–41.

Davi, W. C., & Spelman, D. H. (2020). *Leading with uncommon sense: Slowing down, looking inward, taking action*. Management, Change, Strategy and Positive Leadership. Switzerland: Springer Nature.

Dietert, M., & Dentice, D. (2009). Gender identity issues and workplace discrimination: The transgender experience. *Journal of Workplace Rights, 14*(1).

Flores, A. R., Herman, J. L., Gates, G. J., & Brown, T. N. T. (2017). *How many adults identify as transgender in the United States?* Los Angeles, CA: The Williams Institute 2016.

Grant, J. M., Lisa, A. M., Justin, T., Jack, H., Jody, L. H., & Mara, K. (2011). *Injustice at every turn: A report of the national transgender discrimination survey*. Washington, DC: National Center for Transgender Equality and National Gay and Lesbian Task Force.

Haidt, J. (2006). *The happiness hypothesis: Finding modern truth in ancient wisdom*. New York: Basic Books.

Kozub, S. (2017, March 30). Take a deep breath—No really, it will calm your brain. *The Verge*. Retrieved from https://www.theverge.com/2017/3/30/15109762/deep-breath-study-breathing-affects-brain-neurons-emotional-stat.

Nadal, K. L., Whitman, C. N., Davis, L. S., Erazo, T., & Davidoff, K. C. (2016). Microaggressions toward lesbian, gay, bisexual, transgender, queer, and genderqueer people: A review of the literature. *The Journal of Sex Research, 53*(4–5), 488–508.

Nadal, K. L., Rivera, D. P., Corpus, J. H., & Sue, D. W. (2010). Sexual orientation and transgender microaggressions. *Microaggressions and marginality: Manifestation, dynamics, and impact* (pp. 217–240). Hoboken, NJ: Wiley.

Noguchi, Y. (2019, October 16). *He, she, they: Workplaces adjust as gender identity norms change*. Retrieved from https://www.npr.org/2019/10/16/770 298129/he-she-they-workplaces-adjust-as-gender-identity-norms-change.

Sawyer, K., & Thoroughgood, C. (2017). Gender non-conformity and the modern workplace. *Organizational Dynamics, 46*(1), 1–8. https://doi.org/10.1016/j.orgdyn.2017.01.001.

Sheridan, V. (2009). *The complete guide to transgender in the workplace*. ABC-CLIO.

Speer, S. A. (2005). The interactional organization of the gender attribution process. *Sociology, 39*(1), 67–87.

Steinmetz, K. (2019, December 13). This is why singular 'they' is such a controversial subject. *Time*. Retrieved from https://time.com/5748649/word-of-year-they-merriam-webster/.

Thoroughgood, C. N., Sawyer, K. B., & Webster, J. R. (2020, March–April). Creating a trans-inclusive workplace: How to make transgender employees feel valued at work. *Harvard Business Review*, *98*(2), 114–123.

Valcour, M. (2015, April 27). A 10-minute meditation to help you solve conflicts at work. *Harvard Business Review*. Retrieved from https://hbr.org/2015/04/a-10-minute-meditation-to-help-you-solve-conflicts-at-work.

Walker, M. (2017). *Why we sleep: Unlocking the power of sleep and dreams*. New York: Scribner.

Wilson, T. (2004). *Strangers to ourselves*. Cambridge, MA: Belknap Press.

CHAPTER 11

Gender Equality & Gender Equity: Strategies for Bridging the Gender Gap in the Corporate World

Radha R. Sharma and Sonam Chawla

INTRODUCTION

The sustainable development goals (SDGs), also known as the global goals have "gender equality" as one of the goals which were adopted by 193 member states in UN General assembly in September 2015 for achieving a better future for all. The SDGs came into effect in 2016 and will continue to guide the United Nations Development Program's (UNDP) policy and funding to implement these goals.[1] Each goal is to be measured for its implementation by every country with respect to clearly defined targets. One of the targets to measure the SDG of gender equality

---

[1] http://www.undp.org/content/undp/en/home/sustainable-development-goals.html accessed on 1st August 2020.

R. R. Sharma (✉)
New Delhi Institute of Management, New Delhi, India

S. Chawla
Jindal Global Business School, O.P. Jindal Global University, Sonipat, India

© The Author(s), under exclusive license to Springer Nature
Switzerland AG 2021
J. Marques (ed.), *Exploring Gender at Work*,
https://doi.org/10.1007/978-3-030-64319-5_11

is "ensure women's full and effective participation and equal opportunities for leadership at all levels of decision making in political, economic and public life,"[2] which has policy and practice implications for organizations, institutions, and societies to facilitate the advancement of women to senior leadership positions.

Gender Equality vs. Gender Equity

The terms equality and equity are often used interchangeably, however, the two terms differ from each other significantly, and would depend on the context and country in question. Equality is the process of allocating resources, opportunities, and other facilities in such a manner that both men and women have the same access. That is the same programs; initiatives or policies in the organizations would be applicable in the same way to both men and women. Equality is a relevant concept where the resources, capacities, experiences are the same. This approach believes that both men and women are equal as professionals and need to be treated the same way irrespective of the gender and are capable on contributing and competing equally. Whereas, gender equity has been defined as "fairness, treatment for women and men, according to their respective needs. This may include equal treatment or treatment that is different but which is considered equivalent in terms of rights, benefits, obligations and opportunities," ILO, Geneva, 2000.

Gender equity at the workplace seldom finds mention in the academic literature focused on organizations, as most of the extant studies have focused on gender equality at the workplace. Gender equity, would be based on integration, rather than separation, of professional lives and the private sphere of family and other personal involvements. Though the goal needs to be to explore what would be required to realize such an integration. On the societal level of a given context, activities would be considered as important and valued as professional activities, according to the cultural norms; also, on the part of the individual, it would mean equal commitment to each sphere (Bailyn, 2003).

In the absence of the construct of gender equity in organizations Sharma (2013) empirically evolved the construct of perceived gender

---

[2] http://www.undp.org/content/undp/en/home/sustainable-development-goals/goal-5-gender-equality/targets/ accessed on 15 May 2018

equity and studied its role in work engagement and employee well-being (Sharma & Sharma, 2015). The terms equity in the organizational context has been defined as a composite construct of perceived gender equity (PGE) encompassing organizational policies, practices, and environment leading to gender equitable perceptions among the employees (Sharma, 2013; Sharma & Sharma, 2015). Gender equity, which is different from gender equality and has been an underexplored subject in relation to women's career advancement (Sharma & Sharma, 2015). The construct of PGE comprises of three dimensions, "equity perception through organizational policies," "equity perception through organizational practices" and "equity perception through organizational environment" (Sharma & Sharma, 2015). Accordingly, perceived gender equity'(PGE) and has been defined (Sharma, 2013) as "employees' positive perception of equal opportunity in recruitment, training and development, compensation, career progression, dignified treatment and professional respect through the organizational policies, practices and environment."

Also, in a comprehensive report by McKinsey & Company and Lean In in 2017 it was found that an increasing number of companies are committing to gender equality. 77 Major firms like Apple, IBM, and CVS have also faced major pressure from shareholders in the form of investor proposals to adopt policies promoting gender equality within their firms. Looking at the corporate pipeline, it is evident that inequality begins at the very first promotion and continues to increase at each subsequent step (Women in the Workplace 2017, Lean In and McKinsey and Co., 2017)

The Imperatives for Bridging the Gap

Gender equality has been considered as a pre-requisite to the progress of organizations, economies, nations, and society-at-large (Hausmann, 2009; de Jonge, 2014). Also, from a human rights and dignity perspective, gender inequality prevents women from reaching their potential fully (Greig, Hausmann, Tyson & Zahidi, 2006). According to Catalyst (2019), men are two to three times more likely to be in a senior management position than women. In Standards & Poor's (S&P) 500 companies around the world, there are 36.9% first/mid-level women managers; however, they occupy just 4.6% of CEO positions.[3] The under-representation of women in senior management and corporate board during recent decades has become an area of concern for organizations, economists, policymakers, and the society (Jonge, 2015; Machold, Huse, Hansen & Brogi, 2013), and has started receiving scholarly attention in the recent years. The talent shortage has made it imperative for companies to leverage the female talent to the maximum potential by attracting, retaining, and advancing women (Williams, Kern & Waters, 2016). A lot of women leave their careers mid-way and at critical stages, which entails considerable loss to the organizations because of the investment they have made in their development (Van der Walt, Ingley, Shergill & Townsend, 2006). Apart from the humanitarian and egalitarian considerations, there is also a strong business case for women in the workforce, specifically at all levels in the organizations (Nielsen & Huse, 2010; Wiley & Monllor-Tormos, 2018) as women bring different viewpoints, creativity, and superior problem solving and decision-making, different consumer insights that in turn, help firms to improve performance (Konrad, Kramer & Erkut, 2008). Also, scholars and researchers across the world have been focusing on the benefits of having gender diverse workforce as well as boards and women in decision-making positions (Jonge, 2015), thus building the case for and focus on gender equality and gender equity. The aging population and workforce, makes it vital to leverage and advance female talent and therefore it is no longer an option but an economic necessity today as women constitute half of the population (Corkery, Taylor & Hayden, 2018). A World Bank report[4] explains how the productivity of a nation rises by 25% when the barriers to career advancement of women are completely removed.

Research evidence suggests that career advancement of women is more complex than that of men because of the barriers they face (Chawla & Sharma, 2016). There are a number of factors that are identified as barriers to career advancement of women in management (Barreto, Ryan, & Schmitt, 2009; Burke & Major, 2014; Eagly & Carli, 2007; Naff, 2018; Valian, 1999), thus leading to fewer women in higher ranks and

---

[3] http://www.catalyst.org/knowledge/women-sp-500-companies accessed on 12 June 2018.

[4] https://siteresources.worldbank.org/INTWDR2012/Resources/7778105-129969 9968583/7786210-1315936222006/Complete-Report.pdf, accessed on 17 September 2017.

important decision-making positions in the corporate world. Glass Ceiling (Davidson & Cooper, 1992) is identified as one of the main barriers hindering the advancement of women. Glass ceiling effect implies, other things (education, qualification, experience) being equal, a person is at a disadvantaged position because of the gendered perceptions or notions (Ragins, Townsend, Mattis, 1998). The term glass ceiling was coined nearly 40 years ago but researchers have found that it remains relevant even today (Barreto et al., 2009). The question arises how to quantify the gap that will be explained in the following paragraphs.

Measuring Gender Diversity

Gender can be considered as an "institutionalized system of social practices within society that constitute people as two significantly different categories, men and women, and organize relations of inequality on the basis of this difference" (Ridgeway, 2007). This inequality is a result of two interlinked elements—one is the "unequal distribution and access to resources "and the other is the different meanings that are attributed to femininity and masculinity in different cultures" (Fraser, 2003). Scholars believe that in order to measure gender equality, these different interpretations of the gender processes need to be operationalized in mathematical terms (Harrison & Klein, 2007). Further, the realization and acknowledgement of inequities, and of the importance of measuring them, has led to the development of a number of metrics focused on quantitatively and qualitatively tracing the relationship between gender inequality and national economic growth (Anand & Sen, 1995; Ferrant, 2009; Geske, 2006).

Different gender-related composite indicators have been adopted to measure gender equality, equity, and diversity. These include, for example, the Gender Development Index (GDI) and Gender Empowerment Measure (GEM), both produced by the United Nations Development Program; the Gender Parity Index (GPI) by the United Nations Educational, Scientific and Cultural Organization; the Gender Inequality Index (GII) by the European Union; the Women, Business and the Law Index by the World Bank; the Gender Equality Index (GEI) by Bloomberg; Gender Inequality rankings by McKinsey & Co; and, the central focus of the current chapter- the Global Gender Gap Index (GGGI) by the World Economic Forum (WEF). The 2020 Gender Diversity Index (GDI), which has been tracking female presence on American boards since 2011, notes significant improvements in gender parity in Fortune 1000 boards since tracking began.

The Global Gender Gap Index (GGGI) developed by the World Economic Forum (Hausmann, Tyson, & Zahidi, 2006) considers only gaps that are detrimental to women. Whereas, another indicator developed by the European Institute for Gender Equality, the Gender Equality Index (Humbert, Ivaškaitė-Tamošiūnė, Oetke, & Paats, 2015) states that any kind of gender gap is detrimental, regardless of whether it is women or men that are disadvantaged. The Global Gender Gap Index (GGGI) is regarded as a significant indicator of gender disparities worldwide. It's useful tracking of the extent of access to resources and opportunities, and differences between men and women have been discussed across sectors and levels of decision-making. The index covers critical aspects involving the four sub-indexes (dimensions): economic participation and opportunity, educational attainment, health and survival, and political empowerment. The Global Gender Gap Report (WEF, 2018), also provides a brief overview of country comparisons and rankings. The application of the index can be seen in policy formulation and in consulting.

Gender diversity has been researched in the context of board gender diversity and the two commonly used indexes used by researchers are the Blau Index and the Shannon Index (Boulouta, 2013). Blau index is maximized when the proportion of men and women are maximized. The Blau index is measured as:

$$1 - \sum_{i=1}^{N} P_i^2$$

where i is the percentage of board gender diversity and N is the total number of board members. The scale range from 0 to a maximum of 0.5. It reaches 0.5 when the proportion of men and women in the board is equal. Blau index was developed for measuring biodiversity in ecological-economic settings, but it can be further applied to other measurement of diversity (Campbell & Mínguez-Vera, 2008; Gordini & Rancati, 2017).

Shanon Index is calculated as

$$\text{Shannon Index (H)} = - \sum_{i=1}^{s} p_i \ln p_i$$

In the Shannon index, p is the proportion (n/N) of individuals of one gender found (n) divided by the total number of individuals found (N), ln is the natural log, Σ is the sum of the calculations, and s is the number of species/gender (Shannon, 1948).

The minimum value of the index is zero and diversity is maximized when both genders are present in equal proportions, which gives rise to a value of 0.69 (Shannon, 1948). The properties of the Shannon index are qualitatively similar to those of the Blau index although it will always yield a larger number than the Blau index and is more sensitive to small differences in the gender composition of boards since it is a logarithmic measure of diversity. The index is commonly known as Shannon's "entropy" index due to its formal resemblance to the entropy expression from statistical thermodynamics (Ben-Naim, 2008).

Corporate Governance Codes

As discussed in the preceding sections, gender diversity on boards has been gaining attention from scholars and corporates alike. A gender diverse board has been proven to have positive impact on firm performance (Wiley & Monllor-Tormos, 2018), governance (Orazalin, 2019), creativity, shareholder value, and corporate social responsibility (Dawar & Singh, 2016). Also, in order to attain gender equity and equality, it is important to have fair representation of women in decision-making leadership positions. Therefore, corporate governance codes have been garnering attention, in recent years, as a method of regulating corporate behavior considered to be beneficial to the listed companies and their stakeholders. Initially the codes focused on gaining investor confidence, however, their scope was expanded to include gender diversity and social issues. Codes come in the category of soft regulation as "general principles rather than prescribed rules" and in most of the countries provision of code is voluntary (Klettner, 2016).

Different countries have adopted different strategies involving specific legislations, gender-based quota system, reporting gender composition of the board and corporate governance code. A corporate governance code clarifies the obligation of the Management Board (executive board) and the Supervisory Board to ensure the continued existence of the enterprise and its sustainable creation of value in conformity with the principles of the social market economy (interest of the enterprise). United States was the first country to issue code of good governance in 1978 followed by Hong Kong in 1989. It gathered momentum since 1992 when UK's Cadbury Report was brought out (Cuervo-Cazurra & Aguilera, 2004). "Codes of good governance have become a central issue" (Aguilera & Cuervo-Cazurra, 2009; Brown, Beekes, & Verhoeven, 2011). There is an increasing interest in the diffusion of CG codes across countries" (Brown et al. 2011). There has also been some research evidence that indicates a positive developments and improvements in gender diversity at the board levels by adoption of these corporate governance codes in certain countries (Duh,2017).

Legislation: Company's Act 2013: A Case Study of India

While corporate governance codes are not truly mandatory in their execution, legislations involve legal enforcement by the regulatory body. A few countries have taken a step further w.r.t. having women on board and mandated the same as a part of the law governing the listed companies. An interesting case here is that of India. The Companies Act, 2013 incorporated provisions aimed at strengthening Corporate Governance in companies in India. The Securities and Exchange Board of India (SEBI), the regulatory authority in India, mandated that companies that have a paid-up share capital of INR 10 million[5] or more, or a turnover of INR 3000 million or more have to appoint at least one-woman director on the company's board. This new ruling left the male dominated boards of Indian corporates, struggling to find women directors.[6] Corporate organizations in India have admitted that though they would like to have women directors from the industry, they have limited options as very few women are found in the leadership positions. As on March 29, 2015 (that is a day prior to complying with the norm earlier, later extended) 400 listed companies in India were yet to appoint a Woman Director.[7]

Corporates admitted that though they would like to have women directors from the industry but the options were very limited since there

---

[5] https://www.xe.com/currencyconverter/convert/?Amount=1&From=INR&To=USD, accessed on January 17, 2019

[6] "Indian Companies Scramble to Find Women Directors", *New York Times*, March 27, 2015.

[7] "Nearly 400 listed companies yet to appoint women directors," *Economic Times*, March 29, 2015.

were very few women leaders in the leadership positions. The companies then started exploring the options of having women directors from other fields like government agencies, academic and research institutions, non-profit organizations, as most of the limited eligible women in the corporate world were already part of many boards. Though, most of the companies would have liked to have women directors from the business world as they bring in relevant experience to the decision-making process required at the board level but the scarcity forced them to look outside

This corporate governance norm brought to fore the problem that the companies were ignoring, that of, facilitating the advancement of women to leadership positions. This in some sense "forced" the organizations to put in conscious effort to not only improve gender ratio but also ensure retention and advancement of women to senior positions in the organizations. This required a concerted effort from the companies to help advance women in the organizations.

There are different motivators for organizations for diversity initiatives. However, the strongest motivator is the legal and regulatory push (Langevoort, 2004).

In a last minute rush and the lack of availability of eligible women, more than half the companies appointed family members (wives, daughters and sisters) to meet the requirement of the legislation mandated by SEBI.[8] However, their appointment may have defeated the real purpose of the legislation. Keeping in view the same, in May 2018, SEBI provisioned that each of the top 1,000 listed companies must have at least one-woman independent director by March 2020. As on December 31, 2019, 977 of that top 1,000 companies had a woman director, and 835 of them had a women independent director.[9] Independent Directors have fewer potential conflicts of interest and can thereby operate with greater integrity and can take impartial decisions (Fama 1980; Rosenstein and Wyatt 1997) which may result in better financial performance and governance.

This gender diversity drive has led to some early gains. Women independent directors, usually seasoned professionals, have acted as role

---

[8] https://www.businesstoday.in/current/corporate/wives-women-family-members-appointed-as-directors-sebi-norms/story/217547.html, accessed on 24th July 2020.

[9] https://economictimes.indiatimes.com/news/company/corporate-trends/the-push-to-appoint-women-directors-has-brought-diversity-to-an-all-boys-club.html, accessed on 25th July 2020.

models, ensured the interests of women in the workforce and pushed for hiring of more women, among others. Many professional women had joined company boards as independent directors after the 2013 Company's Act largely as MNCs and professionally run groups took the lead. The share of women directors was a lowly 5% at the end of fiscal 2013. Women's share in boards of Nifty-500 firms has tripled to 15 percent over the past six years.[10] The Nifty-500 index is a proxy for listed firms across the country, as it accounts for roughly 96% of market capitalization on the National Stock Exchange (NSE) in India. It, therefore, gives a fair and representative idea of the representation of women in leadership positions in corporate India. The legislative approach adopted by India has yielded positive results of enhancing gender diversity on the corporate boards.

The Way Forward

The World Development Report 2012 on Gender Equality and Development (WDR, 2012) has provided an approach for enhancing gender equality at the world of work which will add significant development value from an early stage. Also, World Development Report 2013 on Jobs (WDR, 2013) provides detailed frameworks for identifying and addressing gender specific barriers and constraints which can be utilized by policy makers to accelerate gender equality at the workplace.

The view on gender equity at home is also gaining importance especially in the context of work from home arrangements where both partners work (for home as well as the job). Gender equality at work starts with men becoming equal partners at home. Real equity and gender partnership require that men contribute their fair share not only to household chores, childcare but also the emotional labor of planning and tracking activities, and supporting their partner's career (Johnson & Smith, 2018). In the recent years, the issue of mental load or emotional labor of women is coming to fore, highlighting the role of gender equity in the same. Emotional labor includes having to think and plan about a number of things on your mind. For example, women have to remember to stock the grocery, prepare for their kids' school activities, plan and decide the meals in a day and keep a track of the communications from their kids' school (Forbes, 2019). Women, fall of the leadership track not only because

---

[10]data sourced from NSE Infobase.

of what happens in office but also owing to what happens at home. According to a report by Boston Consulting Group (2019),[11] while men are trying to contribute to tasks at home, an average man in a dual career couple is far from sharing equal responsibility at home. This leaves him with enough time to focus on his career- stay late at office, take on stretch assignments, travel for business, and network with colleagues and mentors post office hours. According to Melaku, Smith and Johnson (2020) when men act as equal partners at home contributing to the household chores and sharing other responsibilities, they contribute to gender equity in three important ways. Firstly, it helps women accelerate in their careers by giving them adequate time required to avail of the opportunities. Secondly, by doing so the men also set the expectations for the gender role of their future generations. Thirdly, when they would contribute at home, they would ask for flexibility at work which would make it easier for women to avail of such flexible arrangements at work. This would help in "normalizing" the options of availing parental leave, flexible work or paid leave for women as well.

In countries where the gender divide is greater (like India) the context gender equity becomes important than equality. Gender equity denotes an element of interpretation of social justice, usually based on tradition, custom, religion, or culture (UN Women, 2018); which predominates in the Indian context. Further, in India, economic liberalization has led to an increase in the employment opportunities that has led to upsurge in women employment. But the educated women still face the challenge of growing through the organizational ladder (Khandelwal, 2002).

The chapter has provided a variety of strategies for bridging the gender gap such as gender diversity indices, corporate governance codes, Blau and Shannon index, and gender-based legislation which have been adopted by various countries in recent years. It is time now to scientifically study the impact/effectiveness of these approaches within a country or a cluster of countries in a geographical region based on cultural similarity so that effective measures could be adopted to accelerate the pace of bridging the gender gap across levels and achieving SDG 5 on Gender Equality

[11] https://www.bcg.com/en-es/publications/2019/lightening-mental-load-holds-women-back accessed on 20th Dec 2020.

CHAPTER TAKEAWAYS

- The terms equality and equity are often used interchangeably, however, the two terms differ significantly. Equality is the process of allocating resources, opportunities and other facilities in such a manner that both men and women have the same access. Gender equity pertains to fairness in treatment for women and men, according to their respective needs.
- From a human rights and dignity perspective, gender inequality prevents women from reaching their potential fully.
- Apart from humanitarian and egalitarian considerations, there is a strong business case for women in the workforce at all levels in organizations as women bring different viewpoints, creativity, and superior problem solving and decision-making, different consumer insights that in turn, help firms to improve performance.
- Gender diversity on boards has been gaining attention from scholars and corporates alike. A gender diverse board has been proven to have positive impact on firm performance.
- Different countries have adopted different strategies involving specific legislations, gender-based quota system, reporting gender composition of the board and corporate governance code. A corporate governance code clarifies the obligation of the Management Board (executive board) and the Supervisory Board to ensure the continued existence of the enterprise and its sustainable creation of value in conformity with the principles of the social market economy.
- The World Development Report 2012 on Gender Equality and Development (WDR, 2012) has provided an approach for enhancing gender equality at the world of work which will add significant development value from an early stage.

REFERENCES

Aguilera, R. V., & Cuervo-Cazurra, A. (2009). Codes of good governance. *Corporate Governance: An International Review, 17*(3), 376–387.

Anand, S., & Sen, A. (1995). *Gender inequality in human development: Theories and measurement.* New York: United Nations Development Programme.

Bailyn, L. (2003). Academic careers and gender equity: Lessons learned from MIT 1. *Gender, Work & Organization, 10*(2), 137–153.

Barreto, M. E., Ryan, M. K., & Schmitt, M. T. (2009). *The glass ceiling in the 21st century: Understanding barriers to gender equality* (pp. xvii–334). American Psychological Association.

Ben-Naim, A. (2008). *Entropy demystified: The second law reduced to plain common sense.* World Scientific.

Boulouta, I. (2013). Hidden connections: The link between board gender diversity and corporate social performance. *Journal of Business Ethics, 113*(2), 185–197.

Brown, P., Beekes, W., & Verhoeven, P. (2011). Corporate governance, accounting and finance: A review. *Accounting & Finance, 51*(1), 96–172.

Burke, R. J., & Major, D. A. (Eds.). (2014). *Gender in organizations: Are men allies or adversaries to women s career advancement?* Edward Elgar Publishing.

Campbell, K., & Mínguez-Vera, A. (2008). Gender diversity in the boardroom and firm financial performance. *Journal of Business Ethics, 83*(3), 435–451.

Chawla, S., & Sharma, R. R. (2016). How women traverse an upward journey in Indian industry: Multiple case studies. *Gender in Management: An International Journal, 31*(3), 181–206.

Corkery, J. F., Taylor, M. E., & Hayden, M. (2018). *The business case for quotas.* Women on Corporate Boards: An International Perspective.

Cuervo-Cazurra, A., & Aguilera, R. (2004). The worldwide diffusion of codes of good governance. *Corporate governance and firm organization, 14*, 318–348.

Davidson, M. J., & Cooper, C. L. (1992). *Shattering the glass ceiling: The woman manager.* Paul Chapman Publishing.

Dawar, G., & Singh, S. (2016). Corporate social responsibility and gender diversity: A literature review. *Journal of IMS Group, 13*(1), 61–71.

De Jonge, A. (2015). *The glass ceiling in Chinese and Indian boardrooms: Women directors in listed firms in China and India.* Elsevier.

Eagly, A. H., Eagly, L. L. C. A. H., Carli, L. L., & Carli, L. L. (2007). *Through the labyrinth: The truth about how women become leaders.* Harvard Business Press.

Fama, E. F. (1980). Agency problems and the theory of the firm. *Journal of Political Economy, 88*(2), 288–307.

Ferrant, G. (2009). A new way to measure gender inequalities in developing countries: The gender inequalities index (GII). *JEL classification, 16*, O11.

Forbes. (2019). Let's share women's mental load. *Forbes* https://www.forbes.com/sites/rachelcarrell/2019/08/15/lets-share-womens-mental-load/#493 16556bd61.

Fraser, S. (2003). *Cosmetic surgery, gender and culture.* New York: Palgrave Macmillan.

Geske Dijkstra, A. (2006). Towards a fresh start in measuring gender equality: A contribution to the debate. *Journal of Human Development, 7*(2), 275–283.

Gordini, N., & Rancati, E. (2017). Gender diversity in the Italian boardroom and firm financial performance. *Management Research Review*.

Greig, F., Hausmann, R., Tyson, L. D., & Zahidi, S. (2006). *The gender gap index 2006: A new framework for measuring equality*. The Global Gender Gap Report.

Harrison, D. A., & Klein, K. J. (2007). What's the difference? Diversity constructs as separation, variety, or disparity in organizations. *Academy of Management Review, 32*(4), 1199–1228.

Hausmann, R. (2009). *The global gender gap report 2009*. World Economic Forum.

Hausmann, R., Tyson, L. D., & Zahidi, S. (2006). *The global gender gap report 2006*. Geneva: World Economic Forum.

Humbert, A. L., Ivaškaitė-Tamošiūnė, V., Oetke, N., & Paats, M. (2015). *Gender equality index 2015—Measuring gender equality in the European Union 2005–2012: Report*. Vilnius, Lithuania: European Institute for Gender Equality. Retrieved from http://www.eige.europa.eu/sites/default/files/documents/mh0215616enn.pdf.

Johnson, W. B., & Smith, D. G. (2018). How men can become better allies to women. *Harvard Business Review, 11*.

Khandelwal, P. (2002). Gender stereotypes at work: Implications for organisations. *Indian journal of Training and Development, 32*(2), 72–83.

Klettner, A. 2016. Corporate governance codes and gender diversity: Management-based regulation in action. *UNSW Law Journal, 39*(2), 715–740.

Konrad, A. M., Kramer, V., & Erkut, S. (2008). The impact of three or more women on corporate boards. *Organizational Dynamics, 37*(2), 145–164.

Langevoort, D. C. (2004). Resetting the corporate thermostat: Lessons from the recent financial scandals about self-deception, deceiving others and the design of internal controls. *Geo. LJ, 93*, 285.

Machold, S., Huse, M., Hansen, K., & Brogi, M. (Eds.). (2013). *Getting women on to corporate boards: A snowball starting in Norway*. Edward Elgar Publishing.

Melaku, T. M., Beeman, A., Smith, D. G., & Johnson, W. B. (2020). Be a better ally. *Harvard Business Review, 98*(6), 135–139.

LeanIn.org, & McKinsey&Co. (2017). *Getting to gender equality starts with realizing how far we have to go*. Women in the Workplace 2017, Lean In and McKinsey and Co., https://womenintheworkplace.com/, 2013 Company Act. https://www.mca.gov.in/Ministry/pdf/CompaniesAct2013.pdf. Accessed on July 30, 2020.

Naff, Katherine C. (2018). *To look like America: Dismantling barriers for women and minorities in government*. Routledge.

Nielsen, S., & Huse, M. (2010). Women directors' contribution to board decision-making and strategic involvement: The role of equality perception. *European Management Review, 7*(1), 16–29.

Orazalin, N. (2019). Corporate governance and corporate social responsibility (CSR) disclosure in an emerging economy: Evidence from commercial banks of Kazakhstan. *Corporate Governance: The International Journal of Business in Society.*

Ragins, B. R., Townsend, B., & Mattis, M. (1998). Gender gap in the executive suite: CEOs and female executives report on breaking the glass ceiling. *Academy of Management Perspectives, 12*(1), 28–42.

Ridgeway, G. (2007). Generalized boosted models: A guide to the gbm package. *Update, 1*(1).

Rosenstein, S., & Wyatt, J. G. (1997). Inside directors, board effectiveness, and shareholder wealth. *Journal of Financial Economics, 44*(2), 229–250.

Shannon, C. (1948). A mathematical theory of communication. *Bell Systems Technological Journal, 27*, 379–423.

Sharma Radha, R. (2013). *Development and standardisation of perceived gender equity scale, gender diversity in India: An unpublished report.* Centre for Positive Scholarship. Management Development Institute, India.

Sharma, R. R., & Sharma, N. P. (2015). Opening the gender diversity black box: Causality of perceived gender equity and locus of control and mediation of work engagement in employee well-being. *Frontiers in Psychology, 6*, 1371. Published online 2015 October 9. https://doi.org/10.3389/fpsyg.2015.01371.

UN Women. (2018). *Turning promises into action: Gender equality in the 2030 agenda for sustainable development.* Retrieved from http://www.unwomen.org/-/media/headquarters/attachments/sections/library/publications/2018/sdgreport-gender-equality-in-the-2030-agenda-for-sustainable-development-2018-en.pdf?la=en&vs=4332

Valian, V. (1999). *Why so slow?: The advancement of women.* MIT press.

Van der Walt, N., Ingley, C., Shergill, G. S., & Townsend, A. (2006). Board configuration: Are diverse boards better boards?. *Corporate Governance: The International Journal of Business in Society, 6*(2), 129–147.

Wiley, C., & Monllor-Tormos, M. (2018). Board gender diversity in the STEM&F sectors: the critical mass required to drive firm performance. *Journal of Leadership & Organizational Studies, 25*(3), 290–308.

Williams, P., Kern, M. L., & Waters, L. (2016). Exploring selective exposure and confirmation bias as processes underlying employee work happiness: An intervention study. *Frontiers in Psychology, 7*, 878.

World Bank. (2012a). *Creating jobs good for development: Policy directions from the 2013 world development report on jobs.* Washington, DC: World Bank.

World Bank. (2012b). *World Bank Report 2013: Jobs*. Washington, DC: World Bank. https://doi.org/10.1596/978-0-8213-9575-2.

World Development Report 2012 (WDR). (2012). *Gender equality and development outline*. Washington, DC: World Bank. Available at: http://www-wds.worldbank.org/external/default/WDSContentServer/WDSP/IB/2010/11/03/000334955_20101103062028/Rendered/PDF/576270WDR0SecM1e0only1910BOX353773B.pdf..

World Development Report. (2013). *Jobs*. Accessible at: https://documents.worldbank.org/en/publication/documents-reports/documentdetail/884131468332686103/gender-at-work-a-companion-to-the-world-development-report-on-jobs.

World Economic Forum (WEF). (2018, December). *The future of jobs report 2018*. Geneva: World Economic Forum.

CHAPTER 12

Restoring the Leadership Balance: WOMEN UNITE

Joan Marques and Mercedes Coffman

INTRODUCTION

Women have regularly been described as natural leaders. In the surreal time of the 2020 pandemic, a Harvard Business Review article published data on the fact that countries with women in leadership had six times fewer confirmed deaths from Covid-19 than countries with governments led by men (Chamorro-Premuzic & Wittenberg-Cox, 2020). Chamorro-Premuzic and Wittenberg-Cox claim that there has been an overwhelming number of reports highlighting that female-led countries managed the crisis better. The praise was geared to these female leaders' individual strengths, such as the data-driven trustworthiness of Angela Merkel (Chancellor of Germany), the empathetic rationality of Jacinda Ardern (Prime Minister of New Zealand), and the quiet resilience of Tsai Ing-wen (President of Taiwan). The above trend is not a new one. Hernandez Bark, Escartín, Schuh and Dick (2016) confirmed that female leaders have been known to lead more effectively than male leaders.

J. Marques (✉) · M. Coffman
Woodbury University, Burbank, CA, USA
e-mail: Joan.Marques@woodbury.edu

Hernandez Bark et al. postulate that female leaders generally use more effective leadership styles than men, are financially more valuable for organizations, and bring more philanthropic and corporate social responsibility efforts to organizations they are involved with. Given the current awareness that soft skills, such as empathy, communication, and listening are the most appropriate ones to lead others, it therefore remains amazing that women only hold 21% of C-suite positions (Lipkin, 2019).

A factor to consider in the imbalanced leadership reality is the fact that many companies will claim on their websites and on public forums that they champion diversity, equity, and inclusion, but the compositions of their leadership teams blatantly and categorically deny this claim. The reason, according to King (2020) is denial. All of the 72 male and female senior executives King interviewed stressed the meritocratic nature of their workplace and the equal treatment all employees received. The argument for women to be less successful in reaching the C-Suite was, according to these senior executives, that women made different individual choices or had deviating capabilities. The problem was, in their opinion, not the hostility of their work environments.

Still, whether we choose to perceive women through their physical constitution to procreate, their intuitive skill to yield when necessary, or their innate grit to persevere long after others have given up: women have been the backbone of every human society. "When women succeed, the world succeeds," said House minority leader, Nancy Pelosi, at a 2017 rally on international women's day, March 8th, aimed at stepping up the rights for women (Zavis et al., 2017).

A Disheartening Reality

The fact that women seem to have downplayed their leadership skills for centuries might be explained by several factors. For starters, women have been instructed for the longest time, starting with their upbringing, that it's more suitable to be discreet and even downplay their qualities, compared to men who were encouraged from boyhood on to toot their own horn (Seale, 2019). Women who display any authority are labeled as bossy, whereas men exerting the same behavior are praised for being passionate. In addition, there is a mentorship gap when it comes to grooming women for leadership positions. This gap varies by ethnicity and is greater for black women than for white ones (Seale, 2019). These are all factors that add to the challenge of women making the progress they could have been making if we observe the percentages of college graduates in recent decades. Since 1981–1982, women have outperformed men consistently in the percentages of college graduations with women accounting for 57% of bachelor's degree earnings in 2016–2017 in the US (Matias, 2019). Yet, while women now represent half of the US-educated labor force, their rewards remain low compared to their male counterparts. The average male with a bachelor's degree outearns an equally credentialed woman by about $26,000 per year (Matias, 2019). While the gender gap in pay has narrowed since 1980, it has remained fairly consistent over the past 15 or more years. In 2017, women earned 82% of what men earned (Allen, 2018). While some sources argue that this has to do with the differences in the professional areas women primarily select—indicating that those are usually the lower paid fields—it still turns out that men in similar professions get paid more than women with equal credentials.

Considering the Origins

There is a subtle component that may contribute to the lingering status quo of professional male dominance; one that is not often addressed because it lies deeply in the emotional realm, and that is the fact that women are the bearers of the sons they eagerly want to see prospering, being acutely aware of these upcoming men's inherent limitations and deep-rooted vulnerabilities. Giancaterino (2010) describes the innate vulnerability of men as a paralyzing sense of loneliness and a lingering desire to obtain approval. According to Giancaterino, men have a greater need for belonging and connection, which may be originating from the irrefutable fact that, unlike women who come from women, men don't come from men. This undeniable truth may create a deeper need for connection within males, yet, as they grow up and realize that emotions are considered a sign of weakness, they unplug to an extent that their sensitivity becomes deeply buried under an exterior of stoicism and emotional indifference. McRae, Ochsner, Mauss, Gabrieli and Gross (2008) explain the lesser extent to which men reveal their feelings as a greater level of emotional regulation, and affirm that this doesn't mean that men have less emotional experiences, just that they withhold them more from showing. The above reasoning upholds that women, the bearers of men, are acutely aware of their sons' concealed vulnerabilities, and therefore support and protect them even more than they do other women. A survey by the website Netmums, polling 2,672 mothers led to the finding that more than one in five of the surveyed women (22%) agreed that they let their sons get away with more, turning a blind eye to behavior for which they would reprimand their daughters (*Mothers harder on daughters...*, 2010).

Considering the above issue from an opposite angle may partly address the arising counterargument that women are also the bearers of the daughters who are, till today, ruthlessly oppressed in multiple societies and the professional world, leading up to the question: if women are truly the societal backbone, why would they allow that to happen? The earlier mentioned article (*Mothers harder on daughters...*, 2010) revealed that mothers were twice as likely to be critical of their daughters than their sons (21% compared to 11.5%). The article subsequently alerts its readers that the parental disapproval girls receive growing up may be carried into their professional performance, leading up to self-deprecation, and subconscious preservation of the skewed power dynamics in workplaces.

A Recurring Story of Harsh Treatment

Another clarifying response may be that women are also acutely aware of the inner strength of their own kind, and therefore know that their "daughters," on average, have greater stamina to cope with challenges than the opposite sex. An interesting consideration, which is rather fascinating and conspicuous, is the entrenched competitiveness among women. In a 2016 article, Strauss addresses this issue, and cites a range of sources that support the hypothesis that women are harsher to one another in the workplace. Strauss (2016) mentioned surveys conducted through the years, that yield women rating other women lower 57% of the time, compared to their ratings of male colleagues, and reports that revealed discouraging degrees of workplace bullying from women toward one another than from the opposite sex. Strauss (2016) also mentioned a 2011 report from the American Management Association, which declared that about 95% of women have reportedly been "tormented" by another woman during their careers. University of Arizona management professor Allison Gabriel also conducted a study based on three surveys regarding women's attitudes toward one another in professional environments and found that "female-instigated incivility" (toward one another) is a very real trend. In other words: women are oftentimes meaner toward one another than men are toward them, and meaner than they are toward men (Ang, 2018). The tendency to penalize occurs particularly toward women who try to defy stereotypes, and are thereby seen as violating gender expectations. A resounding example is the case of Hillary Clinton, who received much more support from other women when she was the first lady (the stereotypical role) than when she was running for president (defying the stereotype) (Ang, 2018).

The tendency of women to be harder toward other women may, according to Strauss (2016), originate from a defense mechanism, triggered by perceived competition. Whether or not that is the case, clinical psychologist Seth Meyers (2013) reflects on decades of his work with women across numerous demographic variables, and finds that there is consistency in the harshness of women toward each other, to a greater extent than toward men. He makes reference to the reflections of many women who have explained their encounters with "mean girls" (female bullies) in the workplace, all seeming to have a tendency to socially exclude those they perceive as a potential threat. Indeed, there are many women who will confirm that their harshest critics and least supportive counterparts are not men but other women.

Presenting the term *relational aggression*, Crick and Grotpeter (1995) found that, in a study among 491 third- through sixth-grade children from public schools in the Midwest, this behavioral pattern was more characteristic of girls than of boys. The results of their study indicated that, as a group, girls were significantly more relationally aggressive than boys and, when relatively extreme groups of aggressive and nonaggressive children were identified, girls were more likely than boys to be represented in the relationally aggressive group (Crick & Grotpeter, 1995). These findings were confirmed in a subsequent study (Crick, Bigbee, & Howes, 1996). Meyers (2013), referring to Crick and Grotpeter's studies, infers that women's negative attitudes at work could be considered a manifestation of relational aggression. In support of the earlier presented argument of mothers being harsher toward their daughters than to their sons, Meyers also shares his experiences as a clinical psychologist in that regard, suggesting that women with greater degrees of relational aggression may have been raised by mothers who were excessively critical toward them, and potentially infused a negative mindset about women into them. Meyers finally calls for a deliberate effort from women to teach their daughters positive perspectives about other women, in order to groom them for support rather than opposition of one another in professional settings, as he sees this as the critical way to correct the status quo of women earning less, and holding fewer leadership positions compared to men.

Glass and Pink Ceilings

"The glass ceiling is a metaphor referring to an artificial barrier that prevents women and minorities from being promoted to managerial- and executive-level positions within an organization. The phrase "glass ceiling" is used to describe the difficulties faced by women when trying to move to higher roles in a male-dominated hierarchy. The barriers are most often unwritten, meaning that women are more likely to be restricted from advancing through accepted norms and implicit biases rather than defined corporate policies". (Kagan, 2019)

The glass ceiling was popularized in the 1980s and has been widely perceived as the most common thread for women and minority members to move upward in the corporate world. The term "pink ceiling" has not been addressed formally and expansively as the glass ceiling, but it also entails an informal and often undefined barrier for certain groups. It is based on a homophobic mindset, and forms a resistance to gay and lesbian workforce members in the ascent of their careers (Mitchell, 1999).

Even though there is abundant evidence of the increased quality that a diverse workforce represents for output and the bottom line, glass and pink ceilings are unfortunately still erected, invisible as they are. In addition, there is also a related term, the "glass cliff," which represents the instatement or promotion of women and minorities to positions in times of crisis, when there is an elevated chance for failure (Brooke-Marciniak, 2018; Kagan, 2019).

When glass and pink ceilings are mentioned, there is often a subtle implication that these barriers are erected and maintained by the "good old boys club." There is no doubt that much of these assumptions are correct, given the fact that this club is still very much in control of the C-suite. However, given the earlier mentioned tendencies of bullying, incivility, and relational aggression within the female cohort, the question that may arise is, who are the true designers of these barriers?

Allen (2018) posits that corporate culture and societal norms are definitely impeding factors in pay and positional gaps between men and women, but invites women to consider revisiting their approach in six areas that may contribute to their continued victimization.

1. Women should dare to negotiate harder and ask for extra perks. Allen (2018) states that, while women are superb negotiators, they often question their own value, and subsequently lack the courage to stand up for their own progress, not only in regards to the pay, but also when it comes to incentives.
2. Women should start valuing their talents more, and no longer avoid focusing on hard skills, which are also needed in professional settings. While soft skills are important in human interactions, it's equally advantageous to learn about strategy, finance, budgets, analytics, and performance metrics—factors that come across as impressive at the higher echelons of any organization (Allen, 2018).
3. Women should not shy away from conflict at work. Many women in the workplace fear being seen as overly emotional or aggressive, and subsequently avoid conflict at any cost. Unfortunately, postulates Allen (2018), this profiles them as weaker than they are, and allows others, oftentimes their male counterparts, to demand the credits for bold advocacy.
4. Women should examine their work ethics and their need for more flexibility, which makes their performance less impressive. The Bureau of Labor Statistics reports that men work an average of 14 hours more per month than women (*The Economics Daily*, 2015). Allen (2018) alerts that, while women need more flexible hours for an oftentimes understandable variety of reasons, workplaces are not required to adhere to these needs, and may decide to prefer other takers for demanding jobs. Allen therefore recommends to every woman to deeply consider the demands of a job before taking it on.
5. Women should include appropriate pace in their goals. This means that priorities and sacrifices have to be made, in the understanding that one cannot be everything to everyone at all times (Allen, 2018).
6. Women should be less risk-averse. Allen (2018) observes that performance penalties are a major turn-off to many women, leading to risk aversion, which often means, being stagnant in their performance.

With the six critical areas of attention and necessary attitudinal change in mind, Allen (2018) reiterates that there are many factors keeping the metaphorical ceilings intact, but there is also some work to be done by women in order to shatter them for good. Living in an era of exceptional paradigm transformations, it would befit all stakeholders in professional settings to engage in deep reflection in order to address all issues on the table.

WOMEN UNITE

The next section of this chapter presents ten reflective insights, which are captured in the acronym "WOMEN UNITE." The insights, formulated by the authors on basis of their diverse experiences, insights, and reflections as professional women, educators, supervisors, subordinates, and minorities, are intended as a support system for women who are eager to restore the leadership balance, and do so in a consciously and morally responsible way.

*W alk your talk:*This is an era where mutual support is promoted, and voices are raised for women to stand together. Welsh McNulty (2018) is a major advocate for women to unite and walk the mounting talk of mutual support, but she describes the experiences that led to her current actions and insights in an industry that is still solidly male-dominated at the top: the accounting field. She explains that the greatest downfall for women in many work environments is their lack of supportive action, and also clarifies why this seems to be perpetuated: it is because women who support younger women in workplaces usually get penalized by getting poorer ratings. As this has become widely known, women in higher position have become leery of supporting female protégés. Additionally, there is a space bias about the percentages of women that should be represented in leadership teams. Oftentimes, states Welsh McNulty (2018, companies consider their female top representation sufficient when there are two women in a leadership team of ten. These women at the top sometimes distance themselves from younger ones in order to be more accepted by the senior leadership in-group, thus securing their presence in the limited "space" they consider available for their gender. With a description of percentages for female representatives that steadily drop as we ascend levels in corporations, Welsh McNulty

(2018) also emphasizes the even greater absence of women of color in such circles. She therefore calls for more women support movements in workplaces, greater levels of socializing, and continuing to support younger female entrants until the tendency to be penalized for doing so gets defused. Welsh McNulty also emphasizes the importance of educating new female entrants that their tasks should not be the stereotypical ones—such as always taking care of the coffee—if they were not specifically hired to do so.

Open your heart: It's not easy to climb the career ladder as a woman—not even in these revolutionary times, but once you have landed a leadership position, release grudges and spiteful mannerisms. Turn inward instead, and generously grant others the opportunities that you had to fight for. Carboni, Cross, Page and Parker (2019) provide four useful considerations to women in making the best of their networks, while maintaining relations that provide heartfelt support: (1) Boundary-spanning—whereby it's not the size of a network that makes the positive difference, but the diversity of those one is connected with. Carboni et al. stress that remaining in one small interest world, even if it consists of many people, keeps perspectives and opportunities limited. Breadth in interest areas from a small group of connections is much more rewarding. (2) Efficiency—whereby a critical process of selecting through the many demands on one's time should be implemented in order to reduce stress and a sense of being overexerted. Carboni et al. (2019) posit that being strategic and thoughtful of one's time and well-being is of high importance, and this can only be done when one learns to say "no" more often. (3) Stickiness—whereby women have to understand the importance of maintaining *valuable* relationships—those that are constructive to their well-being and progress—and release connections that don't contribute to their advancement. While it may seem calculated, and Carboni et al. even drop the term "Machiavellian," the deeper and more sensible message here is that it is detrimental to hold on to obsolete relationships, since connections should be organic, and regularly examined on whether they still add value for all parties involved. (4) Trust, which is a critical aspect in any form of human connection. Carboni et al. (2019) distinguish between competence-based trust and benevolent trust. While competence-based trust is more attractive to men, benevolent trust seems to be far more preferred among women. This is the type of trust that garners mutual advancement in an environment of respect, honesty, and reliability.

Motivate others: The progress made by one woman can be a great motivator to others. However, attitude is a major determinant here. Since almost every woman has encountered one or more Queen Bee's in professional settings, and has suffered from relational aggression in more ways than one, there may be legitimate fear among younger women to approach more mature ones for guidance. But here is where some deep soul searching within the more seasoned women should emerge: we can either decide to exude a sense of arrogance by remaining distant, or we can embrace those who approach us for guidance, and help them believe in their ability to succeed.

Studies have revealed that women score lower in power motivation than men (Hernandez Bark et al., 2016). Power motivation describes interpersonal differences in the desire to influence others (McClelland, 1985). Fortunately, literature about transformational leadership has also established that women score higher in transformational leadership than men, which may be attributed to the feminine characteristics that lie at the foundation of this leadership style (Eagly, Johannesen-Schmidt & van Engen, 2003; Hernandez Bark et al., 2016). It is the desire to transform in which we can find influence, mentorship, and a drive to help others excel. Given these innate qualities of women, there is no reason why there could not be a concerted effort made in positively transforming upcoming women in workplaces through motivational practices.

Express your appreciation: We often underestimate how intimidating we may come across onto others, so making some extra effort in showing our sympathetic and supportive side can only do us (and others) a lot of good. Cancialosi (2016) warns that too much complaining, especially at work, brings people down, hurts morale, negatively affects productivity, looks unprofessional, and limits possibilities. Cancialosi (2016) reminds us that we harvest what we focus on, and when we focus on positive energy such as joy, integrity, or trust, we pave the way for these vibes to surround us, and realize that there is much to be appreciated every day anew. Cancialosi recommends to consider a pattern of six daily steps to groom us for greater appreciation: (1) choosing our attitude—regardless of our circumstances, we have the power to do that; (2) paying attention to the way we speak and the things we say—our language use can determine much of what we exude; (3) saying thank you—a simple gesture that can send a lot of positive triggers in the universe; (4) starting a gratitude journal to keep track of all our blessings; (5) asking for feedback to learn how to listen attentively and find out how we come across; and (6) shifting the narrative to positive rather than negative topics.

Nurture constructive habits: One of the main problems with successful people—men and women—is that they have become workaholics, unable to relax, because they have unlearned that part. Yet, what has been unlearned can be relearned. It's not easy, but it's rewarding. Webber (2014) describes the shift made by a software programmer, who was perceived as very successful, as he was making a great salary. Unfortunately, he felt desolate and depressed by his job. He ultimately decided to make the leap toward a more outdoors form of making a living, and found that, while he was making far less money, the quality of his life and his level of gratification was immensely higher. Webber (2014) emphasizes that there is no age barrier for a shift to constructive habits, and studies have revealed that even people over the age of 70 made changes in their lives that provided them a new burst of energy and fulfillment. Understanding your strengths, weaknesses, passions, and story can help you define what you really want in life, causing you to look at the world and match yourself up to opportunities (Webber, 2014).

Understand differences: One critical flaw in many leaders—male and female—is that they prefer team members with similar skills as they have, while they should actually be looking for complementary skills to form a harmonious and strong team. Inclusion of members of underrepresented groups has multiple advantages. It's not only the right thing to do in regards to humaneness, fairness, equity, and opportunity (the social justice case), but it also adds to a competitive advantage, as diverse teams tap from a broader base of insights, can solve problems in more creative ways, and therefore deliver greater innovation and productivity (the innovation case) (Woo & McIntosh, 2016). It's also important to note that diversity should not be limited to lower echelons of organizations, as this is exactly why so many women refrain from rising through the ranks. Surface-level diversity does not lead to creativity and innovation, but when diversity is thoroughly embedded and valued in an organization (deep-level diversity), there will be a clear positive effect on the team's creativity and innovation (Wang, Grand, Cheng, & Leung, 2019).

Navigate the path from here onward:If there's one thing none of us can afford, it's becoming stagnant and stale, especially in the case of women in supervisory positions. We should therefore never consider ourselves too old or too established to be expelled from our current position. Constant learning and evolving are keys to ongoing reinvention. Brenner (2018) offers five ways that can be constructive in regrouping, reprioritizing, renewing, and possibly even reinventing ourselves: (1) streamline your life, and a good way to start that is to declutter our direct surroundings, reorganize our priorities, and re-evaluate our commitments; (2) start something new—this can vary from taking a class, learning a new language volunteer somewhere, in short: doing something different that you consider fulfilling; (3) engage in a new practice—a constructive new, daily habit that can rejuvenate your degree of mindfulness—yoga, meditation, or exercise are some great and inexpensive options; (4) spend time in nature, as this confronts us with the cycle of life and can restore our appreciation for simple joys; (5) take a trip to a place—near or far—that you have not visited before. These outings oftentimes bring a sense of renewed energy and insights.

Instill values into actions: Being true to one's beliefs and values will ensure optimal satisfaction when looking back at a finalized career. Life presents numerous enticements to deviate us from our principles. Yet, we have the space and capacity to consider the many opportunities we receive to demonstrate our commitment. Selig (2018) suggests several ways to determine our primary values, which are the principles that give our lives meaning and allow us to persevere through difficult times. Some of those are, (1) list a large number of values, and then choose our top six to eight; (2) think of a few people (about five) you consider dear or admirable, and ask yourself why they are so important to you: this can reveal a set of values you consider important; (3) observe yourself and ask what you can learn from the choices you made, and (4) consider the highs and lows in your life, as there is a lot of value discovery to be done when evaluating your peaks and valleys.

Tread gently: It can be a tremendous challenge to remain gentle, especially when we had to overcome numerous obstacles on our way to where we currently are, but this doesn't give us a free card to pound on the souls of others. Uzzi (2019) has found that there is a difference between the networks of successful male and female leaders: while men benefit most from the connection points (centrality), women also need an inner circle of close female contacts to guide them through the cultural and political hurdles in workplaces that men don't have to worry about. This inner circle, a group of intimate contacts, should be small, and preferably not connected to similar clusters. Rather, the intimate contacts should derive from diverging circles, so that friction and the rise of potential relational aggression remains minimal. Being part of such an intimate circle of confidantes is an honor for life, and gives us a chance to build a legacy: it is a delicate and precious one, which we should cherish.

Excel where it matters: Getting ahead is great; making much money is admired; achieving the highest rank is commendable, but helping other living beings find happiness is the spice of life. It's therefore important to identify how to make a positive difference, and gear our energy in that direction. That's never a waste of time. Zalis (2019) underscores the success rate that results from women networking with and supporting one another. Referring to the term "power of the pack", she reveals the performance of some large women support groups, such as The FQ Lounge, which doesn't exclude the presence of men, but emphasizes the purpose of supporting females. Unlike an earlier presented statement from Welsh McNulty (2018), Zalis (2019) claims that women who support other women are more successful. She also advises to take the word "work" out of networking, because many women shy away or stress about the requirement to connect with others in order to progress on the corporate ladder. However, when this is done in a meaningful way, it may result in lifelong bonds.

The ten insights above, representing the acronym *WOMEN UNITE*, are intended to encourage female (and male) leaders to reconnect with their empathetic side, and build a legacy that will progressively make them feel happier and fulfilled as they reach the stage of passing the baton.

Chapter Takeaways

- Women have regularly been described as natural leaders and have been confirmed to lead more effectively than male leaders, yet, they only hold 21% of C-suite positions.

  The fact that women seem to have downplayed their leadership skills for centuries could be explained by several factors, some of which are:

  - Women have been instructed for the longest time that it's more suitable to be discreet and even downplay their qualities.
  - There is a mentorship gap when it comes to grooming women for leadership positions.
  - Women are the bearers of the sons they eagerly want to see prospering, being acutely aware of these upcoming men's inherent limitations and deep-rooted vulnerabilities.

- A negative tendency among women is *female-instigated incivility*: 95% of women have reportedly been "tormented" by another woman during their careers. Women are oftentimes meaner toward one another than men are toward them, and meaner than they are toward men.
- Another tendency that women often display against one another is *relational aggression*: studies of school children showed that this behavioral pattern was more characteristic of girls than of boys.
- The phrase "glass ceiling" is used to describe the difficulties faced by women when trying to move to higher roles in a male-dominated hierarchy. Even though there is evidence of the increased quality that a diverse workforce represents for output and the bottom line, glass and pink ceilings are unfortunately still erected, invisible as they are.
- "WOMEN UNITE" is an acronym intended to serve as a support system for women who are eager to restore the leadership balance, and doing so in a consciously and morally responsible way.

  - *Walk your talk*: This is an era where mutual support is promoted, and voices are raised for women to stand together. The greatest downfall for women in many work environments is their lack of supportive action.
  - *Open your heart*: Turn inward and generously grant others the opportunities that you had to fight for.

- *Motivate others:* The progress made by one woman can be a great motivator to others. We can either decide to exude a sense of arrogance by remaining distant, or we can embrace those who approach us for guidance, and help them believe in their ability to succeed.
- *Express your appreciation:* Making some extra effort in showing our sympathetic and supportive side can only do us (and others) a lot of good.
- *Nurture constructive habits:* Understanding your strengths, weaknesses, passions, and story can help you define what you really want in life, causing you to look at the world and match yourself up to opportunities.
- *Understand differences:* Look for complementary skills to form a harmonious and strong team. Inclusion of members of under-represented groups has multiple advantages. It's not only the right thing to do, but it also adds to a competitive advantage.
- *Navigate the path from here onward:* If there's one thing none of us can afford, it's becoming stagnant and stale. Constant learning and evolving are keys to ongoing reinvention.
- *Instill values into actions:* Being true to one's beliefs and values will ensure optimal satisfaction when looking back at a finalized career.
- *Tread gently:* It can be a tremendous challenge to remain gentle, especially when we had to overcome numerous obstacles on our way to where we currently are, but this doesn't give us a free card to pound on the souls of others. Being part of an intimate circle of confidantes is an honor for life.
- *Excel where it matters*: Identify how to make a positive difference, and gear our energy in that direction. That's never a waste of time.

References

Allen, T. (2018, August 25). Six hard truths for women regarding the glass ceiling. *Forbes.* Retrieved from https://www.forbes.com/sites/terinaallen/2018/08/25/six-6-hard-truths-for-women-regarding-that-glass-ceiling/#11694079427f.

Ang, K. (2018, March 5). Why women are meaner to each other than men are to women. *MarketWatch*. Retrieved from https://www.marketwatch.com/story/why-women-are-meaner-to-each-other-than-men-are-to-women-2018-03-05.

Brenner, A. (2018, April 8). 5 Ways to Regroup, Reprioritize, and Renew Yourself Get yourself in rhythm with spring renewal. *Psychology Today*. Retrieved from https://www.psychologytoday.com/us/blog/in-flux/201804/5-ways-regroup-reprioritize-and-renew-yourself.

Brooke-Marciniak, B. (2018). From glass ceiling to glass cliff: Women are not a leadership quick-fix. *Pakistan & Gulf Economist, 37*(52), 83.

Cancialosi, C. (2016, February 16). The surprising power of appreciation at work. *Forbes*. Retrieved from https://www.forbes.com/sites/chriscancialosi/2016/02/16/the-surprising-power-of-appreciation-at-work/#617ac7464681.

Carboni, I., Cross, R., Page, A., & Parker, A. (2019, September). How successful women manage their networks. *Connected Commons*. https://connectedcommons.com/wp-content/uploads/2019/09/how-successful-women-manage-their-networks-v2.pdf.

Chamorro-Premuzic, T. & Wittenberg-Cox, A. (2020, June 26). Will the pandemic reshape notions of female leadership? *Harvard Business Review*. Retrieved from https://hbr.org/2020/06/will-the-pandemic-reshape-notions-of-female-leadership.

Crick, N. R., & Grotpeter, J. K. (1995). Relational aggression, gender, and social-psychological adjustment. *Child Development, 66*(3), 710–722.

Crick, N. R., Bigbee, M. A., & Howes, C. (1996). Gender differences in children's normative beliefs about aggression: How do i hurt thee? Let me count the ways. *Child Development, 67*(3), 1003–1014.

Eagly, A. H., Johannesen-Schmidt, M. C., & van Engen, M. (2003). Transformational, transactional, and laissez-faire: A meta-analysis comparing men and women. *Psychological Bulletin, 129,* 569–591.

Giancaterino, W. (2010, January 11). Are men more vulnerable? Men are so sensitive they literally unplug from their emotional lives. *Psychology Today*. Retrieved from https://www.psychologytoday.com/us/blog/men-and-matters-the-heart/201001/are-men-more-vulnerable.

Hernandez Bark, A., Escartín, J., Schuh, S., & Dick, R. (2016). Who leads more and why? a mediation model from gender to leadership role occupancy. *Journal of Business Ethics, 139*(3), 473–483.

Kagan, J. (2019, October 24). Glass ceiling. *Investopedia: Salaries and compensation*. Retrieved from https://www.investopedia.com/terms/g/glass-ceiling.asp.

King, M. (2020, June 19). Leaders, Stop denying the gender inequity in your organization. *Harvard Business Review*. Retrieved from https://hbr.org/2020/06/leaders-stop-denying-the-gender-inequity-in-your-organization.

Lipkin, N. (2019, November 19). Why women are natural born leaders. *Forbes*. Retrieved from https://www.forbes.com/sites/nicolelipkin/2019/11/19/why-women-are-natural-born-leaders/#515d37d66641.

Matias, D. (2019, June 20). New report says women will soon be majority of college-educated U.S. workers. *National Public Radio, Inc.* Retrieved from https://www.npr.org/2019/06/20/734408574/new-report-says-college-educated-women-will-soon-make-up-majority-of-u-s-labor-f.

McClelland, D. C. (1985). *Human motivation*. Glenview, IL: Scott Foresman.

McRae, K., Ochsner, K. N., Mauss, I. B., Gabrieli, J., & Gross, J. J. (2008). Gender differences in emotion regulation: An fMRI study of cognitive reappraisal. *Group Processes & Intergroup Relations, 11*(2), 143–162.

Meyers, S. (2013, September 24). Women who hate other women: The psychological root of snarky: Women are often harder on each other than men are on each other. *Psychology Today*. Retrieved from https://www.psychologytoday.com/us/blog/insight-is-2020/201309/women-who-hate-other-women-the-psychological-root-snarky.

Mitchell, J. (1999, 06). The pink ceiling: The macho bay street culture can be hostile to anyone who doesn't play by its rules. for gays, the price is often a high one. *Report on Business Magazine, 15*, 78–84.

Mothers 'harder on daughters than sons', poll suggests (2010, October 6). *BBC News*. Retrieved from https://www.bbc.com/news/education-11476561.

Seale, C. (2019, June 14). Why a post about women downplaying their awesomeness went viral. *Forbes*. Retrieved from https://www.forbes.com/sites/colinseale/2019/06/14/why-a-post-about-women-downplaying-their-awesomeness-went-viral/#84202221a4d3.

Selig, M. (2018, November 4). 6 ways to discover and choose your core values. *Psychology Today*. Retrieved from https://www.psychologytoday.com/us/blog/changepower/201811/6-ways-discover-and-choose-your-core-values.

Strauss, K. (2016, July 18). Women in the workplace: Are women tougher on other women? *Forbes*. Retrieved from https://www.forbes.com/sites/karstenstrauss/2016/07/18/women-in-the-workplace-are-women-tougher-on-other-women/#e857347ea9b1.

The Economics Daily. (July 2, 2015). Time spent working by full- and part-time status, gender, and location in 2014. US Bureau of Labor Statistics. Retrieved from https://www.bls.gov/opub/ted/2015/time-spent-working-by-full-and-part-time-status-gender-and-location-in-2014.htm.

Uzzi, B. (2019, February 25). Research: Men and women need different kinds of networks to succeed. *Harvard Business Review*. Retrieved from https://hbr.org/2019/02/research-men-and-women-need-different-kinds-of-networks-to-succeed.

Wang, J., Cheng, Grand H.-L., Chen, T., & Leung, K. (2019). Team creativity/innovation in culturally diverse teams: A meta-analysis. *Journal of Organizational Behavior, 40*(6), 693–708.

Webber, R. (2014, May 6). Reinvent yourself. *Psychology Today*. Retrieved from https://www.psychologytoday.com/ca/articles/201405/reinvent-yourself.

Welsh McNulty, A. (2018, September 3). Power of women supporting each other at work. *Harvard Business Review*. Retrieved from https://hbr.org/2018/09/dont-underestimate-the-power-of-women-supporting-each-other-at-work.

Woo, M., & McIntosh, K. W. (2016). Why diverse teams matter. *EDUCAUSE Review, 51*(3), 54.

Zalis, S. (2019, March 6). Power of the pack: Women who support women are more successful. *Forbes*. Retrieved from https://www.forbes.com/sites/shelleyzalis/2019/03/06/power-of-the-pack-women-who-support-women-are-more-successful/#1630bbf81771.

Zavis, A., King, L., Jarvie, J. & Demick, B. (2017, March 8). 'Women are the backbone of this country': Thousands across the nation skip work, wear red and rally. *Los Angeles Times*—World and Nation. Retrieved from https://www.latimes.com/world/la-na-day-without-a-woman-20170308-story.html.

CHAPTER 13

What Hinders Me from Moving Ahead? Gender Identity's Impact on Women's Entrepreneurial Intention

Eleftheria Egel

What we believe to be possible defines what we are capable of creating.
— Nassim Haramein, Unified Physicist.

INTRODUCTION

The Global Entrepreneurship Monitor (GEM) *2018–2019 Women's Report*, found that the global TEA[1] rate for women is 10.2%—approximately 3/4 of that seen for men. The GEM Report also divides entrepreneurial activity into two categories. First, necessity-driven entrepreneurship, which can be caused by a lack of formal employment

---

[1]Total Entrepreneurial Activity (TEA) represents the % of the adult working-age population (18–64) who are either nascent or new entrepreneurs

---

E. Egel (✉)
Navigating Transformation, Female Entrepreneurship Consultancy, Muellheim, Germany
e-mail: NavigatingTransformation@amfortas.eu

J. Marques (ed.), *Exploring Gender at Work*,
https://doi.org/10.1007/978-3-030-64319-5_13

opportunities in a country or personal necessity (e.g., single mother household), and second, innovation-driven entrepreneurialism, which exists in countries with well-developed formal job markets. Low-income countries report the highest rates of women's necessity-driven TEA at 15.1%. Also more women (27%) around the globe started their businesses "out of necessity," compared to men (21.8%). Conversely, fewer women (68.4%) started their companies "to pursue an opportunity" than men (74%), resulting in what GEM calls a "7% gender gap."

Entrepreneurial intention (EI) is defined as the expressed behavioral intention to become an entrepreneur (Bird, 1988). It is considered as the most critical factor for predicting a business start-up. Therefore, exploring the building blocks necessary to develop entrepreneurial intention is pivotal in understanding or predicting how a person becomes an entrepreneur (Boudreaux, Nikolaev, & Klein, 2019; Tsai, Chang, & Peng, 2016). One of the building blocks of EI is entrepreneurial self-efficacy (ESE). According to a growing body of academic research ESE is a predictor of an individual's propensity to engage in entrepreneurial action (e.g., ; Baron, 2006; Boyd & Vozikis, 1994; Rauch & Frese, 2007; Sequeira et al., 2007; Welpe, Spörrle, Grichnik, Michl, & Audretsch, 2012; Zhao, Seibert, & Hills, 2005).

The concept of entrepreneurial self-efficacy is derived from social cognitive theory (SCT) (Bandura, 1977). Self-efficacy has been defined as a "...belief in one's capabilities to mobilize the motivation, cognitive resources, and courses of action needed to meet given situational demands..." (Wood & Bandura, 1989, p. 408). Self-efficacy is based upon past experience and anticipation of future obstacles and affects one's beliefs about whether or not specific goals are attainable (Gist & Mitchell, 1992). It accordingly influences an individual's choice of activities, goal levels, persistence, and performance in a range of contexts. If self-efficacy is low, an individual will not act, even if there is perceived social approval for that behavior (Boyd & Vozikis, 1994). In the context of entrepreneurship, self-efficacy refers to the belief entrepreneurs have in their own skills and capabilities to start and run new business ventures (McGee et al., 2009). Boyd and Vozikis (1994) were the first who theorized that self-efficacy influences the development of entrepreneurial intentions and hence the probability of venture creation. More recently, Zhao et al. (2005) proposed a predictive model of entrepreneurial intentions in which self-efficacy plays a critical mediating role. Entrepreneurial self-efficacy (ESE) develops over time and is influenced by a number of external and internal factors such as upbringing, economic circumstances, personality traits, and values (Altinay, Madanoglu, Daniele, & Lashley, 2012; Cox, Mueller, & Moss, 2002). It is also affected by national or regional context to the extent that opportunities for gaining confidence through experience and role modelling are prevalent, thereby enhancing ESE, or limited, thereby reducing ESE (Mueller & Goic, 2003).

Personality traits form an important part of individuals' personal identities (Zee, Atsma, & Brodbeck, 2004). In this paper I focus on how personality traits and, consequently, personal identities affect women's ESE.

In the following section I try to elucidate how a female entrepreneur's identity is shaped by their broader self-concept. First, I explain the notion of women's multiple identities from a psychodynamic perspective and second, I explore how these multiple identities shape their entrepreneurial self-efficacy and intention to start a business.

Female Entrepreneurs' Identity

The self is not a unitary whole. Instead, it is a shifting dynamic constellation of core and secondary affective-cognitive self-schemas moving in a continuum between "self-assigned" to "attributed by others"; a form of compromise between preferred and imputed designations, that act as a self-regulating mechanism for behaviors (Lord & Brown, 2001). These self-schemas are called identities (Baumeister, Bratslavsky, Muraven, & Tice, 1998; Snow & Anderson, 1987). Identity refers to subjective knowledge, meanings, and experience, to our ongoing efforts to address the twin questions, "Who am I?" and—by implication—"how should I act?" "Who I am" encompasses the notion of our possible selves, i.e., our ideas about who we might become, would like to become, or fear becoming (Gergen & Gergen, 1988; Markus & Nurius, 1986). The locus of individual identity is neither fully internal (e.g., I determine that I am a leader) nor completely external (e.g., it is not imposed through socioeconomic factors). It depends upon both one's personal identity (physical and psychological attributes) (e.g., height, disabilities, intelligence, extrovert nature) and the social identity that is shaped from one's relationships with others—group identities (e.g., gender, nationality, religion) and role identities (e.g., mother, spouse, entrepreneur). Although individuals have numerous social roles (e.g., student, spouse, and worker) they develop role identities only for those roles that they internalize into their self-concept (Donahue, Robins, Roberts, & John, 1993). These role identities represent the characteristics a person ascribes to him or herself in a particular role. Some individuals develop role identities that vary considerably across roles, whereas others develop role identities that are essentially the same across roles. For example, one woman might see herself as fun, living, and easygoing with her friends but as serious and reserved at work.

The meanings that individuals attach to themselves as a function of their multiple social group and role memberships are called multiple identities. It is obvious that the dynamic and unique interaction among an individual's personal identity and their multiple identities differentiates their self-concept and functions as a resource for personal and work relationships and continued identity development (Rothbard, 2001). The depth and the quality of the interaction among multiple identities is better understood using a psychodynamic lens which takes into account the impact of the unconscious (drives and forces within a person) to the conscious. Whereas Sigmund Freud's psychoanalysis was the original psychodynamic theory, the psychodynamic approach evolved as a whole and today includes all theories that were based on Freud's original ideas; such as, the theories of Carl Jung, Melanie Klein, Alfred Adler, Anna Freud, and Erik Erikson. All these theories—despite their differences—share some common fundamental principles, the most relevant of which for this article are the following: First, the unconscious is largely a vast interior and more primitive domain than the conscious. Second, the conscious is a field of awareness in the everyday waking rational state. Third, identities can be contradictory and in conflict. Fourth, there are psychological defenses that can hinder identity integration and development. Fifth, identity development is not a linear process but rather one that involves gains and losses (DeRue, Ashford, & Cotton, 2009; Ford & Mouzas, 2010; Nicholson & Carroll, 2013; Petriglieri, Ashford, Wrzesniewski, 2019).

How Do These Multiple Identities Impact Women's Entrepreneurial Self-efficacy?

I will try to answer this question by exploring how the five fundamental principles of multiple identities I referred to above play out for female entrepreneurs. The first principle influences—without women realizing it—the way they perceive their choices in their lived reality (second principle), creating, thus, the unseen framework of being (ontology) within which the remaining three principles are manifested. As the female entrepreneur's identity needs to be integrated within their self-concept, if their identity as entrepreneurs is not compatible with their existent multiple identities, this may lead to conflict between their new identity (entrepreneur's) and one or more of their opposing existent multiple identities (e.g., mother's, spouse's, employee's) (third principle). If the conflict is intense, the female entrepreneur may then turn to a defense mechanism to cope with the conflict, such as justification of the conflict (fourth principle). If no integration is achieved that will strengthen their entrepreneurial self-efficacy, the female entrepreneur prefers to discard their entrepreneurial identity (fifth principle) for fear they will not make it. Research has shown that ESE is influenced by how far the entrepreneur believes their own personality traits match the task demands of entrepreneurship as well as on the entrepreneur's perception about the outcome anticipated. ESE, in its turn, impacts EI. Founding and managing a new business venture requires an entrepreneur to fulfil a number of unique task demands or work roles such as innovator, risk taker and bearer, executive manager, relationship builder, risk reducer, and goal achiever (Chen, Greene, & Crick, 1998). If an individual's self-efficacy is low their self-perceived match between their own personality traits and the task demands of entrepreneurship won't be present (Zhao, Seibert, & Lumpkin, 2010). Concerning an individual's perception about the anticipated success or failure of their venture, few people form intentions about engaging in entrepreneurial activities if they believe there is a high probability of failure.

First I will explicate how the unconscious—("the androcentric cosmology") (Bourdieu, 2001, p.6)—influences the conscious (women's gender identity) and consequently women's self-concept. Humans perceive reality as a dualistic system of polarities (univocal determinacy). We use a system of binary oppositions to categorize reality; such as—up/down, above/below, in front of/behind, light/dark, good/bad, outside(public)/inside (private). These categorizations divide our perception of the world into univocal "either/or; i.e., one thing can have only one meaning. Male/female is another opposition which implies that male cannot be female and vice versa. In his "practice theory" (2003), Bourdieu goes one step further to explicate that dualism is prejudiced as it has imposed the androcentric cosmology—also named patriarchy or masculine order—as neutral. As such, it has legitimized (i.e., socially constructed) its arbitrary division of the sexes—which appears to be "in the order of things" and therefore inevitable: sexual division of labor (e.g., doctor/nurse or executive/secretary), the place of activities assigned to each sex (e.g., the market reserved for men, and the house, reserved for women), the life cycle (male moments of rupture and the long female periods of gestation). It has reigned for so long that no one denies its legitimacy. According to Bourdieu, the process of legitimation of masculine dominion has been imposed with "symbolic violence"—"a gentle violence, imperceptible and invisible even to its victims exerted for the most part through the purely symbolic channels of communication and cognition, recognition or even feeling..." (2001, p. 2). Symbolic violence is the moving power of the socially constructed immense symbolic machine that creates and feeds a vicious circle: The gendered and prejudiced deep-rooted social and cultural scripts (i.e., ideas, relationships, power differences) combine with material factors to create social positions and to set the context for social action. They, in their turn, lead to the social reproduction of existing social norms, ideals, and expectations and related systems of belief and individual agency (Foschi, 2000; Sidanius, Pratto, Van Laar, & Levin, 2004). In this (re-)distribution resources and rights are allocated accordingly (Elam, 2014; Ridgeway & Correll, 2004; Ridgeway & Smith-Lovin, 1999). For instance, research on financing of new ventures has shown that when resources are scarce, they are seen as better directed toward more legitimate and established firms, which tend to be businesses led by men. Not to oversee is the fact that men's businesses are often located in higher margin industries whereas women's businesses are primarily concentrated in lower margin industries; mainly retail and services (Brush, Carter, Gatewood, Greene, & Hart, 2004; Edelman, Manolova, & Welter, 2019).

As symbolic violence does not operate at the level of conscious intention, even the best-intentioned men perform discriminatory acts by constructing the diminished situation of women and eventually excluding them. Bourdieu gives some characteristic examples: when women take part in a public debate, they must fight unceasingly for a chance to speak and to keep attention. Concerning the evaluation of male and female activities: whereas being a cook or a seamstress is considered easy and futile when performed by women, when it is performed by a man outside the private sphere it is considered noble and difficult. The man is now called chef and couturier. As a result, every masculine endeavor is considered more important than a feminine one and women, subconsciously accept that their modus operandi is inferior to that of men (Egel, 2020).

The prejudiced domination of the masculine has resulted in entrepreneurship to be generally characterized as a male-type activity in terms of both social structure and influence. Entrepreneurship is heavily influenced by family status and social networks (Ahl, 2004; Baker, Aldrich, & Liou, 1997; Brush, 1992; Jennings & Brush, 2013). Aldrich (1989), for instance, pointed that women hold a different view of reality that emanates from social structures, such as the workplace, marriage, family, and social life. Another outcome is that female entrepreneurs view themselves as limited in the way they understand the world around them and approach other people, but also in their future aspirations (Eddleston & Powell, 2008; Hoang & Gimeno, 2010). It is no wonder, then, that women are, on average, about half as likely as men to start businesses and much less likely to start high-growth, high-profit firms (Acs, Arenius, Hay, & Minniti, 2005; Reynolds, Bygrave, & Aution, 2004). On the other hand, as I explained in the introductory section, women's rates are higher than those of men in necessity-driven entrepreneurship where women are called to carry the family load (GEM, 2018/2019).

Let us now explore how the gendered approach to entrepreneurship impacts women's entrepreneurial self-efficacy and intention to start a business by using the remaining three principles of multiple identities seen from a psychodynamic perspective I referred to above.

A person's entrepreneurship identity is situated within their broader self-concept. In becoming an entrepreneur, people face the challenge of integrating a new entrepreneur identity with their other valued (central) identities. To accommodate their entrepreneur role demands, female entrepreneurs need to modify role definitions (e.g., spouse, employee) and achieve a new synthesis among their multiple important identities (adaptation) (Ashforth & Schinoff, 2016; Nicholson, 1984). When the other identities (e.g., that of a mother) are equally important but the cultures associated with them are not complementary (e.g., being a parent and a spouse) but opposing (e.g., being a parent versus being an entrepreneur), it will more probably lead to interference between these identities, conflict and eventually—if integration is not achieved—to a number of defensive behaviors as a means of coping with conflict (Argyris, 2004; Settles, 2004; Thoits, 1991). For example, women entrepreneurs may distance themselves from their identity as a mother (avoidance of identity conflict). Or, women entrepreneurs may feel shame when they perceive that their entrepreneurial identity is in conflict with a socially valued identity (e.g., spouse). Potential outcomes of dissonance are reduced physical and psychological well-being, self-confidence, work performance, creativity, and work engagement (Cheng et al., 2008; Graves, Ohlott, & Ruderman, 2007; Rothbard, 2001; Settles, Sellers, & Damas, 2002).

Here below, I am using the psychodynamic lens to explore how the multiple identity conflict plays out for female would-be entrepreneurs.

For women aspiring to become entrepreneurs, their complementary traditional identities (e.g., being a mother, a spouse, an employee, a necessity-driven entrepreneur) are opposed to being an innovation-driven entrepreneur. The gendered approach to entrepreneurship as I explained above (first and second principles) creates two obstacles: First, women believe that they do not have the required qualities to succeed; and second, they are afraid that their choice to become entrepreneurs may endanger their social belonging. Both obstacles reduce women's self-efficacy and accordingly their intention to start a business. Entrepreneurship, similarly to traditional leadership- is associated with "male" qualities such as aggressiveness, achievement orientation, dominance, independence, challenge, and high risk-taking (Ahl, 2006; Buttner & Moore, 1997; Egel, 2020; Gupta, Turban, Wasti & Sikdar, 2009; Stewart & Roth, 2001). For instance, women tend to avoid risk or, rather, become less involved in situations with vague success (Orobia & Rooks, 2011; Powell & Ansic, 1997; Sexton & Bowman-Upton, 1990). Van Gelderen, Atsma and Brodbeck (2008) demonstrated that men value challenge and autonomy more than women, while women value financial security and workload. Eagley and Karau (2002) with their role congruity theory showed that men and women choose jobs with characteristics that comply with their individual characteristics. Since men exhibit entrepreneurial characteristics to a higher degree, women anticipate a misfit between their traits and behaviors and those required to become a successful entrepreneur. Hence, self-identification decreases, and cognitive dissonances occur (Haus, Steinmetz, Kabst, & Isidor, 2013; Marlow, 2002; Marlow & Patton, 2005; Shibley Hyde & Kling, 2001). Coming to the second obstacle—that of social belonging—social identity theory states that people define themselves as being members of an in-group that has significantly different attributes from an out-group (Tajfel & Turner, 1986). Members of the in-group evaluate activities by whether they are in line with a social identity prototype—a "fantasy"—and are more likely to conduct activities that fit or approach as much as possible their prototype. Their self-esteem derives from that identity. Its height depends on the extent to which they feel they can live up to that idealized, fantastic image (Ashforth & Kreiner, 1999; Tajfel & Turner, 1986). This idealized image defines what success, achievement, and status mean. Accordingly, it is used by the individual and the in-group to determine who belongs in the group and also the perceived negative attributes of the out-group (Brown & Starkey, 2000). Having a clear idea of expectations and boundaries helps the individual to feel safe and develop a sense of belonging. A perfected ideal to look up to also provides important defenses when individuals confront difficult or impossible tasks (Abrams & Hogg, 1988; Stryker & Burke, 2000). For women, their in-group comprises women who hold traditional roles. Being part of the group and being successful is being in line with the traditional feminine identity prototype—as I described it above (Bourdieu, 2001/2003). The out-group—the vast world of male entrepreneurship—considers female entrepreneurship as less desirable and does not provide adequate normative societal support (Baughn, Chua, & Neupert, 2006) leading to women having less self-efficacy and being afraid to start a business. Bandura (1993) found that social persuasion—ranging from positive encouragement of friends and family to professional support from bankers and accountants—can affect self-efficacy. Individuals who are persuaded verbally that they possess the skills and talent to achieve certain goals are more likely to put forth greater effort than those who may have self-doubts.

That explains partially why women reported having lower confidence levels than men in their capabilities to start a business in the GEM *2018–2019 Women's Report*. Overall, men are about 10% more likely to be undeterred by fear of failure than women. This can also be the reason why women more often pursue opportunities in more competitive, low margin industries or markets. This results in very different business goals, business models, and outcomes. Women also encounter interpersonal dynamics at the business level that reinforce traditional gender hierarchies, male dominance, and undermine personal agency, self-confidence, and professional legitimacy (Hechavarria at al., 2017; Ridgeway & Smith-Lovin, 1999). Research conducted at women-owned businesses aligns with these findings. Women-owned businesses have been found to have lower levels of growth and remain smaller than men-owned businesses (Cliff, 1998; Coleman, 2016; Davis & Shaver, 2012).

How can female would-be entrepreneurs integrate their entrepreneurial identity within their broader self-concept?

Women aspiring to start-up a high growth business need to engage in identity work that will help them integrate their entrepreneurial identity successfully within their existent network of valued personal and social identities. The identity integration process is dynamic and continuous as new events can potentially lead to new forms of identity conflict among multiple identities (Goss &Sadler-Smith, 2018). As I explicated above, women's entrepreneurial identity (esp. for innovation-driven start-ups) is opposing to their other valued identities (e.g., a woman entrepreneur cannot be both a mother and a computer geek). It is only when their entrepreneurial identity becomes complementary (i.e., a woman entrepreneur can be both a mother and a computer geek) and success-fully interacts with the other valued identities (e.g., being a mother offers support to starting an AI venture) (Ibarra, Snook, & Guillen Ramo, 2010; Kets & Vries, 2006) that the female entrepreneur can create a new internal model which comes in terms with and, within limits, influences the various social identities. It is only then that the female entrepreneur has the potential to reach a coherent self-concept (Amiot, De la Sablon-niere, Terry, & Smith, 2007; Down & Reveley, 2009; Petriglieri & Petriglieri, 2010). Nicholson and Carroll (2013) describe the integra-tion process as "identity undoing" (p. 1226). It carries the challenge that-if other identities become destabilized and unraveled—can result in displacing or devaluing a prior or existing identity (identity loss). With the right support, though, identity undoing can release a person's fixed assumptions of gender and entrepreneurship, resist the pressures of conforming to an existing model, and open up possibilities for integrating a new entrepreneurial identity with one's valued identities.

How Do We Make Sure
that Identity Undoing Is Positive?

In order to transform our lived reality, we need to be fully aware of our unconscious beliefs and how they play out to create and reinforce our experiences. I consider that the first step toward this direction is to adopt a different perspective on the way we evaluate reality. That means two things: First, we need to change our system of univocal determinacy which classifies reality into binary oppositions of "either/or"; i.e., what is "male" cannot be "female" and vice versa. Second, we need to redefine the "gender" of entrepreneurship; i.e., that not only "male" qualities (such as aggressiveness) are important for entrepreneurship.

As I explained above, our univocal perception of the world does not allow for reconciliation between antithetical concepts. Male/female is another opposition within a system of homologous oppositions; such as-up/down, above/below, light/dark, good/evil, intelligent/stupid which divides our perception of the world into univocal "either/or" (dualism). In between the antithetical concepts is a hiatus which does not allow for communication and consequently influence. Nowadays, a "male/masculine" cannot be conceived as "female/feminine" and vice versa. If a "male" shows female qualities this is criticized as a lessening of its "masculinity" and not as an "enrichment" of it and vice versa. The reason for that is the prejudiced gender division of the essence and the relationship of "male" and "female." "Female" qualities are considered to be of lesser quality than the "male" ones when we aim at "doing"—success, achievement, and leadership are three examples. Also, the "male" is more powerful than the "female" as it imposes the relational practices to be adopted. Accordingly, being a successful woman in a male domain can be regarded as a violation of gender norms, warranting sanctions. (Fletcher, 2004). The truth of this can be observed in innumerable cases in the business world. For example, women in positions of authority are thought too aggressive or not aggressive enough, and what appears assertive, self-confident, or entrepreneurial in a man often looks abrasive, arrogant, or self-promoting in a woman (Egel, 2020). In the same vein, when women performing traditionally male roles are seen as conforming to feminine stereotypes, they tend to be liked but are not respected. They are judged too soft, emotional, and unassertive to make tough decisions and to come across as sufficiently authoritative (Hellman & Okimoto, 2007).

To overcome this division, I propose that we need to shift from our univocal ("either/or") reasoning into an equivocal "both/end" perception of reality which accepts the space in between with its full relativity (Desmond, 1995/2012; Van den Auweele, 2018). First Plato, in his Dialogues, used the term "metaxu" (it means "in between" in Greek) to describe the experience of the space between our bodily existence and the otherness of consciousness. Postmodern thinkers have taken this concept to develop a new model of reality; the metaxological way of thinking. Metaxological ontology describes the non-dialectical relationality of things; the potencies of being. It leaves the in-between open and emphasizes the interplay between sameness and difference (e.g., Desmond, 2016; Voegelin, 2000). Voegelin (2000) uses "metaxu" to name the participatory mode of consciousness. The philosopher William Desmond, the father of metaxological metaphysics, claims that nothing is defined through itself alone. Beings are defined in a rich ontological intermedium of happening, and are both other-relating and self-relating. He uses the term "porosity" to describe the imagery of the in-between. It is not a neatly bounded moment that fulfils itself in becoming an object. The in-between is a subject that constantly transforms as, by its porous nature, it is not impervious to interaction. In our case, metaxological ontology would shift the prejudiced neutral ontology of patriarchy to a less prejudiced ontology of somewhere in-between in the continuum from male to female. This ontology would be less fixed, more fluid, defined, and shaped continuously through interaction and not progressing teleologically (e.g., Desmond, 2016; Voegelin, 2000). It would allow us to reason that the "male" does not exclude the "female" and the one does not need to fight against the other in order to fit into an ideal stereotypical image of masculinity or femininity which is imbued by power dynamics. It would reduce criticism against a man exhibiting "female" qualities (e.g., compassion) or a woman exhibiting "male" qualities (e.g., assertiveness). Accordingly, both identities could be complementary and not opposing in our self-concept; intermediaries within an endless continuum leading from "male" to "female" and vice versa.

The metaxological reasoning could also enable us to redefine the "gender" of entrepreneurship. Women who want to succeed in entrepreneurship think that they have to internalize a "masculine" approach and suppress their "inferior" "female" qualities (Egel, 2020). As a consequence, female entrepreneurs experience a role conflict trying to adapt to a prototypically male-oriented male entrepreneur identity model (Ely, Ibarra, & Kolb, 2011). If there was no masculine domination the connection of entrepreneurship with male qualities would fade and new models of entrepreneurship closer to a "female" conceptualization would have the potential to come forward. Research has shown that—compared to male entrepreneurs who focus on financial goals—female entrepreneurs tend to pursue noneconomic goals such as balancing work and family roles and have preferences for employee relationship and society satisfiers which in turn may detract from economic performance or growth (Eddleston &

Powell, 2008; Jennings & Brush, 2013). Hitherto, we have criticized such "female" approaches as success is equated with power, individualism, and performance. Since women do not score well in this equation, our collective mindset seems to believe that women are innately doomed to fail. The metaxological reasoning would reduce our fixation with "what is "and "what is not" as unaltered objects and guide us to examine everything in relationship. In that case, we could re-examine the definition of success and the purpose of business. An individualistic, "male" approach to business has been the source of many evils in our societies. It has led to irreparable damage of our social fabric and our environment (e.g., incessant competition, consumerism, depletion of natural resources). A "metaxu" worldview would enable new potentialities; new ways to envision business. For instance, we could reimagine business as a tool to solve societal problems and to allow individuals to express their innate creativity. Has the time come to embrace social entrepreneurship as our mainstream business model? How does that play out in numbers for women?

A few facts to reflect on:

An **OECD** working paper (Huysentruyt, 2014) found out that:

- The "gender gap" in social entrepreneurship was much smaller than the gender gap in "mainstream" entrepreneurship, suggesting that social entrepreneurship can be a powerful tool to increase female entrepreneurship and participation in the labor market.
- Social enterprises led by women and men were very similar in size, profitability, and growth.
- Women took the lead over male social entrepreneurs for new market creation—entering/pioneering new markets. More specifically, 62% of social ventures run by women were the first to provide this kind of service or product in their region, country, or worldwide in comparison with 54% of ventures run by men.

The **GEM 2015** Report on Social Entrepreneurship reported similar findings:

- The gender gap in social entrepreneurial activity was significantly smaller than the roughly 2:1 gender gap in commercial entrepreneurial activity found in some economies (55% male versus 45% female).

- Female-led social enterprises seemed to be *more innovative than men-led enterprises—especially when opening up new markets.* Perhaps due to their specific sensitivity toward social needs, women social entrepreneurs are notable 'lead innovators' when it comes to social innovation."
- Female-led social enterprises were also generally more participatory in terms of management, suggesting "the power of women social entrepreneurs to empower others (and in doing so, enabling colleagues to learn and develop important talents and skills)."

The findings of both reports resonate well with findings drawn from other sources of evidence. For instance, women's participation rate in the nonprofit sector (including paid employment) is higher than men's (Themudo, 2009). And even as commercial entrepreneurs, women seem to emphasize social goals more, and economic goals less relative to their male counterparts (Hechavarria, Renko, & Matthews, 2012). WEstart project initiated by the European Women's Lobby also supports the above findings. Women social entrepreneurs from 11 EU countries were interviewed and responded that their motivation to start a social enterprise was to respond to needs in the community and make a difference. Report further states: "In the countries studied, women described personally experiencing and witnessing unmet needs in their community and looking for innovative solutions that will bring about a specific social impact. They also describe feeling a personal calling towards social issues and a desire to make the world a better place with their work." Interestingly, very few women were interested in making a profit. "At the individual level, for 31% of women, seeking to make a profit was not a motivating factor. In relation to their household situation, the same applied with 47% of women reporting that 'seeking to support myself or my family as a primary earner' was not a motivating factor. Finally, leading a social enterprise appears to be out of choice, since for the majority of women (68%) unemployment or underemployment was not a motivating factor." Even when women considered the profitability of the enterprise to be important—mainly, women who were unemployed or in countries undergoing economic crisis—the social mission of the enterprise remained equally important (WeStart Project, 2018).

The above facts call for further reflection not only by female entrepreneurs but by all those involved in the entrepreneurial ecosystem.

Conclusion

In this study I explored theoretically the question why the number of start-ups by women worldwide still lags that of their male counterparts. I first established the link between entrepreneurial self-efficacy(ESE) and entrepreneurial intention (EI). Research has shown ESE is a predictor of an individual's propensity to engage in entrepreneurial action. Self-efficacy is influenced by personality traits; an important part of individuals' personal identities. Women with low self-efficacy hesitate to start a business; especially when this business is opportunity-driven. Then, I used a psychodynamic lens to look into how the female entrepreneurial identity fits with the other valued identities within a female entrepreneur's broad self-concept. I argued that a prejudiced gendered worldview with deep subconscious biases does not allow women's entrepreneurial identity to be complementary with their other important identities. It is opposing and creates identity conflict. Identity conflict leads to low self-esteem, reduced well-being, and performance. I suggested that women aspiring entrepreneurs need to engage in identity work in order to dissolve the inner conflict and embrace their entrepreneurial identity as being complementary with their other valued identities. I proposed metaxological thinking as an ontology that can assist women reconceptualize their entrepreneurial identity as complementary and not as opposing to their other valued identitities.

Chapter Takeaways

- The locus of individual identity depends upon both one's personal identity (physical and psychological attributes) and the social identity that is shaped from one's relationships with others—group identities and role identities.
- The depth and the quality of the interaction among multiple identities is better understood using a psychodynamic lens which takes into account the impact of the unconscious (drives and forces within a person) to the conscious.
- The prejudiced domination of the masculine has resulted in entrepreneurship to be generally characterized as a male-type activity in terms of both social structure and influence.
- Entrepreneurship is heavily influenced by family status and social networks. Women hold a different view of reality that emanates from

social structures, such as the workplace, marriage, family, and social life.

- Female entrepreneurs view themselves as limited in the way they understand the world around them and approach other people, but also in their future aspirations.
- A person's entrepreneurship identity is situated within their broader self-concept. In becoming an entrepreneur, people face the challenge of integrating a new entrepreneur identity with their other valued (central) identities.
- Women aspiring to start-up a high growth business need to engage in identity work that will help them integrate their entrepreneurial identity successfully within their existent network of valued personal and social identities.
- In order to transform our lived reality, we need to be fully aware of our unconscious beliefs and how they play out to create and reinforce our experiences.

References

Abrams, D., & Hogg, M. A. (1988). Comments on the motivational status of self-esteem in social identity and intergroup discrimination. *European Journal of Social Psychology, 18*(4), 317–334.

Acs, Z. J., Arenius, P., Hay, M., & Minniti, M. (2005). Global entrepreneurship monitor: 2004 executive report. *Babson College and London Business School.*

Ahl, H. (2004). *The scientific reproduction of gender inequality: A discourse analysis of research texts on women's entrepreneurship.* Liber.

Ahl, H. (2006). Why research on women entrepreneurs needs new directions. *Entrepreneurship Theory & Practice, 30*(5), 595–621.

Aldrich, H. (1989). Networking among women entrepreneurs. *Women-Owned Businesses, 103,* 132.

Altinay, L., Madanoglu, M., Daniele, R., & Lashley, C. (2012). The influence of family tradition and psychological traits on entrepreneurial intention. *International Journal of Hospitality Management, 31*(2), 489–499.

Amiot, C. E., De la Sablonniere, R., Terry, D. J., & Smith, J. R. (2007). Integration of social identities in the self: Toward a cognitive-developmental model. *Personality and Social Psychology Review, 11*(4), 364–388.

Argyris, C. (2004). *Reasons and rationalizations: The limits to organizational knowledge.* Oxford University Press on Demand.

Ashforth, B. E., & Kreiner, G. E. (1999). "How can you do it?": Dirty work and the challenge of constructing a positive identity. *Academy of Management Review, 24*(3), 413–434.

Ashforth, B. E., & Schinoff, B. S. (2016). Identity under construction: How individuals come to define themselves in organizations. *Annual Review of Organizational Psychology and Organizational Behavior, 3*, 111–137.

Auweele, D. V. (2018). *Silence, excess, and autonomy. In William desmond's philosophy between metaphysics, religion, ethics, and aesthetics* (pp. 195–207). Palgrave Macmillan, Cham.

Baker, T., E. aldrich, H., & Nina, L. (1997). Invisible entrepreneurs: The neglect of women business owners by mass media and scholarly journals in the USA. *Entrepreneurship & Regional Development, 9*(3), 221–238.

Bandura, A. (1977). Self-efficacy: Toward a unifying theory of behavioral change. *Psychological Review, 84*(2), 191.

Bandura, A. (1993). Perceived self-efficacy in cognitive development and functioning. *Educational Psychologist, 28*(2), 117–148.

Baron, R. A. (2006). Opportunity recognition as pattern recognition: How entrepreneurs "connect the dots" to identify new business opportunities. *Academy of Management Perspectives, 20*(1), 104–119.

Baughn, C. C., Chua, B. L., & Neupert, K. E. (2006). The normative context for women's participation in entrepreneruship: A multicountry study. *Entrepreneurship Theory and Practice, 30*(5), 687–708.

Baumeister, R. F., Bratslavsky, E., Muraven, M., & Tice, D. M. (1998). Ego depletion: Is the active self a limited resource? *Journal of Personality and Social Psychology, 74*(5), 1252–1265.

Bird, B. (1988). Implementing entrepreneurial ideas: The case for intention. *Academy of Management Review, 13*(3), 442–453.

Boudreaux, C. J., Nikolaev, B. N., & Klein, P. (2019). Socio-cognitive traits and entrepreneurship: The moderating role of economic institutions. *Journal of Business Venturing, 34*(1), 178–196.

Bourdieu, P. (2001). *Masculine domination.* Stanford, CA: Stanford University Press.

Bourdieu, P. (2003). Symbolic violence. In *Beyond French Feminisms* (pp. 23–26). New York: Palgrave Macmillan.

Boyd, N. G., & Vozikis, G. S. (1994). The influence of self-efficacy on the development of entrepreneurial intentions and actions. *Entrepreneurship Theory and Practice, 18*(4), 63–77.

Brown, A. D., & Starkey, K. (2000). Organizational identity and learning: A psychodynamic perspective. *Academy of Management Review, 25*(1), 102–120.

Brush, C. G. (1992). Research on women business owners: Past trends, a new perspective and future directions. *Entrepreneurship Theory and Practice, 16*(4), 5–30.

Brush, C., Carter, N., Gatewood, E., Greene, P., & Hart, M. (2004). *Clearing the hurdles: Women building high-growth businesses.* FT Press.

Brush, C., Edelman, L. F., Manolova, T., & Welter, F. (2019). A gendered look at entrepreneurship ecosystems. *Small Business Economics, 53*(2), 393–408.

Buttner, E. H., & Moore, D. P. (1997). Women's organizational exodus to entrepreneurship: self-reported motivations and correlates with success. *Journal of Small Business Management, 35,* 34–46.

Chen, C. C., Greene, P. G., & Crick, A. (1998). Does entrepreneurial self-efficacy distinguish entrepreneurs from managers? *Journal of Business Venturing, 13*(4), 295–316.

Cheng, C. Y., Sanders, M., Sanchez-Burks, J., Molina, K., Lee, F., Darling, E., & Zhao, Y. (2008). Reaping the rewards of diversity: The role of identity integration. *Social and Personality Psychology Compass, 2*(3), 1182–1198.

Cliff, J. E. (1998). Does one size fit all? Exploring the relationship between attitudes towards growth, gender, and business size. *Journal of Business Venturing, 13*(6), 523–542.

Coleman, S. (2016). Gender, entrepreneurship, and firm performance: Recent research and considerations of context. In M. L. Connerley & J. Wu (Eds.), *Handbook on well-being of working women* (pp. 375–391). Dordrecht: Springer Science.

Cox, L. W., Mueller, S. L., & Moss, S. E. (2002). The impact of entrepreneurship education on entrepreneurial self-efficacy. *International Journal of Entrepreneurship Education, 1*(2), 229–245.

Davis, A. E., & Shaver, K. G. (2012). Understanding gendered variations in business growth intentions across the life course. *Entrepreneurship Theory and Practice, 36*(3), 495–515. https://doi.org/10.1111/j.1540-6520.2012.005 08.x.

DeRue, D. S., Ashford, S. J., & Cotton, N. C. (2009). *Assuming the mantle: Unpacking the process by which individuals internalize a leader identity* (pp. 213–232). Exploring positive identities and organizations: Building a theoretical and research foundation.

Desmond, W. (1995). *Perplexity and ultimacy: Metaphysical thoughts from the middle.* New York: SUNY Press.

Desmond, W. (2012). *Art, origins, otherness: Between philosophy and art.* Suny Press.

Desmond, W. (2016). *The intimate universal: The hidden porosity among religion, art, philosophy, and politics.* Columbia University Press.

Donahue, E. M., Robins, R. W., Roberts, B. W., & John, O. P. (1993). The divided self: Concurrent and longitudinal effects of psychological adjustment and social roles on self-concept differentiation. *Journal of Personality and Social Psychology, 64*(5), 834.

Eagly, A. H., & Karau, S. J. (2002). Role congruity theory of prejudice toward female leaders. *Psychological Review, 109*(3), 573.

Eddleston, K. A., & Powell, G. N. (2008). The role of gender identity in explaining sex differences in business owners' career satisfier preferences. *Journal of Business Venturing, 23*(2), 244–256.

Egel, E. (2020). *From "I" to "We": Bringing inclusion and inclusiveness to the next.* Taylor and Francis Group.

Elam, A. B. (2014). *Gender and entrepreneurship.* Cheltenham, UK and Northampton, MA: Edward Elgar Publishing.

Ely, R. J., Ibarra, H., & Kolb, D. M. (2011). Taking gender into account: Theory and design for women's leadership development programs. *Academy of Management Learning & Education, 10*(3), 474–493.

Fletcher, J. K. (2004). The paradox of postheroic leadership: An essay on gender, power, and transformational change. *The Leadership Quarterly, 15*(5), 647–661.

Ford, D., & Mouzas, S. (2010). Interacted service in business networks. In *IMP Group* (Hrsg., 2010), *26th IMP Conference Proceedings.* Budapest.

Foschi, M. (2000). Double standards for competence: Theory and research. *Annual Review of Sociology, 26*(1), 21–42.

Gergen, K. J., & Gergen, M. M. (1988). Narrative and the self as relationship. In *Advances in experimental social psychology* (vol. 21, pp. 17–56). Academic Press.

Gist, M. E., & Mitchell, T. R. (1992). Self-efficacy: A theoretical analysis of its determinants and malleability. *Academy of Management Review, 17*(2), 183–211.

Goss, D., & Sadler-Smith, E. (2018). Opportunity creation: Entrepreneurial agency, interaction, and affect. *Strategic Entrepreneurship Journal, 12*(2), 219–236.

Gupta, V. K., Turban, D. B., Wasti, S. A., & Sikdar, A. (2009). The role of gender stereotypes in perceptions of entrepreneurs and intentions to become an entrepreneur. *Entrepreneurship Theory and Practice, 33*(2), 397–417.

Haus, I., Steinmetz, H., Isidor, R., & Kabst, R. (2013). Gender effects on entrepreneurial intention: A meta-analytical structural equation model. *International Journal of Gender and Entrepreneurship, 5,* 130–156. https://doi.org/10.1108/17566261311328828

Hechavarria, D. M., Renko, M., & Matthews, C. H. (2012). The nascent entrepreneurship hub: Goals, entrepreneurial self-efficacy and start-up outcomes. *Small Business Economics, 39*(3), 685–701.

Hechavarria, D. M., Terjesen, S. A., Ingram, A. E., Renko, M., Justo, R., & Elam, A. (2017). Taking care of business: The impact of culture and gender on entrepreneurs' blended value creation goals. *Small Business Economics,* *48*(1), 225–257.

Hellman, M. E., & Okimoto, T. G. (2007). Why are women penalised for success at male tasks? The implied communality deficit. *Journal of Applied Psychology,* *92*(1), 81–92.

Hoang, H., & Gimeno, J. (2010). Becoming a founder: How founder role identity affects entrepreneurial transitions and persistence in founding. *Journal of Business Venturing, 25*(1), 41–53.

Huysentruyt, M. (2014). *Women's Social Entrepreneurship and Innovation.* OECD Local Economic and Employment Development (LEED) Working Papers, 2014/01, OECD Publishing, Paris. http://dx.doi.org/10.1787/5jx zkq2sr7d4-en.

Ibarra, H. S., Snook, S., & Guillen Ramo, L. (2010). Identity-based leader development. *Leadership: Advancing an intellectual discipline,* 657–678.

Jennings, J. E., & Brush, C. G. (2013). Research on women entrepreneurs: Challenges to (and from) the broader entrepreneurship literature? *Academy of Management Annals, 7*(1), 661–713.

Kets de Vries, M. F. R. (2006). *Leadership archetype questionnaire: Facilitator guide.* Fontainebleau, France: INSEAD Global Leadership Centre.

Lord, R. G., & Brown, D. J. (2001). Leadership, values, and subordinate self-concepts. *The Leadership Quarterly, 12*(2), 133–152.

Markus, H., & Nurius, P. (1986). Possible selves. *American Psychologist, 41*(9), 954.

Marlow, S. (2002). Regulating labor management in small firms. *Human Resource Management Journal, 12*(3), 25–43.

Marlow, S., & Patton, D. (2005). All credit to men? Entrepreneurship, finance, and gender. *Entrepreneurship Theory and Practice, 29*(6), 717–735.

McGee, J. E., Peterson, M., Mueller, S. L., & Sequeira, J. M. (2009). Entrepreneurial self–efficacy: Refining the measure. *Entrepreneurship Theory and Practice, 33*(4), 965–988.

Monitor, G. E. (2018). *GEM 2018/2019 global report.*

Monitor, G. E. (2019). Monitor 2018–2019. *Global Entrepreneurship Research Association* (GERA).

Mueller, S. L., & Goić, S. (2003). East-West differences in entrepreneurial self-efficacy: Implications for entrepreneurship education in transition economies. *International Journal for Entrepreneurship Education, 1*(4), 613–632.

Nicholson, N. (1984). A theory of work role transitions. *Administrative Science Quarterly, 29*(2), 172–191.

Nicholson, H., & Carroll, B. (2013). Identity undoing and power relations in leadership development. *Human Relations, 66*(9), 1225–1248.

Orobia, L., & Rooks, G. (2011). Risk taking and start-up capital: Exploring gender differences in Uganda, through an international comparison. *Journal of Economics and Behavioral Studies, 3*(2), 83–93.

Petriglieri, G., Ashford, S. J., & Wrzesniewski, A. (2019). Agony and ecstasy in the gig economy: Cultivating holding environments for precarious and personalized work identities. *Administrative Science Quarterly, 64*(1), 124–170.

Petriglieri, G., & Petriglieri, J. L. (2010). Identity workspaces: The case of business schools. *Academy of Management Learning & Education, 9*(1), 44–60.

Powell, M., & Ansic, D. (1997). Gender differences in risk behaviour in financial decision-making: An experimental analysis. *Journal of Economic Psychology, 18*(6), 605–628.

Rauch, A., & Frese, M. (2007). Let's put the person back into entrepreneurship research: A meta-analysis on the relationship between business owners' personality traits, business creation, and success. *European Journal of Work and Organizational Psychology, 16*(4), 353–385.

Reveley, J., & Down, S. (2009). Stigmatization and self-presentation in Australian entrepreneurial identity formation. *The politics and aesthetics of entrepreneurship: A fourth movements in entrepreneurship book* (pp. 162–182). Cheltenham, UK: Edward Elgar.

Reynolds, P. D., Bygrave, W., & Autio, E. (2004). *GEM 2003 executive report.* Babson College, London Business School, EM Kauffman Foundation.

Ridgeway, C. L., & Correll, S. J. (2004). Unpacking the gender system: A theoretical perspective on gender beliefs and social relations. *Gender & Society, 18*(4), 510–531.

Ridgeway, C. L., & Smith-Lovin, L. (1999). The gender system and interaction. *Annual Review of Sociology, 25*(1), 191–216.

Rothbard, N. P. (2001). Enriching or depleting? The dynamics of engagement in work and family roles. *Administrative Science Quarterly, 46*(4), 655–684.

Sequeira, J. M., Mueller, S. L., & McGee, J. E. (2007). The influence of social ties and self-efficacy in forming entrepreneurial intentions and motivating nascent behavior. *Journal of Developmental Entrepreneurship, 12*(3), 275–293.

Settles, I. H. (2004). When multiple identities interfere: The role of identity centrality. *Personality and Social Psychology Bulletin, 30*(4), 487–500.

Sexton, D. L., & Bowman-Upton, N. (1990). Female and male entrepreneurs: Psychological characteristics and their role in gender-related discrimination. *Journal of Business Venturing, 5*(1), 29–36.

Shibley Hyde, J., & Kling, K. C. (2001). Women, motivation, and achievement. *Psychology of Women Quarterly, 25*(4), 364–378.

Sidanius, J., Pratto, F., Van Laar, C., & Levin, S. (2004). Social dominance theory: Its agenda and method. *Political Psychology, 25*(6), 845–880.

252   E. EGEL

Snow, D. A., & Anderson, L. (1987). Identity work among the homeless: The verbal construction and avowal of personal identities. *American Journal of Sociology, 92*(6), 1336–1371.

Stewart, W. H., Jr., & Roth, P. L. (2001). Risk propensity differences between entrepreneurs and managers: A meta-analytic review. *Journal of Applied Psychology, 86*(1), 145.

Stryker, S., & Burke, P. J. (2000). The past, present, and future of an identity theory. *Social Psychology Quarterly, 63*(4), 284–297.

Tajfel, H., & Turner, J. C. (1986). An integrative theory of group conflict. *The social psychology of intergroup relations* (pp. 7–24). Chicago: Nelson-Hall.

Themudo, N. S. (2009). Gender and the nonprofit sector. *Nonprofit and Voluntary Sector Quarterly, 38*(4), 663–683.

Thoits, P. A. (1991). On merging identity theory and stress research. *Social Psychology Quarterly, 54*, 101–112.

Tsai, K. H., Chang, H. C., & Peng, C. Y. (2016). Extending the link between entrepreneurial self-efficacy and intention: A moderated mediation model. *International Entrepreneurship and Management Journal, 12*(2), 445–463.

Van Der Zee, K., Atsma, N., & Brodbeck, F. (2004). The influence of social identity and personality on outcomes of cultural diversity in teams. *Journal of Cross-Cultural Psychology, 35*(3), 283–303.

Van Gelderen, M., Brand, M., Van Praag, M., Bodewes, W., Poutsma, E., & Van Gils, A. (2008). Explaining entrepreneurial intentions by means of the theory of planned behaviour. *Career Development International, 13*(6), 538-559.

Voegelin, E. (2000). *Order and history* (vol. 5). In search of order [Collected works of Eric Voegelin, vol. 18].

Welpe, I. M., Spörrle, M., Grichnik, D., Michl, T., & Audretsch, D. B. (2012). Emotions and opportunities: The interplay of opportunity evaluation, fear, joy, and anger as antecedent of entrepreneurial exploitation. *Entrepreneurship Theory and Practice, 36*(1), 69–96.

Westart Project. (2018). *Research project conducted by Women lobby*. Retrieved from site https://womenlobby.org/?lang=en on 15 July, 2020.

Wood, R., & Bandura, A. (1989). Social cognitive theory of organizational management. *Academy of Management Review, 14*(3), 361–384.

Zhao, H., Seibert, S. E., & Hills, G. E. (2005). The mediating role of self-efficacy in the development of entrepreneurial intentions. *Journal of Applied Psychology, 90*(6), 1265.

Zhao, H., Seibert, S. E., & Lumpkin, G. T. (2010). The relationship of personality to entrepreneurial intentions and performance: A meta-analytic review. *Journal of Management, 36*(2), 381–404.

CHAPTER 14

Reviewing Representations of the Ubiquitous "Entrepreneurs Wife"

Robert Smith and Lorraine Warren

INTRODUCTION

The Rose Review of female entrepreneurship (Rose 2019: 2) highlighted an *"unacceptable disparity between female and male entrepreneurship"* in the UK which effects entrepreneurial gender equality, resulting in significant levels of unrealized potential. According to Rose, statistically only one in three UK entrepreneurs are female. Extant research suggests entrepreneurship is embedded in collaborations and relationships between people. Yet to date, too much emphasis has been placed on the "male centric" ideology of entrepreneurship (Ahl & Marlow, 2012; Deacon, Harris, & Worth, 2014); and on the heroic entrepreneur (Anderson & Warren, 2011) when the entrepreneur patently operates within such relationships. Using the statistics of Rose (2019) it is evident that if only in three UK entrepreneurs are female then two-thirds of male

R. Smith (✉)
Aberdeen, Scotland

L. Warren
Southhampton, UK

253

entrepreneurs will have a wife involved in the business to a certain extent. Thus, despite the growing appreciation of the powerbase and dynamics of entrepreneurial activity and a developing academic interest in the socially constructed and gendered nature of entrepreneurial narrative and identity (Al-Dajani, Bika, Collins, & Swail, 2014) the pivotal role played by the wives of entrepreneurs is an under-researched phenomenon. Such wives (Basu, 2004; Bowman, 2009; Martin & Guarnieri, 2014) play a significant role in the lives, achievements, and successes of entrepreneurs and influence their unfolding entrepreneurial identities and narratives. Nevertheless, the ubiquitous *"Entrepreneurs wife"* is a silent, and arguably silenced, entrepreneurial actor, as evidenced the paucity of academic articles on the topic. Moreover, there is a growing literature on how media representations of female entrepreneurs are portrayed (see Achten-hagen & Welter, 2011; Eikhoff, Summers, & Carter 2013; Nicholson & Anderson, 2005; Radu & Redien-Collot, 2008) negatively and trivialized in comparison to their male entrepreneurial peers. We seek to establish if the wives of entrepreneurs are similarly constructed.

The term *"Entrepreneurs wife"* (singular) or *"Entrepreneurs' wives"* (plural) is potentially controversial, possessing as it does a narrow specificity, assuming a patriarchal dominance vis-a-vis the ascribed gender of the entrepreneur. There are only a small number of studies which touch upon the topic such as those of Basu (2004), Bowman (2009), and Martin and Guarnieri (2014) as discussed in the literature review below. This highlights an evident gap in the literature worthy of further research. Thus, what we know at present is that there is a dearth of research into this entrepreneurial category despite there being numerous media representations of said wives that either present them in a less than flattering light, or worse ignores them. This research investigates this research gap to synthesize a protean literature and by examining what the representations actually tell us. Therefore, our main contribution is to posit the *"Entrepreneurs wife"* as an entrepreneurial typology in her own right; and as a construct worthy of further research. Additionally, the significance of this contribution is to shed light on the importance of wives to the success of their partners. Consequentially, we explore an interesting construction of gender at work and neglected gendered identity. We seek to raise awareness of this often invisible, yet stereotypical figure.

This chapter focuses on academic and media representations of *"Entrepreneurs wives"* and in doing so uncovers some generic features relating to the manner in which they are marginalized, exploited, etc.

In the process, we explore an under-researched area of entrepreneurial narrative and identity to shed new theoretical and conceptual light on the "private lives" of entrepreneurs. The research focus is both upon the wives and media representations of them. This makes it necessary to synthesize an explanatory literature. A more nuanced understanding is necessary because at present the wife of an entrepreneur is either ignored or she is treated as an appendage when in reality they play a significant role in the development of the business. This chapter seeks to address two research questions from the literature reviewed, namely—How are "*Entrepreneurs wives*" portrayed in the media and in academic discourse? And—What can we learn from the study?

Some Brief Methodological Considerations

The review methodology used is qualitative in nature and consists of a mixed methodology of netnography (Kozinets, 2009; 2010) and media analysis techniques (as per Altheide & Schneider, 2013) including "ethnographic content analysis." Netnography is helpful for studying under-researched topics, enabling unobtrusive and covert ways to gain deeper insights into opinions, motives, and concerns (Langer & Beckmann, 2005).

We began by examining well-known celebrity entrepreneurs and their wives such as the late Gordon and Ina Baxter, Sir Richard Branson and his second wife *Joan Templeman*; Alan Sugar and his wife Anne Simons; James Caan and his wife Aisha; Peter Jones and his wife Tara; and Sir Philip and Christina "Tina" Green. Lady Green is an entrepreneur in her own right. Ina Baxter was a positive role model for female entrepreneurship (see Smith, 2017). However, issues of selection were complicated by the fact that the iconic Branson was previously married to *Kristen Tomassi; Lady Green was previously married to businessman* Robert Palos; *and because all are high profile celebrity entrepreneurs/CEO's* (See Guthey, Clark, & Jackson, 2009; Muda, Musa, Naina, & Borhan, 2014 for a wider discussion of this phenomenon). It quickly became apparent to us that to better understand the phenomenon we had to conduct an extensive review of such representations and the academic literature.

SYNTHESIZING LITERATURE ON ENTREPRENEURS WIVES

The extant literature on gender and entrepreneurship focuses on the traditional assumption that the entrepreneur is a man (Ahl & Marlow, 2012) albeit there are many ways of doing gender differently (Mavin & Grandy, 2012). Nevertheless, the female as entrepreneur (as an exaggerated expression of femininity) is not the only possible entrepreneurial role available for a woman. Hamilton (2006) argues that the role of women in family businesses is relatively under investigated. This fact underpins our lack of understanding of the role played by the wives of entrepreneurs. One of the issues that obscure wives from view is the fact that at present there is not an appropriate theoretical base in relation to the topic. This may be because too often researchers concentrate on the procedural and business elements of the entrepreneurship paradigm at the expense of the more deeply personal driving forces (see Down, 2007; De Vries, 2009 for examples of significant exceptions). The monograph of Down (2007) was seminal because he incorporated family and personal life of the entrepreneurs he studied as part of his research design. Similarly, the work of De Vries (2009) is refreshing because he considers deeply personal issues such marriage, love, and sex as variables in the life choices of entrepreneurs and CEOs in their quest for authenticity. This review, of necessity focuses on a wide range of topics and themes to highlight the nuances of the "wives" literature and media representations of them. A detailed trawl of extant literature revealed that it was diverse and characterized both by its paucity and specificity. The literature either merely touches upon the topic or deals with specific business issues. Perhaps this is to be expected, given the novel nature of the topic. Indeed, there is an evident dearth of literature that deals specifically with the topic per se. Extant studies span the media and academic domains and although there are many negative representations of wives, overall its focus is on the supportive role of women. We examine both media and academic representations.

Media Representations

Such representations are found in media and press coverage of entrepreneurs including biographies, books, and in the popular press—particularly tabloids. The most visible representations of the

"*Entrepreneurs wife*" are found in biographies and tabloids which concentrate on celebrity, male entrepreneurs.

Biographical and tabloid representations: We restrict our search to a UK based context to avoid cultural and regional factors which may influence the data collected and therefore the nuances of the research. We analyzed these publicly available representations albeit the issue of celebrity may skew the established entrepreneurial narrative because of the nature of journalistic practices (both because of often salacious nature of investigative journalism and the intrusive nature of the paparazzi) and because celebrities are equally celebrated and vilified and accordingly exert an influence that is pervasive, but difficult to evaluate and explain. According to Guthey et al. celebrity actions, personalities and private lives function symbolically to represent significant dynamics and tensions prevalent in the contemporary business environment. In such narratives, the story becomes more than about them and their partners as the inherent themes of heroism, villainy are amplified because of the perennial nature of the manufactured backlash against them. *A scoping-pilot study was conducted using the above named. Emergent themes were of bossy,* overly directive wives and the media stories were often articulated as "slurs," "jibes," and "accusations" against the masculinity or manhood of the male entrepreneur. Accusations of greed, dishonesty largesse, hedonism, extravagant lifestyles, and conspicuous consumption predominated with the anti-capitalist "Fat Cat" slur (Cammett, 2005; Littler, 2007) being commonplace. It was evident that with high profile, celebrity entrepreneurs the stories were more about societal criticisms than about the individuals' legitimate entrepreneurial narrative and that the stories were potentially biased and infused with what "Tabloid Intimacy" (Littler, 2007). Male billionaire entrepreneurs with interests in and expensive investments in horse breeding-racing, vintage cars, yachting, and flying were specifically singled out for vilification by journalists. We surmised that as a theme it was not so much negativity about the entrepreneurs themselves per se but more of a socially constructed societal aversion to hedonism, avarice, and conspicuous consumption. Celebrity entrepreneurs' wives are treated pejoratively and subject to discrimination and prejudice. In biographies of entrepreneurs and in the popular press representations of "*Entrepreneurs wives*" are often pejorative and pervaded by stereotypical representations of a derogatory nature such as the WAG category [Wives and Girlfriends] (Bullen, 2014; Johnson &

Kaye, 2004) and the "Mistress" (Alexander, 1987). Such claims are patri-archal, misogynistic tropes of a derogatory nature and include stereotypes such as gold-digging (Siegal, 2004; Vera, Berardo, & Berardo, 1987) and reflect common sense interpretations of observed and reported behaviors. What such tropes elide is the complexity of the exchange between part-ners as alluded to in this chapter. Partners can clearly exploit each other or be perceived to be doing so. That the wives of celebrity entrepreneurs are used by the media to further their stories, is hardly surprising nor is the fact that much is made of the "trophy-wife" (Vera et al., 1987) and the wife as a mechanism for tax avoidance. Other common stories relate to extravagant lifestyles, hedonism, and conspicuous consumption (Veblen, 2005).

Nevertheless, the majority of stories were positive and relate to fidelity and successful, long-term, loving relationships with childhood sweet-hearts. Fidelity is a strong theme in the narratives, and this resonates with the arguments of Stanley (2000) who found that successful million-aire couples have long-standing marriages. Only a small number relates to infidelity and womanizing. Some wives are cast as "domestic goddesses" and "home-makers." There is a discernible UK media bias in the coverage and many of the themes and their nuances may only be applicable in UK cases.

Representations in the popular press: In the popular press and in the genre of "How to books" there is a focus on women's roles and tensions in personal and business relationships and thus relational dynamics. There is a focus on relationship advice to overcome the challenges and obstacles facing the wives of entrepreneurs. This literature consists of journal-istic articles and books (see Hirshberg, 2010, 2012; Hymowitz, 2012; Williams, 2012). As such the tone and message is different from academic articles. The article of Williams (2012) stresses that the "spouses" of an entrepreneur are critical to their success, but their exploits are often unsung. Williams debunks the myth of an idyllic lifestyle of high income, time off, and extended vacations arguing that the entrepreneurial life is a tornado of long hours, high risk, and uncertainty. Williams stresses that despite good intentions, entrepreneurs can be the world's worst spouses, typically investing the majority of their time and interest in their companies, even during prosperous times. Furthermore, she highlights the high incidence of personal wealth loss, marital troubles, and divorce that can accrue from failed business marriages. Hirshberg (2010) high-lights the high divorce rates of entrepreneurs, citing common causes such as financial strain, neglect, lack of communication, and divergent goals often leading to a toxic cocktail of resentment and anxiety created by putting the family's security constantly at risk. Elsewhere, Hirshberg (2012) addresses topics such as how to handle the failure of a start-up, the strains of serial entrepreneurship, and how to handle extra stresses that happen when a company owner falls ill. She urges entrepreneurs and their families to strive for and focus on the "*magic moments*" which outweigh the negative aspects. In relation to the negative, there are reports of the wealthy wives of businessmen achieving substantial settlements on divorcing their wealthy entrepreneur-husbands (see Baker, 1998). There is also an alternative side to the paradigm as evidenced by Hymowitz (2012) who reported that with the growing rise of female CEO's and entrepreneurs that many husbands choose to become their powerful wives Chief Domestic Officers and "stay-at-home-dads." Chasserio, Lebegue and Poroli (2014) argue that female entrepreneurs often draw upon emotional support from their partners. The literature search only unearthed one academic study of the term "Entrepreneurs husband" carried out by Nikina et al. (2015) who explored the changes in the role of the husband of Scandinavian female entrepreneurs and how these affect the marriage and their relationship with the business. This identified implicit and specific gender-based patterns of dominance between husband and wife which affected levels of marital harmony and spousal support. These changing roles alter marriage dynamics and influence the men's wife–business relationship. Interestingly, such husbands do not face the same negative levels of criticism.

Academic Representations

The propensity of women to be energetically entrepreneurial has been posited by Smith (2009) in the form of the "The Diva" stereotype. In addition, D'Andria and Gabarret (2017) posit the category of women in entrepreneurial careers. Nevertheless, the gender imbalance in entrepreneurial equality as highlighted by Rose is a palpable and well-established facet of the academic literature (Mulholland, 1997, 2003a, 2003b, 1996). Academic representations of women in business generally relate to aspects of gendered entrepreneurial identity, female stereotypes associated with entrepreneurial identity and to life cycles and stages. Such diverse representations include the Co-preneur, The Good Wife, and the Matriarch.

The gender imbalance in entrepreneurial equality: Women entrepreneurs and women in business suffer from a "double bind" (Litz, 2011) having to take care of the twin and often conflicting professional and familio-marital business dimensions. According to Nye (1988) feminist explanatory theories are steeped in the philosophies of men and the patriarchal, practice of misogyny. It is apparent from readings that women are socialized into acceptance of these norms and behaviors and are thus silenced. This gender imbalance begins before the women even marries and is inherent in relation to wealth creation and accumulation in capitalist western societies, particularly in family business (Mulholland, 1997, 2003a, 2003b). Mulholland (1996) challenged the popular image of middle and upper-class women, being beneficiaries and consumers of wealth and of men as the central agents in wealth creation, arguing that while such women were active in the generation of wealth, they do not receive due recognition, marginalizing them in the management and ownership of wealth. Mulholland blames this on a process of wealth formation in which gender relations are underpinned by patriarchal practices. This ordering propels male kin to positions of power and influence while overshadowing females. Moreover, Mulholland (2003a) examined the relationship between domesticity, emotion as absence and enterprise. She drew on Ochberg's (1987) argument that contemporary men merely act out their emotional family role to explore the dynamics of the sexual division of labor and the relationship between home and work. Men generally disinvest in domesticity because work activity is so pervasive it invades and colonizes family life ordering domestic life despite most enterprising men drawing a sharp distinction between work and home. Control of the household falls to wives extending a permutation of capitalist logic to the household. The men's absence from the house and their preference for disengagement from the messy arena of emotional work obscure the extent to which they attempt to regulate. Furthermore, Mulholland (2003b) explored the career paths of husband and wife partnerships in family firms establishing the presence of female kin subordination and male kin domination as wealth is accumulated within the business. Business growth has very different outcomes for wives and husbands. Male partners in parallel with the growth of the business carve out careers as chief executives while female partners are cannot make the transition from the stereotypical image of "helpmate" to company professional. Mulholland suggests that such women are systematically marginalized from the nucleus of organizational power and are excluded from the family business, its managerial structures, specialization of function, and its bureaucratic processes.

The work of Heikkinen (2014) is of note because she argues that a male manager's career unfolds in tandem with their family life, as well as the norms and gender roles related to family. Heikkinen developed a typology distinguishing four types of female spouses, i.e., supporting, balance-seeking, care-providing, and success-expecting types. Women in business possess overlapping identities and try to present a rational and logical persona as business leaders while avoiding being intuitive and emotive because these feminine traits are inappropriate at work. Such traits belong at home but ironically women can express their femininity and maternalism at work because being a "good mother" is a desired ideal embedded in work and at home (Martin, Jerrard, & Wright, 2019).

This stream of literature is important in illustrating the unequal character of the marriage as the business partnership magnifies the contradictions of the class gender nexus in the coordination of the role of wife and business partner in the family enterprise. Women even from a business family background are disadvantaged even before marrying an entrepreneur or starting a business with their partner. In practice, it is not as straight forward as theory suggests because as Hamilton (2006) reported, there is a tension and confusion around authority between the "entrepreneur-husband" and wife stressing that while there is complicity between both, far from being marginalized through the forces of patriarchy or paternalism, wives engage with and narrate alternative gender discourses and practices that paradoxically evidence complicity and resistance to patriarchy. Marital tension is evident in the literature.

The Co-preneurial heroine: When one considers hidden dimensions of the role of women in business and particularly in relation to entrepreneurship theory, the obvious theoretical plank is that of Co-preneurship (Bensemann & Hall, 2010; De Bruin & Lewis, 1994, 2004; Marshack, 1994) whereby couples share ownership, commitment, and responsibility for a business. As it stands the theory is used to represent a heroic union whereby both the male entrepreneur and his wife engage equally in the marriage and the business. However, it is not universally applicable as it does not cover every example of a marriage where the wife is involved in the business. As a theory, it has considerable utility because it is ostensibly asexual and agendered and relates to both heterosexual and homosexual couples, married or not. However, the assumption of gender equality within co-preneurial businesses is merely a taken-for-granted one in that little research has been conducted into the balance of responsibilities in such ventures. The category of *"Fellowship Tales"* (Smith & Neergaard, 2015) is of relevance as it allows a dual entrepreneurial voice to co-preneurial couples.

The Good Wife: Wives can be devoted to both marriage and the business without being a co-preneur. Many wives help their entrepreneur-husbands without having a specified role in the business. Other relevant theoretical categories include *"committed couples"* in business (Ashton-Hodgson, 2005); the *"CEO spouse"* or wives of owner-managers (Poza & Messer, 2001); and the *"good wife"* (Lewis & Massey, 2011). Lewis and Massey looked beyond the *"visible women"* (those running businesses as owner–managers or partners) to a focus on the invisible without clearly acknowledged and/or formalized roles. Such wives play critical, often unseen, unpaid, and unacknowledged *"behind the scenes"* roles in line with the notions of *"wifeliness"* and the *"idealized wife"* (Russell, 2005). Goffee & Scase (2015) refer to the entrepreneurial category of the *"Women in charge"* for whom entrepreneurship is a means to achieve economic and social independence. They refute the notion of a single entrepreneurial experience arguing that the causes and consequences of business start-up are conditioned by the extent to which women are committed to traditionally prescribed roles.

Martin and Guarnieri (2014) highlighted the existence of extensive research into the "assistant" or "helpers" role often assumed by the entrepreneur's wife (Basu, 2004) but nevertheless the literature is underdeveloped. Basu (2004) distinguished between business aspirations in relation to those with business-first, family-first, money-first, and lifestyle-first aspirations, arguing that family background affects entrepreneurs' aspirations and in particular their stage on the family life cycle. Bowman (2009) highlighted the unwritten, gender-based "deal" and explored how wives make sense of the conflicts between their husbands' intense engagement with entrepreneurial business activity and their own belief in the idea of egalitarian intimate relationships. Bowman counselled against looking at family life in isolation from market work, or vice versa because there is a danger of distortion in relation to our understanding of both. Bowman found evidence of the continuation of the gender-based deal in contemporary business practices. She stressed that belief in this deal not only shapes the choices that individual men and women make but shapes the nature of market and non-market life. This so-called deal has become naturalized and inevitable. As a result, the rules that govern resource use and the accumulation of different forms of capital have not been negotiated and remain non-negotiable. The study of Martin and Guarnieri (2014) scrutinized the role of "the wife" of a small business owner in occupational risk management. They found little differentiation in social relationships that characterize the business and the small business owner (and obviously the personal dynamics of their relationship). Martin and Guarnieri established that male entrepreneurs rely heavily on their wives to fulfil regulatory and other business obligations such as complying with risk management and health and safety and regulations. As result, the ubiquitous *"Entrepreneurs Wife"* is expected to take charge of the detail and to delegate tasks to allow her husband to run the business smoothly. The wives possess an elevated status within the family and the business but face resistance, restrictions, and limitations to the performance of their role. Indeed, as a genre, wives are conscientious in fulfilling her duties while overcoming organizational and symbolic challenges.

Also, relevance is the doctoral thesis of Cosson (2017) who studied the roles played by wives weaving the thread of work and family life in crafting a family business. They do so in dynamic, complex, and often invisible ways exercising power in a commonsensical way, circumventing entrepreneurial identity. Cosson suggests that wives are often not comfortable inhabiting an entrepreneurial identity and that the demands of entrepreneurial ideology are met more readily by husbands than wives. Instead, women "reflect back" to men their heroic masculine discourse. Cosson argues that wives exert a powerful force in undermining succession planning and are influential in trying to manage it while crafting the future of the business via a *"discourse of choice."* For Cosson, the uncoupling of gender from traditional precepts is overstated and rather, women achieve uneven recognition and status, highlighting the coexistence of equality with enduring masculine privilege.

The Matriarch: Smith (2014, 2018) posited the stereotypes of the "Matriarch" and "The Dowager" to signify life stages in the evolution of the identity of the wives of entrepreneurs. What unites these stereotypes is that they are both important, positive gendered entrepreneurial role driven identities. In addition, the study of Moult and Anderson (2005) into the mature, enterprising women with reduced domestic responsibilities who exploit specific *"windows of entrepreneurial opportunity"* evident in women's life stages is also of interest. Similarly, Stirzaker and Sitko (2018), using positionality as a lens explored the complexity of the lived multiple identities of older women entrepreneurs (50+) paying attention to how they engage with intersecting discourses surrounding enterprise culture and aging while constructing their identities. The outcomes of these dimensions are largely positive and demonstrate the life enhancing benefits of these overlaps. Again, tension is a key theme in the discourse particularly between the storied identities of *"mother"* and *"entrepreneur."* They demonstrated a synergy between the intersection of older women entrepreneurs' social identities and their entrepreneurial identity, albeit dependent upon the context and stage of life for these women, underpinned by both agency and external factors.

From a comparative close reading of the literatures there are obvious trait-based behaviors evident in the literature—namely acceptance of limitations, commitment, consciousnesses, crafting gender accepted familial narratives, delegation, independence, longevity of relationship, perseverance, responsibility, resistance, and "reflecting back" accepted gender-based roles (the masculine entrepreneurial halo). Several articles focus on relationship advice and overcoming challenges (emotional, financial, organizational, and symbolic) and obstacles (including confusion in relation to issues of power and authority, divorce, the negative perception of female entrepreneurs, marital problems) to entrepreneurial and personal success. All these can be accommodated under the rubrics of external context and individual agency. The overall message is that it is overfocused on the taken-for-grantedness of wives or discriminatory dominant/subordinate relationship. Despite these studies, there is an evident gap in the literature relating to how *"Entrepreneurs wives"* are portrayed in the popular press, media, and academic discourse. Overarching themes include "invisibility" and "indifference." To recap, there are four main obstacles to its acceptance as an established and legitimate research category, or entrepreneurial type in her own right.

1. The invisibility and indifference emanate from media-inspired negative perception of female entrepreneurs in comparison to the eulogized male entrepreneur (and his blinding halo). This underpins the lack of acceptance of wives as serious entrepreneurial actors because if the entrepreneur is considered male-gendered then associated female entrepreneurial types are thus less worthy;
2. The "double bind" whereby women are expected to shoulder domestic responsibilities as well as professional ones prevent the wife from adopting a more visible role. This results in a "gender deal" whereby women who shoulder responsibility for supporting their

husband's entrepreneurial ambitions reflect in that glory and make that narrative their own;

3. This is magnified by male entrepreneurs' overreliance on their wives for domestic and professional tasks thus masking the wife from view in both business and family; and

4. These factors combine to create tensions which accrue around both personal and business relationships and dynamics. There is a definite tension between the forces of marginalization and empowerment and a focus on roles and a tension between performing support and help-based tasks and taking the initiative versus planning and scheming.

Considering Empirical Representations of Entrepreneurs Wives

Smith and Warren (2018) analyzed the "Management Today" *data set* (https://www.managementtoday.co.uk/top100entrepreneurs) consisting of the top 100 UK entrepreneurs (male and female) by wealth, mining it for salient data. It proved difficult to locate details of the male entrepreneur's wives with over half of the entrepreneurs on the list having no publically available information on their wives. It was necessary to extend and expanded the research parameters to include internet searches, searches in the press and biographies to obtain usable data on the wives. They conducted searches to locate internet and newspaper articles on the subjects. This trawl also located Facebook and LinkedIn profiles which were mostly privacy protected. It was necessary to extend the search to company websites to locate a photograph of the subject to confirm and corroborate that the entries related to that individual. When this process failed separate searches of Bloomberg and Companies House helped identify spousal details. Where these searches failed to locate such details, we removed the subjects from the database. It is of note that only eight subjects had photographs of themselves and their wives in the public domain. Data collection proved to be problematic because although we know a lot of background detail on celebrity entrepreneurs who have published biographies, or feature in the press, we know little about less visible entrepreneur and their partners. So, unless the entry related celebrities locating even the names of wives, let alone details of their personal lives was difficult. This phase highlighted that wives are often markedly "invisible." While we appreciate that many female entrepreneurs use "hiding" as a mechanism to remain invisible from critical scrutiny (Weidhaas, 2018), being invisible to the media is not the same as being invisible in a gendered sense. It is a distinct form of invisibility.

One of the problems is that as a category it is quite broad as there is no such thing as the ubiquitous wife. A few stories relate to wives who are entrepreneurial in their own right. A small proportion had other professional careers with no apparent link to their husband's businesses fitting the category of "*The Independent Woman*" (Siegal, 2004). Privacy is a key theme with many of the newspaper or internet articles expressing that the entrepreneurs, their wives, and families were intensely private. Reasons for this include—(1) Many business families avoid interviews with journalists preferring to keep their family stories private and to control their own narratives; (2) Many avoid social media for the same reasons; and (3) In an age of prenups and nondisclosure agreements family secrets remain private. Also, if divorce, turmoil and feuding feature then tabloid press exposure follows with the entrepreneur and family being pilloried. While female entrepreneurs are frequently asked about their domestic arrangements (see for example Hamilton, 2013; Lyer, 2009; Eikhoff et al., 2013) male entrepreneurs are seldom asked about such. Despite the negativity uncovered in representations of wives long-standing spousal relations enhance entrepreneurial performance.

Smith and Warren (2018) also considered the overarching category of "significant others" (Williams, 2012), encompassing a more universal, generic signifier which covers all partners/spouses of entrepreneurs. It avoids the loaded and gendered stereotype associated with wives per se. However, although it is ostensibly asexual and agendered it has yet to feature significantly in either sociological and/or gender research. According to the Collins online dictionary the term "significant other" is defined as "*...a person having importance in, or influence on, another's life*"; and "*a person with whom one has an intimate, often long-term and usually sexual, relationship.*" The term implies intimacy, shared values, and stability. It is surprising that there is an absence of literature on same-sex entrepreneurial couples.

A protean socially constructed typology of "*Entrepreneurs wives*" emerges in the form of an enacted, storied identity with associated trait-based behaviors, ideologically and role-based positions set against obstacles and challenges (see Fig. 14.1 below).

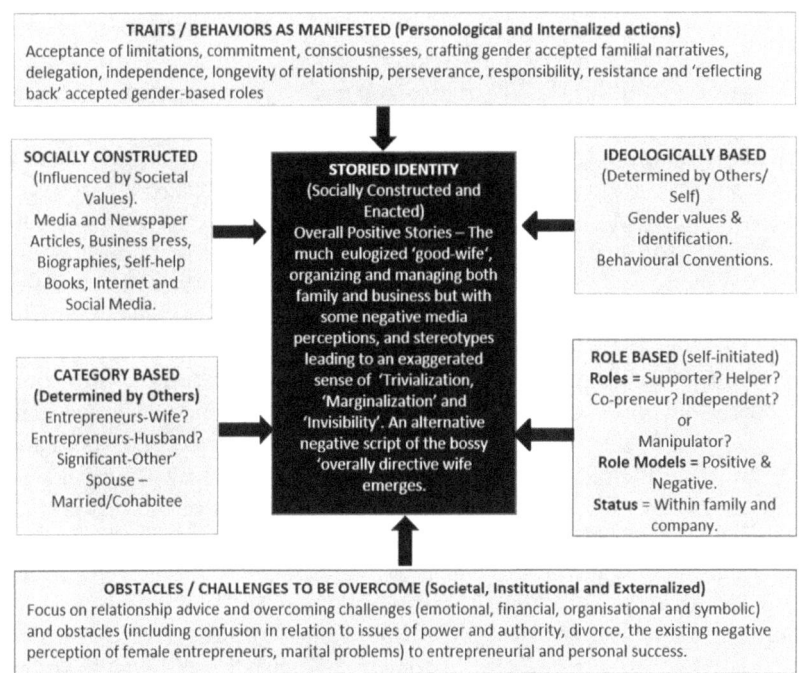

Fig. 14.1 A conceptual model of spousal entrepreneurial identity (*Source* Smith & Warren, 2018)

FURTHER DISCUSSION, INTERPRETATION, AND CONCLUSION

To answer the research questions, it can be argued that representations of "*Entrepreneurs wives*" are socially constructed in academic literature via exposure to the media and particularly the tabloids. There are two main positions for "*Entrepreneurs wives*"—namely to be (1) vilified; and (2) to be invisible. Being invisible is the one most encountered in this study. To be of interest to the media an entrepreneur has to be a high-net worth celebrity and be prone to scandal or other socially prescribed behaviors (such as committing a criminal act, divorce, having an affair, engaging in a family feud, or other personal fall from grace) which make them news worthy. They are hounded, haunted, and humbled by the media. Significant others and extended family are often considered "fair game" by the media losing control of their narrative and their identities and damage to their personal and/or business reputations. However, if the entrepreneur and their family choose to remain private and do not fall foul of personal problems, they can control their own narratives and thus identities by opting for privacy and avoiding the press and social media. So, what can we learn from the study? Obviously, from a behavioral perspective, wives can choose to avoid hedonistic and other negative behaviors in their personal and business lives, behaving legally and morally and avoiding negative publicity which taints identities. However, the majority of entrepreneurs and their wives live ordinary family lives and the media glare. This calls for different, qualitative methodologies to be used to develop our understanding of this important phenomenon.

Moreover, the *"Entrepreneur's Wives"* phenomenon is important because if as identified by Rose (2019) 2/3rds of entrepreneurs in the UK are male then statistically, the vast majority of men will have a wife who contributes formally or informally to the success of the business. If we better understood the ways in which such wives can sustain the success of the business while adding value to the business and wider economy, it would unleash the potential of more women on their entrepreneurial journey. According to Rose (2019: 35) women are as successful as men at sustaining businesses. There is scope to utilize such a potentially skilled and skillful workforce in a business administration and managerial capacity so that they can get the credit, rewards, and recognition that they deserve, positively addressing gender parity. For women becoming an entrepreneur should not be the sole pathway to entrepreneurial success. Tapping into this rich neglected resource is a very real possibility.

One could argue that as a category, *"Entrepreneurs Wives"* is simply too broad to encompass all its sub-types and as such they are not ubiquitous. As a concept, it is certainly a valid one worthy of further study. We have demonstrated that such wives are powerful entrepreneurial actors who perform a variety of roles beyond those of the stereotypical roles of "Mistress" and "Matriarch" (Smith, 2014). Indeed, they perform other traditional archetypal roles of deserving (and sometimes undeserving wives—see Bowman, 2009). Nevertheless, in these days of political correctness and gender (in)equality there is some merit in the "catch-all" category of the "significant-other" as a non-offensive category because from an epistemological, ontological, and axiological perspective human experience cannot always be neatly labelled, nor categorized into discreet entities (Ahl & Marlow, 2012).

CHAPTER TAKEAWAYS

1. This chapter challenges current emphasis on the "male centric" (Ahl and Marlow, 2012; Deacon, Harris, & Worth, 2014) ideology of entrepreneurship; and the entrepreneur as an individual hero (Anderson & Warren, 2011).
2. To be provocative, the ubiquitous "*Entrepreneurs wife*" may well be "a-good-little-helper" and support her husband to achieve his ends, reflecting and basking in his glory but that is only one part of the construct because they exert a hidden agency.
3. This research deepens our understanding of gendered entrepreneurial identities and narratives associated with "*Entrepreneurs Wives*" because developing a deeper understanding of the personal sides of entrepreneurial couples is helpful to policymakers in understanding the entrepreneurial personality (as understood by Chell, 2008) more holistically because of the financial stability that a long-term partnership can bring to an entrepreneurial venture.
4. Moreover, understanding the entrepreneur, and entrepreneurial behavior and practice from a more socialized perspective advances our understanding of entrepreneurial practice and practices.

REFERENCES

Achtenhagen, L., & Welter, F. (2011). Surfing on the ironing board—The representation of women's entrepreneurship in German newspapers. *Entrepreneurship and Regional Development, 23*(9–10), 763–786.

Ahl, H., & Marlow, S. (2012). Exploring the dynamics of gender, feminism and entrepreneurship: Advancing debate to escape a dead end? *Organization, 19*(5), 543–562.

Al-Dajani, H., Bika, Z., Collins, L., & Swail, J. (2014). Gender and family business: New theoretical directions. *International Journal of Gender and Entrepreneurship, 6*(3), 218–230.

Alexander, A. (1987). *Governors' ladies: The wives and mistresses of Van Diemen's land governors*. Tasmania, Australia: Sandy Bay.

Altheide, D. L., & Schneider, C. J. (2013). *Qualitative media analysis*. London: Sage.

Anderson, A. R., & Warren, L. (2011). The entrepreneur as hero and jester: Enacting the entrepreneurial discourse. *International Small Business Journal, 29*(6), 589–609.

Ashton-Hodgeson, K. (2005). Committed couples in business: A delightful dance between work and home. In T. Sayers & N. Monin (Eds.), *The global garage: Home based business in New Zealand*. Thomson-Dunmore Press: Australia.

Baker, D. (1998). Wealthy Wives Tales. *ABAJ*. https://heinonline.org/HOL/LandingPage?handle=hein.journals/abaj84&div=144&id=&page=.

Basu, A. (2004). Entrepreneurial aspirations among family business owners: An analysis of ethnic business owners in the UK. *International Journal of Entrepreneurial Behaviour & Research, 10*(1/2), 12–33.

Bensemann, J., & Hall, C. M. (2010). Copreneurship in rural tourism: Exploring women's experiences. *International Journal of Gender and Entrepreneurship, 2*(3), 228–244.

Bowman, D. (2009). The deal: Wives, entrepreneurial business and family life. *Journal of Family Studies, 15*(2), 167–176.

Bullen, J. (2014). *Framing the wag. In: Media representations of footballers' wives*. London: Palgrave Macmillan.

Cammett, M. (2005). Fat cats and self-made men: Globalization and the paradoxes of collective action. *Comparative Politics, 37*(4), 379–400.

Chasserio, S., Lebegue, T., & Poroli, C. (2014). Heterogeneity of spousal support for French women entrepreneurs. In K. Lewis, C. Henry, E. J. Gatewood, & J. Watson (Eds.), *Women's entrepreneurship in the 21st century. An international multi-level research analysis* (Chapter 11). Cheltenham: Edward Elgar.

Chell, E. (2008). *The entrepreneurial personality: A social construction*. London: Routledge.

Cosson, B. (2017). *Crafting a family business: Wives weaving the threads of work and family life*. Unpublished PhD thesis, Swinburne University. https://researchbank.swinburne.edu.au/file/f181f1b9-b8a0-41eb-81e7-20668c0810d5/1/Barbara%20Cosson%20Thesis%20pdfa.pdf.

D'Andria, A., & Gabarret, I. (2017). *Entrepreneurship and high heels, in building 21st century entrepreneurship*. John Wiley & Sons.

De Bruin, A., & Lewis, K. (1994). Hidden dimensions of women's business: Copreneurship and career constructs. *Work*.

De Bruin, A., & Lewis, K. (2004). Toward enriching united career theory: Familial entrepreneurship and Copreneurship. *Career Development International, 9*(7), 638–646.

Deacon, J. H., Harris, J. A., & Worth, L. (2014). Who leads?: Fresh insights into roles and responsibilities in a heterosexual copreneurial business. *International Journal of Gender and Entrepreneurship, 6*(3), 317–335.

De Vries, M. F. R. (2009). *Sex, money, happiness and death: The quest for authenticity*. Insead Business Press.

Down, S. (2007). *Narratives of enterprise: Crafting entrepreneurial self-identity in a small-firm*. Cheltenham: Edward Elgar.

Eikhoff, D. R., Summers, J., & Carter, S. (2013). Women doing their own thing: Media representations of female entrepreneurship. *International Journal of Entrepreneurial Behaviour and Research, 19*(5), 547–564.

Goffee, R., & Scase, R. (2015). *Women in Charge: The experiences of women entrepreneurs*. London: Routledge.

Guthey, E., Clark, T., & Jackson, B. (2009). *Demystifying Business Celebrity*. London: Routledge.

Hamilton, E. (2006). Whose story is it anyway? Narrative accounts of the role of women in founding and establishing family businesses. *International Small Business Journal, 24*(3).

Hamilton, E. (2013). The discourse of entrepreneurial masculinities (and femininities). *Entrepreneurship & Regional Development: an International Journal, 25*(1–2), 90–99.

Heikkinen, S. S. (2014). How do male managers narrate their female spouse's role in their career? *Gender in Management: An International Journal, 29*(1), 25–43.

Hirshberg, M. C. (2010). *Why so many entrepreneurs get divorced: Why the start of a company so often spells the end of a marriage*. www.inc.com/magazine/20101101/why-so-many-entrepreneurs-get-divorced.html.

Hirshberg, M. C. (2012). *For better or for work: A survival guide for entrepreneurs and their families*. An Inc Original.

Hymowitz, C. (2012). Behind every great woman—*Bloomberg Businessweek Magazine*—sbcf-famlaw.com https://www.sbcf-famlaw.com/wp-content/uploads/2012/03/behind-every-great1.pdf.

Johnson, T. J., & Kaye, B. K. (2004). Wag the blog: How reliance on traditional media and the internet influence credibility perceptions of weblogs among blog users. *Journalism & Mass Communication Quarterly, 81*(3), 622–642.

Kozinets, R. V. (2009). *Doing ethnographic research online*. London: Sage.

Kozinets, R.V. (2010). *Netnography: Doing ethnographic research online*. London: Sage.

Langer, R., & Beckman, S. C. (2005). Sensitive research topics: Netnography revisited. *Qualitative Market Research: An International Journal, 8*(2), 189–203.

Lewis, K., & Massey, C. (2011). Critical yet invisible: The "good wife" in the New Zealand small firm. *International Journal of Gender and Entrepreneurship, 3*(2), 105–122.

Littler, J. (2007). Celebrity CEOs and the cultural economy of tabloid intimacy. In S. Redmond & S. Holmes (Eds.), *2007—Stardom and celebrity: A reader*. London: Sage.

Litz, R. A. (2011). Double roles, double binds? double bind theory and family business research. In A. Carsrud & M. Brännback (Eds.), *Understanding family businesses. international studies in entrepreneurship, 15*. New York, NY: Springer.

Lyer, R. (2009). Entrepreneurial identities and the problematic of subjectivity in media-mediated discourses. *Discourse & society, 20*(2).

Marshack, K. J. (1994). *Love and work: How co-preneurial couples manage the boundaries and transitions in personal relationship and business partnership*. Ph.D. Dissertation, Faculty of the Fielding Institute.

Martin, C., & Guarnieri, F. (2014). The role of the entrepreneurs' wives in the management of occupational risk: A monographic study of the limits of delegation. *Small Enterprise Research, 21*(2), 202–213.

Martin, L., Jerrard, B., & Wright, L. (2019). Identity work in female led creative businesses. *Gender, Work & Organization,*. https://doi.org/10.1111/gwao.12357.

Mavin, S., & Grandy, G. (2012). Doing gender well and differently in management. *Gender in Management: An International Journal, 27*(4), 218–231.

Moult, S., & Anderson, A. R. (2005). Enterprising women: Gender and maturity in new venture creation and development. *Journal of Enterprising Culture, 13*(3), 255–271.

Muda, M., Musa, R., Naina, R., & Borhan, H. (2014). Entrepreneur endorsement and advertising effectiveness. *Procedia—Social and Behavioral Sciences, 130*, 11–20.

Mulholland, K. (1996). Gender power and property relations within entrepreneurial wealthy families. *Gender, Work & Organization, 3*(2), 78–102.

Mulholland, K. (1997). The family enterprise: Business strategies. *Work, Employment and Society, 11*(4), 685–711.

Mulholland, K. (2003a). The entrepreneur's wife and family life: 'It's like being a one-parent family'. In K. Mulholland (Eds.), *Class, gender and the family business* (pp. 111–130). Wiley.

Mulholland, K. (2003b). Gender and the management of family wealth Accumulation: 'He also wants pudding. In K. Mulholland (Eds.), *Class, gender and the family business* (pp. 48–69). Wiley.

Nicholson, L., & Anderson, A. R. (2005). News and nuances of the entrepreneurial metaphor: Linguistic games in entrepreneurial sense-making and sense-giving. *Entrepreneurship, Theory & Practice, 29*(2), 153–172.

Nikina, A., Shelton, L. M., & LeLoarne, S. (2015). An examination of how husbands, as key stakeholders, impact the success of women entrepreneurs. *Journal of Small Business and Enterprise Development, 22*(1), 38–62.

Nye, A. (1988). *Feminist theories and the philosophies of man.* London: Routledge.

Ochberg, R. L. (1987). The male career mode and the ideology of role. In H. Brod (Ed.), *The making of masculinities: The new men's studies.* London: Allen and Unwin.

Poza, E. J., & Messer, T. (2001). Spousal leadership and continuity in the family firm. *Family Business Review, 14*(1).

Radu, M., & Redien-Collot, R. (2008). The social representation of entrepreneurs in the French press: Desirable and feasible models? *International Small Business Journal, 26*(3), 259–298.

Russell, P. (2005). Wife stories: Narrating marriage and self in the life of Jane Franklin. *Victorian Studies, 48*(1), 35–57.

Siegal, D. (2004). *The new trophy wife.* https://www.psychologytoday.com/us/articles/200401/the-new-trophy-wife.

Smith, R. (2009). The diva cycle as an alternative social construction of female entrepreneurship. *International Journal of Entrepreneurship and Gender, 1*(2), 148–163.

Smith, R. (2014). Assessing the contribution of the 'Theory of Matriarchy' to the entrepreneurship and family business literatures. *International Journal of Entrepreneurship and Gender, 6*(3), 255–275.

Smith, R. (2017). Reading liminal and temporal dimensionality in the Baxter family 'public-narrative'. *International Small Business Journal, 36*(1).

Smith, R. (2018). *The 'Dowager' and her role in the governance, and leadership of the entrepreneurial family business.* In V. Ratten, V. Ramadani, L.-P. Dana, R. Hisrich, & J. Ferreira (Eds.), *Gender and family entrepreneurship.* London: Routledge.

Smith, R., & Neergaard, H. (2015). Telling business stories as fellowship-tales. *International Journal of Gender and Entrepreneurship., 7*(2), 232–252.

Smith, R., & Warren, L. (2018, November). *The role of the 'significant other' in the gendered social construction of entrepreneurial identity and narrative.* ISBE.

Stanley, T. J. (2000). *The Millionaire Mind.* Bantum Press.

Stirzaker, R., & Sitko, R. (2018). The older entrepreneurial self: intersecting identities of older women entrepreneurs. *International Journal of Entrepreneurial Behaviour & Research.* https://doi.org/10.1108/IJEBR-12-2017-0497.

The Alison Rose Review of Female Entrepreneurship. (2019). https://assets.publishing.service.gov.uk/government/uploads/system/uploads/attachment_data/file/784324/RoseReview_Digital_FINAL.PDF.

Veblen, T. (2005). *Conspicuous consumption.* London: Penguin.

Vera, H., Berardo, F. M., & Berardo, D. H. (1987). On Gold Diggers: Status gain or loss in age—Heterogamous marriages. *Journal of Aging Studies, 1*(1), 51–64.

Weidhaas, A. D. (2018). Female business owners hiding in plain sight. *International Journal of Gender and Entrepreneurship, 10*(1), 2–18.

Williams, D. K. (2012, August 19). The entrepreneurial spouse: The vital role of the significant other. *Forbes*. https://www.forbes.com/sites/davidkwilliams/2012/08/19/the-entrepreneurial-spouse-the-vital-role-of-the-significant-other/#4860aec630e6.

CHAPTER 15

Strategies to Build Women Leaders Globally: Think Managers, Think Men; Think Leaders, Think Women

M. S. Rao

INTRODUCTION

You may encounter many defeats, but you must not be defeated. In fact, it may be necessary to encounter the defeats, so you can know who you are, what you can rise from, how you can still come out of it.

—Maya Angelou

When we think about managers we think about men. However, when we think about leaders do we think about women? We must think about women because women are better leaders than men in several aspects. Most men talk about women empowerment and equality of women but in reality, a few of them walk their talk and advocate gender equality globally.

Although leadership is not gendered specific, we find only a few women leaders globally due to cultural, religious, social, and other factors

M. S. Rao (✉)
MSR Leadership Consultants, New Delhi, India

© The Author(s), under exclusive license to Springer Nature Switzerland AG 2021
J. Marques (ed.), *Exploring Gender at Work*,
https://doi.org/10.1007/978-3-030-64319-5_15

including the glass ceiling. The good news is that currently women are smashing through the glass ceiling and excelling globally to carve a niche for themselves. Despite several constraints, women are proving their credentials and capabilities on par with men. They are not behind in any way when compared with male leaders.

Research shows that women take failures to their hearts and take a little longer time to move on from their failures. They are hard on themselves and love to be perfectionists. They fail to claim their achievements and make noise publicly especially on social media because of gender and cultural aspects. Additionally, they fail to leverage their networks and groups thus hindering their career prospects. Women fail to network for fear of being misunderstood by others. Women often ruminate about their failures more than men. They are harder on themselves than men. They are better at multitasking than men.

Research further shows that compared to men, women are better at interpersonal skills, soft skills, emotional intelligence, empathy, flexibility, and sociability. In a 2017 survey, Deloitte found that organizations with diverse and inclusive cultures tend to be six times more innovative, six times more agile in anticipating and responding to change, and twice as likely to meet or exceed financial targets. Organizations truly committed to gender diversity look at if not as a means of virtue signaling, but something as important as any business issue. It is observed that women get senior positions when companies are in a downturn and riddled with challenges. Women can troubleshoot effectively and can lead during crisis effectively. A series of experimental studies showed that a female candidate is more likely to be appointed to a leadership position when the position is risky and there is an increased risk of failure.

Myths and Truths About Women Leaders

Myths are major challenges globally. They are unrealities that hold the people back. They create wrong assumptions leading to wrong conclusions. They adversely affect society. Hence, they must be debunked with facts and figures. When you look at women and women leaders, several myths prevent them from contributing their best. They prevent them from achieving amazing success. Here are some myths with truths about them.

- Myth #1: Women are not ambitious. Truth: Women are equally ambitious like men but they are more relationship-oriented, unlike men who are more task-oriented. Women care for their families and children. Hence, it is improper to label them as non-ambitious.
- Myth #2: Advancement of women leaders is a threat to men leaders. Truth: Usually men often compete with men while advancing their careers. With the entry of women leaders, men must compete with men and women while advancing their careers. There is no change in competition except in gender. There is nothing to be concerned as long as men are strong in their knowledge, skills, and abilities.
- Myth #3: All men are against women's empowerment. Truth: No. Only a few men are against women's empowerment who cannot digest the fact that women should be treated equal to men in all aspects. It takes time for them to empathize and understand to respect women and empower them finally. Additionally, some men encourage women empowerment and advocate gender equality globally—#HeForShe.
- Myth #4: Women cannot execute tasks effectively. Truth: The truth is that women can execute tasks effectively and can also multitask, unlike men who can execute one task at a time effectively.
- Myth #5: Women cannot lead. Truth: Leadership is not gender-related. Anyone one can lead irrespective of their community, creed, caste, color, and gender.
- Myth #6: Women are unsuitable to occupy senior positions. Truth: Women are equal to men and can occupy all positions and handle issues with a cool demeanor. When you look at Indra Nooyi she proved as a successful CEO for PepsiCo for many years.
- Myth #7: Women are unfit for some military roles and operations. Truth: Although women have certain biological health issues, they can contribute to the way men contribute. Hence, gender is not an excuse to deny them equal opportunities to serve in the military.
- Myth #8: Women burst under pressure. Truth: In fact, women can work under pressure better than men. Men often burst when they are under pressure whereas women remain calm and composed under pressure. Additionally, women explore ideas rather than to brood over issues, unlike men.
- Myth #9: Women cannot manage money. Truth: It is only a perception that women spend money carelessly on shopping. But they are more cautious while spending money. They search for value

for their money and are better investors than men. Men are often emotional while investing money while women are often analytical while investing money.

- Myth #10: Women are part of the problem. Truth: In fact, women are part of the solution. When men create problems, women create solutions to overcome them.
- Myth #11: Women must remain at home. Truth: That was the philosophy in the Stone Age, not now. Women must come out of their homes to lead and provide better directions to societies. No society can grow without the support of women. In fact, behind the success of every man, there is a woman. Women lead at the home. Margaret Thatcher once remarked, "Any woman who understands the problems of running a home will be nearer to understanding the problems of running a country." Imagine the kind of world we would create when women come out and lead outside with men.

Strengths of Women

Women work harder than men to prove themselves in the male-dominated corporate world. They don't like to be scapegoated by male leaders. Hence, they work harder than men. They stand up for what they believe in and work with flexibility and adaptability. They are collaborative while men are competitive by nature. Collaboration is essential for the smooth functioning of organizations and equally essential is a competitive spirit without which organizations cannot succeed. Blending both collaboration and competition is essential to achieve organizational excellence and effectiveness. Here are some strengths of women: Biologically women have a huge potential and are compassionate by nature. They empathize with others and are sensitive to others' feelings. They are experts in interpersonal skills and soft skills. They can handle stress better than men. By nature, men are aggressive. However, women are soft and well-behaved. Women are also experts in hidden data of communication. That is why they know the knack of understanding male egos, emotions, and feelings better and act accordingly. Women are leaders at home. They lead their spouses and children effectively. They are more responsible for work.

Women vs. Men Leadership Styles

Leadership is fundamentally based on the individual, environment, and situation. Although leadership is leadership, it differs from person to person and between men and women. The way people lead differs from leader to leader. The way women lead is different from men. Women leaders emphasize more on the democratic process to build consensus. They make decisions after weighing all options by thinking coolly. They emphasize more on collaboration, not competition. They are empathetic and good listeners. They apply different strokes to different men as all men are not alike. However, they don't take many risks like men. Here is some characteristic of women that make them lead differently from men. Women are tender, moral, cooperative, and trustworthy. They are imaginative, empathetic, and open to listen from all sources. They give more importance to emotions and feelings. They emphasize inspirational motivation and adopt a transformational leadership style in the workplace to accomplish organizational objectives. In a nutshell, they adopt more of transformational leadership than transactional leadership and more of soft leadership than hard leadership.

Women vs. Men Communication Styles

Conflicts occur in all aspects of our life. They cannot be eliminated. However, they can be minimized to a great extent, if adequate precautionary measures are taken. Approaches to addressing the conflicts differ between the genders and on the situation.

Whenever conflicts arise women act differently from men. In fact, women act while men react to conflicts. Men often settle their scores instantly while women take a little longer time to settle their scores. While men forget most of their negative experiences, women remember and ruminate about them. It is a well-admitted fact that men share negative experiences, observations, and information with a few of their close connections while women share with more connections. Hence, there is a possibility of women spreading information more than men.

The communication styles differ from person to person and between genders. Here are some differences between women and men in their approaches toward resolving conflicts. Women seek more information than men to arrive at their conclusions. They can decode and encode data more effectively than men. They are more emotional than men and enjoy talking more than men. They often see things from multiple perspectives, unlike men who often see from own their perspective. Women are indirect while men are direct in their approaches. Women use cell phones more than men and text more than men.

Research shows that humans demonstrate more than 10,000 facial expressions. But women use more facial expressions than men. Women are less likely to interrupt others. Women smile more often than men. Women are often more demanding than men and it is challenging to please women. Above all, women are more assertive while men are more aggressive in their communication styles. Understanding these differences helps you address conflicts effectively.

Whenever there was a miscommunication, change your approach, not your attitude; attack the issues, not individuals. While addressing conflicts both genders must note that neither aggressiveness nor submissiveness works but it is the assertiveness that works. Hence, be proactive to overcome the conflicts and be assertive to address the conflicts to resolve them amicably.

The differences between genders make approaches to resolving conflicts differently. Hence, both men and women must understand gender differences and adopt their styles according to the situation to address conflicts and ensure smooth communication to achieve organizational productivity and performance.

Challenges Holding Women Leaders Back

Several factors are holding women leaders back within the global organizations—stereotypes, structural obstacles, lifestyle issues, institutional mindsets, and individual mindsets to name a few. There are several barriers to the advancement of women leaders including glass ceiling, prejudices, the old boy network, gender discrimination, sexual harassment, and lack of mentors to name a few. Research shows that women are less consulted and receive less recognition than men in organizations. Here are some reasons that are holding women back to reach senior-level positions. C-suite women executives express that their gender cost promotion. Most women don't aspire to avoid pressure and stress at the top level. Most women work in staff roles, not line roles thus losing out in the race to the top.

It is a fact that women outperform men consistently in all aspects including curricular and extracurricular activities. Here are some solutions to overcome the challenges. Offer equal access to developmental experiences that would prepare women for senior levels. Make HR policies women-friendly. HR feedback helps them assess and improve themselves. Encourage mixed-gender management teams.

Previously people talked about the biological differences between men and women. However, presently they are vocal about other issues including women empowerment, equality, and pay parity. There is a dramatic shift in the expectations and aspirations of women leaders. Hence, global organizations must address the causes that hold women back earnestly to empower women to achieve organizational excellence and effectiveness.

Overcome 'Queen Bee' Syndrome

There is a special place in hell for women who don't help other women.
—Madeleine Albright

Women encounter several challenges to establish and become successful. Mostly they encounter challenges from their male superiors and colleagues. In rare cases, they find challenges especially suppression from the same sex which is known as "Queen Bee" Syndrome. Cecilia Harvey, a London-based consultant and founder of global showcase platform Tech Women Today unfolds, "Queen Bees are adult versions of the mean girls from school—but now they have grown up and are more calculating. These socially aggressive behaviors include gossiping, social exclusion, social isolation, social alienation, talking about someone, and stealing friends or romantic partners." The derogatory[1] "queen bee" label is given to women who pursue individual success in male-dominated work settings (organizations in which men hold most executive positions) by adjusting to the masculine culture and by distancing themselves from other women. Queen bees are the successful senior women who don't allow other ambitious princesses to succeed in the workplace. Worse, they prevent young women from reaching senior positions. Their attitude and approach hurt the interests of other ambitious young women leading to decreased morale and increased litigations within the organizations. Their

[1] https://ppw.kuleuven.be/cscp/documents/artikels-colette/the-queen-bee-phenomenon.pdf.

behavior adversely affects organizational performance and productivity. Therefore, Queen Bee Syndrome can be defined as the practice where the successful senior women prevent ambitious princesses from reaching the senior positions.

Professor Allison Gabriel[2] remarked, "Women are ruder to each other than they are to men, or than men are to women. This isn't to say men were off the hook or they weren't engaging in these behaviors. But when we compared the average levels of incivility reported, female-instigated incivility was reported more often than male-instigated incivility by women in our three studies." The examples of queen bees include Margaret Thatcher and Indira Gandhi who were former Prime Ministers to UK and India, respectively. In traditional Indian society, mothers-in-law usually turn out queen bees for their daughters-in-law.

Women are more ambitious to fast-track their careers than to advance the careers of their female colleagues and subordinates. There are several reasons for women turning into queen bees. They want young women to struggle and suffer because they struggled and suffered to reach their senior positions. They lack empathy and sympathy toward the same gender. They turn out to be hard and their leadership style becomes autocratic. There may be psychological reasons, their personality type, and the environment in which they were brought up. At times, they behave themselves more like men and distance themselves from other women thus endorsing the glass ceiling. A few women turn into queen bees to flow along with the malestream to fast-track their careers.

Queen Bee Syndrome is a controversial topic that cannot be substantiated with research findings because it is based on perceptions. It may be a generational perception rather than gender perception. Therefore, it is essential to bust the myth that there is something inherent in women that hinders the growth of other women.

Queen bees must learn that great leaders pave the way for others by laying the ladder. To empower women and ensure their career advancement, we need righteous women, not queen bees. The young women must not give up their goals when odds are stacked against them including from the same sex. They must demonstrate their grit and determination to excel in all aspects of life to leave their marks for others to follow.

---

[2] https://www.bustle.com/p/what-is-queen-bee-syndrome-it-might-explain-why-some-women-are-uncivil-to-each-other-at-work-8402852.

Impart Soft Skills Training for Women Leaders

Soft skills are essential for everyone irrespective of rank, position, and gender. They are essential, especially for women to excel as leaders and C-level executives. There is a myth that soft skills are closely connected with gender. The truth is that soft skills are not gender-related. They are essential from janitors to the highest positions in the organizations.

Soft skills are the skills, abilities, and traits about your personality, attitude, and behavior. There are several skills that collectively constitute soft skills such as self-management skills, communication skills, speaking skills, writing skills, reading skills, listening skills, leadership skills, teambuilding skills, decision-making skills, conflict-management skills, problem-solving skills, time management skills, career management skills, critical thinking skills, customer service skills, negotiation skills, networking skills, entrepreneurial skills, analytical skills, interpersonal skills, emotional intelligence, and initiative to name a few.

You can acquire soft skills by various means including observation, reading, training, experience, and practice. Soft skills training equips you with skills, abilities, and knowledge. However, your interaction with others helps acquire soft skills greatly. Since soft skills are behavioral skills, people must learn by trial and error method by using their emotional intelligence, and through flexibility and adaptability. You must be practical, realistic, and situational to acquire soft skills. Above all, you must learn from your failures to improve your behavior to get along well with others effectively.

You must develop emotional intelligence and interpersonal skills. You must observe and understand people and their behaviors. Travel unknown destinations to understand people. Talk to them to get along with them. Understand their cultures and behaviors. Traveling teaches tolerance and improves soft skills. When you travel to unknown destinations and communicate in a non-native language, you will be able to improve soft skills effectively.

Reading soft skills is one aspect and applying them is another aspect. Attending workshops and training programs help you understand what are soft skills and how you will be able to acquire them as such programs conduct role-plays to bring out behavioral improvement.

The dearth of soft skills will adversely affect accommodation, food services, retail, health, and social work sectors in the future. Therefore, there must be coordinated and integrated efforts from all stakeholders including individuals, organizations, intellectuals, educational institutions, policy-makers, thought leaders, government, and nonprofits to promote soft skills in all spheres.

Equip Networking Skills for Women Leaders

It is not *what* you know but *who* you know matters in this networked world. Having connections helps you greatly to fast-track your career. Some people get quick visibility while some remain incognito forever. Some people even leave this world as unsung heroes and heroines. Therefore, having connections helps you greatly to achieve success.

LeanIn.Org and McKinsey & Company[3] found in their major new study—with almost 30,000 employees across 118 companies that women's odds of advancement are 15% lower than men's. A study[4] explains "Women and men agree that sponsorship is vital to success and advancement, with two-thirds describing it as 'very' or 'extremely' important. Yet they do not have the same type of professional networks, which may result in different levels of support." It is obvious from these research findings that women lack strong networking skills to excel socially, professionally, and virtually. Hence, they receive the news of employment opportunities much later than men. In fact, most employment opportunities are not available through newspaper advertisements. They are filled mostly through connections and referral recruitments. The people who work in the companies know about the openings and refer their close connections who get shortlisted and selected. The incentives are directly credited into the accounts of the people who referred the candidates. Things have changed from the conventional methods of recruitment to advanced methods of recruitment. People who know the top people can get access to opportunities for employment. After joining the organizations, the employees who have strong connections with the top hierarchy in the organizations get promoted quickly.

Currently, 3Cs are essential to succeed in all spheres—content, communication, and connections. Content is king while communication is queen. When your content is strong, you earn respect from others. At

[3] https://www.mckinsey.com/featured-insights/gender-equality/women-in-the-workplace-2017.

[4] https://www.huffingtonpost.com/marilyn-nagel/women-network-differently_b_8259538.html.

the same time, you must have strong communication skills to convey your content to reach the right audiences. Connections are the people who spread a word about your content and communication. Hence, having content, communication, and connections helps you achieve amazing success in all spheres.

Networking is an art, not rocket science. Anybody can network if they acquire basic tools and techniques. Here are some tools for women to network with others successfully. Women must diversify network development strategies. They must treat other women as allies, not enemies to build strong networks. They must network with both women and men equally. They must not seek favors immediately. They must extend their hands and explore opportunities. Currently, there is more of "boys club" than "girls club" in the organizations. Hence, they must network with both clubs to advance their careers.

Whenever you get an opportunity, seize it to deliver a speech to get noticed. You must come forward to deliver their talks during public events, functions, and award ceremonies. It enhances visibility and offers innumerable opportunities. Remember to emphasize quality connections. Instead of networking with too many people, choose a few people especially 2–3 people with positive body language in the events and talk to them. Take their business cards and give your business cards to them. Follow-up. Note down their email ids and send them an email with a thank-you note. In case, if there are any opportunities, your email helps them connect back with you. In a nutshell, to be a successful networker, you must be an attentive listener, empathize with others, emotionally intelligent, ask the right questions, respect the listener, add value to the listener and make a difference.

Internet and technology have thrown tremendous opportunities for ordinary individuals to excel as extraordinary individuals. If people know how to create original content and share it with their audiences on social media with the right hashtags at the right time, they can be seen easily and promoted quickly. Some ordinary people showcase their skills, knowledge, abilities, and talents through YouTube channel and get recognition instantly. They build networks and create a fan base. They build their leadership brands.

If a raindrop falls into an ocean, it loses its significance; if the same raindrop falls into a shell, it becomes a pearl. The right people must connect with the right people at the right time to achieve the right outcomes. The difference between the lucky people and the unlucky people is that lucky people have connections while the unlucky people don't have any connections.

Close the Gender Pay Gap Globally

Globally the gender pay gap is a burning topic but very few take it seriously to bridge the gap earnestly. If women are equipped with negotiation skills the gender pay gap can be minimized in organizations. Women find it hard to negotiate their salary. They are behind men in expressing and expecting the desired outcomes in salary and compensation.

Women must learn how to negotiate their salaries to end up rich at the end of their careers. Failing to do so will result in undervaluing their resumes, low productivity, and low morale in the workplace. They must remember that unless they ask, they don't get what they want. While negotiating pay compensation men are direct and women are indirect in their approaches. At times it becomes difficult for employers to understand what women want. Therefore, women must communicate clearly about their expectations.

Women must remember that gender stereotypes are pervasive. They are often at a disadvantaged position at the negotiation table thus adversely impacting negotiations. Hence, they must ask what they want during negotiations. They must not react negatively across the negotiating table. They must maintain neutral body language; avoid expressing eagerness to get employment or overexcitement if offered more salary, and keep cool and composed. They must focus on their core skills and strengths and bargain from the position of strength.

Salary negotiation is a collaborative process between the employer and the employee. It must be a win-win outcome to ensure employee engagement effectively and achieve organizational excellence and effectiveness.

Be realistic when you negotiate your salary. Research to find out the prevailing salaries paid in your current position in your industry. Ask for a reasonable hike. Don't quote sky high as you lose the chances of getting employment offer. Fix low and high figures on your mind and negotiate to make it win-win. A win-win outcome is always better than a lose-win or win-lose outcome. If you are convinced that others are getting salaries better than you, be assertive to ask for it. If you find that the present employer doesn't pay as your abilities, explore employment opportunities elsewhere to get a higher salary. When you know your true worth and the prevailing salaries in your industry, you can negotiate from a position of strength.

Countries including Iceland, Norway, Finland, Sweden, and Denmark have taken appropriate measures to close the gender pay gap. For instance, Iceland fines for companies with gender wage gaps; Norway pays mandatory paternal leave; Finland and Sweden offer flexible schedules, and Denmark provides partially subsidized and affordable childcare. Global companies including Starbucks, Intel, Salesforce.com, GoDaddy, and Accenture have taken the right steps to bridge the gender pay gap.

Ensure Work-Life Integration for Women

Work-life integration is a challenging issue for both men and women. It is more challenging for women as they must take a break for their motherhood and take care of their children at home. Currently, the employees work very hard to earn their livelihood and beat the competition. Hence, taking care of all aspects is not an easy thing. If anybody has it all, they are truly blessed.

For women, there is often a conflict between the biological clock and career clock. Balancing both is a challenging task for them. Companies including Facebook and Google encourage work-life integration which encourages some leisure time for their employees to pursue their hobbies or to relax during the working hours to enable them to recharge.

Instead of searching for work-life balance, women must reframe their minds and integrate work and life to lead a complete life. Previously people worked hard for more than 8 hours a day for 6 days a week. Presently people work smart for 8 hours a day for 5 days a week. In the future, people will work wise 6 hours a day for 4 days a week. Therefore, we are looking forward to a world where people eat the cake and have it too. That means, they enjoy during work hours and achieve peak performance in the workplace.

Build a Team of Connections Globally

When you want to achieve amazing success globally you must build a team of strong connections and networks. After completion of your education, parents have a limited role to play in your life except in supporting your family and finance. However, when you want to fast-track your career, you must build a team of connections globally to add value to them and leverage their connections.

Connections are crucial for your career and leadership success. They help you keep in the right place at the right time. They help you timely and immensely. When a raindrop falls into an ocean, it loses its significance. In contrast, if the same raindrop falls into a shell, it becomes a pearl. Right connections, coaches, and mentors help you fast-track your career.

Even if you don't have money, your connections help you greatly. That is one of the major reasons why people invest their time, energy, and resources to build connections. Some people attend events and functions to network with others. There are networking events at the end of each program to connect with like-minded people to explore opportunities. It is a well-admitted fact that behind the success of every person there is someone who laid the ladder for their success. Therefore, success is not a solo game. It is a confluence of various factors including hard work, persistence, and connections. Here are some tools to build your network. Don't be shy to talk with strangers. Be comfortable to open up with them. Don't be overly conscious about making mistakes. Be cheerful. Smile to connect with others. Start your conversation based on your knowledge, skills, and abilities. Also, initiate your conversation by outlining others' areas of interest. Be a good listener first. Don't interfere when others converse with you. Present a positive body language to connect with others. Adopt mirroring techniques to connect with others quickly. Avoid interfering with their personal issues and lives. Your conversation must be professional with an emphasis on ethics and etiquette.

People prefer to pursue an education in prestigious institutions. Apart from acquiring knowledge from the best faculty and exchanging knowledge with their peers, they enjoy quality connections. Some of their connections reach higher positions in the long run. They help themselves since they hail from the same institution. The alumni from these institutions help their institutions to grow stronger and greater. In this way, they elevate their brand and strengthen their connections. Additionally, if you want to stay rich forever, one of the best ways is to acquire quality education in prestigious institutions as the alumni extend their help among themselves. Remember, a single contact with the right person at the right time will keep you in the right place to touch your tipping point.

In this cutthroat competitive world what makes the successful and unsuccessful is the ability to network with others effectively. There are people who became stars due to their connections. Subsequently, they worked hard; built their skills and abilities; and retained their positions. Hence, don't underestimate the power of networks and connections. In fact, "who you know" matters more than "what you know" in this cutthroat competitive world.

It is observed that some people are very strong in their areas but they don't know how to build connections and showcase them with others. They find it challenging and remain unnoticed and unrecognized throughout their lives. On the other hand, some people have the right connections and showcase whatever the little they have and achieve recognition and success quickly. Hence "who you know" certainly matters more than "what you know." If "what you know" is the king of success, "who you know" is the queen of success. Both the king and queen are essential to run your career empire successfully.

Leverage Social Media

Social media has played a crucial role to highlight various social issues including women empowerment. It has highlighted many unnoticed issues. It has connected the people globally and brought democracy virtually. Although it has created chaos in some aspects, it has transformed society by highlighting social justice and bringing social change. Women are better informed than ever before due to the internet and advanced technology. There is growing awareness and assertiveness to fight for their equality.

You can communicate with anybody on social media across nations, time zones, and demographics. You can share your vision, mission, and execution and your knowledge, skills, and abilities. It is an open platform for everyone either to agree or disagree with what you have posted. It is a democratic platform to exchange ideas, insights, opinions, and views. It is a great opportunity thrown open to humans by technology. Therefore, women leaders must express their ambitions early in their careers to reach top positions and spread their words on social media to get noticed. To be successful in social media, you must be consistent in your content and communication. It takes lots of effort, energy, and time to build your brand. It requires loads of passion, patience, and perseverance.

Technology has become both a boon and bane and it all depends on how you view it. Instead of viewing it as your enemy, you must treat it as your ally to harness it effectively to achieve human progress and prosperity. Many people viewed it as an ally and participated in social media to share their knowledge, ideas, insights, and opinions. Some people leveraged social media to build their brands and fast-track their careers. Women leaders including Oprah Winfrey, Sheryl Sandberg, and Arianna Huffington have successfully leveraged social media to brand and market themselves. Hence, women must know how to leverage this amazing platform to fast-track their careers.

If you are a novice, here is how you can proceed on social media. Understand the basics of all social media platforms and their pros and cons. Shortlist the ones that suit your profile, area, and image. Stick to those platforms and share your ideas, insights, thoughts, knowledge, skills, and abilities regularly. Gradually people will notice and follow you. Comment on their posts and they will reciprocate if they find the time and feel that your posts or comments are interesting. Be consistent in your posts and messages. Build your credibility. Be persistent because it takes a lot of time. At the same time don't get addicted to social media. Fix some time every day and use it judiciously without hampering your core activities and assignments. Use your filler time in the day such as traveling while you commute to your office. In this way, you can leverage your traveling time judiciously to build your brand and market yourself. Here are some tools for women leaders to adopt to excel personally, professionally, and socially. Don't shy to market and brand yourself. Be visible on social media to showcase your strengths and achievements. Make a noise whenever you achieve something worthwhile to enable the people to notice you and to become an inspiration for others. Here is a caution: Be careful about what you are posting. Avoid posting sensitive issues related to religion and politics. Avoid kicking up controversies for getting short-term fame.

Social media highlighted women empowerment and atrocities on women thus advocating gender equality globally. It unfolded many things that were unknown to many people. Therefore, women must use social media judiciously to fight for their rights and fast-track their careers.

Humanize Your Leadership Brand

These are the days of branding and marketing whether you are a spiritual leader, religious leader, business leader, political leader, or academic leader. With the advent of social media, people started using technology aggressively to build their credibility and enhance visibility. There are celebrities including film stars, cricketers, and sportspersons who hire marketing people and social media managers to click photographs with their pets and post on social media. They meet poor people in developing nations and the less fortunate; click photos and upload on social media platforms especially on Instagram to enhance their visibility. They want to show visually that they are committed to making a difference. Are they honestly humanizing their brands?

By leveraging social media, ordinary individuals excelled as extraordinary individuals by branding and marketing aggressively. Several celebrities bank on the support of other celebrities to leverage their brands rather than to extend opportunities to the average individuals and upcoming ambitious individuals. Such celebrities hardly humanize their brands.

When you look at Mahatma Gandhi, Mother Teresa, Martin Luther King Jr, and Nelson Mandela they worked for their causes, not applauses. They walked their talk. They did not crave for publicity and visibility. It was the people who spread their ideals and ideas, and struggles and sacrifices through word of mouth and built their credibility and enhanced their visibility. However, in this internet age, most celebrities pump their money to build their brands and market themselves aggressively to create more wealth. They hardly walk their talk and make a difference in the lives of people.

Humanizing your brand means giving a human dimension to your brand by connecting with your audience and touching their lives. It is to connect with your audience emotionally, not mechanically. It is to convert invisible elements into visible elements and intangible aspects into tangible aspects. It is to include emotions with a humane touch to your brand. It gives a competitive edge to your leadership brand.

When everyone involved in social media is human why cannot you humanize your brand? To humanize your brand, you must emphasize emotions, egos, and feelings. Therefore, brand humanization can be defined as the process of giving a human dimension to your brand by involving emotions, egos, and feelings to connect with your audience quickly to touch their lives and make a difference. In this age of automation, it is essential to emphasize human elements to your brand due to the dearth of physical proximity. Humanizing your brand is a marathon, not a sprint. It requires regular efforts, energy, enthusiasm, and time to humanize your brand. Here are some tips to humanize your brand. Emphasize social issues to bring social change. Take up a few core issues globally and highlight them. Focus on average individuals and their issues to explore ideas. Include emotional elements to touch their hearts and offer inspiring ideas to ignite their minds. Accept your mistakes and apologize. Don't worry about flaws. Accept flaws and failures because nobody is perfect in the world. Keep people before profit. Avoid short-term temptations. Be agile and active. Engage your audience on your social media platform. Encourage agreement and disagreement. Be honest and transparent. Observe ethics and etiquette. Build trust and goodwill in the audience. Build social media warriors and soldiers. Build brand ambassadors and evangelists. Walk your talk and go the extra mile. Above all, learn, unlearn, and relearn to humanize your leadership brand constantly.

Some people kick up controversies to get noticed on social media. They want instant fame on social media. Such tactics don't help them in the long run because a consistently growing graph is essential to build your brand on social media. However, there will be occasional setbacks in career graphs. When you look at the authentic influencers, they mean business and grow consistently on social media with meaningful dialogues and discussions by sharing great content consistently and adding value to their audiences.

If you think that brands are like humans on the move, you will personalize, engage, and inspire your audiences effectively and successfully. When you look at global companies including Google, Apple, Facebook, Nike, Coca-Cola, South West Airlines, McDonald's, and Starbucks, they humanized their brands successfully. They emphasized customer delight which is far ahead of customer satisfaction. When you humanize your brand, you can achieve customer delight.

People have become much wiser and smarter than ever before because social media has thrown everything open to assess individuals and their activities. It reviews and offers feedback instantly. The audiences watch their leaders from all spheres; branding and marketing tactics, and assess authenticity. Hence, ordinary individuals who aspire to excel as extraordinary individuals and successful individuals who intend to become more influential must add value to others by humanizing their brands and making a difference to the world.

Smashing Through the Glass Ceiling

> There is no great force for change, for peace, for justice and democracy, for inclusive economic growth than a world of empowered women.
> —Phumzile Mlambo-Ngcuka

We cannot force men to sacrifice their careers for women. Instead, we can implore men to support women in whatever the best possible way to achieve women's empowerment and advancement. Women must realize that playing a gender card does not work in any away. Instead, they must participate and work hard and smart in developmental activities. They must chart their paths to prove themselves identifying their inner talents and understanding their limitations. They must take initiative to move forward as nobody invites them to lead from the front. They must express their ambitions in the early stage of their careers; build connections; seek help from others; and help other women leaders to accomplish their goals.

To summarize, when you want to achieve growth and prosperity it is imperative to encourage women participation in developmental activities. A bird cannot fly with one wing because it needs two wings to fly. Similarly, when you want society to progress, you must advocate women empowerment and participation who constitute half of the global population. When both men and women participate, imagine the type of society we will pass on to the next generation. Hence, men must support women wholeheartedly to build a prosperous world. To conclude, women must smash through the glass ceiling. They must not shy away from shouldering responsibilities. They must stay in the game by learning and leading. They must break structural obstacles and build connections to fast-track their careers.

Chapter Takeaways

- Currently women are smashing through the glass ceiling and excelling globally to carve a niche for themselves.
- compared to men, women are better at interpersonal skills, soft skills, emotional intelligence, empathy, flexibility, and sociability.

- Women work harder than men to prove themselves in the male-dominated corporate world.
- Women leaders emphasize more on the democratic process to build consensus. They emphasize more on collaboration, not competition. They are empathetic and good listeners.
- Communication styles differ from person to person and between genders. Women seek more information than men to arrive at their conclusions. They can decode and encode data more effectively than men.
- Several factors are holding women leaders back within the global organizations—stereotypes, structural obstacles, lifestyle issues, institutional mindsets, and individual mindsets to name a few.
- Women encounter several challenges to establish and become successful. Mostly they encounter challenges from their male superiors and colleagues. In rare cases, they find challenges especially suppression from the same sex which is known as "Queen Bee" Syndrome.
- Queen Bee Syndrome is a controversial topic that cannot be substantiated with research findings because it is based on perceptions.
- Soft skills are essential for everyone irrespective of rank, position, and gender. They are essential, especially for women to excel as leaders and C-level executives.

References

Additional Readings

https://www.coastal.edu/media/administration/.../pdf/Cinardo_Communication.pdf.

http://www.uky.edu/ofa/sites/www.uky.edu.ofa/files/uploads/Gender%20Styles%20in%20Communication.pdf.

https://pdfs.semanticscholar.org/4698/d2a6dfa8bd81975d8a20707c7157f95c6e97.pdf.

https://ppw.kuleuven.be/cscp/documents/artikels-colette/the-queen-bee-phenomenon.pdf.

https://www.bustle.com/p/what-is-queen-bee-syndrome-it-might-explain-why-some-women-are-uncivil-to-each-other-at-work-8402852.

https://www.mckinsey.com/featured-insights/gender-equality/women-in-the-workplace-2017.

https://www.huffingtonpost.com/marilyn-nagel/women-network-differently_
    b_8259538.html.
https://www.theguardian.com/society/2017/nov/01/gender-pay-gap-217-
    years-to-close-world-economic-forum.
https://www.forbes.com/sites/shelleyzalis/2018/10/30/lessons-from-the-wor
    lds-most-gender-equal-countries/#376cab727dd8.
https://www.forbes.com/sites/selenarezvani1/2018/04/13/six-companies-hac
    king-the-gender-wage-gap/#5dc8075f7055.
https://www.amazon.com/Build-Your-Dream-Network-Hyper-Connected/dp/
    0143111485.
https://www.forbes.com/sites/nextavenue/2014/09/11/are-women-too-
    timid-when-they-job-search.
www.grantthornton.cn/upload/IBR_2013_Women_in_senior_manage
    ment_EN.pdf.
https://engage.kornferry.com/womenceosspeak.
https://hbr.org/2016/04/do-women-make-bolder-leaders-than-men.
https://www.ddiworld.com/DDI/media/trend-research/holding-women-
    back_tr_ddi.pdf?ext=.pdf.
https://images.dowjones.com/wp-content/uploads/sites/137/2017/07/311
    53316/WITW_2015_JournalReport.pdf.
https://www.deakinco.com/uploads/news/Anneli_Blundell_whitepaper.pdf.

CHAPTER 16

Feminism: Legitimate, Fearful, or Feared

Amelia F. Underwood and Debra J. Dean

INTRODUCTION

Forbes has an annual award for The World's 100 Most Powerful Women with names such as Angela Merkel, Christine Lagarde, and Nancy Pelosi. The British Broadcasting Corporation (BBC) also had a list of 100 women for 2019 that included Precious Adams, Parveena Ahanger, and Piera Aiello. There are awards for the Woman of the Year offered by magazines such as Glamour, Harper's Bazaar, and Vogue. There is no shortage of such awards offered annually by businesses, communities, and schools. This chapter examines the women of the Bible as if they were being awarded such a noble prize. In total, there are fewer than 200 women whose words appear in the Protestant Bible, which consists of 66 books. According to Frank (2019), there are 10,000 words spoken by 86 women; 44 are named and 42 are unnamed. Hannah (2015) stated

A. F. Underwood
School of Business and Leadership, Regent University, Virginia Beach, VA, USA

D. J. Dean (✉)
Department of Business, Leadership, and Information Systems, Regent University, Virginia Beach, VA, USA
e-mail: debrdea@regent.edu

J. Marques (ed.), *Exploring Gender at Work*,
https://doi.org/10.1007/978-3-030-64319-5_16

297

there were 93 women in the Bible; including 14,056 words by 49 named and 44 unnamed. Bible Gateway lists 176 women in the Bible. In the Roman Catholic Canon of the Bible there are 73 books with 333 women (Camille 2017).

WHO'S WHO OF WOMEN IN THE BIBLE

According to Hannah (2015), there are 14,056 words spoken by 93 women in the Bible. Of those 93 women, only 49 were named (Hannah). Eve only spoke 74 words in the Bible. Mary, the mother of Jesus spoke 191 words. In her research, Hanna found 61 words for Mary Magdalene and 141 words for Sarah. The woman with the most words in the Bible was Judith with 2689.

LEGITIMATE

According to Pelikan (1996), Mary, the mother of Jesus Christ, has inspired more people than any other woman in history. In his book, *Mary Through the Centuries: Her place in the history of culture*, Pelikan posits that Mary embodies the polar struggle of modesty and sensuality that many women still struggle with today. She is a complex woman portrayed as virgin and mother, model of purity and shelter for sinners, God-bearer and sheltered nun, and Monarch of heaven and mother of all (Morgan 2005). As a teenager, Mary was told she would give birth to the savior of the world. In modern society, Mary would have a choice of keeping her fetus or aborting it. Thankfully for all of us, she chose to continue with the pregnancy despite the fact she would have hardships as an unmarried, betrothed woman. In the days of Mary, it was normal for women to be engaged or betrothed prior to their wedding day. In the days of Mary and Joseph, a betrothed woman was legally married, yet remained in her father's home until her wedding day. During the betrothal period, a woman was to abstain from sexual relations. The betrothal period was not only a time to prove virginity, it was also a time for family negotiations to occur. The future groom would compensate the bride's father since he was taking a working member of the family away. Although the bride and groom were not living in the same house, they were legally considered married for all intents and purposes. Therefore, in the case of Mary becoming pregnant prior to moving in with Joseph, this was grounds for divorce. Joseph had a decision to make too. If he divorced Mary, she would be unable to care for herself and the child because women were not permitted to handle money or have jobs during that time. Regardless if he stayed with Mary or not, her reputation as a virgin was on the line.

Mary Magdalene may be the most misunderstood woman in the Bible. Unfortunately, she has a "foul stigma" attached to her name; however, she has supporters that claim she is the only woman of the Bible that "superseded Mary in her devotion to the Master" (BibleGateway, n.d.). A major controversy surrounds this woman as some claim she was a prostitute; however, there is not a shred of evidence in scripture that infers she had an unsavory reputation. In comparison to other women through the centuries, one might wonder how many women have lived a life with a reputation they did not deserve. Her introduction in Luke 8: 2 describes Mary Magdalene as one of the women with Jesus and the twelve disciples. In that passage, the women are described as followers that were "healed of evil spirits and infirmities." Specifically, Mary Magdalene had seven demons. She is mentioned fourteen times in the gospels (Matthew 27: 56, 61; 28: 1; Mark 15: 40, 47; 16: 1–19; Luke 8: 2; 24: 10; John 19: 25; 20: 1–18). In eight of those instances, she is listed with other women and her name tops the list. In the one instance where her name does not top the list it is because she is alongside Jesus' mother and aunt (John 19: 25). In the five times she is mentioned alone, it is in connection with Jesus' death and resurrection (Mark 16: 9, John 20: 1, 11, 16, 18).

FEARFUL

Proverbs 31: 30 states, "Charm is deceptive, and beauty is vain; but a woman who fears the Lord is to be praised." This scripture passage calls into question the definition of fear as we know it today. At first thought, a fearful woman may be one that is beyond submissive allowing emotional, physical, or sexual abuse to take place out of fear their relationship will fall apart. The word fear refers to awe, calamity, danger, fright, intimidation, respect, revere, and terror. Nelson (2019) believes the word "fear" is used in reference to God at least 300 times in scripture. The phrase "Fear of the Lord" is used 25 times in the New American Standard Bible and appears more in the book of Proverbs than any other book of the Bible. Fear infers honor and respect for the Lord; whereas, wisdom is the beginning of knowledge. Therefore, this section of the chapter examines fearful women as those seeking wisdom to grow in spiritual maturity. Psalm 139: 14

states, "I praise you because I am fearfully and wonderfully made; your works are wonderful, I know that full well."

Edwards (2017) documented the following ten women of biblical times that exceeded expectations: Huldah, Jehosheba, Lydia, Phoebe, Priscilla, Puah, Rahab, Shiphrah, Tamar, and the women that witnessed the resurrection of Christ. Joseph (2015) wrote of the following five "seemingly insignificant" women that, amid crisis, stood up bravely against the violence: Miriam, Moses' Mother, Pharoah's Daughter, Puah, and Shiphrah. This section selects a few of these cases to examine in further detail.

Two women, never mentioned again in the Bible, are praised for saving thousands of lives while disobeying government authority. Puah and Shiphrah were Hebrew midwives commanded by the King of Egypt to kill all firstborn male Hebrew children (Exodus 1: 15–22). Instead of following the order of the king, the two women feared God more than Pharaoh and resisted the evil regime. According to Kadari (2009), the midwives "did not obey the royal edict because they feared God" and "God rewarded them for their actions."

A woman was the first Christian in all of Europe. Lydia of Thyatira was a wealthy businesswoman. She made and sold purple cloth. Elliott (2008) explained that the color purple was indisputably signified as a magnificent sacrifice and royal wealth noting that the wealthy would flaunt their purple goods when they went to the marketplace. Criswell (1983) proclaimed that all things of the Judeo-Christian faith come out of history and he explained that prophecy is unique to the Judeo-Christian religion. The history of Lydia is no different. Lydia is the first Christian convert in Macedonia (Acts 16: 11–15). After her conversion, she was baptized right away and invited Luke, Paul, and Silas to her home.

Women were the first to see Jesus after he raised from the dead. Setzer (1997) argues the validity of an argument over female witnesses and the law since witnessing the absence of a body in the tomb was "hardly a legal context." However, many scriptural references affirm that some men were slow to listen and adhere to the directive of the women to meet Jesus in Galilee. Yet, Setzer reveals that "someone believed them" as "the disciples made their way to Galilee to the mountain to which Jesus had summoned them" (Matthew 28: 15). Other disciples relayed the message saying the tomb was empty "just as the women had said" (Luke 24: 22–24). In general, this event where Mary Magdalene, Joanna, Mary the mother of James, and other women reported to the tomb, found it empty, encountered and received a message from Jesus Christ, and proceeded to tell others as instructed is a huge display of fearing God, rejoicing, worshiping, and becoming joyful (Setzer, pp. 266–267).

WICKED WOMEN

Spangler (2015b) explained that "One of the things that makes Scripture so believable is that the unsavory stories remain part of it. In truth, the Bible never attempts to clean up the stories or whitewash its characters" (p. 10). In her book, Wicked Women of the Bible, Spangler included wicked women as in (a) morally evil, and (b) very, very good. Her book opens with Eve, the first woman of all times. She also includes Abigail, Bathsheba, Deborah, Delilah, Esther, Gomer, Hannah, Herodias, Jael, Jezebel, Mary Magdalene, Michal, Miriam, Naomi, Peninnah, Rahab, Ruth, Salome, Sarah, Tamar, the Medium of Endor, the Woman of Samaria, and the Woman who wiped the feet of Jesus. Spangler (2015a) guest authored a list for Bible Gateway demonstrating how "the most ancient of books has shaped and formed the history of our world." Her list included Athaliah, Delilah, Eve, Gomer, Herodias, Jezebel, Lot's wife, Potiphar's wife, the witch of Endor (also known as the medium of Endor), and the woman of Samaria. Coming in at number one on both lists was Eve, "the original baddie." Spangler stated she selected Eve as number one because of "all the evil she and her husband unleashed on the world" (2015a). Although Eve was the perfect woman, she knew both good and evil. She knew what it was like to "feel every sense satisfied, every need cared for" and she "knew the immensity of love" (Spangler 2015b, p. 14). Yet, Eve also experienced how "sin could lurk at your door, waiting for a chance to beat you down and shatter you into a thousand jagged pieces, each on a thorn and a barb" (p. 15). Eve also knew "deceit, blame, want, shame, and terrible grief" (p. 16).

D'Ror Chankin-Gould, Hutchinson, Hilton Jackson, Mayfield, Schulte, Schneider, and Winkelman (2008) exegete 2 Samuel 11: 2–4 to understand Bathsheba's character and clear her reputation of what some call whore and others consider a rape victim (p. 352). Their scholarly interpretation of the text points to Bathsheba's "action on the roof, her ethnic identity, and her character" (p. 350). The scholars focus on the following three words in the Hebrew Bible pericope: *roheset* (washing), *mitqaddeset* (self-sanctifying), and *mittumatah* (from her uncleanness). The first word, *roheset*, is found 77 times in the Hebrew Bible and is never used in connection with a woman bathing after her menstrual cycle, according to D'Ror Chankin-Gould, et al. (p. 342). The scholars note that this type of reactive washing occurs when something is in need of being cleaned. Such bathing could include hygiene or to remove dirt. It could also mean cleansing oneself or another person for hospitality, emotional cleansing, or preparing for ritual sacrifices. The authors note that menstruation at the time of Bathsheba's famous washing would not necessitate a bath for women because at that time, a woman would social distance for seven days due to her period and return with sacrifices of doves or pigeons (Leviticus 15: 19–30). However, if a man came in contact with a woman's blood, they were to bathe. The second word, *mitqaddeset*, is used in Ezekiel 38: 23 when God declares He is great, holy, and will make himself known to many nations. It is only used once by a human, causing the scholars to consider Bathsheba in a position of God cleansing her for the sake of Israel's lineage (p. 348). The last word, *mittumatah,* does not refer to uncleanliness due to menstruation, but could refer to a male or female needing to clean for the sake of touching a dead body or sleeping with a person that is not their spouse (pp. 348–349). The scholar's interpretation reveals that Bathsheba was likely not an Israelite because she proactively bathed. D'Ror Chankin-Gould, et al. explain that the word *roheset* also "signals Bathsheba's legitimacy to become a mother of a future leader of Israel" (p. 351). They also explain that *mitqaddeset* refers to her action of laying with David and in contrast, Bathsheba is "the only individual human to self-sanctify herself" signifying again her "acceptability as a mother of a future leader of Israel" (p. 351). Finally, *mittumatah* reaffirms the self-sanctification due to the sexual encounter. The scholars explain that reactive washing could simply be due to intercourse and the body fluids that arise from such an event. In the end; however, D'Ror Chankin-Gould, et al. explain that "The author of Kings ultimately proves Bathsheba's status as a clean, sanctified, legitimate mother of Israel" noting 1 Kings 1: 15–40 where "she, at the instigation of Nathan, enthrones her son, the next Israelite king" (D'Ror Chankin-Gould, et al. p. 352).

Biblical Women in Leadership Roles

Deborah had a heart fixed on God and is the only female judge of Israel and one of a few prophetesses mentioned in the Bible. During the period of Judges (1382–1063 B.C.) God appointed 12 Judges; their role was not elected nor anointed. Deborah served 20 years before and 40 years after a time of conflict where the Israelites defeated Canaan and Sisera's army in 1216 B.C. Deborah was a key spokesperson for the victory as she listened to God's strategic instruction and commanded 10,000 men to battle against 100,000 soldiers and 900 iron chariots. Her colleague respected her fear for God and divine wisdom so much that he said, "If you go with me, I will go; but if you don't go with me, I won't go" (Judges 4: 8). Nielson (2018) explains that when reading Judges 4–5 one will see that Deborah had a God-inspired strength within her. As a prophetess, she had the ability to discern the mind and purpose of God and speaks God's word. In addition to speaking God's word, she obeyed it, and she sang God's word giving credit to God for the victory. Marrone (2019) explains that Deborah lived during a time before there were kings and after there were deliverers. Her charismatic leadership style and fear of God provided her with sound judgment, divine wisdom, and outstanding character qualities. Marrone said she had high moral character and integrity. She was highly intelligent, cunning, witty, smart, and intuitive. She was also a military leader, warrior, poet, wife, and mother. Others trusted her and saw her as fair, open, and a person that refused to show partiality.

The book of Esther has the distinction of being the only book of the Bible named after a woman. This Old Testament book portrays the history of a beautiful and faithful Jewish girl orphaned at youth and raised by her cousin Mordecai during the time of Jewish exile. Considering her Jewish heritage and her status as a captive of the Persian Empire, Esther represents an unlikely candidate to become Queen during the reign of King Ahasuerus 484–464 B.C. However, Esther's courageous journey to become the leader and the rescuer of her people serves as a useful illustration of the practice of spiritual discernment and leadership during a period of extreme duress. The events in the book of Esther take place during the period of Jewish exile; notably, the Diaspora Jews descended from those driven into exile in Babylon and Egypt following the fall of Jerusalem in 586 B.C. (Bell 1998, p. 21). While some Jews returned to rebuild Jerusalem with Nehemiah in 536 B.C., many other Jews continued to practice their faith and maintained their unique identity as exiles in a foreign land (Bell 1998, p. 21). Walvoord and Zuck (1985) articulated that the book of Esther served to "encourage the returned Jewish exiles by reminding them of the faithfulness of God who would keep His promises to the nation" (p. 701). The book opens by chroni-cling how King Ahasuerus removed the reigning queen, Vashti, for failing to obey his direct command; moreover, the queen's behavior represented a direct challenge to the existing patriarchal structure of this society as "the queen's behavior [would] be made known to all women, causing them to look at their husbands with contempt" (Esther 1: 17). The king then ordered his officers to gather all the beautiful young girls in the provinces in order that "the young woman who pleases the king [would] be queen instead of Vashti" (Esther 2: 4).

Considering that Esther "had a beautiful figure and was lovely to look at... [she] was also taken to the king's palace and put in custody of Hegai, who had charge of the women" (Esther 2: 7–8). During this initial twelve months stay at the king's palace, Esther remained secluded in the king's harem while awaiting her introduction and subsequent opportunity to please the king. Prior to her departure, however, Mordecai, commanded Esther to not disclose her Jewish heritage. Interestingly, the name Esther means secret or hidden (Hitchcock 1996). While the scriptures do not indicate that Esther had a choice to comply, most scholars agree that Esther understood the ramifications of this decision because "by law, Esther was not to marry a pagan or have sexual relations with a man who was not her husband, and yet this was the purpose of her being included in the harem" (Waalvoord and Zuck 1985, p. 704). While the text omits any discussion of Esther's inner struggle with her situation, the writer does acknowledge Esther's willingness to obey the sound advice of Mordecai by remaining silent concerning her Jewish heritage (Esther 2: 10). Additionally, Esther chose to adopt a favorable disposition and atti-tude despite her circumstances which gained her favor with Hegai who managed the harem while she also "won favor in the eyes of all who saw her" (Esther 2: 15). When she was finally presented to the king, "the king loved Esther more than all the women, and she won graced and favor in his sight...so that he set the royal crown on her head and made her queen instead of Vashti" (Esther 2: 17).

As the story continues, Mordecai informed Esther of an impending plot hatched by the king's top advisor, Haman, which would destroy all Jews in the kingdom of Ahasuerus; specifically, Haman convinced the King that Jews in Persia refused to obey the laws of the land (Esther 3: 1–9). Moreover, Mordecai implored Esther to go before the king to "beg his favor and plead with him on behalf of her people" (Esther 4: 8). Esther carefully measured her response to Mordecai and she reminded him that "if any man or woman goes to the king inside the inner court without being called, there is but one law—to be put to death" (Esther 4: 11). While Esther's response may have appeared selfish at the surface, some scholars noted that Esther demonstrated foresight in questioning how she could serve her people if she exposed herself to certain death by approaching the king without being summoned (Nixon 2015, p. 334). On the other hand, Mordecai admonished Esther for being overly concerned for her own life in his statement, "Do not think to yourself that in the king's palace you will escape any more than all the other Jews. For if you keep silent at this time, relief and deliverance will rise for the Jew from another place, but you and your father's house will perish" (Esther 4: 13–14).

As this historical event unfolded, Esther effectively employed a discernment strategy that enabled her to effectively process the complexity of her situation and develop a strategic course of action to rescue her people. According to Thomas, Clark, and Gioia (1993), perceived threats or crisis situations often restrict the number of alternatives considered by decision-makers; additionally, the authors stated that threat interpretation "may distort information processing…and cause rigidity in decision processing that limits organizational responses" (p. 244). Discernment; however, requires leaders to seek God's wisdom; therefore, they must intentionally "forfeit any short-range or less-than-free solution that relieves the tension, settles the chaos, makes a decision, moves to action, makes oneself feel good, enhances the bottom line, gets someone off your back" (Delbecq, Mostyn, Nutt and Walter 2004, p. 157). Esther now exercised her legitimate power as queen and leader of her people to initiate a plan of her own which began with a request for the Jews to conduct a three day fast on her behalf while she personally fasted and prayed for guidance from God. In this decision to first pause and commune with God, Esther clearly recognized her need for spiritual guidance and courage to approach her decision-making process with an open mind and creativity; moreover, after this period of fasting and prayer, Esther communicated her willingness to intervene on behalf of her people regardless of the consequences stating "If I perish, I perish" (Esther 4: 16). According to Delbecq et al. (2004), spiritual discernment requires reverent listening and a posture that remains "attentive to emerging deep feelings…not transient emotions or anxieties, but rather the deep and persistent inner voice of truth" (p. 159); likewise, Esther placed herself in a receptive posture prepared to respond to God's revealed truth.

Esther orchestrated a strategic and risky plan to foil Haman's plot and rescue her people. Adopting a humble and unassuming bearing, Esther rejected the king's offers of personal gifts and favors in preparation for her ultimate request as an intervention to spare her and her people. With great emotion and poise, Esther honorably presented her request stating, "For we have been sold, I and my people, to be destroyed, to be killed, to be annihilated. If we had been sold merely as slaves, men and women, I would have been silent, for our affliction is not to be compared with the loss to the king" (Esther 7: 4). Moreover, Esther cleverly presented her petition using Haman's own words, thereby leading the king to the conclusion that he had been tricked by Hamen.

Who's There, yet Missing in the Bible

Is a name all that important? Names identify the person. Historically, a name was much more than a label; it claimed a person's identity, such as "Daughter of Abraham" or "Wife of Moses." A person's authority, character, ownership, reputation, will, and worth were determined by the name. Today, many people want their name to be popular, celebrated, or immortalized in some way as to be famous. Reflection of names in today's culture reveals some of ancestral significance, such as being named after a grandmother; historical relevance, such as being named after a princess, and then there are names on the Outrageous Baby Name List such as Tesla, Lucifer, and Lemon. Scripture confirms that to enter heaven, one must believe in Jesus Christ and in doing so, their name is written in the Book of Life (Revelation 3: 5) and every child will have a new name in heaven (Isaiah 49: 16, Revelation 2: 17).

The Unnamed Women of the Bible

According to Bible Gateway, there are 107 unnamed women in the Bible and "thousands upon thousands of unnamed men." However, it is challenging to really know how many women are not named and what their role in history has been. Human creation started with Adam and Eve. While Eve was named in the Sacred Text, her daughters were not; however, their part in modern-day history is not to be taken lightly. God blessed Adam and Eve and told them to be fruitful and multiply (Genesis 1: 28) and then their sons are named as Cain, Abel, and Seth. In Genesis 5: 4, scripture quickly speaks of Adam and Eve having other sons and daughters. Without the daughters, it would have been impossible for Cain and Seth to have children. It is believed that Abel did not have any children. Adam's children numbered 33 sons and 23 daughters (Josephus, Whiston and Maier 1999, p. 53).

In the New Testament, it is interesting that Jesus' sister's names are unknown; however, many of the women he associated with are; the most loyal nonfamily member being Mary Magdalene. Jesus has many encounters with unnamed women. This section of the chapter will look at the woman who anoints Jesus with a highly valued jar of perfume and the Samaritan woman that Jesus meets at a water well. Both women serve Jesus. In Luke 7: 36–50, an unknown woman approaches Jesus with an alabaster jar of pure perfume. The value of the perfume is extremely high. Some scholars believe the price of the perfume would be equivalent to the annual earnings of an average Roman worker during the time of Jesus (Ottuh 2015). The unnamed Samaritan woman who meets Jesus at the well has 151 words recorded in scripture documenting their interaction as he stopped; "tired from his journey" (John 4: 1–26).

Ultimately, in believing that scripture is God breathed, one may wonder why some women are mentioned and others are not. One may wonder why some have as many words documented as Judith, while others have no words recorded. While we may never know these answers this side of heaven, one can rest with assurance that God included the women scripture because they hold equal value as do men and children.

Biblical Reference to Equality

Bird (2017) suggested that the creation accounts in Genesis 1–3 attempted to describe the essential nature of man and woman; furthermore, the author stated that the origin account in Genesis 1 reflected a shared embodiment of humankind symbolized by the divine image of God (p. 271). While man served as the model, the author stated that the grammar in the text designated the species as a whole—both man and woman made in the image of God (p. 271). However, the author suggested that the historic gendered existence of men and women as evidenced in the New Testament has promoted gender differentiation of roles, values, and authority (p. 271). Based on these gendered interpretations of Hebrew Scripture, male authority structures within ancient Israel, and the early church elevated the male perspective and status that persists to this day (p. 271). Consequently, biblical interpretations regarding the biological and cultural differences of human beings (gender, race, class, and ethnicity) as "equally characteristic of the species" (p. 271) pose challenges for contemporary theologians. Hence, the author argued that theological anthropology in the Hebrew Scriptures, as well as theological anthropology derived from the Hebrew Scriptures, presents an explicitly or implicitly male view of humans created in the image of God (p. 271). The author's feminist approach reflects present-day efforts to reconcile ancient Hebrew interpretations with New Testament applications of Hebrew texts that continue to shape the dialogue regarding roles, responsibilities, and status in the modern-day Church.

Malina (2001) identified the concepts of honor and shame as paramount cultural identifiers in the first-century Mediterranean world; specifically, the author argued that honor established a person's status and place in society. Individuals who failed to live up to societal expectations experienced humiliation or defeat (pp. 48–49). Paul routinely dealt with issues of status, honor, and shame when ministering to a diverse body of believers dispersed across a vast area of the Mediterranean during the first century. In Fiorenza's (1997) discussion of Paul's leadership among the diverse community of believers in Galatia, the author employed socio-cultural hermeneutical analysis to explore the meaning of unity in ethnic, gendered, and class terms. Addressing a mixed congregation of Jewish and Gentile believers who contested the necessity of circumcision for inclusion into the body of Christ, Paul stated, "You are all sons of God through faith. For as many of you as were baptized into Christ have to put on Christ. There is neither Jew nor Greek, there is neither slave nor free, there is no male and female, for you are all one in Christ Jesus" (Galatians 3: 26–2).

Employing the structural functionalism model, Fiorenza (1997) argued that Paul's stance on equality represented a radical departure from the recognized societal structure of Jewish and Gentile communities during this period. The author stated that Paul's declaration of religious equality for all believers included both the individual's standing before God as well as their social status and function in society (p. 226). Furthermore, the author noted that kinship lines would now be drawn on the basis of faith in Jesus Christ rather than racial and national inheritance as a believer's baptism in the name of Jesus Christ established an individual's equal status among believers in the body of Christ (pp. 226–227). Paul's declaration in Galatians 3: 28 represented a formal challenge to the established societal structure at this time as even male converts into

Judaism could not claim the status of the male Israelite in society (p. 226). For Jewish and Gentile Christian women, this claim equal status among men fundamentally subverted societal understandings of the role and status of women. Moreover, Kahl (2000) argued that Paul's emphasis on oneness as opposed to otherness openly challenged the masculine identity of male members of the Galatian congregation and introduced confusion concerning established gender roles in their society (pp. 47–48).

Huizing (2011) examined the prescribed roles of women in the early church that continue to influence the debate over leadership roles for women in the church today (pp. 18–21). In 1 Timothy 2, Paul addressed appropriate behaviors for believers in the church at Ephesus during times of worship and preaching to include lifting of hands, modest dress, and the roles of students and teachers of the scriptures. The author argued that Paul encouraged women to be "equal learners" (p. 17) so long as they followed the cultural practice of respectful submission to the teacher (p. 17). The author suggested that Paul primarily wanted to protect the church from false doctrine while also addressing behaviors of prominent women in the Ephesian church that where not in alignment with the proclamation of the gospel message (Huizing, pp. 19–20).

From a present-day standpoint, Paul's command against women teaching men in the church has incited much debate over the accepted leadership roles for women in the church. According to Huizing, (2011), authentic servant leadership "shares authority and develops others" (p. 21); furthermore, the author pointed out that the introduction of secular leadership principles under the guidance of the Holy Spirit may result in alterations to the existing Biblical model of leadership (p. 21). From a historical and cultural perspective, Paul's academic experiences as a highly educated Jewish scholar and his familiarity as a student under the most prominent all-male Pharisaic rabbis possibly shaped his decision-making process regarding the exclusion from women teachers in the church (Philippians 3: 4–6, Acts 22: 3).

In his discussion of the role of ideology when interpreting texts, Vanhoozer (1998), indicated that feminist criticism has demonstrated "greater sensitivity to the political implications of language and interpretation" (p. 167). Fiorenza (1983) stated that "feminist theory insists that all texts are products of an androcentric patriarchal culture and history" (p. xv). Therefore, Vanhoozer (1998) stated that the challenge for feminist readers includes interpreting the Bible in a fashion where "its oppressive potential is neutralized while its liberating power is released" (p. 180).

The author suggested that "feminist interpretation seeks to liberate the text from its own ideological limitations" (Vanhoozer, p. 181) thus situating the interpretative authority "outside the text in those social practices that encourage the liberation of women" (Vanhoozer, p. 181).

Wolters (2000) emphasized that ideological criticism refers to how the author's social location (race, class, gender, sexual orientation) influences the interpretation of that author's writing (p. 101). The author offered the example of how feminist biblical scholars remain alert to the presence of bias rooted in gender (Wolters, p. 101). Examples of feminist interpretation include Trible's (1978) discussion of Hosea 1–3 where Hosea used the imagery of a female harlot to denounce Israel's lack of faithfulness; the use of degrading female sexual images in Ezekiel 23; and the association of woman with wickedness and her removal from the restored land in Zechariah 5: 7–11 (Wolters, pp. 101–102).

Dube (1997) stated that among biblical and theological feminist readers, women from Two-Thirds World settings most frequently address the challenge to read postcolonially for decolonization (pp. 20–21). The author questioned how passages like Matthew 28: 18–20, Luke 24: 46–47, and John 20: 21 demonstrate the construction of power relations in the encounter with the Other and whether these passages "propose relationships of liberating interdependence between races, genders, cultures, and nations or do they propose a model of unequal inclusion" (Dube, p. 21). Moreover, Edet and Ekeya (1988) argued that among African people "there is alienation because evangelization has not been that of cultural exchange but of cultural domination and assimilation" (p. 3).

CONCLUSION

This chapter exegetically examined the role of women and the relationship between the historical context and modern-day presumptions that exist. Research confirmed there were named men and unnamed men, just as there are named women and unnamed women. Women in the Bible were faced with similar issues that modern-day women are faced with such as the polar struggle of modesty and sensuality. Today, just as in Biblical times, women face adversity where some are not trusted or believed, some are given horrendous reputations they do not deserve while others carry scarlet letters they have rightfully earned, and all are tempted with sinful desires. However, scripture demonstrates that women

do overcome such adversities with fear of God and prayerful consideration. Ultimately, women of the Bible are similar to women of modern
day in that they can be leaders and followers just as good or bad as men.
As good, they are characterized with words such as committed, courageous, high moral character, hospitable, integrity, loyalty, problem solver,
selflessness, self-sacrificing, and visionary.

CHAPTER TAKEAWAYS

The takeaways from this chapter are numerous. Overall, the idea is to see
that some women are mentioned in the Bible, and some are not. In understanding that women had pivotal roles in history, one can discern that
they maintain such valued places in modern-day society. And, while we
may not understand why some women are mentioned and some are not
revealed by name; nor may we understand why some historical events are
included, while others are not, we take refuge in knowing that scripture
is God breathed and perfect just the way it is.

REFERENCES

Bell, A. A. (1998). *Exploring the New Testament World: An illustrated guide
to the World of Jesus and the first Christians.* Nashville, TN: Thomas Nelson
Publishers.

BibleGateway. (n.d.). Retrieved from: https://www.biblegateway.com/resour
ces/all-men-bible/Great-Host-Unnamed-Bible-Men.

BibleGateway. (n.d.). Retrieved from: https://www.biblegateway.com/resour
ces/all-women-bible/Chapter-2-Alphabetical.

BibleGateway. (n.d.). Retrieved from: https://www.biblegateway.com/resour
ces/all-women-bible/Chapter-3-Nameless-Bible-Women.

BibleGateway. (n.d.). Retrieved from: https://www.biblegateway.com/resour
ces/all-women-bible/Mary-Magdalene.

Bird, P. A. (2017). Theological anthropology in the Hebrew Bible. In L. G.
Perdue (Ed.), *The blackwell companion to the Hebrew Bible,* (pp. 258–275).

Camille, A. (2017). Naming the 333 women in the Bible. Retrieved from:
https://www.uscatholic.org/articles/201703/naming-333-women-bible-
30948.

Criswell, W. (1983). Lydia: God's businesswoman. Retrieved from: https://wac
riswell.com/sermons/1983/lydia-god-s-businesswoman/.

D'Ror Chankin-Gould, J., Hutchinson, D., Hilton Jackson, D., Mayfield, T. D., Schulte, L. R., Schneider, T. J., & Winkelman, E. (2008). The sanctified 'adulteress' and her circumstantial clause: Bathsheba's bath and self-consecration in 2 Samuel 11. *Journal for the Study of the Old Testament, 32*(3), 339–352. https://doi.org/10.1177/0309089208090805.

Delbecq, A. L., Liebert, E., Mostyn, J., Nutt, P. C., & Walter, G. (2004). Discernment and strategic decision making: Reflections for spirituality of organizational leadership. *Research in Ethical Issues in Organizations, 5,* 139–174.

Dube, M. (1997). Toward a post-colonial feminist interpretation of the Bible. *Semeia, 78,* 11–26.

Edet, R. & Ekeya, B. (1988). Church women of Africa: A theological community. In V. Fabella & M. Oduyoye (Eds.), *With passion and compassion. Third World women doing theology: Reflections from the Women's Commission of the EATWT,* (pp. 3–13). Maryknoll, NY: Orbis.

Edwards, K. (2017, August 1). 10 women in the Bible who exceeded expectations. Retrieved from: https://www.crosswalk.com/faith/bible-study/10-women-in-the-bible-that-broke-stereotypes.html.

Elliott, C. (2008). Purple pasts: Color codification in the ancient world. *Law & Social Inquiry, 33*(1), 173–194. https://doi.org/10.1111/j.1747-4469.2008.00097.x.

Fiorenza, E. S. (1983). *In memory of her: A feminist theological reconstruction of Christian origins.* New York, NY: Crossroad.

Fiorenza, E. S. (1997). The praxis of coequal discipleship. In R. A. Horsley (Ed.), *Paul and empire: Religion and power in Roman imperial society,* (pp. 224–241). Harrisburg, PA: Trinity Press International.

Frank, C. (2019). Biblical women—The named and the nameless. Retrieved from: https://www.tomorrowsworld.org/woman-to-woman/biblical-women-the-named-and-the-nameless.

Huizing, R. L. (2011). What was Paul thinking? An ideological study of 1 Timothy 2. *Journal of Biblical Perspectives in Leadership, 3*(2), 14–22.

Hannah, L. (2015). Study finds there are 93 women in the Bible—but they speak just 1.1% of the time. Retrieved from: https://www.dailymail.co.uk/news/article-2940774/Study-finds-93-women-Bible-speak-just-1-1-cent-time.html.

Hitchcock, R. (1996). Esther.*Hitchcock's Bible names dictionary.* Retrieved from: https://www.blueletterbible.org/search/Dictionary/viewTopic.cfm.

Joseph, C. (2015). Be brave. Retrieved from: https://womenlivingwell.org/2015/01/be-brave/.

Josephus, F., Whiston, W., & Maier, P. L. (1999). *The new complete works of Josephus.* Grand Rapids, MI: Kregel.

Kadari, T. (2009). *Shiphrah, Midrash and Aggadah*. Jewish women: A comprehensive historical encyclopedia. Retrieved from: https://jwa.org/encyclopedia/article/shiphrah-midrash-and-aggadah.

Kahl, B. (2000). No longer male: Masculinity struggles behind Galatians 3: 28? *Journal for the Study of the New Testament, 79*, 37–49.

Malina, B. J. (2001). *The New Testament World: Insights from cultural anthropology*. Louisville, KY: Westminster John Knox Press.

Marrone, J. (2019). Characters of the Bible series: Deborah. Retrieved from: https://www.youtube.com/watch?v=tkpkJDjtMNM.

Morgan, E. (2005). Mary and modesty. *Christianity and Literature, 54*(2), 209–233. https://doi.org/10.1177/014833310505400206.

Nielson, K. (2018). What makes a woman strong: How God prepared Deborah to lead. Retrieved from: https://www.desiringgod.org/articles/what-makes-a-woman-strong.

Nelson, S. (2019). A woman who fears the Lord is to be praised. Retrieved from: https://womanofnoblecharacter.com/fears-the-lord/.

Nixon, M. (2015). Servant leadership: Queen Esther and Mary Kay Ash. *Proceedings of ASBBS, 22*(1), 331–341.

Ottuh, J. (2015). Measurement, evaluation and exegesis of the value of the ointment poured on Jesus in Mark 14: 3–9: A contemporary application in Nigeria. *American International Journal of Research in Humanities, Arts and Social Sciences*, 69–76.

Pelikan, J. (1996). *Mary through the centuries: Her place in the history of culture*. New Haven: Yale University Press.

Setzer, C. (1997). Excellent women: Female witness to the resurrection. *Journal of Biblical Literature, 116*(2), 259–272. https://doi.org/10.2307/3266223.

Spangler, A. (2015a). The Bible's top-10 wicked women. Retrieved from: https://www.biblegateway.com/blog/2015/10/the-bibles-top-10-wicked-women/.

Spangler, A. (2015). *Wicked women of the Bible*. Grand Rapids, MI: Zondervan.

Thomas, J. B., Clark, S. M., & Gioia, D. A. (1993). Strategic sensemaking and organizational performance: Linkages among scanning, interpretation, action, and outcomes. *Academy of Management Journal, 36(2)*, 239–270.

Trible, P. (1978). *God and the rhetoric of sexuality*. Philadelphia, PA: Fortress Press.

Vanhoozer, K. J. (1998). *Is there a meaning in this text? The Bible, the reader and the morality of literary knowledge*. Grand Rapids, MI: Zondervan.

Walvoord, J. F., & Zuck, R. B. (1985). *The Bible knowledge commentary*. USA: Victor Books.

Wolters, A. (2000). Confessional criticism and the night visions of Zechariah. In C. Bartholomew, C. Greene, & K. Moller, (Eds.) *Renewing Biblical Interpretation*, (pp. 90–117). Grand Rapids, MI: Zondervan.

PART IV

Cultural Influences and Gender

CHAPTER 17

If Iceland Is a Gender Paradise, Where Are the Women CEOs of Listed Companies?

Ásta Dís Óladóttir, Þóra H. Christiansen,
and Gylfi Dalmann Aðalsteinsson

INTRODUCTION

In 1908 more than 15,000 female garment workers went on strike in New York City, their goal was to secure higher wages, shorter hours, and better working conditions. Hundred years later we still have a long way to go according to the Gender Social Norms Index 2020. Despite decades of progress toward closing the equality gap between men and women, close to 90% of men and women hold some sort of bias against women,

Á. D. Óladóttir (✉)
Department of Business Administration, University of Iceland, Reykjavik, Iceland
e-mail: astadis@hi.is

Þ. H. Christiansen
School of Business, University of Iceland, Reykjavik, Iceland

G. D. Aðalsteinsson
Human Resource Management, University of Iceland, Reykjavik, Iceland

© The Author(s), under exclusive license to Springer Nature Switzerland AG 2021
J. Marques (ed.), *Exploring Gender at Work*,
https://doi.org/10.1007/978-3-030-64319-5_17

providing new clues to the barriers that women face in achieving equality, and a potential path forward to shattering the glass ceiling (UNDP 2020).

Research has shown (cf. Gregoric, Oxelheim, Randoy and Thomsen 2017; Pechersky 2016) that even though it has been demonstrated that participation of women in corporate management has generally beneficial effects, there is still resistance and barriers to women reaching positions of power. Furthermore, corporate boards tend to be more effective when gender ratios are even, which in turn affects company image, earnings and even leads to more professional practices (Adam and Ferriera 2009; Carter, Simkins and Simpson 2003). Nevertheless, women´s attainment of senior positions is lagging across the globe, according to the glass-ceiling index for 2019, women in the OECD hold 25.4% of seats on boards and are in 32.5% of managerial positions (Economist 2020).

The report on the progress toward the Sustainable Development Goals of the Secretary-General in 2019 states that gender inequalities persist. Women represent less than 40% of those employed, occupy only about a quarter of managerial positions in the world and face a gender pay gap of 12%. The world can not achieve the 17 Sustainable Development Goals without also achieving gender equality and the empowerment of women and girls (United Nations 2019).

The Gender Gap Index for 2020 reveals that for the eleventh year in a row Iceland has topped the list and made the greatest progress toward closing the gender gap, or 87.7% (WEF 2020). Icelandic women have been making great strides toward equality, for example representing 46% of the boards of directors in listed companies (EIGE 2020). A key reason for their gains in board membership is the enactment of gender quota legislation in 2010, stipulating a minimum ratio of 40% of either gender on the boards of companies with over 50 employees. However, of the 20 companies listed on the Icelandic Nasdaq exchange in 2020, none were headed by a woman CEO.

The objective of the study is to gain understanding of this conundrum and to that end we explore the beliefs of women business leaders regarding why no woman is CEO of a listed company in Iceland and what actions they deem feasible to increase the number of women in senior positions in Iceland. We also explore whether and why they support the enactment of gender quota legislation on executive positions in Icelandic companies.

First we give an overview of our theoretical background, gendered hiring, and explanations for uneven gender ratios framed as supply and demand factors, followed by discussion of gender quota legislation. Next, we describe the Icelandic context and our research methods, present main findings and discuss their implications and, finally, give some takeaways.

EXPLANATIONS FOR THE GENDER GAP IN SENIOR POSITIONS

In the 1980s the glass ceiling concept was coined to describe the invisible barriers facing women seeking top corporate positions. As women increasingly managed to break through this ceiling the focus shifted to other obstacles, for instance, what has been termed the labyrinth to leadership, conceptualizing the many obstacles and challenges women have to navigate on their path to success. Eagly and Carli (2007) conceived this metaphor to emphasize that although some women have reached the top, various barriers remain at many levels and they are not invisible to women.

Uneven gender ratios in executive positions can be explained in terms of supply and demand, that is, whether the reason lies with the women themselves or with the employers and their hiring procedures. If this imbalance is explained by supply, then not enough women seek senior positions. This explanation maintains that women are less inclined to apply for executive positions, possible reasons being that they put family first rather than their career, that they are less interested in positions of power, or that they avoid competition (Kleinjans2009). Gneezy, Niederle, and Rustichini (2003) claim that women are less self-confident than men and therefore need more support and encouragement, especially if they work in highly competitive environments. Kleinjans (2009) maintains that women are less interested in competitive jobs than men, and that they prefer less competitive jobs even though remuneration may be lower, rather than diving head-on into the competition where income is higher.

If demand is the explanation, then the reason is that employers are less inclined to hire and promote women than men, possibly because men tend to favor other men, especially where men are in the majority (Koch, D'Mello and Sackett 2015; Gabaldon, De Anca, Mateos de Cabo and Gimeno 2016). Findings that support demand-side explanations include a study on the Swedish labor market that found that the main reason for hiring more men than women as CEOs was that men select other men over women, not because they have negative attitudes toward women, but rather because they lean toward certain types of men (Holgersson2013). Kanter (1977) reached a similar conclusion; individuals tend to view similar others as more competent. Holgersson and Tienari (2015) conclude that the exclusion of women from senior positions is not the result of direct discrimination, but rather that a certain type of men who supposedly have the right background, are the right age, have the right lifestyle and looks, are preferred. Holgersson (2013) also points out that men's weaknesses may even be redefined as strengths.

The concepts *homosociality*, defined as preference for relations with persons of the same gender as oneself, and *homosocial reproduction*, when men in positions of power prefer those they perceive as similar to themselves, have been used to explain why a homogenous group of men occupies top positions (Kanter 1977). These groups, typically high status white men, afford their members access to social capital based on their membership in this "old boys' club," while excluding nonmembers (McDonald 2011). Kleinjans (2009) showed that ambitious and assertive women who seek to join the higher ranks are often seen as pushy harpies who are difficult to work with, whereas men are rewarded for the same behavior. Consequently, companies that are managed mostly by men and where men are the majority of board members tend to bring in more men. This could explain why so few women sit on company boards or hold senior positions, namely, that men prefer to hire other men (De Anca and Gabaldon 2013).

Axelsdottir and Halrynjo (2018) examined the attitudes of senior managers in Norway and Iceland toward demand- and supply-side explanations of gender bias. No difference was found in the views of male and female managers on whether the gender bias was due to supply or demand. Men, in general, were slightly less of the opinion that the explanation was found on the demand side but were nonetheless not more likely to support the supply argument. Men in CEO positions were, however, more likely to support the supply-side explanation. Interestingly, Icelandic women in the study were more likely than other participants from both Iceland and Norway to favor the view that too much hiring was done through informal network connections.

When considering whether demand-side or supply-side factors explain gendered hiring, it is important to keep in mind that the explanations need not be either one or the other, in fact, a mix of demand and supply factors are likely to explain gender imbalance (Axelsdottir and Halrynjo 2018). Many scholars have claimed that both demand-side and supply-side forces contribute to differences between females' and males' careers.

They have used frameworks from economics to synthesize diverse theoretical arguments into a single paradigm (Brands and Fernandez-Mateo 2017; Fernandez-Mateo and Fernandez 2016; Wang, Holmes, Devine and Bishoff 2018).

The different gender roles for men and women furthermore influence how men and women are perceived to perform in certain jobs or roles (Eagly and Karau 2002) although there are indications that the perceptions of gender differences may be decreasing (Paustian-Underdahl, Walker and Woehr 2014). Women are still more likely than men to shoulder more responsibility for family (Juliusdottir, Rafnsdottir and Einarsdottir 2018). Women's networks tend to be less developed than men's and they experience being discriminated against in wages, promotions, and executive positions (Carli and Eagly 2016).

Traditionally and around the globe, men rather than women have held the majority of seats on corporate boards. In an effort to achieve gender parity, several countries have enacted gender quotas on corporate boards. The implementation varies between countries as does the extent to which different types and sizes of companies are subject to these regulations, whether the quotas are binding, and whether and how penalties for noncompliance are included.

Gender Quotas

Norway was the first country worldwide to institute gender quotas for company boards of directors in 2003. At that time, women constituted only 20.3% of board members in listed companies. The laws came into compliance in 2006 to 2008 and by year-end 2008 the ratio of women had reached around 43% (EIGE 2020).

Considerable debate took place, e.g. within the European Parliament in 2011, on whether gender quotas on corporate boards of directors were the means to balance the gender ratio (European Commission 2016). But even though the European Union did not enact such laws at the time, several European countries have followed the Nordic precedent including Spain, Italy, Greece, France, the Netherlands, Austria, and Belgium. In the US the first step has been taken to set gender quotas with Californian law requiring companies with headquarters in California to have at least one woman on their board of directors starting in 2019 (Saba 2018).

At the height of the gender quota debate in Iceland around 2010, many were opposed to such quotas. Those most opposed to gender quotas consider them to impede active market competition and the maxim of appointing the best candidate, believing that companies should be left alone to decide who are best suited to direct them and that the most competent candidate should always be hired (Rafnsdóttir, Einarsdóttir & Snorrason, 2014). Ahern and Dittmar (2012) showed that companies that had to increase the number of women on their boards of directors were in some cases appointing women who had less experience than the men that would otherwise have been chosen. Accordingly, these women had only found a seat at the table because of their gender. Those in favor of gender quota laws asserted that women had a constitutional right to equal the men on company boards and that obstacles would likely disappear (Terjesen, Aguilera and Lorenz 2015). Those who argued the profitability point of view pointed out that a more even gender ratio could lead to better utilization of both genders' qualifications thus increasing the profitability of the companies (Rafnsdóttir et al. 2014).

Einarsdottir, Rafnsdottir, and Valdimarsdottir (2019) examined the connection between Icelandic managers' views on gender quotas and what they think might explain the gender imbalance in senior positions. Women in the study were more in favor of gender quotas; 56.1% of women versus 17.4% of men agreed that *"gender quotas are an important way to attain gender equality in any corporation management"* (p. 16). Furthermore, those respondents who thought the gender bias could be explained by environmental factors, or the demand aspect, were more likely to support gender quotas. Women were also more likely to hold the view that the gender bias was explained by external factors on the demand side rather than on the supply side.

The Icelandic Context

Women have historically been significantly underrepresented on boards of directors in Icelandic companies, spurring demands for gender quotas. In March of 2010, Icelandic law was amended such that either gender should constitute at least 40% of the board of directors in companies with more than 50 employees. These changes entered into force forthwith for Official Public Limited Companies, but Public Limited Companies were given a grace period until September of 2013. A law setting the same requirements for boards of directors of Pension Funds was passed in September 2011 and allotted the same grace period. Iceland was the second country in the world, after Norway, to implement such quotas.

These gender quota laws have had significant effects on the gender composition of corporate boards, resulting in more women sitting on boards than previously.

Men nonetheless continue to outnumber women as board chairmen. In 2000, women chaired 10% of the boards at medium-sized companies, i.e. with 50 to 99 employees, and that ratio increased only to 13% in 2017. The greatest increase was at the largest companies where the ratio rose from 6% in 2000 to 18% in 2017, and in the very largest companies where no woman was a board member in 2000 to 13% in 2017 (Statistics Iceland, n.d.). The trend in the gender composition of the boards of companies listed at the Icelandic Nasdaq stock exchange, depicted in Fig. 17.1, shows that the gender quota laws worked the way they were intended.

As Fig. 17.1 shows, women held only 4% of the board seats in 2003 and none were chairs. In 2010, when the gender quota laws were enacted, the ratio of women board members was around 16%. In 2020, the ratio of women board members had reached 46% (EIGE 2020). Still, in April 2020, of 20 board chairs, only 2 were women.

A small nation like Iceland with close to 364,000 inhabitants cannot afford to consider only half the pool of qualified candidates for senior positions. A total of 92,400 women were in the labor force in February 2020, a participation rate of just under 75%, while that of men was 81% (Statistics Iceland, n.d.). Icelandic women have been very active in the labor force since the 1980s and since the 1990s their participation rate has never gone below 70%. This is considerably higher than the average OECD rate of 57% (OECD 2019).

According to data from Statistics Iceland (n.d.), women are more commonly CEOs of small companies with 1 to 10 employees, and as companies get bigger, their numbers decrease. Figure 17.2 depicts

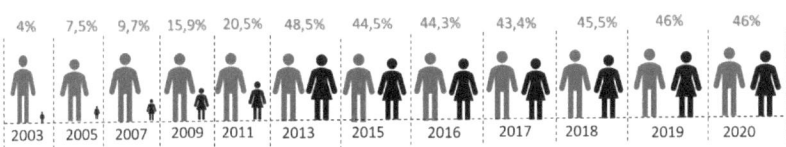

Fig. 17.1 The ratio of women as board members of registered companies from 2003 to 2020. (European Institute for Gender Equality [2020], Authors' presentation)

Fig. 17.2 Number of women and men Chief Executive Officers in Iceland by firm size (Statistics Iceland n.d.)

numbers of men and women CEOs by size of the company in terms of number of employees, from 2000 to 2017.

The situation has certainly improved since 2000 when only one woman (or 2%) was CEO of a company with more than 250 employees, but in 2017 that ratio had reached 13% (Statistics Iceland, n.d.).

Katrin Jakobsdottir, the prime minister of Iceland, addressed this issue in 2019:

> Although Iceland is at the forefront in gender equality worldwide, the status of women in management shows that there is significant room for improvement in companies with 50 or more employees as well as within the 100 largest Icelandic companies. (Government of Iceland March 29, 2019)

METHODS

The objective of the study is to explore the beliefs of Icelandic women business leaders on why no woman is CEO of a listed company in Iceland, what actions can be taken to increase the number of women in executive positions, and whether they support the enactment of gender quota on corporate executive positions. The study focuses on the lack of women CEOs in listed companies for three reasons. First, because no woman is CEO. Second, because listed companies are subject to strict regulations on transparency in their reporting. And third, because of their dispersed ownership, from individuals to institutional investors such as pension funds.

The study seeks to answer the following research questions:

1. What do Icelandic women business leaders believe are the main reasons for no woman being CEO of a listed company in Iceland?
2. What actions do Icelandic women business leaders think should be taken to increase the number of women in executive positions in Icelandic companies?
3. Do Icelandic women business leaders support the enactment of gender quota on executive positions in Icelandic companies?

Study Participants and Procedure

To elicit responses from women who have experience of leadership and management, convenience sampling was applied (Katz 1972).Two associations were deemed suitable for the study, FKA, the largest association of businesswomen in Iceland, and Excedra, an exclusive membership of "influential women in Icelandic business, politics and the public sector." Both associations maintain closed Facebook groups, with 1100 and 225 members, respectively. The survey was posted in February 2019 and was open for one week. A total of 189 women responded, a 14% response rate. While this is a low response rate, it was deemed acceptable for this exploratory study and not significantly different from the response rate that Saunders, Lewis, and Thornhill (2012) report for mail surveys, or between 10 and 20%. Analysis of respondents revealed that over half of the respondents hold an executive position in an organization and of those, two thirds were CEOs. Broken down by sector, 78% work in the private sector, 17% in the public sector, with 5% listing "other."

Instrument and Analysis

The survey included open-ended questions on why no women are CEOs of listed companies in Iceland and what needs to be done to increase the number of women CEOs, in addition to questions on whether gender quota on executive positions should be enacted and questions on demographics. The survey was pilot tested on a small group of women managers and adjusted according to their feedback. Links to the survey were posted on the closed Facebook pages of the two associations. To participate, respondents clicked on the link which took them to the web page of the survey. Responses were totally anonymous and untraceable.

In this chapter we report on the responses to three open-ended questions and one yes/no question: "What do you believe are the main reason(s) for no women being CEOs of listed companies in Iceland," and "What actions do you believe should be taken to increase the number of women in executive positions in Icelandic companies." These questions were followed by a yes/no question: "Do you agree that a gender quota should be enacted on executive positions in Icelandic companies." Finally, an open-ended question gave the women the opportunity to rationalize their yes or no answer to the question on the enactment of gender quota. All of the answers to the open-ended questions were analyzed thematically by the researchers, identifying both recurrent themes and unique insights. The resulting themes were then discussed and verified with regard to theory. Themes and descriptive statistics for the yes/no question are presented in the results.

RESULTS

The Lack of Women CEOs of Listed Companies

When asked to elaborate on what the main reasons are for there not being any women CEOs of listed companies in Iceland, half of the women's answers fell under the theme of the old boys' club. The second strongest theme explained women not receiving a chance because of the glass ceiling, stereotypes, outdated attitudes and culture. The third theme entails women's shortcomings.

The strongest theme encompasses the explanation that the old boys' club is alive and well on top of the glass ceiling. The largest category of explanations identified by the women centered on men. While only a couple used the term "*patriarchy*," a majority referred to some version of the old boys' club, men's world, men's network, or men's cronyism. Many elaborated their answers by saying that men already hold the positions of power and seem unwilling to look further than their network of friends and acquaintances. They felt that men prefer to hire other men, distrust women and do not want women because they think and act differently than men, thus the status quo prevails.

The respondents tended to view men's networks as exclusionary and unwilling to consider hiring anyone from outside the group, or, if women are hired: *"Women are still only hired to improve the company image."* They seemed to experience being outnumbered by men and hold little hope of breaking into the network: *"The men either manage or own all the money and therefore hold the power to hire CEOs that are favorable. Their network is made up of men."* They even referred to *"cliques,"* indicating that the men receive undeserved preferential treatment from each other:

> It seems like there is a very small group or clique who sits on the boards of most companies in this country, so when it's time to hire for executive positions, someone who is well known within the group gets selected. Among men, the pool of candidates chosen from is usually mostly filled by other men.

Others expressed a clear experience of exclusion by men; that the old boys' club was made up of men who distrust women and are actively trying to keep the women out: *"Men are still defending their territory and hire each other for these positions."* Furthermore, if they felt the top echelons might not be impenetrable, that access may only be temporary: *"The old boys' club still prevails, the competition is fierce and women are not allowed in. If a woman manages to gain access, she is practically shut out until she herself chooses to leave."*

The second theme maintains that the explanation lies in corporate cultures, often based on outdated attitudes, practices, and gender stereotypes. While these are distinct concepts, the women clearly felt that the interplay of attitudes, stereotypes, and values often created a culture that excludes women: *"The cultures of corporate boards and organizations and the attitudes towards the characteristics required for these positions and the attitudes towards women in executive positions."* One respondent pointed out that role models are needed to eradicate the stereotypes held by those who hire: *"Lack of role models. Those who hire for the positions cannot envision women in these positions."* Other answers included references to stereotypical thinking such as*: "Old ideas about women not being capable of handling these jobs."*

The third theme attributes the reasons to women themselves, focusing on their shortcomings. These respondents compared women to men, finding that women come up short because they are not behaving enough like men. They viewed women as not wanting these positions enough, not self-assured enough, not interested enough, not determined enough: *"Women are not good enough at promoting themselves," "they lack experience and networks,"* and *"women also must be more courageous and willing to take on the top positions, they often want to be number 2 rather than the top manager."* Some of the answers overlapped with the theme on stereotypes, such as: *"women are too nurturing and neither as aggressive nor self-assured as men."* Comments also turned the attention toward the women sitting on corporate boards. Some respondents felt disappointed by the lack of progress, they had not seen the anticipated trickle-down effect on executive positions: *"because the women whohave attained seats on the boards, they haven't stepped up and hired in competent women."*

Actions to Increase the Number of Women in Executive Positions

The open-ended question on actions needed garnered a variety of responses, ranging from changing norms and attitudes, requiring advertisements of open positions, a more transparent hiring process, women's empowerment and women's solidarity, to enacting gender quotas on executive positions. Three main themes emerged with strong support. The strongest support was for changing attitudes and norms. The second strongest support was for gender quotas on executive positions. Third was the need for women to change.

The theme on changing attitudes had a focus on both societal attitudes and the attitudes of those who make the decisions on hiring and promotions. The respondents overwhelmingly felt that attitudes need to change away from outdated gender norms toward a new way of thinking that appreciates women's contributions: *"Prejudice against women as executives must be eradicated."* Only a couple of the answers specifically addressed the need for men's attitudes toward women to change and that they need to take part: *"Men must accept women as equals and their attitudes towards women as CEOs must change."* As a way to engender the change, some respondents called for a dialogue on skills and competencies, for men to take part in the dialogue on the benefits of gender diversity in company leadership: *"New thinking is sorely needed, that companies take the responsibility and realize the advantage of having both men and women in the top management team. Men have to join the discussion and take responsibility."*

They also felt that an understanding of the value of diversity was needed: *"Both the culture and attitudes must be changed, realizing that gender diversity in company management is the best solution like countless studies of organizations have pointed out."* The respondents felt that companies must improve outdated practices, in particular the hiring process. They believed that increasing the transparency of the process, advertising top positions and more professionalism could possibly overcome the rampant cronyism and impenetrability of the old boys' club: *"Make the hiring process more transparent and advertise open positions."*

The second theme advocated for gender quotas and many respondents were very direct and simply recommended quotas without going into details on implementation: *"The only solution is to enact a gender quota."* Some had experienced a change of heart since the enactment of gender quota on corporate boards a decade ago and explained how they had arrived at their current opinion:

> Enact quotas, I was completely against them first, but now I fully support them. Nothing else works, especially since the boards are not effective and the largest shareholders in the market are completely passive, and by that I mean the pension funds. Obviously they are mostly governed by male CEOs. Some changes are needed there too.

While many saw this as a rather extreme measure, they felt that to change the system, a disruption was needed: *"Gender quota to disrupt the pattern."* A clear focus was on the need for quotas because the women felt that other measures had been exhausted and without the quota there would be no change. They explained how they envisioned the quota would work *"to generate new thinking and give women an opportunity."* They based their opinion on experience and there was a sense that their patience has been exhausted:

> Experience has proven that legislation encourages positive change towards equality, although we would rather achieve change through normal development. But history has shown us that this takes a lot of time and often progress is reversed if legislation is not enacted to improve equality and equity.

The answers that fell under the third theme echoed many of the stereotypical views on women's shortcomings, such as lack of self-confidence and willingness to apply for the top jobs and can be summarized as "fix the women." Most of these respondents used language like *"they must"* or *"women have to,"* which may mean that they do not include themselves, since the majority of respondents either run their own business or are in management positions. There was a clear sense that women needed to adopt more masculine behaviors: *"They must pursue it – and then 'fight for it' using the same tricks as the men."* The necessity of fighting was echoed in a number of answers: *"A larger number of courageous women who are ready to fight against the current."* They also pointed out specific shortcomings that they felt women need to work on: *"Probably women have to seek CEO positions harder, be better at using networks and make themselves known."* Finally, they alluded to women perhaps not having the same desire for these positions as men do.

Other comments under this theme focused on the need for more solidarity and how women who already hold seats on corporate boards must take responsibility and step up their support of other women: *" Women on the boards of Icelandic companies – often minimum 40% - must care about the issue."* Some voiced disappointment with the performance of women board members and clearly felt that more should have been accomplished as the numbers of women on corporate boards have increased:

> This is a small community and cronyism, networking and such seem to prevail/determine everything. Why don't women on corporate boards stand their ground when CEOs are hired? I don't believe that there are not enough competent women to fill these positions.

Thus the women who have attained seats on corporate boards also must be "fixed," not just to make them more like men, but to make more effort to support other women: *"The women on corporate boards must be more determined to enable women to reach the CEO and executive positions."*

ENACTMENT OF GENDER QUOTA ON EXECUTIVE POSITIONS IN ICELANDIC COMPANIES

Following the open-ended questions on explanations and actions needed to increase the number of women in senior positions, the respondents were asked directly about their support for gender quota. To that question 59.3% of respondents answered yes, and 40.7% answered no. When offered to elaborate on their answers, those who opposed tended to base their answer on objection to government interference in the market; they would rather see the change happen through corporate efforts or soft quotas: *"Rather achieve this through the corporate governance statement – addressing gender ratios in executive positions."* Opponents also felt that a quota would be demeaning for women, they would not be viewed as having achieved their position based on merit but because of the quota: *"I would want to achieve such a position based on my own merit – not because I was the woman. It devalues women's leadership appointments if the assumption is that it was because of gender quotas."*

The supporters overwhelmingly explained their position by stating that *"Everything else has been tried"* and *"What we are doing now is not working, we have stalled and it's time to take action."* These respondents felt that none of the current efforts are working and that an intervention would be needed to force the needed changes: *"Sometimes external pressure is needed to force people to think differently."* Others supported their argument with references to the enactment of gender quota for corporate boards: *"The change is not occurring organically. The same action is needed as with the corporate boards."* Finally, many of the supporters proposed a temporary quota might be the answer:

> We must take action because otherwise the changes will take too long time. The gender quota would probably need to be in effect for some years until we reach a balance and then the next generation will not be used to anything different. Simple as that.

Discussion

According to the WEF, gender equality will not be achieved for another hundred years. Despite Iceland's leading position, full gender equality in senior positions appears beyond reach. Our objective was to explore the insights of Icelandic women business leaders into what can explain why no woman is CEO of a listed company in Iceland and what women believe should be done to increase the number of women in corporate leadership. Our findings reveal that overwhelmingly, our respondents explain the bias through demand-side factors, particularly exclusion by men's networks, what Kanter (1977) termed *homosocial reproduction*, and outdated attitudes and practices. This supports and extends the findings of Einarsdottir, Rafnsdottir, and Valdimarsdottir (2019); women experience the greatest barriers on the demand side, and our respondents believe those barriers are due to men's actions. Although some feel that women face discrimination and outdated stereotypes (Carli and Eagly 2016; Eagly and Karau 2002), most of the respondents describe the decision-makers as a network of men (Gabaldon et al. 2016) who simply don't consider candidates outside of their own network, which happens to consist of other men (Axelsdottir and Halrynjo 2018; Holgerson 2013; Holgerson and Tienari 2015). A minority opinion attributes the bias to supply factors such as women's lack of assertiveness or interest in senior positions (Gneezy et al. 2003; Kleinjans 2009). As Eagly and Carli (2007) maintained, the barriers are complex and they are visible to these women.

Gender quota legislation for corporate boards was enacted in 2010, resulting in a much more even gender ratio on corporate boards. The anticipated outcome was a trickle-down effect on the number of women CEOs and executives, but that has not materialized. In 2020 no woman is CEO of a listed company in Iceland and women represent only 13% of the CEOs and C-suite of large companies in Iceland. Corporate boards of the listed companies in Iceland are composed of both men and women, at least two women on each 5-member board. Women chair two of the boards and hold the majority of four boards. Since 2010, at least 15 companies have hired new CEOs, and among them only one woman which has stepped down.

Our findings also clearly indicate that the respondents feel that changes are needed. They call for a change in corporate cultures such as work hours and hiring practices (Juliusdottir et al. 2018). Primarily they support measures to increase the demand and the responsibility for that lies with the company leadership; management, which tends to be male-dominated (Koch et al. 2015) and boards, which are more balanced. The respondents feel that the needed changes are not occurring organically, they have seen the effects of the already enacted gender quota on corporate boards, consequently, they are calling for a gender quota on executive positions.

The support for gender quota aligns very closely with the findings of Einarsdóttir, Rafnsdóttir, and Valdimarsdóttir (2019)—our findings contribute insights into why the women support gender quota on executive positions. It is because in their experience, the old boys' club will not budge, therefore the change will have to be forced. The experience of the gender quota on corporate boards has also managed to change the minds of many women who were opposed to quotas, but the arguments against quota align closely with the objections that were voiced against the corporate board quota (Rafnsdóttir et al. 2014). They furthermore believe this gender quota need only be temporary because its enactment will disrupt the prevailing attitudes and norms, allowing more women a chance to prove themselves and become role models. Role models that are needed both to encourage other women to seek senior positions and to demonstrate to the decision-makers that women are capable of handling these roles. They envision that once an equal ratio of men and women will be sharing the leadership that will be the new norm.

Addressing the problem of gender inequality in the world, UN Secretary-General António Guterres recently called for the redistribution of power, *"power that has been jealously guarded by men"* and concluded:

> It is time to stop trying to change women and start changing the systems that prevent them from achieving their potential. Our power structures have evolved gradually over thousands of years. One further evolution is long overdue. The twenty-first century must be the century of women's equality. (UN News 2020)

Our findings show that our participants agree with Secretary-General Guterres that we must turn away from trying to change women and start focusing on changing the power structures. The experiences of these women have convinced them that men will continue to guard the power by supporting other men. The glass ceilinghas been broken but the jagged edge of glass shards still remains as a formidable barrier that only a few women manage to overcome unscathed. Our participants' solution is a temporary gender quota on executive management positions to bring about the disruption needed to eradicate outdated attitudes and stereotypes.

As is globally evident, there is no shortage of internationally agreed upon instruments, national laws, and declarations on gender equality goals, yet gender inequalities still persist in all countries. SDG 5 and its targets set out the requisite collective action to create conducive environments toward substantive equality for all women and girls. In order to attain the SDG 5 target of ensuring women's full and effective participation and equal opportunities for leadership, measures are needed to challenge the persistent gender inequalities in general. Implementing gender-responsive measures within political parties' constitutions, internal rules and regulations on processes to identify, nominate, and select candidates for leadership positions are essential to achieve the SDG 5 targets.

CHAPTER TAKEAWAYS

Despite a progress toward closing the Gender gap, societies around the world have a long way to go. Forty years ago, in 1980, Vigdís Finnbogadóttir was elected president of Iceland, becoming the first woman in the world to be democratically elected as head of state. Vigdís served as president until 1996 and remains a role model for women worldwide. In 2020 women lead many nations and during the current crisis, similar to previous crises, women play a pivotal role. According to research, the banks that were led by women and countries that had more women at the forefront of the financial sector suffered less from the global economic crisis in 2008. Another global crisis, now in 2020, people are looking for true leadership examples. From Iceland to Taiwan or Germany to New Zealand, women are stepping up to show the world how to manage a pandemic. When given a chance to apply their leadership skills, it seems that these women have what it takes to lead their nations through crisis. These national leaders are case study sightings of the seven leadership traits men may want to learn from women (Wittenberg-Cox 2020). The time has come to trust women to also take over the CEO position.

REFERENCES

Adam, R. B., & Ferreira, D. (2009). Women in the boardroom and their impact on governance and performance. *Journal of Financial Economics, 94*, 291–309.

Ahern, K. R., & Dittmar, A. K. (2012). The changing of the boards: The impact on firm valuation of mandated female board representation. *Quarterly Journal of Economics, 127*(1), 137–197.

Axelsdóttir, L., & Halrynjo, S. (2018). Gender balance in executive management: Top-managers' understanding of barriers and solutions from the demand-supply perspective. *Social Politics: International Studies in Gender, State & Society, 25*(2), 287–314.

Brands, R. A., & Fernandez-Mateo, I. (2017). Leaning out: How negative recruitment experiences shape women's decisions to compete for executive roles. *Administrative Science Quarterly, 62*(3), 405–442. https://doi.org/10.1177/0001839216682728.

Carli, L. L., & Eagly, A. H. (2016). Women face a labyrinth: An examination of metaphors for women leaders. *Gender in Management: An International Journal, 31*, 514–527.

Carter, D. A., Simkins, B. J., & Simpson, W. G. (2003). Corporate governance, board diversity, and firm value. *The Financial Review, 38*, 33–53.

De Anca, C., & Gabaldon, P. (2013). Female directors and the media: Stereotypes of board members. *Gender in Management: An International Journal*, 29(6), 334–351.

Eagly, A. H., & Carli, L. L. (2007). *Through the labyrinth: The truth about how women become leaders*. Boston, MA: Harvard Business School.

Eagly, A. H., & Karau, S. J. (2002). Role congruity theory of prejudice toward female leaders. *Psychological Review, 109*(3), 573.

Economist. (2020). Iceland leads the way to women's equality in the workplace. Retrieved from: https://www.economist.com/graphic-detail/2020/03/04/iceland-leads-the-way-to-womens-equality-in-the-workplace.

Einarsdóttir, P. J., Rafnsdóttir, G. L., & Valdimarsdóttir, M. (2019). Structural hindrances or less driven women? Managers' views on corporate quotas. *Politics & Gender*, 1–29.

European Institute for Gender Equality (EIGE). (2020). *Gender statistics database*. Retrieved from: https://eige.europa.eu/.

European Commission. (2016). *Gender balance on corporate boards. Europe is cracking the glass ceiling*. Belgium: European Commission.

Fernandez-Mateo, I., & Fernandez, R. M. (2016). Bending the pipeline? Executive search and gender inequality in hiring for top management jobs. *Management Science, 62*(12), 3636–3655. https://doi.org/10.1287/mnsc.2015.2315.

Gabaldon, P., De Anca, C., Mateos de Cabo, R., & Gimeno, R. (2016). Searching for women on boards: An analysis from the supply and demand perspective. *Corporate Governance: An International Review, 24*(3), 371–385.

Gneezy, U., Niederle, M., & Rustichini, A. (2003). Performance in competitive environments: Gender differences. *The Quarterly Journal of Economics, 118*(3), 1049–1074.

Government of Iceland. (2019, March 29). Forsætisráðherra undirritar samning við Félag kvenna í atvinnulífinu um Jafnréttisvogina. Retrieved from: https://www.stjornarradid.is/efst-a-baugi/frettir/stok-frett/2019/03/29/Forsaetis radherra-undirritar-samning-vid-Felag-kvenna-i-atvinnulifinu-um-Jafnvaegisvo gina/?fbclid=IwAR3MG03K8ZCW6NQRpG1hWVRaW9g9sVvv1MqkCauH JTxAcF-EhBAsmNmzx6U.

Gregoric, A., Oxelheim, L., Randoy, T., & Thomsen, S. (2017). Resistance to change in the corporate elite: Female directors' appointments onto Nordic boards. *Journal of Business Ethics, 141*, 267–287.

Holgersson, C. (2013). Recruiting managing directors: Doing homosociality. *Gender, Work & Organization, 20*(4), 454–466.

Holgersson, C., & Tienari, J. (2015). 'This is just the way it is': Executive search and gendered careers. In A. Broadbridge & S. Fielden (Eds.), *Handbook of gendered careers in management: Getting in, getting on, getting out* (pp. 123–139). Cheltenham: Edward Elgar.

Júlíusdóttir, Ó., Rafnsdóttir, G. L., & Einarsdóttir, Þ. (2018). Top managers and the gendered interplay of organizations and family life: The case of Iceland. *Gender in Management: An International Journal, 33*(8), 602–622.

Kanter, R. M. (1977). *Men and women of the corporation.* New York: Basic Books.

Katz, D. (1972), Some final considerations about experimentation in social psychology. In C. G. McClintock (Ed.), *Experimental social psychology.* New York, NY: Holt, Rinehart & Winston.

Kleinjans, K. J. (2009). Do gender differences in preferences for competition matter for occupational expectations? *Journal of Economic Psychology, 30,* 701–710.

Koch, A. J., D'Mello, S. D., & Sackett, P. R. (2015). A meta-analysis of gender stereotypes and bias in experimental simulations of employment decision making. *Journal of Applied Psychology, 100*(1), 128–161.

McDonald, S. (2011). What's in the "old boys" network? Accessing social capital in gendered and racialized networks. *Social Networks, 33*(4), 317–330.

OECD. (2019). Employment rate 2018. Retrieved from: https://data.oecd.org/emp/employment-rate.htm#indicator-chart.

Paustian-Underdahl, S. C., Walker, L. S., & Woehr, D. J. (2014). Gender and perceptions of leadership effectiveness: A meta-analysis of contextual moderators. *Journal of Applied Psychology, 99*(6), 1129–1145.

Pechersky, A. (2016). Diversity in board of directors: Review of diversity as a factor to enhance board performance. *Studia Commercialia Bratislavensia, 9*(33), 88–101.

Rafnsdóttir, G. L., Einarsdóttir, T., Snorrason, J. S., De Vos, M., & Culliford, P. (2014). Gender quota on the boards of corporations in Iceland. In M. De Vos & P. Culliford (Eds.), *Gender quotas for company boards* (pp. 147–158). Cambridge, United Kingdom: Intersentia.

Saba, J. (2018). Breakingviews—California boardroom gender quota is useful nudge. *Reuters.* Retrieved from: https://www.reuters.com/article/us-california-board-breakingviews/breakingviews-california-boardroom-gender-quota-is-useful-nudge-idUSKCN1MB3PE.

Saunders, M., Lewis, P., & Thornhill, A. (2012). *Research methods for business students.* Harlow: Pearson.

Statistics Iceland. (n.d.). *Women and men.* Retrieved from: https://statice.is/statistics/society/social-affairs/women-and-men/.

Terjesen, S., Aguilera, V. R., & Lorenz, R. (2015). Legislating a woman's seat on the board: Institutional factors driving gender quotas for boards of directors. *Journal of Business Ethics, 128*(2), 233–251.

United Nations Development Program. (2020). Almost 90% of men/women globally are biased against women. Retrieved from: https://www.undp.org/content/undp/en/home/news-centre/news/2020/Gender_Social_Norms_Index_2020.html.

United Nations. (2019). Special edition: Progress towards the sustainable development goals report of the secretary-general. Retrieved from: https://und ocs.org/E/2019/68.

UN News. (2020). Make this the century of women's equality: UN chief. Retrieved from: https://news.un.org/en/story/2020/02/1058271.

Wang, G., Holmes, R. M., Devine, R. A., & Bishoff, J. (2018). CEO gender differences in careers and the moderating role of country culture: A meta-analytic investigation. *Organizational Behavior and Human Decision Processes, 148,* 30–53. https://doi.org/10.1016/j.obhdp.2018.04.002.

Wittenberg-Cox, A. (2020). *What do countries with the best coronavirus responses have in common? Women leaders.* Retrieved from: https://www.forbes.com/sites/avivahwittenbergcox/2020/04/13/what-do-countries-with-the-best-coronavirus-reponses-have-in-common-women-leaders/#42dcaf103dec.

World Economic Forum. (2020). *The Global Gender Gap Report 2020.* Retrieved from: https://www3.weforum.org/docs/WEF_GGGR_2020.pdf.

CHAPTER 18

Senior Executive Women's Views on Female Solidarity: The Role of Perceived Gender Salience

Belgin Okay-Somerville and Gamze Arman

INTRODUCTION

Despite much progress, women are still underrepresented in the top managerial positions. While attention has been given to the study of glass ceiling, women's struggles in managerial careers do not end as they achieve higher ranks. Female senior executives are often expected to assume the role of change agents for improving women's representation at the top-level management (Mavin, 2006a, 2006b). Such solidarity with female career development (Kanter, 1977) is regarded as the 'women in management mantle' (Mavin, 2006a, 2006b). Those who do not conform to solidarity expectations are labeled as 'Queen Bees' who actively oppress

B. Okay-Somerville
Adam Smith Business School, University of Glasgow, Glasgow, Scotland, UK

G. Arman (✉)
Department of Health and Social Sciences, University of the West of England (UWE Bristol), Bristol, UK
e-mail: Gamze.Arman@uwe.ac.uk

© The Author(s), under exclusive license to Springer Nature Switzerland AG 2021
J. Marques (ed.), *Exploring Gender at Work*,
https://doi.org/10.1007/978-3-030-64319-5_18

junior women's career development (Rodriguez, 2013) or 'as a "bitch" who stings other women if her power is threatened' (Mavin, 2008, p. 75).

Female solidarity in organizations is often studied from a Social Identity Theory (SIT; Tajfel & Turner, 1979, 1986) perspective, according to which we hold multiple social identities on, for instance, personal, family, and national levels. We then tend to favor others who belong to the same in-group as ourselves, over out-group members—to the extent of sometimes discriminating against the latter. The solidarity perspective expects senior women to display strong gender-based in-group identification and, therefore, actively support their career advancement by taking the role of change agents (Mavin, 2006a, 2006b, 2008). Mentoring female subordinates, challenging the organizational culture, policies, and practices, and actively advocating for women's rights in career advancement are cited as more specific behaviors associated with female solidarity (Korabik & Abbondanza, 2004). It has been shown that female leaders are more likely than male leaders to adopt mentoring (Sheppard & Aquino, 2017) and coaching roles (Ye, Wang, Wendt, Wu, & Euwema, 2016), and to be benevolent toward female subordinates (Arvate, Galilea, & Todescat, 2018). Moreover, several social initiatives (such as Sisters Mentoring Sisters Program or the Women in Business networks) exist where women are encouraged to network with and mentor each other with the aim of advancing female careers.

Despite stereotypical gender expectations of communality, women in management are not necessarily friends (Mavin, Grandy, & Williams, 2017). For instance, in the workplace, women report being subjected to more female- (rather than male-)instigated incivility (Gabriel, Butts, Yuan, Rosen, & Sliter, 2018). At the very extreme, women "who achieve career success by derogating other women while simultaneously emphasizing their own career commitment and masculine qualities" (Derks, Van Laar, Ellemers, & de Groot, 2011, p. 520) are referred to as Queen Bees. This is manifested in gender stereotyping of other women's abilities and career commitment, masculine self-descriptions, and active oppression of women's career advancement (Derks et al., 2011).

Female executives' solidarity behaviors are likely to depend on several factors at multiple levels, such as personality and former experiences of receiving support at the individual level, culture and climate at the organizational level, and other contextual factors. Building on recent calls for better understanding of the gendered context which influences women's career advancement (Derks, Van Laar, & Ellemers, 2016), this chapter aims to explore the relevance of context in senior executive women's views on female solidarity.

WHY DOES CONTEXT MATTER?

Contemporary research on the negative intra-gender relations in organizations gives us reason to explore the role of larger contextual influences. More specifically, the overarching gendered context within which senior women operate may impose the acceptable norms of intra-gender relations. For instance, Veldman, Meussen, Van Laar, and Phalet (2017) show that within organizations positive diversity climate alleviates gender-work identity conflict that results from gender-dissimilarity with the team. On the one hand, although both men and women experience same-sex conflict at work, it is the women who are often penalized in career development (Sheppard & Aquino, 2017). On the other hand, women and minorities in general are penalized with poorer performance ratings if they engage in diversity-valuing behavior in the workplace (Hekman, Johnson, Foo, & Yang, 2017). Reduced cooperation with subordinates among female leaders has been observed when the legitimacy of the female leader's position is questioned, which instigates a cycle of illegitimacy for the female leader (Vial, Napier, & Brescoll, 2016). This suggests that senior executive women's negative intra-gender relations may be due to accepting/satisfying the expectations of the gendered organizational contexts and a response to the social identity threat experienced by women in career advancement (Derks et al., 2016). Moving beyond organizations, in this study we explore justifications based on national context in senior executive women's views on female solidarity.

DELVING INTO THE ROLE
OF CONTEXT: THE CASE OF TURKEY

Turkey is among the top 15 countries in the world with the most women sitting on boards (ILO, 2017). Nevertheless, Turkey struggles with gender equality in society and in the workplace. For instance, women still lag behind men in access to education and the labor market (30.4% vs 71.4% for women and men, respectively) (ILO, 2017). Persistently low gender egalitarianism in Turkish society is rooted in patriarchal norms (Gunduz-Hosgor & Smits, 2008) and reflected in strong traditional gender roles, which prescribe the role of the 'breadwinner' to the man and that of the 'homemaker' to the woman (Aycan, 2004a): on average, Turkish women spend nine times more on household and family care work than men (ILO, 2017). Below, we provide an overview of key socioeconomic trends with implications for women's place in Turkish society.

Achieving gender egalitarianism has been a priority of Ataturk, the founder of modern Turkey. This ambition was reflected in numerous reforms to the legal system since the establishment of the Republic in 1923 and was likened to 'state feminism' (Kabasakal, Aycan, Karakas, & Maden, 2011). Successive legislative changes instilled an emphasis on educating girls as the professionals of the future. This has contributed to favorable increase in participation rates of women in professional positions (Özbilgin & Healy, 2004). However, such positive change had the greatest impact on a small group of elite women, from middle-/upper-class family backgrounds (Zeytinoglu & Bonnabeauis, 2015).

Active government intervention for gender egalitarianism has considerably slowed down with the transition to a neoliberal economy in the 1980s (Zeytinoglu & Bonnabeauis, 2015). A rising tide of conservatism, reflecting religiosity, and patriarchal norms, has been observed in Turkish society (Carkoglu & Kalaycioglu, 2009). Within the workplace, this is manifested in multiple ways all of which either exclude women from the labor market (e.g., negative attitudes toward working women) or limit their opportunities (e.g., beliefs about roles most suitable for women) (Zeytinoglu & Bonnabeauis, 2015).

Deregulation of markets since the 1980s has served to weaken the emphasis placed on gender equality (Ozbilgin & Healy, 2004) and heighten that on meritocracy. Meritocratic attitude attributes Turkish women's underrepresentation at senior managerial positions to domestic responsibilities and individual preferences (Tabak, 1997). Lack of policy intervention for achieving gender equality at work in Turkey served to institutionalize gendered organizational contexts and reinforced the male-breadwinner family structure (Ilkkaracan, 2012).

While the Republican era represented more collectivistic values of 'fulfilling a national duty' (Kabasakal et al., 2011, p. 318), more individualistic career motivation is observed since the 1980s (Kabasakal, Karakas, Maden, & Aycan, 2016). Turkish women were found to accept traditional gender roles in negotiating employment and to compensate for structural barriers (e.g., by living close to grandparents for handling childcare responsibilities) (Beşpınar, 2010). Overall, far from demonstrating solidarity, Turkish women utilize individual strategies for negotiating and justifying their labor market position, the majority of which serve to reinforce patriarchal norms (e.g., unmarried women wearing a wedding ring to show they are "under the protection of a man" [Bespinar, 2010, p. 530]). In line with the individualistic career strategies, middle/top-level managerial women in Turkey attribute their success largely to individual factors (such as decisiveness and integrity) and perceive no systematic barriers to women's career advancement in Turkey (Aycan, 2004b).

The current government that has been in power since 2002 is known for its Islamist tendencies. Examples of legislation which had considerable implications for women's inclusion and advancement in working life include: generous severance pay for women who voluntarily quit their jobs in the first year of marriage, providing increasing financial support to mothers for each child they produce and paying women minimum wage for elderly care duties at home. A key outcome of these policies is the declining women's labor market participation (from 72% in 1955 to 32.5% in 2016) (Karaalp-Orhan, 2017) and reinforcement of the patriarchal norm that a woman's most suitable roles are that of a wife/mother (Zeytinoglu & Bonnabeauis, 2015). This clearly contradicts the historical Republican and neoliberal trends toward maintaining gender egalitarianism and meritocracy in the workforce, respectively.

In sum, Turkey represents a unique context where strong patriarchal norms govern all areas of life and socioeconomic developments have competing impact on women's inclusion in the labor market and career advancement. Such strong gendered social context gives us reason to expect both positive and negative views on supporting female careers. On the one hand, reflecting more Republican views to women's place in society, as the oppressed of the two sexes in everyday life in Turkish society, women in senior executive positions may in fact identify with the other women in organizations and demonstrate positive views on female solidarity with the aim of increasing female representation in top managerial positions. This is already evidenced in the increasing numbers of non-governmental organizations for improving women's place in society (Kabasakal et al., 2016). Maintaining a critical mass in the boardroom has been shown to be of benefit to the Turkish senior executive women, e.g., for feeling more comfortable and being heard in the boardroom (Erkut, Kramer, & Konrad, 2008). On the other hand, as the highly educated, elite members of society, senior executive women are clearly different from the majority of women in Turkey and may not identify with the experiences of other women: they may deny any influence of gender in progression. In this study, we therefore explore which norms senior executive women refer to (if any) for justifying views on female solidarity.

METHOD

The study is based on semi-structured in-depth interviews with 29 Turkish female senior managers/executives in Istanbul, Turkey. All participants worked in private sector organizations. The positions they held included two CEOs, 12 general managers, and 15 vice presidents (see Table 18.1 for a summary). Interviews consisted of four main open-ended questions which covered participants' (1) career history (i.e., previous positions until the day of the interview and barriers faced in progression); (2) their perception of the barriers women face in career development in Turkey; (3) support for female subordinates' career progression (i.e., whether they support junior women in their organizations; if so, their reasons and the kinds of support they engage in; and (4) views on what can/should be done to facilitate women's career development.

We used two-step template analysis (King, 2004) for identifying themes (see Table 18.2). The first step sorted the transcripts based on participants' positive and negative views on supporting female career development. Building on the sociopolitical developments in Turkey with implications for women's career development, we actively scanned the transcripts for the Republican; neoliberal; and the Conservatist views that women may use to justify solidarity or lack thereof. Any emerging elements of the context that arose beyond these themes were added to the template. These were industry characteristics, paternalistic organizational culture, and diversity programs. Categorizations and themes were compared and negotiated to ensure inter-rater reliability at each step.

TO SUPPORT OR NOT TO SUPPORT: VIEWS ON FEMALE SOLIDARITY

Results suggested a clear divide of positive and negative views on supporting female careers. Participants with positive views (supporters) often used the pronoun 'us,' whereas those with negative views (non-supporters) used 'them' in discussing female careers. As observed in Table 18.2 supporters' ($n = 9$) scripts consisted of positive views on individual, organizational, and national levels of support for female career development. Non-supporters' ($n = 20$) negative views were largely personal and based on organizational rhetoric with no references to larger national context.

Table 18.1 Sample description

	Position[a]	Sector	Ownership[b]	Size[c]	Age	Marital status[d]	Children
P1	VP	Finance	N	L	58	M	2
P2	GM	Tourism	MN	L	41	D	0
P3	GM	Tourism	MN	L	50	M	1
P4	GM	Public relations	N	S/M	50	D	1
P5	VP	Finance	N	L	37	S	0
P6	VP	ICT	MN	L	52	M	2
P7	GM	Textile	N	S/M	50	M	1
P8	VP	Finance	N	L	40	M	1
P9	VP	Education	N	SME	53	D	1
P10	VP	Finance	N	L	47	M	1
P11	VP	Entertainment	N	SME	47	D	1
P12	GM	HR	MN	L	33	S	0
P13	VP	Finance	MN	L	50	M	2
P14	GM	Finance	MN	L	40	M	1
P15	CEO	PR	N	SME	47	D	1
P16	GM	Health	FO	SME	34	S	0
P17	GM	Entertainment	N	SME	44	S	1
P18	VP	Finance	N	L	50	M	1
P19	VP	Manufacturing	MN	L	46	M	0
P20	GM	Finance	MN	L	46	M	2
P21	CEO	Advertising	N	SME	49	M	2
P22	VP	Finance	MN	L	56	M	1
P23	VP	Fast Moving Goods	MN	L	41	S	0
P24	VP	Advertising	N	L	38	M	1
P25	GM	Finance	MN	L	46	M	2
P26	GM	Advertising	MN	L	57	S	0
P27	VP	ICT	N	L	43	S	1
P28	VP	Fast Moving Goods	N	L	41	M	1
P29	GM	ICT	MN	L	39	M	2

Note [a]VP = vice president, GM = general manager, CEO = chief executive officer; [b]MN = multinational, N = national, FO = family owned; [c]M = married, S = single, D = divorced; [d]S = small, M = medium, L = large

EXPLORING THE POSITIVE VIEWS

Supporters believed that being 'the educated and successful women of this country' (P13) it was their moral obligation to assist younger generations in career development (e.g., 'we are only a handful of women here. There

Table 18.2 Template analysis

Step 1: Positive views for supporting female career development

	Illustrative positive quotes	Illustrative negative quotes
Individual level	I definitely have a discriminatory attitude. I'm a feminist. I believe in positive discrimination, until we close the gender gap	There are people I actively mentor, but this includes both men and women. I enjoy doing this, too. As much as I can, I am trying to transfer my experience but it's really up to the individual. This is not about gender, it's about personal development
Organizational level	Communication within organizations is very important. These days there are plenty of media to communicate the importance of overcoming the barriers women face in careers. There are HR magazines, websites, social media, etc. The message needs to focus on raising awareness on the barriers women face. I think communication is very important	This is where senior management's values become very important. If the organization values equal opportunities not only on gender but also on other characteristics and is open to diversity, then as much as possible performance should be based on measurable criteria to provide opportunities for everyone
National/policy level	A lot needs to be done at the national level! I support non-governmental organizations. Women need to be educated, then trained. I try to support these initiatives as much as I can. In our society, we need to invest in women and that is partly through educating the men	N/A

(continued)

are many more women outside of this bubble' [P16]). Three pointed out that they support positive discrimination 'until the gender gap is closed' (P4). All of the supporters ($n = 9$) referred to the lack of gender equality

Table 18.2 (continued)

Step 2: Justification of views on female solidarity

Republican view	*Neoliberal view*	*Patriarchal view*
Sense of duty	Merit-based decision-making	Complying with the requirements of religion
Own privileged status	Organizational performance	Jobs for men and women
Praising women's abilities and commitment	Attitudinal barriers in women's progression[a]	Gender stereotyping of other women
Structural barriers in women's progression	Personal sacrifices[a]	It's the women's weakness
Attitudinal barriers in women's progression	Female-dominated industry is advantageous[b]	
	Turkey vs Western world[b]	
	Paternalistic work culture[b]	
	Diversity programs in place[b]	

Note Themes included under Step 2 are those driven from the socioeconomic trends in Turkey; [a]Consolidated theme as a result of inter-rater reliability agreement; [b]other emergent themes

in Turkey yet reported a positive future outlook for improving women's lives, in society and at work. P17's description below exemplifies this:

> There are many dimensions to women's disadvantaged status. Views that women should not be visible, should be the home-maker and the primary care-giver are still dominant in our country. ... We experience discrimination in every aspect of our lives. Centuries of being second-class citizens through gender socialization is still affecting our lives. But I think the future is in the hands of the women. (P17)

Supporters repeatedly praised working women for their skills and capabilities and believed that (i) women were more hardworking and dedicated in comparison to men ($n = 7$); (ii) motherhood enhances women's managerial capabilities ($n = 6$); and (iii) that women in Turkey face serious attitudinal and structural barriers in labor market entry and progression ($n = 8$). For instance, P8 discusses women's place in the labor market as:

> There are currently no female general managers in insurance. I strongly believe this will change in the near future. When I was a student, 70% of my cohort were women, who all ended up in good managerial positions.

> We are more ambitious and have a better work ethic than men. ... Men are like short distance runners, whereas women are ready for the marathon. (P8)

Most supporters revealed experiencing attitudinal and/or organizational barriers in career progression (e.g., explicit biases in recruitment and selection such as questions about family planning intentions). These barriers are attributed to lack of trust in women's capabilities, commitment, and authority. They, therefore, argued that managerial career progression for men and women in Turkey is 'not a game of equals.' P17's experience below illustrates this:

> When I first started here there was a gentleman who headed sales and marketing. After about a month he said to me 'I like you a lot. I think you can produce great work. However, I have to resign as I cannot work for a female manager. It's nothing personal.' I wished him good luck. (P17)

Curiously, none of the supporters revealed intentions/actions to personally challenge the status quo inside organizations (e.g., 'I don't believe that personal advocacy makes any difference. I don't believe personal initiatives will go far. Societies need to change. Strength in numbers! Particularly in a country like ours, you really need to put a good fight' [P23]). Their support was reflected in intentions to actively argue for women's rights in Turkey and to support women in their personal development upon retirement. Most ($n = 6$) were members of voluntary organizations. Those who supported positive discrimination at the workplace were also more strongly involved in these societal initiatives (e.g., 'I was personally involved in the recent changes to civil code in Turkey. I also attended the women's congress in Belgium. I never give up on this battle' [P4]). Five stated that they mentor female subordinates, particularly in lobbying tactics to increase their visibility and in managing interpersonal relations within the organization.

Exploring the Negative Views

Negative views on female solidarity were more prevalent among the sample; twenty participants revealed varying degrees of negative views on female solidarity in managerial careers. The overarching theme was meritocracy and how performance-based decision-making within organizations renders gender irrelevant. Nevertheless, within such meritocracy-based arguments, participants also discussed (i) women's need to put in more effort than men; (ii) their own personal sacrifices; and (iii) certain organizational (e.g., diversity programs and paternalistic cultures) and industry/organization characteristics (e.g., female-dominated industries). At the very extreme, a minority ($n = 5$) of participants discussed meritocracy while demeaning women's attributes and life choices. These participants showed stronger negative views on female solidarity than those who only based their discussion on meritocracy.

Impact of meritocracy. Non-supporters discussed the irrelevance of gender for career progression (e.g., 'There is no distinction between men and women. You leave your women-ness and men-ness outside and show consistently good performance' [P10]). Although individual performance was argued as the key to promotion and progression, managerial discretion in performance ratings was also mentioned ($n = 4$).

Such subjective rating system within what is described 'as a highly objective system' (P25) appears to have been internalized. For instance, P9 describes a 'highly transparent' performance management system, where performance criteria are agreed between the employee and the manager. She then introduces managerial discretion:

> The manager only has 15% discretion over your performance ratings. This may be where discrimination occurs, but I don't think any manager would use this for discriminating against women. I have never seen this happen. (P9)

Organizational performance/profits were discussed ($n = 9$) in justifying the importance of merit. It was argued that support, including some of those mandated by law (e.g., maternity leave) contradicts organizational goals and does not make 'business sense,' as organizations 'want to hold onto people who demonstrate good performance, regardless of gender' (P14). Nine (out of 20 non-supporters) engaged in mentoring of both men and women. This was another way of underlining the role of employee performance on organizational profits ('this is both for the organization's and my own benefit, because they'll perform better' [P3]).

Personal sacrifices and meritocracy. A minority of non-supporters ($n = 6$) discussed the sacrifices they made for their career in their justification of how meritocracy works in favor of women's progression. For instance,

P12 discusses below her negative reaction toward policies favoring women (e.g., positive discrimination and/or gender quotas):

> It was a costly journey to the top and I paid all my dues. ... Such policies supporting women cannot apply for progression to top level management. If you want to reach the highest level in organizations, then you need to be ready to pay the price. (P12)

The sacrifices made were mostly around keeping family life distinct from work life (e.g., having to take very short maternity leave, missing children's special occasions) and prioritizing work over family (e.g., 'if the woman's priorities are work and career, then you can't even begin to imagine that she had kids at home' [P6]). Two participants revealed that they made a conscious decision not to have children in order to progress. For instance, P5 justifies lack of support for female solidarity by arguing that marriage and children are personal problems:

> Maybe if I were married, my husband may not let me travel for work or stay up late. This would be my problem, not my organization's problem. The root of the problem would be my personal life, not my organization's policies. (P5)

Other workplace characteristics that make gender irrelevant. In addition to meritocracy, there was also a discussion of industry as a differentiator of whether gender is a problem. Particularly those in multinational corporations (MNCs) discussed diversity programs being in place. A minority of participants also discussed paternalistic cultures (in SMEs) as removing gender as an issue at the workplace.

Six participants in female-dominated industries (e.g., textile and recruitment) discussed how the industry itself was an advantage for women. Women were praised for stereotypical characteristics, especially their communal attributes (e.g., 'Women are much better at customer relations. This provides an advantage in our industry. Although top management is mostly men' [P2]).

Alongside industry characteristics, some non-supporters ($n = 4$, all in MNCs) also discussed how Turkey is doing much better compared to the developed world. Both references to industry and international comparisons were used to describe the gender problem as existing elsewhere. P13's comparison of her colleagues in the US and the UK with her position in Turkey exemplifies this:

> Because if you look at our managers in parts of the US or in London, you can't see too many women at top management. Men are dominant because these are men's jobs. Certain organizations have unwritten rules and these include degrading women. This is more prominent elsewhere in the US/the UK in comparison to Turkey. (P13)

All but one of the 13 participants from MNCs mentioned that their organization had in place diversity and/or flexible-working programs but the focal point of these was to maintain employee commitment at lower levels in the organization (e.g., 'To be perfectly honest with you it is difficult for these systems to be genuine. If the woman is ambitious, she won't care for these. She will put in the maximum effort, not flexible but hard effort' [P25]). There was also the belief ($n = 4$) that such support would disadvantage the women because men do not need these initiatives to progress (e.g., 'it would make [women] look weak in the eyes of the organization' [P9]).

In justifying why gender is not an issue in their organizations, some non-supporters ($n = 4$) referred to the paternalistic work culture. Participants argued that being like a family, particularly for SMEs, means that employees can reveal and discuss anything with the knowledge that management will listen and help. Non-supporters mentioned that no female subordinates reported any concerns due to being a woman in career progression. This was therefore justification for lack of support for female solidarity.

Gender stereotyping of other women. Another reason for not supporting female career development was that women's underrepresentation was attributed to their own attributes and/or choices. A minority of participants ($n = 4$) discussed how some women do not have the confidence to break the patriarchal expectations and this was depicted as their main weakness. At a very broad level P3 summarizes her views on women's lack of progression in managerial careers as follows:

> If women stop seeing themselves as second class citizens they can actually go far. Turkish women enjoy being comfortable. They think 'it's OK if I don't earn as much or even work, because my husband will take care

of me.'... There are barriers women set for themselves. ... Moreover, men are more rational at work. Whereas women can be very emotional and take things personally. I see women's lack of progress as their own incompetence and lack of motivation – especially if they are being emotional about this. (P3)

Gender stereotypical attributes were also discussed by five women as influencing women's progression. Jobs for men and women were mentioned both in relation to women's household responsibilities (e.g., childcare), marital status (e.g., husband may not give permission for travel), and women's abilities. For instance, P5 summarizes this below for the insurance industry:

At the lowest levels we have 60-70% women. Men dominate top levels. Men choose more operational roles. Men are more ambitious and approach work with better discipline, especially under pressure. Some men also stay up late, for instance, until 4am in the morning without worrying about permission from the wife! Women are better at routine work, which doesn't require much decision-making. (P5)

Implications for Understanding Senior Executive Women's Views on Female Solidarity

This study explored how senior executive women contextualized their views on female solidarity. In our analyses, we actively searched for themes relevant for fulfilling a duty (the Republican view), meritocracy (neoliberal view), and patriarchy and/or religion (the Conservatist view). Neoliberal, meritocratic values were more prominent in justification of negative views on female solidarity. Republication values were referred to in support of female solidarity. Hence, we have reason to argue that perceived gender salience of organizational and national context is relevant for understanding senior executive females' views on female solidarity.

Gender becomes salient as men and women interact (Tatli, Ozturk, & Woo, 2017). Within the workplace, Kanter (1977) argues that as women reach top positions in organizations their visibility as the members of the minority group increases and hence gender becomes more salient. From a social identity theory perspective (Tajfel & Turner, 1986), previous research argues that women may perceive identity threat due to such visibility, especially in sexist organizational cultures, which may negatively influence their support for the junior women in the organization (Derks et al., 2016; Sterk, Meeussen, & Van Laar, 2018). For most women at top managerial positions, issues of legitimacy of power and tokenism due to male-dominance of organizations are relevant (Vial et al., 2016). The findings show that when women anchor their views on the meritocratic context which expects men and women to be treated equally, they are less likely to be positive about female solidarity. A neoliberal/meritocratic justification was the most common in the study.

The study's findings can be also discussed in line with the ongoing debate on the standards of merit for female career development. As also observed in this study, a discourse of meritocracy denies gender as relevant in managerial progression (Lewis & Simpson, 2010). Decisions based on merit (e.g., education, skills, and work performance) are regarded as relatively objective and fair allocation of resources and distribution of rewards (Kumra, 2017). Meritocracy is therefore assumed to be the rational choice in decision-making and emphasizes the importance of a 'level playing field' and hard work for progression in managerial careers. This places the blame on women's underrepresentation in top managerial positions to personal choice and preference, and may undermine the reasons for the gender problem (Broadbridge & Simpson, 2011; Hakim, 2002). There is an element of subjectivity in determining the standards of merit (e.g., Simpson & Kumra, 2016; Thornton, 2007; Van den Brink & Benschop, 2012).

Merit that is void of the social context replicates the attributes of the dominant group and therefore runs the danger of reinforcing existing inequalities. For instance, Banihani and Syed (2020) show how in Jordan women's opportunities for work engagement, a key determinant of work performance, are limited due to patriarchal expectations, e.g., not being able to work late hours. Most non-supporters in our study discussed meritocracy alongside women's need for impression management to convince the decision-makers against stereotypical attributes (e.g., rational decision-making) and gender role expectations (e.g., prioritizing family over work). Confirming previous research which shows that discourses of meritocracy as diluted by impression management in order to appear as ambitious and available as male counterparts (Kumra & Vinnicombe, 2010) and mediated by personal choice (Simpson, Ross-Smith, & Lewis, 2010), we may question the level playing field associated with notions of meritocracy in Turkey's neoliberal context.

There were also some striking findings which we did not anticipate. Firstly, there was a clear divide between positive and negative views on female solidarity. The former is anchored in where gender is most visible in everyday life (i.e., on the patriarchal values of Turkish society), while the latter is anchored in where gender is regarded as most irrelevant (i.e., on meritocracy). The former was also more likely to mention gender-related obstacles they experienced in their own progression. These findings may be explained in future research by the upper echelons theory (Hambrick & Mason, 1984), which argues that senior executives' agency on different employee-related issues is largely influenced by the way they interpret the problem, based on their individual characteristics, such as values. For instance, we observed the patriarchal context to be evident in most scripts, both among supporters and non-supporters (e.g., in references to Turkish women's need to put in extra effort to breaking patriarchal expectations, such as needing permission from the husband for work-related travel). For non-supporters these were not recognized as barriers against women's career progression. Hence, the difference between positive and negative views is not in experience of the patriarchal context but on whether women find this relevant for organizational careers based on experience.

Secondly, although we observed differences in views, none of the participants in this study reported solidarity behaviors within their organizations as assumed by SIT (Tajfel & Turner, 1979, 1986): that women actively cooperate in increasing female in-group representation at the top management level (Kanter, 1977). We also did not record any evidence of active oppression of female subordinates' careers, as would be described by the 'Queen Bee' syndrome (although this was not actively asked about in the interviews). There was, however, some reference to the perceived inefficiency of individual endeavors in challenging organizational cultures. Future research may benefit from extending the theoretical lens to take into account the perceived behavioral control/self-efficacy women have for influencing women's career development. This may help control for possible reservations due to tokenism.

Lastly, our findings show no evidence of strong patriarchal values held by senior women in justification of views on female solidarity. In our theorizing we associated such strong gender-based values with the rising Conservatist/Islamist tendencies in Turkish society and discussed the implications for women's labor market participation, let alone progression. We can speculate here that the sample may be somewhat skewed, in that those women who hold strong patriarchal values may choose to (or be oppressed to) either stay at home or take up lower levels jobs that do not interfere with family life.

PRACTICAL IMPLICATIONS

Initiatives, such as diversity/flexible-working programs, may work for the benefit of women at lower skilled work, in terms of providing continuous employment. They were, however, perceived to be incompatible with managerial careers by the majority of participants in this study. Watts (2009) calls this the 'diversity paradox'; one that has limited application for women aiming for senior managerial positions yet serves to the well-being of those at the lower levels. Especially in a high gender salient context such as Turkey, welfare reforms may be more important in tackling the issue of women's employment and career progression, alongside organizational interventions for (un)conscious bias.

CHAPTER TAKEAWAYS

- Perceived gender salience informs senior female executives' views on female solidarity in managerial careers. Patriarchal norms that prescribe clear gendered distribution of roles are omnipresent in Turkey.
- Meritocratic values are associated with negative views on female solidarity, while Republican values are relevant for support.
- The evidence for female solidarity and women being natural allies in management is limited.
- At the organizational level, gendered context of larger society may be considered in assigning standards of merit.

REFERENCES

Arvate, P. R., Galilea, G. W., & Todescat, I. (2018). The queen bee: A myth? The effect of top-level female leadership on subordinate females. *The Leadership Quarterly, 29,* 533–548. https://doi.org/10.1016/j.leaqua.2018.03.002.

Aycan, Z. (2004a). Key success factors for women in management in Turkey. *Applied Psychology, 53,* 453–477. https://doi.org/10.1111/j.1464-0597. 2004.00180.x.

Aycan, Z. (2004b). *Uç boyutlu cam tavan: Kadınların kariyer gelişiminde kim, kime, neden engel oluyor?* Paper presented at the 2nd Summit of Women Managers, Istanbul, Turkey.

Banihani, M., & Syed, J. (2020). Gendered work engagement: Qualitative insights from Jordan. *The International Journal of Human Resource Management, 31*, 611–637. https://doi.org/10.1080/09585192.2017.1355838.

Bespinar, F. U. (2010). Questioning agency and empowerment: Women's work-related strategies and social class in urban Turkey. *Women's Studies International Forum, 33*, 523–532. https://doi.org/10.1016/j.wsif.2010.09.003.

Broadbridge, A., & Simpson, R. (2011). 25 years on: Reflecting on the past and looking to the future in gender and management research. *British Journal of Management, 22*, 470–483. https://doi.org/10.1111/j.1467-8551.2011.00758.x.

Carkoglu, A., & Kalaycioglu, E. (2009). *Turkiye'de dindarlık: Uluslararası bir karsilastirma*. Monograph. Istanbul: IPM (Istanbul Politikalar Merkezi), Sabancı University.

Derks, B., Van Laar, C., & Ellemers, N. (2016). The queen bee phenomenon: Why women leaders distance themselves from junior women. *The Leadership Quarterly, 27*, 456–469. https://doi.org/10.1016/j.leaqua.2015.12.007.

Derks, B., Van Laar, C., Ellemers, N., & de Groot, K. (2011). Gender-bias primes elicit queen-bee responses among senior policewomen. *Psychological Science, 22*, 1243–1249. https://doi.org/10.1177/0956797611417258.

Erkut, S., Kramer, V. W., & Konrad, A. M. (2008). Critical mass: Does the number of women on a corporate board make a difference? In S. Vinnicombe, R. J. Burke, D. Bilimoria, & M. Huse (Eds.), *Women on corporate boards of directors: International research and practice* (pp. 350–366). Cheltenham, UK: Edward Elgar Publishing.

Gabriel, A. S., Butts, M. M., Yuan, Z., Rosen, R. L., & Sliter, M. T. (2018). Further understanding incivility in the workplace: The effects of gender, agency, and communion. *Journal of Applied Psychology, 103*, 362–382. https://doi.org/10.1037/apl0000289.

Gunduz-Hosgor, A., & Smits, J. (2008). Variation in labor market participation of married women in Turkey. *Women's Studies International Forum, 31*, 104–117.

Hakim, C. (2002). Lifestyle preferences as determinants of women's differentiated labor market careers. *Work and Occupations, 29*, 428–459. https://doi.org/10.1177/0730888402029004003.

Hambrick, D. C., & Mason, P. A. (1984). Upper echelons: The organization as a reflection of its top managers. *Academy of Management Review, 9*, 193–206. https://doi.org/10.5465/amr.1984.4277628.

Hekman, D. R., Johnson, S. K., Foo, M. D., & Yang, W. (2017). Does diversity-valuing behavior result in diminished performance ratings for non-white and female leaders? *Academy of Management Journal, 60,* 771–797. https://doi.org/10.5465/amj.2014.0538.

Ilkkaracan, I. (2012). Why so few women in the labor market in Turkey? *Feminist Economics, 18,* 1–37. https://doi.org/10.1080/13545701.2011.649358.

ILO. (2017). *The gender gap in employment: What's holding women back?* Retrieved from https://www.ilo.org/infostories/en-GB/Stories/Employment/barriers-women#header.

Kabasakal, H., Aycan, Z., Karakas, F., & Maden, C. (2011). Women in management in Turkey. In M. J. Davidson & R. J. Burke (Eds.), *Women in management worldwide: Progress and prospects* (pp. 317–338). London: Gower.

Kabasakal, H., Karakas, F., Maden, C., & Aycan, Z. (2016). Women in management in Turkey. In R. J. Burke & A. M. Richardsen (Eds.), *Women in management worldwide* (pp. 226–246). New York, NY: Routledge.

Kanter, R. M. (1977). *Men and women of the corporation.* New York: Basic Books.

Karaalp-Orhan, H. S. (2017). What are the trends in women's labour force participation in Turkey? *European Journal of Sustainable Development, 6,* 303–312. https://doi.org/10.14207/ejsd.2017.v6n3p303.

King, N. (2004). Using templates in the thematic analysis of texts. In C. Cassell & G. Symon (Eds.), *Essential guide to qualitative methods in organizational research* (pp. 256–270). London: Sage.

Korabik, K., & Abbondanza, M. (2004). *New theory supplants queen bee notion of woman in management.* Report by Almina Ali, Office of Research, Ontario Ministry of Education & Training.

Kumra, S. (2017). Really saying something: Exploring conceptions of merit in women's experience of career based tensions inspired by my friend Ruth Simpson. *Gender in Management: An International Journal, 32,* 468–475. https://doi.org/10.1108/GM-05-2017-0067.

Kumra, S., & Vinnicombe, S. (2010). Impressing for success: A gendered analysis of a key social capital accumulation strategy. *Gender, Work & Organization, 17,* 521–546. https://doi.org/10.1111/j.1468-0432.2010.00521.x.

Lewis, P., & Simpson, R. (2010). Meritocracy, difference and choice: Women's experiences of advantage and disadvantage at work. *Gender in Management, 25,* 165–169. https://doi.org/10.1108/17542411011036374.

Mavin, S. (2006a). Venus envy: Problematizing solidarity behaviour and queen bees. *Women in Management Review, 21,* 264–276. https://doi.org/10.1108/09649420610666579.

Mavin, S. (2006b). Venus envy 2: Sisterhood, queen bees and female misogyny in management. *Women in Management Review, 21,* 349–364. https://doi. org/10.1108/09649420610676172.

Mavin, S. (2008). Queen bees, wannabees and afraid to bees: No more 'best enemies' for women in management? *British Journal of Management, 19,* S75–S84. https://doi.org/10.1111/j.1467-8551.2008.00573.x.

Mavin, S., Grandy, G., & Williams, J. (2017). Theorizing women leaders' negative relations with other women. In S. R. Madsen (Ed.), *Handbook of research on gender and leadership* (pp. 328–343). Cheltenham, UK: Edward Elgar Publishing.

Ozbilgin, M., & Healy, G. (2004). The gendered nature of career development of university professors: The case of Turkey. *Journal of Vocational Behavior, 64,* 358–371. https://doi.org/10.1016/j.jvb.2002.09.001.

Rodriguez, J. K. (2013). Joining the dark side: Women in management in the Dominican Republic. *Gender, Work & Organization, 20,* 1–19. https://doi. org/10.1111/j.1468-0432.2010.00541.x.

Sheppard, L. D., & Aquino, K. (2017). Sisters at arms: A theory of female same-sex conflict and its problematization in organizations. *Journal of Management, 43,* 691–715. https://doi.org/10.1177/0149206314539348.

Simpson, R., & Kumra, S. (2016). The Teflon effect: When the glass slipper meets merit. *Gender in Management: An International Journal, 31,* 562–576. https://doi.org/10.1108/GM-12-2014-0111.

Simpson, R., Ross-Smith, A., & Lewis, P. (2010). Merit, special contribution and choice: How women negotiate between sameness and difference in their organizational lives. *Gender in Management: An International Journal, 25,* 198–207. https://doi.org/10.1108/17542411011036400.

Sterk, N., Meeussen, L., & Van Laar, C. (2018). Perpetuating inequality: Junior women do not see queen bee behavior as negative but are nonetheless negatively affected by it. *Frontiers in Psychology, 9,* 1690. https://doi.org/10. 3389/fpsyg.2018.01690.

Tabak, F. (1997). Women's upward mobility in manufacturing organizations in Istanbul: A glass ceiling initiative? *Sex Roles, 36,* 93–102. https://doi.org/10. 1007/BF02766240.

Tajfel, H., & Turner, J. C. (1979). An integrative theory of intergroup conflict. In W. G. Austin & S. Worchel (Eds.), *The social psychology of intergroup relations* (pp. 33–47). Monterey, CA: Brooks-Cole.

Tajfel, H., & Turner, J. C. (1986). The social identity of intergroup relations. In S. Worchel & W. G. Austin (Eds.), *Psychology of intergroup relations* (pp. 7–24). Chicago: Nelson-Hall.

Tatli, A., Ozturk, M. B., & Woo, H. S. (2017). Individualization and marketization of responsibility for gender equality: The case of female managers in China. *Human Resource Management, 56,* 407–430. https://doi.org/10.1002/hrm.21776.

Thornton, M. (2007). Otherness' on the bench: How merit is gendered. *Sydney Law Review, 29,* 391–413.

Van den Brink, M., & Benschop, Y. (2012). Gender practices in the construction of academic excellence: Sheep with five legs. *Organization, 19,* 507–524. https://doi.org/10.1177/1350508411414293.

Veldman, J., Meeussen, L., Van Laar, C., & Phalet, K. (2017). Women (do not) belong here: Gender-work identity conflict among female police officers. *Frontiers in Psychology, 8,* 130. https://doi.org/10.3389/fpsyg.2017.00130.

Vial, A. C., Napier, J. L., & Brescoll, V. L. (2016). A bed of thorns: Female leaders and the self-reinforcing cycle of illegitimacy. *The Leadership Quarterly, 27,* 400–414. https://doi.org/10.1016/j.leaqua.2015.12.004.

Watts, J. H. (2009). Leaders of men: Women 'managing' in construction. *Work, Employment and Society, 23,* 512–530. https://doi.org/10.1177/0950017009337074.

Ye, R., Wang, X. H., Wendt, J. H., Wu, J., & Euwema, M. C. (2016). Gender and managerial coaching across cultures: Female managers are coaching more. *The International Journal of Human Resource Management, 27,* 1791–1812. https://doi.org/10.1080/09585192.2015.1075570.

Zeytinoglu, G. N., & Bonnabeauis, R. F. (2015). From Atatürk to Erdoğan: Women in modern Turkey. In S. Safdar & N. Kosakowska-Berezecka (Eds.), *Psychology of gender through the lens of culture* (pp. 93–112). Cham: Springer.

CHAPTER 19

Gender Quota for Workplace Inclusivity: A Mere Band-Aid?

Vartika

INTRODUCTION

If they don't give you a seat at the table, bring a folding chair.
—Shirley Chisholm (First African American Women elected to the US congress)

"Exclusion" is a word that women are too familiar with. It often gives them the impression that the social contract is only between the males of the society and the females will only have to register protest to get into it. It has been a century since women got their first universal suffrage (women in New Zealand got the right to vote in 1893 even as their peers around the world were waiting for a movement to start), and half a century since the first equal pay legislation got underway in the US. However, when we talk about the inclusivity of women at the workplace, we are nowhere compared to the quantum leaps and progress that we have made in technology in the same timeframe. It seems easier to go on

Vartika (✉)
Jawaharlal Nehru University, New Delhi, India

© The Author(s), under exclusive license to Springer Nature Switzerland AG 2021
J. Marques (ed.), *Exploring Gender at Work*,
https://doi.org/10.1007/978-3-030-64319-5_19

361

Mars than to change societal constructs and gender biasness. The reality is that the world still underpaid and overlooks half of its talent pool (Parker, 2016). The World Economic Forum's global gender gap index studies the historical trends and changes in gender gap for 109 countries and estimates that it will take the World 118 more years to close the gender gap (World Economic Forum, 2016). If this means that women will have to wait 118 more years for a seat at the decision maker's table, then it probably is time to start one more movement.

The conspicuous absences of women from corporate boards have drawn the attention of academics (Hillman, Shropshire, & Cannella, 2007), policymakers (OECD, 2009), practitioners, and business analysts (Grant Thornton Report, 2014). Academics have assigned this shortage often to the "pipeline problem" that means a lack of qualified women in lower and mid-level leadership roles led to the lack of a talent pool. This shortage has been attributed to the variety of causes, like women's domestic responsibilities (Greenhaus & Parasuraman, 1999) and lack of adequate display of the traits and motivations that are necessary to attain and achieve success in high-level positions by women due to the way they are brought up (Browne, 1993). Proponents of social role theory attribute this pipeline problem to differences in societal roles that lead men and women to demonstrate and value different types of interpersonal behaviors (Eagly & Johannesen-Schmidt, 2001). According to this theory, men tend to value and engage in more assertive, competitive and agentic behaviors, whereas, women tend to value and engage in more communal behaviors and hence, traditionally have been occupying more caretaking roles (Koenig, Eagly, Mitchell, & Ristikari, 2011). This stereotypical perception is shared by individuals in most societies and gives legitimacy and consensual nature to exclusion of women from leadership roles. Applying the above reasoning, in the context of the workplace and more pointedly in corporate boardroom, women are, therefore, more likely than men to hold positions at low levels in hierarchies of status and authority, and are less likely to be at the decision-making table (Eagly & Wood, 2012; Heilman, 2001), where agency is expected.

While there is some merit to these arguments, data also points toward the fact that the number of women attaining a university degree has gone up drastically, and so has the number of women joining the workforce. However, the corresponding figures for women in leadership positions in the corporate world remain stubbornly dismal. This disturbing absence of women from the boardrooms despite their proven academic abilities and high share in workforce sparks the discussion on gender quotas. One has to wonder whether it will take mandatory quotas for the rich men's club to finally share some power with their female counterparts. At the same time, corporate governance debates have shifted from "independence" to "gender diversity". The lack of evidence that conventional measures of board independence matter (Adams, Hermalin, & Weisbach, 2010) have led to arguments that independent boards will continue to be as ineffective as old composition if they are dominated by the "Old-Boys Club". Since women are not part of this club, the next step in corporate governance debates have been inclusion of women and making boards more gender diverse to let in new perspectives. Scholars have tried to establish if and how women directors are different from their male counterparts and if this difference affects organizational outcome (Anja Kirsch School of Economics and Business, Germany). Some scholars point out that appointing women directors tends to affect the nature of board processes and outcomes, and by extension, firm outcomes (Terjesen, Sealy, & Singh, 2009). However, the determinants and effects of board composition are intertwined (Adams et al., 2010), making it very difficult to convincingly link the characteristics of directors, including their gender, to firm outcomes (Johnson, Ellstrand, & Daily, 1996; Withers, Hillman, & Cannella, 2012).

This chapter studies three aspects of the gender quota debate. First of all, through literature review and available data, this chapter tries to establish whether organizations are really gendered and if there is a genuine bias working against women preventing them from entering corporate boardrooms, or if it is the sum total of socio-cultural obstacles and the pipeline problem. Secondly, we ask what the perceived and actual benefits of gender diversity in corporate boardrooms are and if those benefits are lucrative enough to push through the biases against women to give them a share in power. Thirdly, is gender quota necessary and if implemented, can it get the desired results, is a question we ask. In this part, we study the Norwegian social experiment of mandatory gender quota. While analyzing global data and literature, this chapter tries to put in place India's position in all three aspects.

The Gendered Business Model

It is universally acknowledged that capitalism thrives on profit motive. The sole purpose of a business organization engaged in any economic activity is to earn profit. The most prevalent business model currently in big business is of public limited companies which are run by a board of directors. Since the corporate board is the most important body in a company's functioning, it is natural to assume that decisions to appoint the board would be made keeping in mind the efficacy of the proposed board. This in turn entails that merit would be the deciding factor, which means that corporate boards' gender ratio should at the very least be reflective of its workforce composition, if not of gender equality. Let us have a look at global data for corporate leadership and workforce participation.

This data of the World Economic Forum report, 2016 reveals that the global average for females on corporate boards is 28%. However, this is a 2016 average which has outliers in the form of countries like Norway, which have already implemented mandatory gender quota as well as countries like France, Sweden, etc. that have adopted some form of quota guidelines in their company regulations. However, the picture varies country-wise. Women form less than 17% of the Fortune 500 board seats in the US, and one-tenth of those companies do not have any female Director on board. Similarly, in Australia women representation on board averages around 18.2%, in Canada 15.9%, and 21.6% in the UK. Asian countries paint yet more dismal pictures with China having only 8% female board representation, India 5% and Japan 2% in 2012 (Grant Thornton IBR, 2014). There does seem to be a pipeline problem as women in senior management roles average only 15% globally. That does bring out the point, Is the improved average of female representation on corporate boards a product of steps being taken by countries to improve gender diversity? Since women's representation in senior management falls dramatically to 15% from 24% in mid-level roles and 33% in junior roles. The problem is further accentuated by the fact that globally only 9% women lead these companies as CEOs. Thus, while board representation might have improved due to quota, letting women lead does not come naturally to the old boys' club. If we analyze the date at line and staff roles we find that women are under-represented in line roles in Mobility, Information and Communication Technology, Energy and Basic and Infrastructure, with line roles more likely to equip women with the skills and experience that would prepare them for senior positions. This may be one of the barriers to top level positions.

The same World Economic Forum Survey also studied the gender wage gap as well as barriers to women recruitment, and a look at the same will throw some light at the way the corporate world has created space for women.

Table 19.2 reveals that the gender wage gap is persistently higher across sectors barring the exception of Art, Design, Entertainment, Sports & Media, where the gap is comparatively lower. However, when it comes to difficulty in recruiting women (since across all industries, companies reported that they found women harder to recruit), it is directly proportional to the existing gender composition of the industry. However, it needs to be ascertained if these difficulties are solely due to socio-cultural barriers to female integration in the workforce or if there is a systematic bias that leads to perceived difficulty.

Unconscious bias among managers seems to be the overbearing barrier, which reinforces the idea that when it comes to integration of females into the workforce, biases work as barriers. Lack of female role models reported by 39% is a vicious circle that needs to be broken through external intervention.

One more important aspect to ascertaining the presence of bias against females is to crosscheck if the excuse of lack of talent pool has any credibility. Figures for female enrollment in tertiary education don't reflect so. As per a UNESCO 2013 study, the global ratio for enrollment of females to 100 males in tertiary education was 108 in 2012, an increase of 24% from 1980s. The same study showed that this ratio has increased in almost all countries of the world. In North America it was 140, in Latin America 127, in European Union 126, in Asia pacific 107. If we look at India particularly, it was 78; nowhere near the dismal representation women had on board in the same year. One can argue that it will take some time for the achievements in tertiary education to transform into a greater role for women in businesses. However, there is no issue in using the talent pool to get the work done as is evident from the current share of women in junior & staff roles at 33 and 36%, respectively (Table 19.1). It is the sharing of power that is the actual issue. The presence of gender wage gap (Table 19.2) as well as respondent's agreement to presence of bias (Fig. 19.1) just solidifies the proof toward existence of a problem. Hence, unless we are alright with the argument that women who clear graduate schools with flying colors suddenly lose their shine in the business world, there is no way we can justify the extreme gaps between women in the work force and women in management roles. Hence, we need to explore the possibility that there are considerations much different than merit and profitability that limit the access women have to management roles. There

Table 19.1 Percentage (%) of female workforce across industries

Industry group	CEOs	Board members	Senior roles		Mid-level roles		Junior roles		Line roles		Staff roles	
			Current	2020	Current	2020	Current	2020	Current	2020	Current	2020
Industries Overall	9%	28%	15%	25%	24%	33%	33%	36%	30%	34%	35%	39%
Basic & Infrastructure	2	35	9	17	13	21	22	29	14	23	20	27
Consumer	10	21	16	24	26	33	33	37	31	34	37	41
Financial Services & Investors	0	32	11	20	19	27	24	27	19	25	22	30
Healthcare	6	–	15	28	31	44	39	46	44	49	41	48
Information & Communication Technology	5	19	11	20	21	29	32	34	23	32	33	38
Media, Entertainment & Information	13	22	25	33	25	32	35	36	38	43	47	46
Mobility	9	17	13	21	21	30	28	33	25	31	34	36
Professional Services	9	23	22	34	33	40	39	43	44	44	44	46

Source Future of Jobs Survey, World Economic Forum, 2016

Table 19.2 Gender gap by job family

Job family	Share of women (%)	Gender wage gap (%)	Relative ease of recruitment	
			Current	2020
Architecture & Engineering	11	27	−1.18	−0.27
Art, Design, Entertainment, Sports & Media	48	12	−0.21	0.07
Business & Financial Operations	43	30	−0.42	−0.16
Computer & Mathematical	23	28	−0.91	−0.13
Construction & Extraction	10	48	−1.48	−0.64
Installation & Maintenance	8	24	−1.43	−0.20
Management	25	34	−0.84	−0.03
Manufacturing & Production	20	32	−0.99	−0.12
Office & Administrative	54	36	0.21	0.31
Sales & Related	41	35	−0.42	−0.03

Source Future of Jobs Survey, World Economic Forum
Note Relative ease of recruitment measured on a quantitative −2 ("much harder") to + 2 ("much easier") scale. Gender wage gap refers to the share of responses in the affirmative

appears to be an undeniable bias working against women and it may be for several socio-economic reasons but it doesn't relate to merit. Thus, the current business model shows signs of gender bias and fuels the discussion on the need for gender quota.

Does Gender Diversity at the Workplace Work?

It is an established fact that men dominate the boardrooms as discussed above through the available data. Finding the impact of gender diversity on firms working and performance is a difficult task when there is no diversity to begin with (Adams, 2016). It is also easy to dismiss the idea of benefits associated with gender diversity after a token comparative

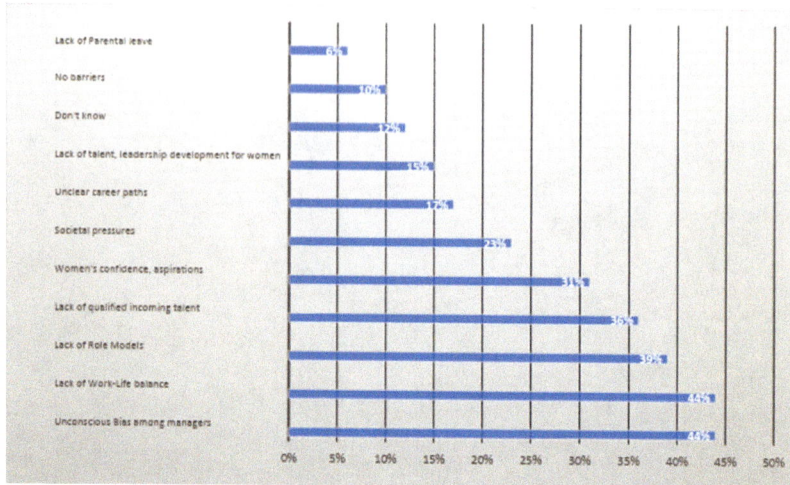

Fig. 19.1 Significance of barriers to gender parity across industry (Percentage) Share of respondents reporting barrier. (*Source* Future of Jobs Survey. World Economic Forum)

study ignoring the importance of achieving a critical mass for results to be visible. This is what has been happening to academic studies related to gender diversity. Evidence of benefits of gender diversity are murky at best. Some researchers also point out that the murky evidence may be a result of varying context and different board structures (Carter, D'Souza, Simkins, & Simpson, 2010). Other studies point to critical mass acts merely as token members on board and goes by the majority opinion instead of enforcing their viewpoint or taking any independent stand (Rose, 2007). Only after a critical mass of about 30% or more is achieved can positive effects be associated with gender diverse boards in comparison to an all-male board (Kanter, 1977; Joecks, Pull, & Vetter, 2013).

Literature review of available research does not point out conclusively in favor or against gender quota. While there are researches associating negative value with gender quota there are yet others that suggest that gender diversity leads to positive performance. Boards with more female directors have higher economic performance measured by stock price growth, return on equity and Tobin's Q (Mckinsey & Company, 2007).

Not only this, but a gender diverse board also leads to improvement in accounting quality. Firms with a greater number of females on board showed higher earning quality measured by return on asset & return on investment (Erhardt, Werbel, & Shrader, 2003). In short, improved gender diversity improves oversight function of the board (Srinidhi, Gul, & Tsui, 2011). Some research also points that the male executives make more takeover bids and issue more debt than female executives. A study based on S&P 1500 companies during 1997–2009 concludes that each female director is associated with 7.6% fewer bids and with each additional female director the board reduces the bid premium paid by 15.4% (Levi, Li, & Zhang, 2014). This reflects that the female directors help in creating shareholder's value by making thorough acquisition decisions.

Another way to gauge the impact of gender diversity on a firm's performance is to examine changes in performance on appointment of a new female director. Here also there is no conclusive evidence for a one-sided verdict. A study based on US fortune 500 data from 1990 to 2000 suggests that there is no significant abnormal return on announcement of addition of new female directors to board (Farrell & Hersch, 2005). On the other hand, another study shows that appointment of a new female director is associated with better operating performance compared to that of a new male director appointment (Dieleman, Qian, & Ibrahim, 2013). Another study based in Spain shows that stock markets react positively to the appointment of female directors on board (Campbell & Vera, 2010).

If economic performance alone cannot push through the ideas of gender diversity, there are social good objectives too that have been visited by academicians. With increased number of women on board corporate social behavior such as charitable giving, community involvement, and employee recognition improves (Broome & Krawiec, 2008). This heightened social responsibility can be attributed to men & women behaving as per roles associated with them through gender stereotypes. While women are considered more "communal", men are considered more "agentic" (Bakan, 1966). Globally, women are associated with traits like being caring, compassion, being interested in actualizing values in relationships of importance (Boulouta, 2012). That's why companies with gender diversity in their corporate boards are more likely to be listed on Ethisphere Magazine's "World's Most Ethical Companies" list (Bernardi, Bosco, & Columb, 2009).

Women are also better at following rules and regulations. Studies support that the presence of women on corporate boards reduces earnings management and improves overall accounting quality (Lara, Osma & Penalva, 2009). Moreover, women tend to be more financially risk-averse than men, which leads to lesser securities fraud on average with gender diverse boards (Cabo, Gimeno & Nieto, 2012). Therefore, the idea of increased participation of women has started gaining ground. A widely discussed panel at a World Economic Forum in Davos posed the question: "Would the world be in this financial mess if it had been Lehman Sisters?" (Bennhold, 2009). A large number of participants at Davos believed that the answer was "NO" as women were "more prudent" and less "ego driven" than men in financial management contexts (ibid.). Thus, while empirical research is inconclusive on its verdict about the effect of gender diversity on firm's performance, it shows that there are positive benefits of a gender diverse board when it comes to corporate governance. However, as is well known, business enterprises are guided solely by profit motive. Hence, in absence of concrete evidence of positive impact of gender diversity on firm's performance, it would be unwise to expect enterprises around the world to become more open and accommodating toward having women on their boards. However, policy makers around the world seem to be convinced that more gender diverse boards are more effective and there are not enough women on boards to bring this effectiveness (Adams, 2016). Hence, the discussion around gender quota, a regulatory inference to open the old boys' network to the women. While the world was discussing gender quota, its need and effectiveness, Norway took a giant leap in 2003 making provisions for gender equality in the boardroom and subsequently making them mandatory in 2008. Thus, the world is looking to Norway and it is not disappointing.

The Norwegian Experiment and the Verdict on Gender Quota in Business

In 2003, Norway introduced an amendment to its Public Limited Companies Act and became a pioneer in the field of economic emancipation of women. The amendment required Public Limited Companies to have at least 40% directors from both genders. Amidst resistance from shareholders, some European countries followed suit. However, most of the world gawked and waited for the verdict on Norwegian experiment before taking action. Norway, on the other hand, moved ahead and seeing slow pace of adoption through voluntary quotas made it mandatory in 2008. The target was to achieve 40% board membership for females by 2009 and non-complying firms could face severe penalties including liquidation. Not only this, the government further expanded the quota requirement to state-owned companies in 2004 and municipality-owned and cooperative companies in 2009. The amendment known as Gender Equality law has served its purpose of improving female representation on board in Norway from 6% in 2002 to 40.5% in 2014 (Grant Thornton IBR, 2014).

The Norwegian experiment did not go down well with the shareholders and the 2003 announcement- of 40% target of female representation on board when there were only 9% at the time of announcement—led to significant drop in stock price and a large decline in Tobin's Q in the next few years (Ahern & Dittmar, 2012). It also led to younger and less experienced boards, increasing leverage in acquisitions and decreasing operating performance (ibid.). After the Norwegian government announced the penalty of liquidation for non-compliance, half the firms excited to an organizational form not exposed to the law (Øyvind & Staubo, 2014). This response suggests that the cost of involuntary board restructuring is higher than abandoning exposed organizational form (ibid.).

On the positive side, despite fear from businesses about dearth of qualified women to fill the top position research shows that new reserved seats were filled by women who were observably more qualified to serve on board than women who were appointed before, reflecting that there was indeed a glass ceiling at work stopping qualified women from rising to the top positions (Bertrand, Black, Jensen & Lleras-Muney, 2015). Even the fear that quotas will lead to staffing of several boards with same female over achievers—known disparagingly as "golden skirts"—is unwarranted. In large listed companies, "golden trousers" are as common as "golden skirts", 15% of male directors sit on three or more boards compared to 19% of female directors (*The Economist*, 2018). Studying the effect of quota on corporate policy decisions, a research concluded that Norwegian firms undertook fewer workforce reductions compared to other Scandinavian unaffected firms (Matsa & Miller, 2013).

Norway's success in achieving 40% gender quota and its firms' success in finding qualified females to sit on boards makes a compelling case about the existence of glass ceilings and the need for external push to break it.

However, as the Economist points out in its article, only 7% of biggest Norwegian firms have female bosses. Therefore, quota is not the organic way to achieve gender equality in boardrooms and the economic power arena; however, it is one of the steps in a long arduous journey that needs to be taken. Several socio-economic notions need to be changed and supportive legislations need to be enacted to make gender equality in economic decision making a reality.

Gender Quota in Boardrooms: The Dominos Effect

The conspicuous absence of women from the top of the corporate ladder without any substantial reason brought to the forefront, the need for strict action to ensure diversity at the top. While chartering into controversial territory of gender quotas even women at times have hesitated to resort to tokenistic measures instead of getting individual talents recognized but attitudes have changed. As Christian Lagarde, Managing Director IMF who has admitted to resisting the idea of quotas all her professional career put it, "there was no way we were going to jump the right step" (Grant Thornton IBR, 2014). Different countries dealt with the issue of diversity differently. The most prominent tool has been one or another form of gender quota. Norway was the first country to implement a gender quota in 2003 in its pursuit of Gender Equality. Referred to as Gender Equality Law, it was voluntary, applied only to public limited companies and required them to achieve 40% female board membership by 2009 (Sweigart, 2012). In 2011, France, Italy, and Belgium implemented binding gender quotas. A 2011 French law requires a minimum 20% corporate board seats to be filled by female members by 2014 and 40% by 2017. Italy's law required at least 33% of each gender on the board by 2015, insisting on a target of 20% in the four transition years. In Belgium the law requires a minimum of 33% representation of each gender on the board of public and state-run companies by 2018. All these countries have sanctions and fines attached to non-compliance (Choobineh & Neeka, 2016).

Other countries like Spain, Iceland, the Netherlands, Germany, Malaysia, and India have implemented gender quotas without sanctions. In 2007, Spain passed a law that encouraged large publicly traded companies to reach a board ratio of 40% women by 2015. Iceland followed suit in 2010 by recommending that all publicly listed companies and companies with more than 50 employees have at least 40% of each gender on board by 2013. In 2011, the Netherlands implemented a comply or explain mechanism for public and private firms with more than 250 employees, requiring them to have at least 30% of each gender on their supervisory and executive board. In 2015, Germany passed a law requiring large publicly traded companies to reserve 30% of new board seats for women in 2016, pushing the ratio to 50% by 2018.

However, countries elsewhere are also in pursuit of gender equality in economic leadership. In 2011, Malaysia instituted a quota targeting 30% women on corporate boards in the next five years. In 2013, India mandated all public limited companies to have at least one female director on board. The Austrian government in 2012 called for ASX 200 companies to voluntarily reach a target of 30% female board membership by 2018. Israel, Kenya, Brazil have issued directives for gender equality in economic leadership.

Boardrooms in India

Traditionally Indian boardrooms have been a lonely place for females and it has not changed yet. Female representation on board of NIFTY 500 companies was 5% in 2012 and increased to mere 13% in 2017. This is when the new Companies Act 2013, made it mandatory to have at least one independent woman director on boards of the companies listed on the National Stock Exchange (NSE). However, experts say the spirit of the reform is yet to see the light of day. At 13% women are still under-represented on Indian boards when compared to other large economies. India is the seventh largest economy in terms of GDP (nominal). The corresponding figures for other six large economies are US 22%, China 38%, Japan nine%, Germany 14%, UK 20% (IBR, 2014), and France 34% (Institutional Investor Advisory Services India Limited, 2017). The small progress that India has achieved can be mostly attributed to the newly introduced companies act as most companies tend to be filling only the mandatory "one woman" quota. Only 26 on NIFTY 500 boards had three or more female directors as on 31 March, 2017. 15 companies were still non-compliant with no females on board, the corresponding figure is only 6 for S&P 500 companies in the US. Thus, Indian boards not only need to travel a long way to be competitive in the global race for gender diversity, but it appears a lot needs to be changed in terms of socio-economic conditions for ensuring economic emancipation of women.

The Need and Push Toward Gender Quota in India

Girls Education is the single most powerful investment towards development. When you educate a girl, you educate a nation.—UNICEF

India inherited a very poor literacy rate from its colonial masters and hence education as a whole was a mammoth task for the nation builders. However, being the archetype patriarchal society, special efforts were needed to educate women in India. The efforts of the past have started paying off and female tertiary education participation that revolved somewhere around 40% in the 1980s has climbed to 78% in 2011. More and more women are acquiring higher education and joining the workforce. In 2017, female workforce participation was 27% in India. However, as is the trend globally, improved workforce participation does not transform into improved participation in senior management. In March 2012, female representation on boards in NIFTY 500 companies, a benchmark for gauzing female participation in senior management, was only 5%. In the next two years it remained static at 6%. Only after the new Companies Act came in force in 2014 did it give fillip to female participation in boards and the figures jumped to 11% in March 2015. In the next two years, it again grew by only 1% per year to reach 13% in March, 2017. The sad part is that even after the new Act and SEBI listing rules, there are companies that choose to ignore the mandatory requirements. In 2015, SEBI fined 530 companies for missing multiple deadlines to meet the quota (Bhalla, 2015). This suggests that the fine for listed companies of $2240 plus $78 per day may not be enough to persuade companies to abide by the mandatory requirement of having at least one female on board (ibid.). Looking at the talent pool available in the country, the dearth of eligible female candidates does not seem to be the issue. Something more than a mere issue of merit seems to be blocking the adoption of the idea of gender diversity and the need of the hour seems to push the agenda strictly.

Toward Gender Diversity on Indian Boards: The First Few Steps

In the year 2013, India enacted the New Companies Act, which came into force from 1 April 2014. Section 149(1) of the act provides that "such class or classes of companies as may be prescribed, shall have at least one female director." Accordingly, Companies (Appointment and qualification of directors) rules 2014 provide that "Every listed company and every other public company having paid-up share capital of at least Rs.100 crore or turnover of at least Rs.300 crore shall appoint at least one, woman director." Subsequently the Securities and Exchange Board of India amended its listing regulations to introduce a quota for female directors. Regulation 17 (1)(a) of SEBI (LODR) Regulations, 2015 mandates that "board of directors shall have an optimum combination of executive and nonexecutive directors with at least one-woman director and not less than fifty percent of the board of directors shall comprise of non-executive directors."

The recent legislative and regulatory push has given impetus to otherwise stagnant strides of females upward the corporate ladder. Females comprised 13% of NIFTY 500 board of directors, up from a meagre 5% in 2013. In absolute numbers, 622 female directors are there on the board of NIFTY 500 companies. If we account for multiple directorships, the number turns out to be 477 unique women directors on board of top Indian companies—that is, 477 women with the ability to influence and inspire change and motivate a whole generation of new female employees. Almost all sectors, with an exception of the energy sector that has an average of 8%, have no large variance in proportion of female directors, indicating that there is no sector-specific limitation in appointment of female directors on board. With the new regulations in place 485 of NIFTY 500 companies are compliant with the mandatory requirement of one female member on board. 107 of these companies exceeded the mandatory quota requirement. Only 15 companies had no female director on board as of March 2017 and bulk of these i.e., 11 were Public Sector Undertakings. Delays in appointments were due to pending approval from the ministry.

Female Directors on Indian Boards

As per the IIAS Research 2017, female directors on boards of NIFTY 500 companies had an average tenure of 4.6 years compared to the 9.0 years of their male counterparts. They had an average age of 56.6 years compared to 62.5 for males; average number of directorships held was 5.3 against 5.9 held by men and average attendance was 78% against 81% for men. The only place where the female directors seem to be lagging behind their male counterparts is experience. They have a smaller average tenure of 4.6 years but that can be attributed to the fact that most of them got entry into boardrooms only after the Companies Act mandated it in 2013.

On the introduction of the mandatory quota, there were concerns that not enough competent women would be available to fill the vacant seats or the new women directors would belong to the promoter family and work in non-executive capacity. Over the years those concerns have been found to be unwarranted. As of March 2017, only 16% of the female directors were Promoter Directors and 50% of these were driving the company in leadership capacity as Executive Directors. 60% of the female Directors were Independent Directors. Thus, instead of providing mere lip service to the new regulations, the companies are actually putting effort complying and bringing forward eligible female talent.

However, there are certain issues that come with quotas. Ensuring a seat at the table does not necessarily mean that the women are getting a share in power. Only 3% boards among the NIFTY 500 companies are headed by women. Although it is comparable to the European average of 4% chairmanship, it underlines a larger issue. Quotas can take women only so far. Similarly, only 7% of the executive directors are female. So, even a quota is not able to confirm promotions and larger responsibility for female executives. As far as Independent Directors are concerned, only 16% of Independent Directors in India are female. This is much lower than European average of 34%. However, this may be because the proportion of female directors on board is also low in India compared to Europe. Majority of women inducted on the board after quota have been Independent Directors in India as well as globally. In India, 60% of female directors are Independent Directors.

Women on Board: Has India Done Enough?

As this chapter points out in the beginning, the effects of gender diversity on economic performance are murky at best, and this may be due to lack of enough gender diverse boards to prove a point. It is also true that without profits to back it up, the argument for gender diversity will not hold up and companies will not pick it up on their own. The only other way is to resort to quota, which most of the countries have been doing. But, quota is just a quick fix to a structural problem. As we saw in Table 19.1, while the gender quota on corporate boards has taken the ratio of women to 28%, only 9% of the companies internationally are being headed by women CEOs and the ratio of women in senior management roles globally is a dismal 15%. Thus, the issues and biases that were holding women back from decision-making roles are still in place and gender quota for corporate boards has just given it a nudge in the right direction.

If we look at India, the affirmative action of one woman on corporate board as a requirement under companies' act has brought significant change in board compositions but it can't impact the decision making much. One woman on board is not enough critical mass to show the benefits of diversity. It is not even enough representation to bring about women centric policies in the corporate environment. The absence of women as CEO and in senior management positions is much more conspicuous in India. Women in the country face several barriers that need to be broken before we leave meritocracy to take its course for fair representation. In the next section, the chapter examines the steps that need to be taken to positively impact workplace inclusion of women. Gender quota is just the beginning; the end is to reap the benefits of inclusion of the remaining 50% population in economic activities.

What More Needs to Be Done

India has traditionally been a patriarchal society with women's working to earn becoming acceptable only in the recent past. It was an achievement when India adopted universal adult franchise. Thus, granting women the right to vote much before many of the first world nations. However, that didn't usher in an era of women empowerment and our socio-political dynamics still promotes exclusion of women from the public sphere. Thus, while policies for economic inclusion are good, they can't work in silo. Following are few actions that need to be looked at if India wants to have full contribution of its female population in the GDP.

1. Investment in Female Education:

India still has a very poor female literacy rate. This just reflects the attitude of society toward educating its female members. We need policies that will promote female literacy and it will be more effective if continuing education becomes easier for women. Male is to female enrollment ratio in tertiary education in India was 78% which is much below the global average. Higher education for girl children is still a secondary priority in most families in India. Hence, India needs better public schools and cheaper higher education for girls.

2. Safety in Public Places:

Being a patriarchal society, allowing women to work is a very momentous decision in a lot of families and a lot depends on their perception of security in the work environment. A lot of women leave jobs because their jobs require night shifts or staying late. While the presence of a lesser number of women in the public sphere is probably one of the reasons this lack of safety ensues from, it is a vicious circle that needs to be broken. Safety in public places will go a long way in bringing more women into workplaces.

3. Gender Inclusive Policies:

As it is said, "Equality doesn't mean equal treatment to all it means equal treatment to people with similar circumstances." This is true for women at work places. While working late nights and night shifts has become the norm in the corporate sector, policies should be made so that women are not left out of working at these places. Requirements like pick up and drop facilities for women working late, proper security at workplace, lesser or no night shifts for women considering their convenience will help women whose families frown letting them work late or women who have small kids and are primary caretaker of the family.

Another issue that takes away precious years of women's careers and is often blamed for the lesser number of women progressing to senior management is motherhood. "Motherhood" is a happy experience and the reason for society's continuation. It should not be turned into a career killer for women. There should be policies in place that would provide women ample maternity leave without harming their career progression. In fact, establishing parity between maternity and paternity leave will ensure that men also involve themselves in parental duties and are provided breaks from work in lieu of parenthood. It will remove the stigma from maternity leave if it is parenting leave.

4. Promoting Female Entrepreneurs:

It is often seen that the families are not supportive of those women who would like to start their own business venture and even society is not very welcoming and friendly in India, to women-led businesses. However, more women entrepreneurs will mean more role models and mentors for young women. Also, women will not be asking a seat at board but rather providing one. It can be achieved if lending as well as startup policies give special impetus to female-led businesses. Business incubation labs in the country can be encouraged to take up women-led projects.

Conclusion

This chapter started on a quest to determine whether gender-based exclusion is a reality in the corporate sector and if so, whether gender quota can help in achieving gender diversity in corporate boardrooms. On examining available data and literature review, it was concluded that the data indeed points to gender-based exclusion from corporate boards. Review of literature on benefits of gender diverse boards suggested that there was not enough evidence to substantially establish that gender diversity positively impacts firm's performance. In absence of substantial evidence to relate gender diversity and economic performance, gender quota remains the undisputed method to achieve the target of gender diversity on corporate boards. However, the chapter also examined whether gender quota was enough to ensure diversity and found out that while a mandatory quota would ensure enough women get representation on board, it cannot ensure that those voices would ever get heard. It also cannot ensure a trickledown effect. Hence, the chapter concludes that a lot more needs to be done than just gender quota to ensure workplace inclusion of women in an organic manner. Some of the suggestions mentioned in the last section of this chapter can be effective in achieving the same. Thus, to achieve the overall goal of gender diversity at the workplace and to ensure that a large section of the population is not unutilized or underutilized in GDP creation, we need to go a step beyond gender quota and ensure socio-economic transformation.

Chapter Takeaways

- When we talk about the inclusivity of women at the workplace, we are nowhere compared to the quantum leaps and progress that we have made in technology in the same timeframe.
- Data of the World Economic Forum report, 2016 reveals that the global average for females on corporate boards is 28%. However, this average has outliers in the form of countries like Norway, which have already implemented mandatory gender quota as well as countries like France, Sweden, etc. that have adopted some form of quota guidelines in their company regulations.

- The gender wage gap gets persistently higher across sectors barring the exception of Art, Design, Entertainment, Sports & Media, where the gap is comparatively lower.
- Unconscious bias among managers seems to be the overbearing barrier, which reinforces the idea that when it comes to integration of females into the workforce, biases work as barriers. Lack of female role models reported by 39% is a vicious circle that needs to be broken through external intervention.
- As a forerunner, Norway achieved success in achieving 40% gender quota on boards. Still, only 7% of biggest Norwegian firms have female bosses.
- Different countries dealt with the issue of diversity on corporate boards differently. The most prominent tool has been one or another form of gender quota.
- Traditionally Indian boardrooms have been a lonely place for females and it has not changed yet.
- On the introduction of the mandatory quota, there were concerns that not enough competent Indian women would be available to fill the vacant seats or the new women directors would belong to the promoter family and work in non-executive capacity. Over the years those concerns have been found to be unwarranted.

References

Adams, R. B. (2016). Women on boards: The superheroes of tomorrow? *The Leadership Quarterly, 27*(3), 371–386. https://doi.org/10.1016/j.leaqua.2015.11.001.

Adams, R. B., Hermalin, B., & Weisbach, M. (2010). The role of boards of directors in corporate governance: A conceptual framework and survey. *Journal of Economic Literature, 48*(1), 58–107. https://doi.org/10.1257/jel.48.1.58.

Ahern, K. R., & Dittmar, A. K. (2012). The changing of the boards: The impact on firm valuation of mandated female board representation. *The Quarterly Journal of Economics, 127*(1), 137–197. https://doi.org/10.1093/qje/qjr049.

Bakan, D. (1966). *The duality of human existence: Isolation and communion in western man.* Boston, MA: Beacon Press.

Bennhold, K. (2009, February 1). Where would we be if women ran Wall Street? *The New York Times.* Retrieved from https://www.nytimes.com/.

Bernardi, R. A., Bosco, S. M., & Columb, V. L. (2009). Does female representation on boards of directors associate with the 'most ethical companies' list? *Corporate Reputation Review, 25*(3), 270–280. https://doi.org/10.1057/crr.2009.15.

Beroutsos, A., Andrew, F., & Kehoe, C. F. (2007, January). *What public companies can learn from private equity.* USA: Mckinsey & Company. Retrieved from https://www.mckinsey.com/business-functions/strategy-and-corporate-finance/our-insights/what-public-companies-can-learn-from-private-equity.

Bertrand, M., Black, S. E. and Jensen, S. & Lleras-Muney, A. (2015, March). Breaking the Glass Ceiling. *SSRN Electronic Journal.* CEPR Discussion Paper No. DP10467, https://doi.org/10.2139/ssrn.2488955.

Bhalla, N. (2015, July 14). Indian regulator fines 530 companies for delay in appointing women directors. Thomson Reuters Foundation News. Retrieved from https://news.trust.org/item/20150714165315-d1eda/https://news.trust.org/item/20150714165315-d1eda/.

Boulouta, I. (2012). Hidden connections: The link between board gender diversity and corporate social performance. *Journal of Business Ethics, 113*(2), 185–197. https://doi.org/10.1007/s10551-012-1293-7.

Broome, L. L., & Krawiec, K. D. (2008). Signaling through board diversity: Is anyone listening? *University of Cincinnati Law Review, 77*, 431–464. UNC Legal Studies Research Paper No. 1132884, Forthcoming. Available at SSRN: https://ssrn.com/abstract=1132884.

Browne, A. (1993). Violence against women by male partners: Prevalence, outcomes, and policy implications. *American Psychologist, 48*(10), 1077–1087. https://doi.org/10.1037/0003-066X.48.10.1077.

Browne, K. (1999). *Divided labors: An evolutionary view of women at work.* New Haven, CT: Yale University Press.

Cabo, R. M., Gimeno, R., & Nieto, M. J. (2012). Gender diversity on European banks' boards of directors. *Journal of Business Ethics, 109*(2), 145–162. https://doi.org/10.1007/s10551-011-1112-6.

Campbell, K., & Vera, A. M. (2010). Female board appointments and firm valuation: Short and long-term effects. *Journal of Management and Governance, 14*(1), 37–59. https://doi.org/10.1007/s10997-009-9092-y.

Carter, D. A., D'Souza, F., Simkins, B. J., & Simpson, W. G. (2010). The gender and ethnic diversity of US boards and board committees and firm financial performance. *Corporate Governance: An International Review, 18*(5), 396–414. https://doi.org/10.1111/j.1467-8683.2010.00809.x.

Dieleman, M., Qian M., & Ibrahim, M. (2013). Singapore Board Diversity Report 2013—Time for women to rise. Centre for Governance, Institutions and Organisations.

Eagly, A. H., & Johannesen-Schmidt, M. C. (2001). The leadership styles of women and men. *Journal of Social Issues, 57*(4), 781–797. https://doi.org/10.1111/0022-4537.00241.

Eagly, A. H., & Wood, W. (2012). Social role theory. In P. van Lange, A. Kruglanski, & E. T. Higgins (Eds.), *Handbook of theories in social psychology* (pp. 458–476). Thousand Oaks, CA: Sage.

Erhardt, N. L., Werbel, J. D., & Shrader, C. B. (2003). Board of director diversity and firm financial performance. *Corporate Governance: An International Review, 11*(2), 102–111. https://doi.org/10.1111/1467-8683.00011.

Farrell, K. A., & Hersch, P. L. (2005). Additions to corporate boards: The effect of gender. *Finance Department Faculty Publications, 18,* 85–106. https://digitalcommons.unl.edu/financefacpub/18.

Grant Thornton International Business Report. (2014). *Women in business: From classroom to boardroom.* Grant Thornton International Business Report 2014, United Kingdom. Retrieved from https://www.grantthornton.global/globalassets/1.-member-firms/global/insights/article-pdfs/2014/ibr2014_wib_report_final.pdf.

Greenhaus, J. H., & Parasuraman, S. (1999). Research on work, family, and gender: Current status and future directions. In G. N. Powell (Ed.), *Handbook of gender and work* (pp. 391–412). Thousand Oaks, CA: Sage.

Heilman, M. E. (2001). Description and prescription: How gender stereotypes prevent women's ascent up the organizational ladder. *Journal of Social Issues, 57*(4), 657–674. https://doi.org/10.1111/0022-4537.00234.

Hillman, A. J., Shropshire, C., & Cannella, A. A. (2007). Organizational predictors of women on corporate boards. *Academy of Management Journal, 50*(4), 941–952. https://doi.org/10.5465/amj.2007.26279222.

Institutional Investor Advisory Services India Limited. (2017). *Corporate India: Women on boards.* Retrieved from https://docs.wixstatic.com/ugd/09d5d3_bff9bfcbf6604b948bd8464a0a84d8e6.pdf.

Joecks, J., Pull, K. & Vetter, K. (2013). Gender diversity in the boardroom and firm performance: What exactly constitutes a "Critical mass?" *Journal Bus Ethics, 118,* 61–72. https://doi.org/10.1007/s10551-012-1553-6.

Johnson, J. L., Ellstrand, A. E., & Daily, C. M. (1996). Boards of directors: A review and research agenda. *Journal of Management, 22*(3), 409–438. https://doi.org/10.1016/S0149-2063(96)90031-8.

Kanter, R. M. (1977). Some effects of proportions on group life. In Rieker P. P. & Carmen E. (Eds.), *The gender gap in psychotherapy.* Boston, MA: Springer. https://doi.org/10.1007/978-1-4684-4754-5_5.

Koenig, A. M., Eagly, A. H., Mitchell, A. A., & Ristikari, T. (2011). Are leader stereotypes masculine? A meta-analysis of three research paradigms. *Psychological Bulletin, 137*(4), 616–642. https://doi.org/10.1037/a0023557.

Lara, J. M. G., Osma, B. G., & Penalva, F. (2009). Accounting conservatism and corporate governance. *Review of Accounting Studies, 14*(1), 161–220. https://doi.org/10.1007/s11142-007-9060-1.

Levi, M., Li, K., & Zhang, F. (2014). Director gender and mergers and acquisitions. *Journal of Corporate Finance, 28*, 185–200. https://doi.org/10.1016/j.jcorpfin.2013.11.005.

Matsa, D. A., & Miller, A. R. (2013). A female style in corporate leadership? Evidence from Quotas. *American Economic Journal: Applied Economics, 5*(3), 136–169. https://doi.org/10.1257/app.5.3.136.

OECD. (2009). *Gender and sustainable development: Maximizing the economic, social, and environmental role of women.* Paris: OECD. Retrieved from https://www.oecd.org/social/40881538.pdf.

Øyvind, B., & Staubo, S. (2014). Does mandatory gender balance work? Changing organizational form to avoid board upheaval. *Journal of Corporate Finance, 28*(C), 152–168. https://doi.org/10.1016/j.jcorpfin.2013.12.005.

Parker, C. (2016). Women and work. The system is broken, so how can we fix it? *World Economic Forum.* Retrieved from https://www.weforum.org/agenda/2016/03/women-and-work-the-system-is-broken-so-how-can-we-fix-it/.

Rose, C. (2007). Does female board representation influence firm performance? The Danish evidence. *Corporate Governance: An International Review Wiley Blackwell, 15*(2), 404–413. https://doi.org/10.1111/j.1467-8683.2007.00570.x.

S. C. (2018, September 3). Are gender quotas good for business? *The Economist.* Retrieved from https://www.economist.com/the-economist-explains/2018/09/03/are-gender-quotas-good-for-business.

Srinidhi, B., Gul, F., & Tsui, J. (2011). Female directors and earnings quality. *Contemporary Accounting Research, 28*(5), 1610–1644. https://doi.org/10.1111/j.1911-3846.2011.01071.x.

Sweigart, A. (2012). Women on board for change: The Norway model of boardroom quotas as a tool for progress in the United States and Canada. *Northwestern Journal of International Law and Business, 32*(4), 81–105. Retrieved from https://scholarlycommons.law.northwestern.edu/njilb/vol32/iss4/6/.

Terjesen, S., Sealy, R., & Singh, V. (2009). Women directors on corporate boards: A review and research agenda. *Corporate Governance: An International Review, 17*(3), 320–337. https://doi.org/10.1111/j.1467-8683.2009.00742.x.

Withers, M. C., Hillman, A. J., & Cannella, A. A. (2012). A multidisciplinary review of the director selection literature. *Journal of Management, 38*, 243–277. https://doi.org/10.1177/0149206311428671.

Creating Inclusion for Transwomen at Work Through Corporate Social Responsibility: The Contributions of Bandhu in Bangladesh

Enrico Fontana

INTRODUCTION

"If [a] new transgender generation were given work opportunities, I am sure they will not be a part of the so-called *Hijra* culture [...] We want [the] opportunity to work for both public and private sectors so that we can resolve our issues ourselves" (Tanisha Yeasmin Chaity, transwoman and official at the Bangladesh National Human Rights Commission, cited in Cassell, 2018).

In late 2013, the Bangladeshi government acknowledged transwomen and transmen (transgender individuals) as a separate gender. While their recognition has been acclaimed globally for its promise to alleviate their suffering and vulnerability, to date, transwomen in Bangladesh continue

E. Fontana (✉)
Sasin School of Management, Chulalongkorn University, Bangkok, Thailand
e-mail: enrico.fontana@sasin.edu

Mistra Centre for Sustainable Markets (MISUM), Stockholm School of Economics, Stockholm, Sweden to struggle with limited access to the labor market and pervasive discrimination (Anam, 2015; Hossain, 2017; Jebin & Farhana, 2015). Knight (2016), for instance, highlights that their "employment opportunities are often limited to begging or sex work" (p. 7). When transwomen secure jobs in private and public organizations, on the contrary, they are quickly dismissed due to their often gender non-conforming orientation that stirs disapproval and social exclusion (Alizai, Doneys, & Doane, 2017; Stenqvist, 2015; Wallen, 2020). As a result, many transwomen in Bangladesh give up their hope of a different life and resign themselves to serving their own community for survival (Haq, 2015; Jebin, 2019).

With the purpose of better understanding how to create inclusion in organizations for transwomen in South Asia and specifically in Bangladesh, this chapter showcases the contribution of Bandhu.[1] Bandhu is a Bangladeshi non-governmental organization (NGO) that is fully community-based and entirely devoted to the provision of services on sexual and reproductive health and rights and to ensuring the well-being of the gender diverse[2] population (Bandhu, 2019). Focusing on Bandhu holds particular relevance because of its pioneering achievements and its ongoing contribution to the lives of transwomen and the United Nations Sustainable Development Goals 1 (No Poverty), 3 (Good Health and Well-Being), 5 (Gender Equality), 10 (Equality), 16 (Peace, Justice and Stronger Institutions), and 17 (Partnerships) (Bandhu, 2017, 2020).

To better understand Bandhu's contribution, however, this chapter uncovers the life stories and challenges of Shima and Dilruba before and after finding employment. They are two transwomen and the first beneficiaries of a corporate social responsibility (CSR) project[3] where Bandhu holds a leading and implementing function since 2018. While explicitly centered on creating inclusion for transwomen at work, this

---

[1] Bandhu is an abbreviate form of Bandhu Social Welfare Society.

[2] The term "gender diverse" is assigned in medicine to people for whom "the assumption that one's gender identity will accord with assigned sex (where a penis is taken as indicating a male and a vagina is taken as indicating a female) is incorrect" (Riggs, Coleman, & Due, 2014, p. 230).

[3] CSR projects can be defined as those projects that a company conducts in cooperation with relevant stakeholders and that pertain to the integration of social, environmental, ethical, and philanthropic responsibilities toward society into its operations, processes, and core business strategy (Rasche, Morsing, & Moon, 2017).

CSR project is implemented by Bandhu in collaboration with USAID—a US-based international development organization—and Denim Expert Ltd.—a company in Chittagong specializing in the manufacture and export of denim bottom apparel and garment washing.

While shedding light on Bandhu's approach as part of the CSR project to navigate Shima and Dilruba's challenges after their recruitment, this chapter highlights Bandhu's overall contribution to empower and improve the lives of transwomen in Bangladesh. Hence, it represents an important learning tool for those interested in human rights and in understanding how to better create inclusion for transwomen at work in South Asia.

Literature Review

Transwomen and the Hijra Community in South Asia

While transgender individuals are broadly defined in sociology as "people whose gender identity does not necessarily correspond to the sex category" (Schilt & Lagos, 2017, p. 427), male-to-female transwomen in South Asia are often recognized as *third gender* (Kalra & Shah, 2013; Khan et al., 2008). This label comprises individuals who are neither male nor female and have an inner psyche and behavior that is nonconforming, often above and beyond the bipolar gendered society (Anam, 2015; de Lind van Wijngaarden, Schunter, & Iqbal, 2013; Hamzić, 2019). Nonetheless, what makes transwomen in South Asia different from transwomen in the Western world is a shared and collective culture that is manifest through an institutionalized system defined as the *Hijra* community or *Hijra* culture (Abdullah et al., 2012; Goel, 2016; Hossain, 2018; Sultana & Kalyani, 2012). This has existed in South Asia for millennia (Aziz & Azhar, 2019; Haq, 2015) and has generated significant fascination among scholars due to its "strong historical fairy-tale inceptions" (Goel, 2016, p. 535). Originated in India from Hinduism, this culture was credited with the ability to bless households with prosperity and fertility, but also to curse them with misfortune if they do not meet their demands (Alizai et al., 2017; Nanda, 1999; Reddy, 2005). While transwomen in the *Hijra* community have been studied for sacrificing their male genitalia and for their impotence (Aziz & Azhar, 2019; Nanda, 1986), today they take very different decisions about their bodies

(Alizai et al., 2017; Goel, 2016). Hossain (2012), for instance, differentiates between non-emasculated or *janana* and emasculated or *chibry* transwomen in Bangladesh. However, their heterogeneous degree of gender nonconformity and body decisions fuel confusion. For instance, many transwomen in South Asia are incorrectly equated with other gender minorities such as the *Kothis*, or men who enjoy sex with men (Boyce, 2007; Kalra & Shah, 2013). Still, both in public and in the literature, they are all essentialized as part of the *Hijra* community and are often labelled as *Hijra*. Although the majority of transwomen in South Asia are connected with the *Hijra* community, not all of them are and want to be called *Hijra*. This lack of detail was recently highlighted by Tanisha Yeasmin Chaity, a transwoman and government official working in the National Human Rights Commission of Bangladesh. During an interview, she argued that "I describe myself as a transwoman, but traditionally we are called *Hijra*. But *Hijra* is a culture, not an identity [...] I wanted a normal life" (Cassell, 2018).

Despite the allegorical image of the *Hijra* community in history, transwomen in South Asia today have become "the most excluded of the excluded" (Khan et al., 2009, p. 448). They suffer from poverty, social marginalization, and discrimination that are often caused by the dislike of their non-conforming orientation and its alleged connection with sexual amorality (Hall, 1997). Saeed, Mughal, and Farooq (2018, p. 1067), for instance, note that transwomen often suffer from a systemic bias and a higher level of stigmatization in comparison to their LGB counterparts because they "have been consistently associated with sex work."

Notably, their suffering starts during childhood. As they begin to exhibit girlish behavior, they are both humiliated and ridiculed by peers and relatives (Wallen, 2020). Both Saeed et al. (2018) in Pakistan and Khan et al. (2009) in Bangladesh, for instance, pinpoint that feminine boys are scolded by parents because they are afraid of their neighbors' criticism, which is perceived to potentially dent the honor of their household.

As they begin transitioning, transgender girls are abandoned by their family and are forced to drop out of school (Jebin, 2019; Wallen, 2020). Although many get breast implants and undergo hormone therapy later in life, transitioning for many South Asian transwomen is not necessarily associated with gender reassignment surgery but with decisions pertaining to clothing, lifestyle, and gender orientation. This happens at a much younger age compared to transwomen in the Western world—often between ten and fifteen years old (Nanda, 1986). Hossain (2012, p. 497), for instance, explains that transwomen take a decision about genitalia later in life, but these are also personal and do not accord them a "more authentic status." Due to the lack of social and material support, transgender girls seek informal assistance in their districts from similar peers who help them connect with a maternal leader or *guru* (Hamzić, 2019; Haq, 2015; Sultana & Kalyani, 2012). The *Hijra* community is characterized by a relational system that hinges on seniority and that is administered by a guru. She retains the right to allow new members into the *Hijra* community as one of her followers or *chelas* (de Lind van Wijngaarden et al., 2013). Because they are expected to provide lifelong services and earn money for the guru, the acceptance of a new *chela* hinges on her ability to bring in money. As Nanda (1999, p. 44) synthetizes, "the connection of guru to *chela* is the foundation of the economic benefits gained by joining the *Hijra* community." In Bangladesh, transwomen in the *Hijra* community collect money though their *Hijragiri* rituals. These are public performances as *badhai*—singing and dancing as a form of blessing for babies—or *cholla*—demanding money on the road, during weddings and other events (Hossain, 2012, 2017). In exchange for their work, *chelas* are expected to be taken care of by their guru, who trains them and ensures a welcoming environment for them in the *Hijra* community (Aziz & Azhar, 2019). Nonetheless, gurus often take advantage of them. They demand their *chelas* to continuously pay money as part of their implicit relation, often forcing them to engage in sex-related and illicit activities to maximize their income. Khan et al. (2009, p. 445), for instance, highlights that transwomen in the *Hijra* community in Bangladesh are "forced to have sex with men who paid money to gurus." On the contrary, transwomen who disrespect their guru are expelled, with little opportunity to return (Nanda, 1999; Sultana & Kalyani, 2012). Although the *Hijra* community symbolizes a contested environment, it has a double connotation for transwomen facing exclusion in society. On the one hand, it has a physical and material meaning, being linked with the shared buildings or *dera* where transwomen dwell and feel at home. Concurrently, it offers a social space where transwomen spend time with each other and learn how to comply with those seniority principles that guide internal promotion (Abdullah et al., 2012; Hamzić, 2019). Subsequently, accessing the *Hijra* community is often portrayed as an opportunity for transwomen and their only way to survive (Khan et al., 2009; Knight, 2016).

The Problem of Employment for Transwomen in Bangladesh

While transwomen in all South Asia suffer from discrimination, their inclusion in organizations as possible avenues for emancipation lacks scrutiny. Bangladesh is an important context of inquiry because of the government's recent (2013) acknowledgment of transgender individuals as having a separate gender. This has represented a major change in direction for a country where section 377 of the Code of Criminal Procedure condemns carnal intercourse between same biological individuals (Islam, 2019; Stenqvist, 2015). Although some scholars have accused this acknowledgment as having brought little improvement to transwomen (Anam, 2015; Knight, 2016), it is also recognized for potentially engendering new job opportunities in private and public organizations (Hossain, 2017; Jebin & Farhana, 2015). To date however, Bangladeshi transwomen struggle to access jobs and retain them (Hossain, 2016) even though they openly disclose their wish to be hired (Alizai et al., 2017; Khan et al., 2009). Officially, their difficulty in finding jobs is predominantly attributed to their lack of formal education and training, which they could not obtain because of bullying from colleagues and teachers (Abdullah et al., 2012). According to Stenqvist (2015), education is, however, a pretext for not hiring transwomen. Regardless of their school attendance or current abilities, transwomen in Bangladesh are frequently perceived to be "not valuable as employees or as the receivers of training efforts" (p. 32). This is often exacerbated by their feminine behavior at work but also their flamboyant way of living that creates misunderstandings, social exclusion, and violence (Jebin, 2019; Wallen, 2020). Because of their inability to work, most transwomen keep serving their gurus or engage in sex work (Haq, 2015; Stenqvist 2015). Only a few transwomen who come from wealthier families continue to study. These eventually cover positions in human rights NGOs such as Bandhu and conduct an independent life detached from the *Hijra* community (Cassell, 2018; Hossain, 2018).

Bandhu: A Human Rights Pioneer in Bangladesh

Bandhu was founded in 1996 with a mission to provide services on sexual and reproductive health and rights and to ensure the well-being of the gender diverse population in Bangladesh. With more than 300 part-time staff, Bandhu formulates a strategic plan every five years (the current one lasting until 2021) and is now focused on:

- improving access to quality health services,
- protecting human rights and ensuring access to justice,
- allowing access to social entitlements and social protection.

Bandhu aims to achieve these pillars by building capacity for communities and stakeholders, advocating for affirmative action to create an enabling environment for the sexual and gender diverse population (mainly via policy changes) and developing other organizations' capabilities and knowledge management (Bandhu, 2020). Apart from its pioneering efforts in ensuring health and human rights for the gender diverse population in Bangladesh, Bandhu is of core importance due to three key competencies that make its performance superior vis-à-vis other NGOs in the country:

- *Community-based structure.* Bandhu is a fully community-led NGO. It manages 34 field health centers in 22 districts of Bangladesh and collaborates with a capillary network of 26 community-based organizations (CBOs) by training them and continuously communicating with them. For instance, one of these CBOs is "Sustha Jiban," which is famous for its executive director Miss Boby *Hijra,* and which aims to eradicate discrimination, ensure equal rights in society while also ensuring the sexual health of transwomen in the *Hijra* community in Dhaka and adjacent areas (Mamun, Heyden, & Yasser, 2016; Shustha Jibon, 2010). By collaborating with CBOs, Bandhu controls the territory and ensures that transwomen in Bangladesh have access to basic health and consultation services. As the director for policy advocacy and human rights at Bandhu explained:

  We work in particular with community-based organizations. These are organizations providing services and sensitization at the local level. We want to develop their capacity and it is through them that we ensure our services. We mainly focus on transwomen and the *Hijra* community, but when we design any capacity building training, we include all gender minorities.

- *Human potential.* Bandhu is constituted by a body of highly motivated individuals who often are part of the gender diverse populations it aims to empower. While acting as a reference for the gender diverse population, Bandhu provides direct and indirect opportunities for those who have enough education and seek to make a change in their life and in the lives of other minorities. For instance, Tanisha Yeasmin Chaity worked as one of Bandhu's employees in Dhaka before becoming a government official in the Bangladeshi National Human Rights Commission (Cassell, 2018). Bandhu's human potential is summarized by the project manager, specialist, and civil society advisor of USAID in Bangladesh who is cooperating with Bandhu:

> Bandhu is the champion here in addressing the issues of the gender diverse population. Its expertise, policies, and processes are very advanced and proactive for Bangladesh. But its staff are the key. In particular, their excellent leadership and commitment. They have been serving with Bandhu for a long time. Also, they are both professionals and activists at the same time. Their whole organizational vision, mission and the passion through which they pursue goals such as inclusion and rights of transgender people is what makes Bandhu a strong and competent civil society organization.

As a Junior officer at Bandhu also noted:

I discovered Bandhu during for my first HIV test. They suggested me to join and I found many friends. Bandhu is our own organization. Here we can talk about anything—our life, our problems. And we get answers. Bandhu is a pioneer organization in Bangladesh for our transgender rights. This is the first and last place where we share our feelings. We expect a lot from Bandhu and Bandhu is doing a lot for us.

- *Collaborative planning.* With the specific purpose of protecting human rights and ensuring access to justice for the gender diverse population, Bandhu also collaborates with different partners and organizes consultations based on the involvement of stakeholders in Bangladesh. This is both to sensitize stakeholders at different levels, and also to urge the enactment of laws. These range, for instance, from talks with the Ministry of Social Welfare of the Bangladesh government and with the National Human Rights Commission, to meetings with district judges and law enforcement agencies to sensitize them and raise awareness of the rights of the gender diverse population (Bandhu, 2019). As the executive director of Bandhu noted:

> We do advocacy programs by inviting important stakeholders from different sectors. We invite the Ministry of Social Welfare, the Police Department, the Education Ministry. We actually have consultations with the government to produce the anti-discriminatory laws of the country for the third gender. But we are not alone. We take the lead but there are some human rights-based organizations that collaborate with us. Some have limited skills but we support their growth and they support us.

Bandhu's Implementing Function in the CSR Project and the Lives of Transwomen

As part of its collaboration with stakeholders, Bandhu received a grant in 2015 from USAID. This is an international development organization based in the US, focused on promoting and demonstrating democratic values abroad, and advancing a free, peaceful, and prosperous world (USAID, 2020). Part of the grant was assigned to creating education on transwomen issues, improving their access to public services, and advocating for human rights. Together with USAID, Bandhu co-organized a job fair in 2017 with about 20 apparel companies. This was purposed to sensitize them about the vulnerability of the transgender population but also to discover if they wanted to host a CSR project focused on offering new employment opportunities for transwomen. In this CSR project, Bandhu acted as implementer, trainer, and expert. During this event, Bandhu and USAID communicated with Denim Expert Ltd., which agreed to partake in the CSR project. With about 1,900 workers, Denim is a company in Chittagong specializing in the manufacture and export of denim bottom apparel and garment washing. Shima and Dilruba are the first two beneficiaries of the CSR project and the first two transwomen hired in September 2018.

Tales of Transwomen: The Life of Shima

Shima was raised in a village in Noakhali district (between Dhaka and Chittagong) in a large and middle-income family. Her father was a primary school teacher and her mother was a housewife. They had other sons and daughters. Between the age of ten and eleven years old, her parents realized that her femininity was not temporary. Although she was biologically male, Shima was always convinced she was a girl and her parents, who tried to be accommodating, also addressed her as a girl. To avoid any suspicion about her orientation, they prevented her from spending time outside the house and meeting with others apart from her close friends. During her adolescence she discovered she was not a girl. As Shima revealed:

> I knew my body was different, but I still thought I was a girl. At the age of 14 my girlfriends had menstruation. But I did not have it. Then my mom said: "Don't worry, it will happen. And if it doesn't happen, don't worry. But don't tell others about it." I thought: "Why should I tell lies?" Then I realized my mom was hiding something from me. In this way, I understood I am a transwoman.

Although Shima's parents knew about her orientation, they did not abandon her. With the unexpected death of her father after she passed her intermediate exams at school at the age of eighteen, the situation changed. Shima's brothers and sisters started to voice their fears about not being able to marry and that their relationships with neighbors were at risk because of her. Subsequently, Shima decided to move to Chittagong where she was hosted by other relatives. During that period, she kept looking for jobs but she could not find any. One day, she saw some transwomen begging for money on the road. She stopped and talked to them. After they realized she could be one of them, they introduced her to their guru who agreed to take her in the *Hijra* community as a *chela*. Shima was sent to Bandhu right after that to receive a medical checkup and test for possible sexually transmitted diseases. Bandhu provides immediate support for all members of the *Hijra* community and represents a point of reference. Shima's *Hijra* community was composed of 400 transwomen. Shortly after her arrival, however, the guru asked her to work as sex worker. Although she did not want to do it, she was compelled to serve her guru. As Shima noted:

> The guru was living in one room but had four extra rooms. This is where we did the entertainment. She asked for 5000, 4000 or 3000 taka for three or two hours. The clients were truck drivers, private sector men and students. The guru called us: "You come". We could not do anything against her will and she was getting the money.

After six months, she decided she did not want to live with the other transwomen in the community. She could not accept the impositions of her guru and, because she came from a middle-income family, she struggled with the poor hygienic conditions in the *dera*. Most transwomen could not shower for days and lived in very precarious conditions. At the same time, Shima longed for an autonomous life outside the community, where she could be seen as an independent woman "with dignity" and not just as a *Hijra* community member. Although she eventually managed to convince her guru to let her live outside the *dera*, she was still expected to send in money periodically. During one of her periodical health checks, Bandhu informed her about a new position at Denim Expert Ltd. Excited, she immediately applied through Bandhu and received an offer of employment shortly thereafter.

Tales of Transwomen: The Life of Dilruba

Dilruba was born as biological male in Mirpur, Dhaka, in an underprivileged household. While her father worked in a small shop, her mother was a housewife and she had two sisters. When she was nine years old, her mother passed away and her father decided to remarry. At that time, she started to feel that she was not a boy. She wanted to be like her sisters and started to behave in a more feminine way. With the goal of shifting her orientation, her stepmother started to beat and torture her. At twelve years old, when she started to transition and wear feminine garments in public, her stepmother abandoned her. Alone and without any support, Dilruba started to beg among the shops and markets in Mirpur. Fortunately, she met an older transwoman who agreed to accept her in her house. As Dilruba described:

Parents have responsibility for their children until age eighteen. But for poor families, it does not matter. And we were a poor family. After my stepmother abandoned me at twelve years old, I met one transwoman begging in the street. That transwoman had a home near where I lived. She agreed to give me shelter.

That transwoman communicated with other peers until the guru in a *Hijra* community in Chittagong decided to welcome her. After only five days, Dilruba was sent there and started a new life as an active member of the *Hijra* community. She started to earn money for her guru while engaging with *badhai* and *cholla*. A few months after her initiation, she started to feel confused. Her guru sometimes treated her like a daughter, but she also felt she was being taken advantage of by her guru. For instance, she was asked to clean the floors in the *dera* but when she tried to resist, she was beaten by the other transwomen. Although she collected 25000 taka (about 300 US dollars) from the street every month, she had to hand that money over to her guru. She could not go to school and be educated and her guru did not allow her to walk to other places alone. She always had to be with a group of peers. At night, she had to drink and engage in entertaining activities with clients. Exhausted both physically and mentally, Dilruba escaped from her *Hijra* community and left Bangladesh to go to Punjab, India. However, after three months, the guru in Chittagong managed to transfer her back. As Dilruba explained:

> I could not stand the pressure and I crossed the border illegally. I went to India for three months. I learned Hindi and I joined the *Hijra* community there. They also do a lot of dancing, singing when a child is born. And I survived by asking for money during these activities. But the gurus are interconnected. They are powerful and have a strong network. When the Bangladeshi guru circulated my picture on social media, the Punjab guru understood that I was hiding. She sent me back.

Although Dilruba desired to live on her own and be recognized as independent woman, she could not leave the community. For almost ten years, she served her guru. During one of her health checkups with Bandhu, when she was 22 years old, Dilruba was notified by Bandhu employees about a new CSR project starting at Denim Expert Ltd. and the fact they were looking to employ transwomen in the factory. Attracted by the opportunity to start a new life on her own, Dilruba managed to prepare a CV and to hand it over to Bandhu, which helped her receive a job offer.

CREATING INCLUSION
FOR TRANSWOMEN IN ORGANIZATIONS

The Challenges of Shima and Dilruba After Their Recruitment

Today, Shima works as a product safety assistant and has also been assigned as manager of the housekeeping department. Similarly, Dilruba supervises 35 cleaning operators and assists all officers' material needs. After their recruitment by Denim Expert Ltd., however, they faced three main challenges:

- *Challenge of gurus.* When Bandhu confirmed their new appointments, Shima and Dilruba were introduced to each other and decided to share an apartment near the factory to commute more easily. Due to fear, both Shima and Dilruba did not let their gurus know about their decision to work and live independently. They changed phone numbers and official residences, hoping their guru would have somewhat understood their wish. But the gurus found out about them through their own Hijra network. They sent their *chelas* to search for them and, after discovering what had happened, they threatened to abduct and kill them. The aggressive reaction of the gurus is exacerbated by the fact that *chelas* represent an important source of income that is necessary for them to manage the *Hijra* community. As highlighted by the training and counselling manager at Bandhu:

  > Gurus depend on their *chelas*. The *chelas* go out and collect money. Most of it is given to their gurus. So, if her *chelas* are allowed to have jobs and leave the *Hijra* community, who will work for the gurus? Although some gurus support employment, most gurus do not accept to let them go.

- *Challenge of workers.* When joining Denim, Shima and Dilruba entered an environment to which transwomen had never had access before. Shima and Dilruba struggled because of the pervasive lack of knowledge and poor acceptance of their gender non-conforming orientation. While many workers expressed their fears, fueled by stereotypes and traditional beliefs, others refused to speak with them. The manager of human resources and compliance at Denim Expert Ltd. synthetized it like this:

> Harassment against transwomen at work is persistent in Bangladesh—verbal and physical. This is mostly in the apparel sector where thousands of people who could not afford to go to school work together. Initially, when Shima and Dilruba joined our factory, our workers said: "No. If you recruit transwomen, we will not work." Many workers have the perception that: "Oh my god, transwomen. They are coming. Let's leave this place."

- *Challenge with lack of social network.* Because transwomen in Bangladesh are often abandoned by the families, the *Hijra* community often represents the only safe space where they can establish social relations with similar peers and forge friendships. As a consequence of their departure from the *Hijra* community, this social structure also went missing. Shima and Dilruba started to struggle with loneliness, with the difficulty of keeping in touch with their past friends and meeting other transgender individuals in society, possibly leaving a lasting imprint on their psyche and mental health. The brief account of Dilruba indicates the vulnerability associated with the lack of a social network:

> When I lived in the *Hijra* community in Chittagong, I had so many friends. We were always together. Now I am alone. I don't know many mainstream people. I had a relationship with a guy, but he took my money and left me. I particularly miss my best friends—five transgender girls. We were like family members in the Hijra community and they loved me so much. I don't see them anymore.

Bandhu's Approach to Facilitating Transwomen Inclusion in the CSR Project

In line with Shima and Dilruba's experiences, Fig. 20.1 summarizes the challenges transwomen face upon recruitment, but also Bandhu's approach in mitigating them and enabling the CSR project. Bandhu's approach is clarified in Fig. 20.1.

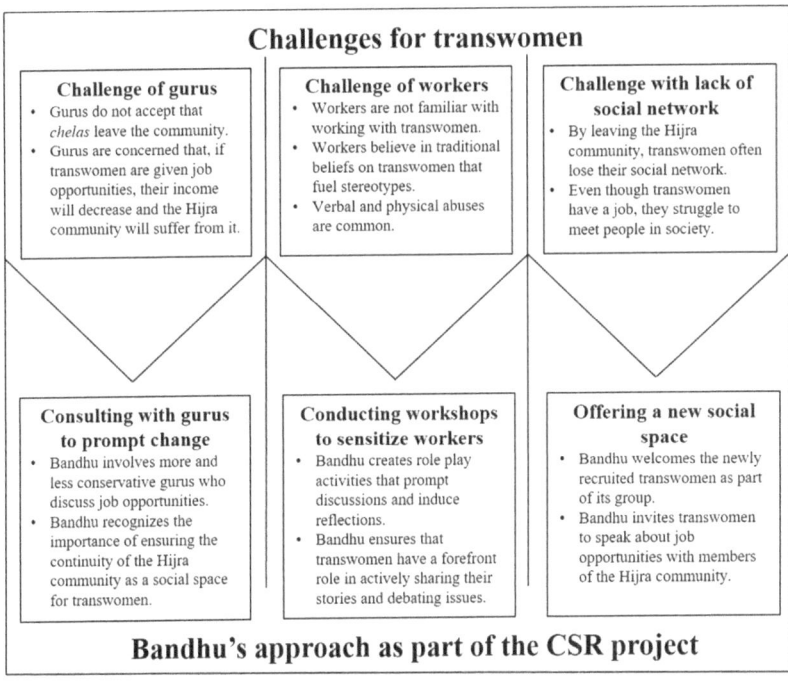

Fig. 20.1 Challenges for transwomen and Bandhu's approach as part of the CSR project

Consulting with gurus to prompt change. Bandhu aims to overcome the challenge of gurus through consultations and the creation of an ongoing collaboration with them. These meetings are predominantly focused on shifting mindsets and helping them understand the importance for transwomen to find employment in society and to be recognized as independent individuals. Simultaneously, Bandhu is also keen to ascertain the continuity of the *Hijra* community in the future as key social spaces that many transwomen need to overcome the most difficult period of their lives, when they are abandoned and face poverty. Although this is a long-term solution, this helped Shima and Dilruba gain support and respect for their decision from the broader Hijra community. The team leader at USAID in Bangladesh, who works on transwomen inclusion and participated in Bandhu's consultations with gurus, underlined that:

As transwomen communities in Bangladesh are often led by senior leaders called hijra gurus, it is critical to work with them and help them understand disadvantages of Hijra begging over employment. Bandhu got the acceptance of Denim Expert Ltd. to employ more transwomen community members, while also organizing a training for Denim workers to ensure necessary tranwomen workplace integration. However, as many gurus oppose longer-term employment over begging, Bandhu played a critical role in helping them understand the advantages of decent employment. They organized one event with the progressive and the less progressive gurus and facilitated discussion on hijra employment. One important feature of Bandhu's consultations is that they often bring community members, who are the best in telling their life stories and in advocating for specific issues. This approach proved to be effective in increasing awareness and supporting changes by engaging community members instead of just having outsiders speaking about certain issues.

Conducting workshops to sensitize workers. Bandhu creates workshops in the factory to sensitize workers about what it means to be transwoman and the challenges associated with it. Most of the workshops, to date, have been centered on role play activities where workers can pose questions, explain their disagreements but also enjoy their time together. These were helped by the presence of expert trainers from Bandhu who were leading the sessions and engaging workers. Crucially, Shima and Dilruba have been taking a leading role during these workshops, revealing their stories, and taking questions from workers and discussing their situations. Although it would be improper to claim this is enough to erase all verbal or physical abuses again them, these workshops contribute to breaking the ice and helping Shima and Dilruba gain respect. The executive director of Bandhu explained one of the sessions that he helped administer:

> We provided first an orientation to the senior members and the workers at Denim on sexual orientation, gender identity and human rights. We also invited the transwomen from the *Hijra* community. We generally do it so that a dialogue can start. The workers expressed their fears, the reasons for their attitudes. Shima and Dilruba responded very well, asking why perceptions are so negative for transgender individuals only. Through this ongoing and hands-on process, we improve relationships with workers and minimize cases of harassment.

Offering a new social space. In order to alleviate the social exclusion that comes with leaving the *Hijra* community, Bandhu tries to make sure that transwomen are not left alone and tries to involve them in its organization as part of its transgender group. In this way, it helps them create new connections and make sure that they can have a life outside the Hijra community. Shima and Dilruba, for instance, keep in touch with other transwomen employees. They are involved in activities focused on the improvement of transgender individuals as a whole, particularly those aimed at sensitizing transwomen on the importance of actively seeking work and having jobs. In the specific case of Shima, being with Bandhu helped her understand she has a mission in life and that is about creating change for other transwomen. As she noted:

> When Bandhu does any meeting with transwomen inside or outside the *Hijra* community, they call me. I am very excited about that. I can go with Bandhu and provide motivational speeches, as I did before in Bashundhara (Dhaka). Bandhu keeps me informed about trainings and its activities. Now my life has changed. Because I have no one in my life, I want to help others through Bandhu. I want transwomen in Bangladesh to change their life and work outside the *Hijra* community.

Conclusion and Chapter Takeaways

This chapter sheds light on the work of Bandhu and its implementing function in a CSR project for transwomen. Specifically, it analyzed the contribution of Bandhu to create inclusion for transwomen in Bangladesh through the life stories and challenges of Shima and Dilruba—the first two transwomen involved in the CSR project and their primary beneficiaries. Finally, this chapter offers four important takeaways for industry practitioners, government professionals, activists, and educators interested in human rights and how to better create inclusion for transwomen at work in South Asian contexts:

1. *Sensitizing gurus without jeopardizing the Hijra community.* This chapter unveils the exploitative behaviors against transwomen of many gurus, which prevent them from seeking jobs. However, it also highlights the relevance of the *Hijra* community as a social space where transwomen can be together and forget about the discrimination they suffer in their daily life. This conforms with the scholarly accounts that accuse gurus of misbehavior and violence (Knight,

2016; Stenqvist, 2015), but also adds to the literature that high-lights the essentiality of the *Hijra* community for the survival of transwomen (Hossain, 2012; Jebin, 2019; Khan et al., 2009). The example of the ongoing consultation of Bandhu with gurus shows that organizations and individuals should be aware of the impor-tance of involving gurus when seeking to facilitate transwomen inclusion in South Asia, without, however, compromising the conti-nuity of the Hijra community.

2. *Transwomen inclusion should align with training workers on gender nonconformity.* This chapter illustrates that the lack of education and awareness of gender nonconformity among workers can easily nullify inter-organizational efforts. The case of transwomen in Bangladesh adds evidence to the literature that highlights the problem of transwomen in retaining jobs because they are often ridiculed and harassed at work for their femininity and non-binary orientation (Jebin, 2019; Stenqvist, 2015). While drawing on the continuous efforts of Bandhu to sensitize workers, this chapter indicates that organizations and individuals must be aware that creating inclu-sion requires a major change in the organizational environment. Achieving this goal in South Asian contexts might be particu-larly difficult given the existence of pervasive and traditional beliefs against transwomen that fuel stereotypes and represent a major barrier to their emancipation.

3. *Collaboration is key for change.* Although this chapter was specifically focused on the implementing function of Bandhu, it was thanks to the collaboration developed with USAID and Denim Expert Ltd. that Bandhu was able to advance transwomen inclusion as part of the CSR project. As Bandhu understood that supporting transwomen and the gender diverse population in Bangladesh is hardly achievable on its own (Bandhu, 2019), this chapter prompts organizations and individuals to focus on inter-organizational collaboration as a more effective means to initiate sustainable change for gender minorities at work.

4. *Transwomen are individuals and not all of them are "Hijra."* The stories of Shima and Dilruba in this chapter exhibited their desire to be respected as individuals who have their own gender and sexual orientation as well as identity beyond the *Hijra* commu-nity. This somewhat aligns with Tanisha Yeasmin Chaity's claim that transwomen in Bangladesh should be respected for their own

identity regardless of their connection with the *Hijra* community (Cassell, 2018). Although the *Hijra* community is a core social foundation, this chapter indicates that essentializing all transwomen in South Asia as *Hijra* is incorrect and violates the desires of those who aim to be viewed as different. Organizations and individuals should assign great importance to the way they frame their communication when addressing transwomen in South Asia. Downplaying their individual orientation while aggregating them in line with collective and cultural traditions can inversely fuel a rhetoric of disempowerment that dents their emancipation and reinforces stereotypes.

Acknowledgements I owe my gratitude to Shale Ahmed—Executive director at Bandhu—and his team for their continuous support and for sharing their experiences and insights. I thank Ohidul Islam (Parboti) for her precious assistance and constructive advices during the interview process in Dhaka. I am particularly grateful to Mostafiz Uddin—Managing Director of Denim Expert Ltd. as well as Founder and CEO of the Bangladesh Apparel exchange—for his admirable CSR initiatives with transgender inclusion in Chittagong. Despite the difficulties due to the rise of Covid-19, I am confident that his continuous efforts to create positive change for the people of Bangladesh will not go unnoticed. I am also indebted to a number of experts at USAID and Denim Expert Limited who were willing to devote their time to discuss about their CSR project. Last but not least, I would like to express my deepest gratitude to Shima and Dilruba for letting me hear their stories and for the inspiring conversations that have informed this chapter. This would have never materialized without their courage and contribution. I completed part of this research while I was a post-doctoral fellow at the Centre for Social and Sustainable Innovation (CSSI) at the Gustavson School of Business, University of Victoria, British Columbia, Canada. CSSI receives funding from Newmont Goldcorp Inc. Any inaccuracies or omissions are entirely my own.

REFERENCES

Abdullah, M. A., Basharat, Z., Kamal, B., Sattar, N. Y., Hassan, Z. F., Jan, A. D., & Shafqat, A. (2012). Is social exclusion pushing the Pakistani

Hijras (transgenders) towards commercial sex work? A qualitative study. *BMC International Health and Human Rights, 12*(1), 32–41.

Alizai, A., Doneys, P., & Doane, D. L. (2017). Impact of gender binarism on Hijras' life course and their access to fundamental human rights in Pakistan. *Journal of Homosexuality, 64*(9), 1214–1240.

Anam, T. (2015). *Transgender rights, Bangladesh style. New York Times.*

Aziz, A., & Azhar, S. (2019). Social exclusion and official recognition of Hijra in Bangladesh. *Journal of Research on Women and Gender, 9,* 3–19.

Bandhu. (2017). *A tale of two decades: 20-year achievements leading to impact.* Dhaka, Bangladesh: Bandhu Social Welfare Society.

Bandhu. (2019). *Moving beyond level: 2018 annual report.* Dhaka, Bangladesh: Bandhu Social Welfare Society.

Bandhu. (2020). *Organizational strategic plan: Guidance for every 5 years.* Retrieved August 4, 2020 (https://www.bandhu-bd.org/about-2/organizational-strategic-plan/).

Boyce, P. (2007). 'Conceiving Kothis': Men who have sex with men in India and the cultural subject of HIV prevention. *Medical Anthropology, 26*(2), 175–203.

Cassell, H. 2018. Trans Bangladeshi official signals changes. *The Bay Area Reporter.*

de Lind van Wijngaarden, J. W., Schunter, B. T., & Iqbal, Q. (2013). Sexual abuse, social stigma and HIV vulnerability among young feminised men in Lahore and Karachi, Pakistan. *Culture, Health & Sexuality, 15*(1), 73–84.

Goel, I. (2016). Hijra communities of Delhi. *Sexualities, 19*(5–6), 535–546.

Hall, K. (1997). 'Go suck your husband's sugarcane': Hijras and the use of sexual insult. In A. Livia & K. Hall (Eds.), *Queerly phrased: Language, gender, and sexuality* (pp. 430–460). New York, NY: Oxford University Press.

Hamzić, V. (2019). The Dera paradigm: Homecoming of the gendered other. *Ethnoscripts, 21*(1), 34–57.

Haq, K. (2015). The Hijra comes in from the heat and dust. *Wasafiri, 40*(3), 3–7.

Hossain, A. (2012). Beyond emasculation: Being Muslim and becoming Hijra in South Asia. *Asian Studies Review, 36*(4), 495–513.

Hossain, A. (2016). Transgender woman in Bangladesh: 'I'm not a burden to society'. *British Broadcasting Corporation.*

Hossain, A. (2017). The paradox of recognition: Hijra, third gender and sexual rights in Bangladesh. *Culture, Health & Sexuality, 19*(12), 1418–1431.

Hossain, A. (2018). De-Indianizing Hijra: Intraregional effacements and inequalities in South Asian queer space. *Transgender Studies Quarterly, 5*(3), 321–331.

Islam, S. (2019). A theoretical analysis of the legal status of transgender: Bangladesh perspective. *International Journal of Research and Innovation in Social Science, 3*(3), 117–119.

Jebin, L. (2019). Status of transgender people in Bangladesh: A socio-economic-analysis. *South Asian Journal of Policy and Governance, 42*(1), 49–63.

Jebin, L., & Farhana, U. (2015). The rights of Hijra in Bangladesh: An overview. *Journal of Nazrul University, 3*(1 and 2), 1–9.

Kalra, G., & Shah, N. (2013). The cultural, psychiatric, and sexuality aspects of Hijras in India. *International Journal of Transgenderism, 14*(4), 171–181.

Khan, S. I., Hussain, M. I., Gourab, G., Parveen, S., Bhuiyan, M. I., & Sikder, J. (2008). Not to stigmatize but to humanize sexual lives of the transgender (Hijra) in Bangladesh: Condom chat in the AIDS era. *Journal of LGBT Health Research, 4*(2–3), 127–141.

Khan, S. I., Hussain, M. I., Parveen, S., Bhuiyan, M. I., Gourab, G., Sarker, G. F., et al. (2009). Living on the extreme margin: Social exclusion of the transgender population (Hijra) in Bangladesh. *Journal of Health, Population, and Nutrition, 27*(4), 441–451.

Knight, K. (2016). *I want to live with my head held high: Abuses in Bangladesh's legal recognition of Hijras*. New York, NY: Human Rights Watch.

Mamun, A. A., Heyden, M. L. M., & Yasser, Q. R. (2016). Transgender individuals in Asian Islamic countries: An overview of workplace diversity and inclusion issues in Pakistan, Bangladesh, and Malaysia. In T. Köllen (Ed.), *Sexual orientation and transgender issues in organizations* (pp. 167–180). Zurich, Switzerland: Springer International Publishing.

Nanda, S. (1986). The Hijras of India. *Journal of Homosexuality, 11*(3–4), 35–54.

Nanda, S. (1999). *Neither man nor woman: The Hijras of India* (2nd ed.). Belmont, CA: Wadsworth Publishing Company.

Rasche, A., Morsing, M., & Moon, J. (2017). Corporate social responsibility: Strategy, communication and governance. In A. Rasche, M. Morsing, & J. Moon (Eds.), *Corporate social responsibility: Strategy, communication and governance*. Cambridge, UK: Cambridge University Press.

Reddy, G. (2005). Geographies of contagion: Hijras, Kothis, and the politics of sexual marginality in Hyderabad. *Anthropology & Medicine, 12*(3), 255–270.

Riggs, D. W., Coleman, K., & Due, C. (2014). Healthcare experiences of gender diverse Australians: A mixed-methods, self-report survey. *BMC Public Health, 14*(1), 230–235.

Saeed, A., Mughal, U., & Farooq, S. (2018). It's complicated: Sociocultural factors and the disclosure decision of transgender individuals in Pakistan. *Journal of Homosexuality, 65*(8), 1051–1070.

Schilt, K., & Lagos, D. (2017). The development of transgender studies in sociology. *Annual Review of Sociology, 43*, 425–443.

Shustha Jibon. (2010). *Shustha Jibon*. Shyampur, Dhaka.

Stenqvist, T. (2015). *The social struggle of being Hijra in Bangladesh: Cultural aspiration between inclusion and illegitimacy*. Malmö, Sweden: Malmö University.

Sultana, A., & Kalyani, M. K. (2012). Femaling males: Anthropological analysis of the transgender community in Pakistan. *The Journal of Humanities and Social Sciences, 20*(1), 93–108.

USAiD. (2020). *Mission, vision and values*. Retrieved July 4, 2020 (https://www.usaid.gov/who-we-are/mission-vision-values).

Wallen, J. (2020). Pride and persecution: The rise and fall of the world's oldest transgender community. *The Telegraph*.

CHAPTER 21

Working While Homosexual in South Africa: Where Are We Now?

Lusanda Sekaja, *Ikraam Kraft*, *Catherine Lötter,*
Nadia Daniel, M. Christina Meyers, and Byron G. Adams

L. Sekaja (✉) · I. Kraft · C. Lötter · N. Daniel · B. G. Adams
Department of Industrial Psychology and People Management, University of Johannesburg, Johannesburg, South Africa
e-mail: lsekaja@uj.ac.za

M. C. Meyers
Department of Human Resource Studies, Tilburg University, Tilburg, The Netherlands

B. G. Adams
Department of Social Psychology, Tilburg University, Tilburg, The Netherlands

Department of Work, Organization and Society, Ghent University, Ghent, Belgium

Department of Work and Organizational Psychology, University of Amsterdam, Amsterdam, The Netherlands

407

Introduction

This chapter illustrates the lived experience of homosexual (gay and/or lesbian) individuals in the South African workplace. It also focuses on how discrimination of homosexual individuals and religion are intertwined. Religious institutions, through their scriptures and elders, often condemn homosexuality. This may translate into stereotypes, prejudice, and discrimination. We examine and integrate three unpublished dissertations undertaken in the last five years on the discriminatory experiences of gay and/or lesbian individuals in the South African workplace. The first study examined the discriminatory experiences of gay and lesbian South Africans at work (see Lötter, 2015). The second study sought to understand the nature of prejudice and discrimination that gay men experience from heterosexual members of their own religion (Muslims and Protestant Christians[1]; see Daniel, 2020). The final study looked at the influence of an individual's religion and their own experience of discrimination on their own attitudes toward homosexual individuals (see Kraft, 2017). From these three studies, we map out how gay and lesbian participants experience stereotyping, prejudice, and discrimination.

Homosexuality in South Africa

South Africa has a multiethnic population of about 58.8 million (Statistics South Africa, 2019). In the last census count, the country was 79.2% Black, 8.9% Colored (people of mixed ethnic/racial descent), 2.5% Asian/Indian, 8.9% White, and 0.5% other (Statistics South Africa, 2011a). It is made up of various religious groups, the most common being Christianity (84.2%), no religion (5.5%), ancestral and traditional African religion (5.0%), and Islam (2.0%; Statistics South Africa, 2014). Approximately 634,000 (~1.1%) adult South Africans identify as lesbian, gay, bisexual, or other (Nyeck, Shepherd, Sehoole, Ngcobozi, & Conron, 2019).

Since the advent of colonization and the adoption of Christianity and Islam, being homosexual in Africa has long had serious consequences—from imprisonment to death. Homosexuality is only legal in 19 out of 54 African countries, including Benin, Gabon, Madagascar, Lesotho, and South Africa (Amnesty International UK, 2018) and attitudes suggest a

---

[1] Protestant Christian and Christian are used interchangeably.

prevailing sense of homonegativity (see Hagopian, Rao, Katz, Sanford, & Barnhart, 2017; Jones, 2019; Oberth & Mondry 2014; Quinn & Dickson-Gomez, 2015; Wike et al. 2013). However, South Africa stands out in the African context because it has one of the most progressive post-democratic constitutions. It is the only African country where homosexual individuals enjoy equal rights to their heterosexual counterparts (Government Gazette, 1996; Oberth & Mondry 2014; UNESCO, 2016). In fact, it was the first country in the world to promulgate legislation to protect homosexual individuals from discrimination based on their sexual orientation (Pillay, 2018). For example, the constitution states that "The state may not unfairly discriminate, directly or indirectly, against anyone on one or more grounds, including, race, gender, sex, pregnancy, marital status, ethnic or social origin, color, *sexual orientation*, age, disability, religion, conscience, belief, culture, language and birth" (Government Gazette, 1996, p. 4). Stemming from the constitution, various other acts have been promulgated to ensure the equal treatment of all historically disadvantaged groups, including homosexual individuals.

Despite these progressive policies, the liberal constitution may sometimes be at odds with the beliefs of the conservative population. This is evident in that conservative political, religious, and cultural leaders have shown attitudes or behaviors that are not in keeping with the legislation. For example, former President Jacob Zuma, while still deputy president of the ruling party proclaimed during Heritage Day celebrations, "When I was growing up, *unqingili* (a gay person) would not have stood in front of me. I would knock him out," and that same-sex marriages were "a disgrace to the nation and to God" (eNCA, 2015; Sokupa & Majova, 2006). King Goodwill Zwelithini, who enjoys considerable influence over the Zulu culture, which represents 22.7% of the population, the largest in the country, stated that "Traditionally, there were no people who engaged in same-sex relationships. There was nothing like that, and if you do it, you must know that you are rotten" (eNCA, 2015). He has also referred to homosexuality as a form of moral decay (Vincent & Howell, 2014). Therefore, while the law protects the rights of homosexual individuals, influential leaders and role models do not uphold the sentiments of the law, which is also reflected in the attitudes of the public (Kotzé & Loubser, 2018).

Attitudes Toward Homosexuality in South Africa

Various studies in the South African context have indicated that people generally have negative attitudes toward homosexuality. To illustrate, within the South African context, a Pew Research Global Attitudes Project (2013) survey with 815 English-, Afrikaans-, Sotho-, Xhosa-, and Zulu-speaking participants found that 61% of participants believed that society should not accept homosexuality. Benjamin (2019) states the key concerns for the LGBTQ+ community include stereotyping based on their gender identity, gender policing, or disclosing their sexual orientation. Lastly, in a survey of attitudes toward gays and lesbians, Sutherland, Roberts, Gabriel, Struwig, and Gordon (2016) found that 61% of straight people held negative attitudes toward homosexuals, stating that they are disgusting.

When compared to the general public, highly religious individuals most strongly agreed that being gay or lesbian is wrong or disgusting. Moderately religious individuals tended to be the most tolerant. However, although moderately and highly religious individuals were less likely to keep away from gays and lesbians than the general population, they reported more or less the same levels of violence against nonconforming men and women. Of particular interest for this chapter is the treatment of working homosexual individuals in South Africa by both the general population as well as their religious counterparts, in particular, where stereotypes, prejudice, and discrimination are concerned.

This will be examined through three studies conducted in the last five years by Lötter (2015), Daniel (2020), and Kraft (2017), presented in Table 21.1. The first study examined the general discriminatory experiences of five gay and five lesbian South Africans (see Lötter, 2015). The second study sought to understand the nature of prejudice and discrimination that gay men experience from heterosexual members of their own religion (Muslim and Protestant Christians; see Daniel, 2020). The final study looked at the influence of an individual's religion and their own experience of discrimination on their own attitudes toward homosexual individuals (see Kraft, 2017). Below we offer a closer look at the stereotypes, prejudices, and discrimination experienced by gays and lesbians at work.

Table 21.1 Details of the anchor studies

	Study Purpose	Nature of study	Sample	No. of participants	Example of sectors sampled
Study 1 Lötter (2015)	Discriminatory experiences of gay and lesbian South Africans	Qualitative	Gays Lesbians	10	Information technology, Financial, Higher education
Study 2 Daniel (2020)	Prejudice and discrimination that gay men experience from heterosexuals members of their own religion	Qualitative	Muslim gays Protestant Christian gays	12	Financial, Retail, Photography
Study 3 Kraft (2017)	The influence of an individual's religion and their own experience of discrimination on their own attitudes toward homosexual others	Quantitative	Catholic heterosexuals Muslim heterosexuals Protestant Christian heterosexuals	449	Safety and security, Financial services, Government services, Media, Healthcare

Gaining an Integrated View on the Experiences of Gay and Lesbian Employees Derived from Both Data and the Literature

The data shows us that although stereotypes, prejudice, and discrimination are three separate phenomena, they are interlinked. Each of these starts with the notion of "otherness" (Augé, 1987; Fedor, 2014), where a subgroup is seen as distinct from the rest of the group (gays and lesbians are distinct from straight people). In some instances, this othering can be as severe as excluding or eliminating the subgroup from the rest of the group (sometimes straight people do not want to associate with gays and lesbians). Ultimately, stereotypes appear to lead to prejudice, which, in turn, leads to discrimination.

Stereotypes

According to the data from Lötter (2015), from a generic point of view, stereotypes can be seen as the general assumptions straight people make about gay and lesbian individuals. For instance, straight people hold assumptions about what a lesbian looks like. If a lesbian does not fit that mold, they may be faced with comments such as "*You're too pretty to be lesbian....*" Other comments that lesbians are faced with at work reveal that some straight people assume that being homosexual is a response to a traumatic event in the past. These assumptions tend to influence how straight people behave toward gay participants. In Daniel (2020), stereotypes were seen as false generalizations about gay individuals from the point of view of straight, religious individuals.

> I think a lot of people think a gay person is going to be prancing around like a queen or a lady ... they think that's going to be me and be like doing all the stereotypical gay things that people think gay people do which is a whole lot of junk.

Another common stereotype pertains to the competence of minority groups such as gays and lesbians. A gay participant from Lötter (2015) recalled how he was accused of not doing a part of his job well. "*They said that I'm not managing the temp staff very well. So I then had to go for a huge disciplinary hearing which obviously proved otherwise.*" A similar incident happened to a different gay employee:

> ...and somebody else was brought into my division, into my department. He started actually taking over a lot of my responsibilities as well. They started moving me away from my previous responsibilities and giving me smaller things to do, not to keep me involved in the running of the IT division.

The literature supports this notion of othering. Othering begins by making assumptions about individuals based on the social group to which they belong (Brink & Nel, 2015; Colquitt, Lepine, & Wesson, 2014). In most instances, stereotypes are held by the dominant group in society about a minority group (Tung, King, & Tse, 2020), even when these beliefs are based on misconceptions or falsehoods (Taylor, Guy-Walls, Wilkerson, & Addae, 2019). For example, a gay man will not hit on a straight male colleague if he befriends him. It is not uncommon for gay and lesbian individuals to face gender misrepresentation. They are often stereotyped as gender nonconforming, where gays are expected to be feminine and lesbians masculine (Blashill & Powlishta, 2009; Mize & Manago, 2018). Current literature suggests that gay and lesbian individuals generally face negative sentiments about them, accompanied by a number of social disadvantages (Herek & McLemore, 2013), at work and elsewhere. Here, competence stereotypes may exist where those who are assumed to be less competent are given less work, influence, and opportunities to speak, and are less likely to be employed (Correll, Benard, & Paik, 2007; Correll & Ridgeway, 2003; Mize & Manago, 2018). Beliefs about competence are influenced by perceptions of masculinity vs. femininity as well as a group's social status (Mize & Manago, 2018). Even if stereotypes may be false, they are still perpetuated by groups, and this may lead to prejudice.

Prejudice

Data from Lötter (2015) and Daniel (2020) showed that prejudices are negative feelings and attitudes toward gays and lesbians. For instance, in Lötter (2015), a lesbian participant explained how a straight colleague expressed disdain toward homosexuals as a minority group.

> So I was talking to one of the ladies about my weekend plans, and I was like, "oh I'm going to Pride," and she was like, "oh, what's that?" and so I explained to her that it's a gay and lesbian march, you know, and she goes, "I don't like those people," and I'm like, "oh, I'm one," and then ja, we'll probably never discuss it again.

A gay participant from Lötter (2015) expressed how open the prejudice had been displayed, even by senior members of the organization who should be setting a positive example for others.

> One of the executives from the bank stood up and admitted what was said and they did not appreciate me being in there because obviously, they were not comfortable having a gay person there in their circle, an openly gay person within their circle within their organization.

Similarly, in Daniel (2020), a gay participant expressed how Christian colleagues in his workplace looked down on gay people. "*They would see*

*gay people as almost a lesser [human being] or not necessarily good enough...
where I saw this was more when it came to team socials."*

According to literature, prejudice is a hostile attitude that is based
on a flawed generalization of those who have been othered (Durrheim,
Quayle, & Dixon, 2016). On the one hand, the social context matters
as the people in one's surroundings can influence these attitudes (Hjerm,
Eger, & Danell, 2018). For example, Muslim heterosexual individuals feel
a societal pressure to behave in a particular (negative) manner toward
gay individuals. This societal pressure is believed to be influenced by the
Islamic religion and its condemning view of homosexuality. As a result,
coming out to people of one's religion may not be easy. On the other
hand, as per Crandall and Eshleman (2003), although an individual may
hold prejudicial views, these may be restrained by the individual's beliefs,
values, and social norms. Even though the constitution is superior to religion, this has not stopped religious individuals from discriminating against
gays and lesbians. After all, the majority of South Africans are religious
(Statistics South Africa, 2011b).

Discrimination

An analysis of the two studies by Lötter (2015) and Daniel (2020)
revealed that discrimination took the form of negative treatment of
gays and/or lesbians by their straight colleagues. This treatment ranged
in severity from mild incidents to harsher, more aggressive ones. One
example of subtle discrimination included how a gay employee perceived
that members of his organization started treating him differently and
excluding him from work activities.

> I never disclosed to my company that I was gay but it was a family-oriented
> business. From that time that the managing director found out I was gay, I
> was treated differently, I was excluded from certain things, certain meetings
> that were important at the time.

One lesbian participant from Lötter (2015) reported how hugging her
girlfriend within the work premises was a problem for her and not for
straight people:

> One day my girlfriend fetched me from work, and she got out of the car,
> opened the door for me, gave me a hug and then I got in the car and

went home. And the next day, my team leader called me into a meeting. I was told it was inappropriate for me to greet my girlfriend at the time by giving her a hug in that way.

Another lesbian participant from Lötter (2015) recounted a more severe incident:

...There was a guy who was attacked at a plant, at a manufacturing plant. He was beaten up. He was gay. He was gay, and he was attacked, and he was in [the] hospital for like a month, and you know he wasn't the same after that at all.

Other experiences comprised gossiping, sabotage, isolation, fear of physical assault, changing an employee's job, and ignoring ideas.

From a religious perspective, Daniel (2020) found that some Christians did not like to associate themselves with gay people. "*You can tell that these people are Christians based on how they interact [with] me and try not to associate themselves with me.*" Daniel (2020) also found reports of bullying in the workplace by religious others to include a lack of acknowledgment, jokes being made, and unsupportive superiors.

Literature tells us that negative attitudes toward gays and lesbians (i.e., prejudice) are often expressed through discrimination, that is, judgements, verbal or physical aggression, and symbolic violence (Tombolato, Maia, Uziel, & Santos, 2018). Because homosexuality falls outside the norm, gays and lesbians are seen as deviant in different social spaces (Tombolato et al., 2018). As a result, gay and lesbian employees often experience discrimination, both covertly and overtly. Covert discrimination tends to be more subtle, less visible, hard to link to an individual's prejudice, and, therefore, easily overlooked (Lennartz, Proost, & Brebels, 2019). Overt discrimination, on the other hand, is more openly expressed, easily linkable to prejudice toward the "other," and thus challenging to deny (Lennartz et al., 2019). Prejudiced individuals may make an effort not to express their prejudice overtly, but even so, they may still unwittingly exhibit bias (Fric, 2019). Both interpersonal and institutional discrimination of sexual minorities such as gays and lesbians are linked to the life experience of mental health issues (Bostwick, Boyd, Hughes, & West, 2014; Hatzenbuehler, Keyes, & Hasin, 2009).

Across the anchor studies of Lötter (2015) and Daniel (2020), there seemed to be no real tangible difference in how people experienced discrimination from straight people in comparison to straight religious people. This can be explained by the fact that Lötter's study did not explicitly ask for the religious identities of those that discriminated against her participants. Yet, they very well could have been stereotyping and showing their prejudice and discrimination based on their own religious belief.

Religion and Prejudice

In the third anchor study, Kraft (2017) investigated how a person's religion and their personal experience of discrimination may influence their attitudes (or for this chapter, prejudice) toward gay and lesbian individuals. What he found was that, in line with prior research, identifying with and adhering to religion is likely to bring about prejudice (see Anderson & Koct, 2015; Reygan & Moane, 2014). This was especially true for Muslims and Catholics. This is because, much like the beliefs that South African political and religious leaders tout, homosexuality is considered impure and unnatural. The negative attitudes stem from their respective sacred scriptures, where homosexuality is openly condemned (Ring, 2016; Roggemans, Spruyt, van Droogenbroeck, & Keppens, 2015). This notion is confirmed by Janssen and Scheepers (2019), who state that religiosity is a strong determinant of the rejection of homosexuality, which happens through social agents such as religious institutions.

Managerial Implications

As gay and lesbian employees continue to be subjected to stereotypes, prejudice, and discrimination at work, South African organizations are advised to invest in creating more inclusive workplaces since inclusion has positive implications for wellbeing (Adams, Meyers, & Sekaja, 2020). This is a highly complex task as stereotypical and prejudiced beliefs are often deeply ingrained and difficult to change. One of the most important ways forward is to stimulate all members of the workforce to collect individuation information about one another to disconfirm stereotypes (van Dijk, Meyer, van Engen, & Loyd, 2017). On the one hand, this can be achieved by fostering a climate of discovery and learning that includes strong norms about learning from and about each other at work. van Dijk et al. (2017) suggest, for instance, that organizations can foster such a climate by challenging employees to find out at least one thing they did not know about their colleagues each week. On the other hand, collaborating with diverse others toward a common goal can help to disconfirm stereotypes and reduce prejudiced and discriminatory behavior (van Dijk et al., 2017). To ensure that diverse individuals collaborate toward a common goal, organizations could introduce team performance goals next to or instead of individual performance goals throughout the organization. In addition, temporary, multifunctional project teams with clear common goals may increase mutual respect and understanding among employees in South Africa.

In order to combat discrimination, organizations are moreover strongly advised to hold managers at all levels accountable for diversity targets (Kalev, Dobbin, & Kelly, 2006). This is paramount because other initiatives to counter discrimination (e.g., diversity training) will only show desired effects if paired with such accountability structures (Kalev et al., 2006). Once the accountability structures are established and anchored in, for instance, the annual performance management cycle, organizations can start to invest in broader diversity training. Often in South Africa, diversity training is limited to race and gender differences. So arguably, people may not always know what is appropriate in terms of behavior when it comes to sexual orientation. Thus, training needs to expand to include this important right also enshrined in the constitution.

An additional implication, outside of the influence of managers or organizations, is that religious institutions have a role to play in promoting higher tolerance among their congregations. Even though concepts like benevolence, respect, and compassion appear to be critical virtues in many religions, religious groups do not always behave in a virtuous way toward others, in particular, homosexual individuals. Similarly, we see an important role for educational institutions to challenge the heteronormative, homonegative views that many young people in South Africa hold due to conservative upbringing, vicarious learning, and religious teachings.

Taken together, we believe that it will take targeted initiatives from educators, religious, and organizational leaders to produce psychologically safe climates (in organizations and elsewhere) that make members of sexual orientation minority groups feel fully accepted and included.

Future Research Directions

Given the complexity of the lived experiences of gays and lesbians and other members of the LGBTQ+ community, we would like to consider a few recommendations important for future research. In the above, we have presented qualitative data from the perspective of gays and lesbians. At the same time, the quantitative study provided some insight into the attitudes of people who define themselves as "straight." In future research, we would advise the use of observational studies. Here, researchers could evaluate the inclusion and diversity climate within an organization as it pertains to many different groups and in particular members of the LGBTQ+ community. This might provide more objective perspectives on how people who identify as "other" may experience the workplace.

Second, we would recommend that the effectiveness of diversity and inclusion initiatives across different South African organizations needs to be evaluated. It might be that some organizations are faring much better than others when it comes to creating an inclusive organizational culture. Researchers need to establish which aspects within these organizations drive this culture of inclusivity. Qualitative analyzes of the corporate policies and practices would be informative about how different organizations within different industries deal with integrating people who identify as "other" into their organizations.

One other key aspect that we have observed in conducting these studies was that members of the LGBTQ+ community are still quite reluctant to speak out about their experiences. It is vital that researchers, in general, advocate for safe spaces where people from the LGBTQ+ community might feel invited to share their experiences. Higher education institutions, or research institutes, and government need to set up centers dedicated to the lived experiences of members of the LGBTQ+ community. This would mean working very closely with LGBTQ+ organizations and communities, determining their needs, and aligning research initiatives with these needs. In this chapter, we have only scratched the surface of the lived experiences of LGBTQ+ community by focusing on gay and lesbian people. However, given the diversity within these communities, more directed research initiatives would be instrumental for gaining a better understanding of more, if not all, members of the LGBTQ+ community, not just in the workplace but throughout their lives in general. Individuals who identify as other beyond gay and lesbian, are even less likely to be understood in the South African society and they likely face even more discrimination.

Finally, so far, the scientific knowledge we have gained on the discrimination of homosexual individuals is from the perspective of homosexual employees. The other side of the coin is yet to be explored, that is, the perpetrators of discrimination. To tackle issues of prejudice and discrimination, we need to understand them in their entirety, that is, the type of upbringing that elicits this type of discriminatory behavior and what it would take to reverse the thinking associated with discrimination.

CONCLUSION

Although there are persistent moral and religious belief systems that prevent gay and lesbian people in South Africa from exercising and enjoying their rights to just be, there seems to be some hope that these stereotypes, prejudices, and discriminations may diminish slowly over time. In fact, there is one encouraging observation in Daniel's (2020) study where she found that although stereotypes, prejudice, and discrimination were prevalent for some of her participants, there was also a trend emerging where gay participants noted that they did not detect negative sentiments and behaviors directed toward them. This does not necessarily indicate that stereotyping, prejudice, and discrimination is not present, as it may still exist, albeit in more covert forms. While there is no other literature from the past five years in South Africa to support this finding, other international studies do suggest that attitudes toward gay and lesbian individuals have become more positive over time even if prejudice against them still exists (Herek & McLemore, 2013; Mize & Manago, 2018). Creating more positive attitudes will be possible through increased exposure to gays and lesbians (we fear what we do not know) and, importantly, through being taught acceptance by educational and religious institutions from an early age. Once people reach the age where they start to work, their inclination to stereotype, prejudice, and discrimination has already been solidified. At this stage, one needs workplace interventions such as diversity training coupled with hardline approaches (i.e., accountability structures) that reprimand those that do not respect the gays' and lesbians' rights that are enshrined in the constitution.

CHAPTER TAKEAWAYS

1. Legislatively, South Africa has all the makings of a homosexual-inclusive society. But it is also a highly religious country, and teachings of religions are not in keeping with the constitution. These teachings often encourage negative stereotyping, prejudice, and discrimination, which hinder the ideals of the constitution.
2. We still see the differential treatment of gays and lesbians at work, both in the anchor studies and in literature. Further, stereotypes bring about prejudice, which in turn fosters a culture of discrimination, whether covert or overt.
3. There are real proven ways for organizations to foster inclusion that go beyond the mundane diversity training, which is often costly but does not work.
4. There are key research gaps that are yet to be explored in this context that illuminate the experiences of other members of the LGBTQ+ community.

REFERENCES

Adams, B. G., Meyers, M. C., & Sekaja, L. (2020). Positive leadership: Relationships with employee inclusion, discrimination, and well-being. *Applied Psychology: An International Review, 69*(4), 1145–1173. https://doi.org/10.1111/apps.12230.

Amnesty International UK. (2018). *Mapping anti-gay laws in Africa.* Retrieved from https://www.amnesty.org.uk/lgbti-lgbt-gay-human-rights-law-africa-uganda-kenya-nigeria-cameroon.

Anderson, J., & Koct, Y. (2015). Exploring patterns of explicit and implicit anti-gay attitudes in Muslims and Atheists. *European Journal of Social Psychology, 45*(6), 687–701. https://doi.org/10.1002/ejsp.2126.

Augé, M. (1987). Qui est l'autre? Un itinéraire anthropologique. *L' Homme, XXVII, 3,* 7–26.

Benjamin, N. (2019). *What will it take to build LGBT inclusive workplaces in South Africa?* Retrieved from https://lrs.org.za/articles/What-will-it-take-to-build-LGBT-inclusive-workplaces-in-South-Africa

Blashill, A., & Powlishta, K. (2009). Gay stereotypes: The use of sexual orientation as a cue for gender-related attributes. *Sex Roles, 61,* 783–793.

Bostwick, W. B., Boyd, C. J., Hughes, T. L., & West, B. (2014). Discrimination and mental health among lesbian, gay, and bisexual adults in the United

States. *American Journal of Orthopsychiatry, 84*(1), 35–45. https://doi.org/10.1037/h0098851.

Brink, L., & Nel, J. A. (2015). Exploring the meaning and origin of stereotypes amongst South African employees. *SA Journal of Industrial Psychology, 41*(1), Art. #1234, 13 pp. https://doi.org/10.4102/sajip.v41i1.1234.

Colquitt, J. A., Lepine, J. A., & Wesson, M. J. (2014). *Organizational behavior: Improving performance and commitment in the workplace* (2nd ed.). New York, NY: McGraw-Hill.

Correll, S., Benard, S., & Paik, I. (2007). Getting a job: Is there a motherhood penalty? *American Journal of Sociology, 112*, 1297–1338.

Correll, S., & Ridgeway, C. (2003). Expectation states theory. In J. DeLamater (Ed.), *Handbook of social psychology* (pp. 29–51). New York, NY: Kluwer Academic.

Crandall, C., & Eshleman, A. (2003). A justification-suppression model of the expression and experience of prejudice. *Psychological Bulletin, 129*(3), 414–446. https://doi.org/10.1037/0033-2909.129.3.414.

Daniel, N. (2020). *Exploring the perceived attitudes and discrimination of heterosexual individuals towards gay men within the same religious group in the workplace* (Unpublished master's dissertation). University of Johannesburg, Johannesburg, South Africa.

Durrheim, K., Quayle, M., & Dixon, J. (2016). The struggle for the nature of "prejudice": "Prejudice" expression as identity performance. *Political Psychology, 37*(1), 17–35.

eNCA. (2015, May). *Maimane, Zuma and other 'anti-gay' statements in SA politics*. Retrieved from https://www.enca.com/south-africa/maimane-zuma-and-other-anti-gay-statements-sa-politics

Fedor, C.-G. (2014). Stereotypes and prejudice in the perception of the "other". *Procedia—Social and Behavioral Sciences, 149*, 321–326.

Fric, K. (2019). How does being out at work relate to discrimination and unemployment of gays and lesbians? *Journal for Labour Market Research, 53*, 14. https://doi.org/10.1186/s12651-019-0264-1.

Government Gazette. (1996). Constitution of the Republic of South Africa Act No. 108 of 1996. Republic of South Africa, Pretoria, 18 December, 1996.

Hagopian, A., Rao, D., Katz, A., Sanford, S., & Barnhart, S. (2017). Anti-homosexual legislation and HIV-related stigma in African nations: What has been the role of PEPFAR? *Global Health Action, 10*(1), 1306391. https://doi.org/10.1080/16549716.2017.1306391.

Hatzenbuehler, M., Keyes, K., & Hasin, D. (2009). State-level policies and psychiatric morbidity in lesbian, gay and bisexual populations. *American Journal of Public Health, 99*, 2275–2281.

Herek, G. M., & McLemore, K. A. (2013). Sexual prejudice. *Annual Review of Psychology, 64*, 309–333.

Hjerm, M., Eger, M. A., & Danell, R. (2018). Peer attitudes and the development of prejudice in adolescence. *Socius: Sociological Research for a Dynamic World, 4,* 1–11. https://doi.org/10.1177/2378023118763318.

Janssen, D.-J., & Scheepers, P. (2019). How religiosity shapes rejection of homosexuality across the globe. *Journal of Homosexuality, 66*(14), 1974–2001. https://doi.org/10.1080/00918369.2018.1522809.

Jones, T. (2019). South African contributions to LGBTI education issues. *Sex Education, 19*(4), 455–471. https://doi.org/10.1080/14681811.2018.1535969.

Kalev, A., Dobbin, F., & Kelly, E. (2006). Best practices or best guesses? Assessing the efficacy of corporate affirmative action and diversity policies. *American Sociological Review, 71*(4), 589–617. https://doi.org/10.1177/000312240607100404.

Kotzé, H., & Loubser, R. (2018). Christian ethics in South Africa: Liberal values among the public and elites. *Scriptura, 117,* 1–10.

Kraft, I. (2017). *Attitudes towards homosexuality based on religion and workplace discrimination* (Unpublished master's dissertation). University of Johannesburg, Johannesburg, South Africa.

Lennartz, C., Proost, K., & Brebels, L. (2019). Decreasing overt discrimination increases covert discrimination: Adverse effects of equal opportunities policies. *International Journal of Selection and Assessment, 27,* 129–138. https://doi.org/10.1111/ijsa.12244.

Lötter, C. (2015). *The nature of perceived discriminatory experiences of gay men at work* (Unpublished master's dissertation). University of Johannesburg, Johannesburg, South Africa.

Mize, T. D., & Manago, B. (2018). The stereotype content of sexual orientation. *Social Currents, 5*(5), 458–478. https://doi.org/10.1177/2329496518761999.

Nyeck, S. N., Shepherd, D., Sehoole, J., Ngcobozi, L., & Conron, K. J. (2019). *The economic cost of LGBT stigma and discrimination in South Africa.* Retrieved from https://williamsinstitute.law.ucla.edu/wp-content/uploads/Cost-Discrim-So-Africa-Dec-2019.pdf.

Oberth, G., & Mondry, L. (2014). *Lesbian, gay, bisexual, transgender and intersex human rights in Southern Africa.* Johannesburg, South Africa: Hivos Local Office in South Africa.

Pew Research Global Attitudes Project. (2013). *The global divide on homosexuality: Greater acceptance in more secular and affluent countries.* Retrieved from https://www.pewglobal.org/2013/06/04/the-global-divide-on-homosexuality/.

Pillay, R. (2018). *South Africa still hasn't won LGBTQ+ equality. Here are 5 reasons why.* Retrieved from https://www.weforum.org/agenda/2018/11/south-africa-road-to-lgbtq-equality/.

Quinn, K., & Dickson-Gomez, J. (2015). Homonegativity, religiosity, and the intersecting identities of young black men who have sex with men. *AIDS and Behavior, 20*(1), 51–64. https://doi.org/10.1007/s10461-015-1200-1.

Reygan, F., & Moane, G. (2014). Religious homophobia: The experiences of a sample of lesbian, gay, bisexual and transgender (LGBT) people in Ireland. *Culture and Religion, 15*(3), 298–312. https://doi.org/10.1080/14755610.2014.942329.

Ring, T. (2016). *Pope Francis's report a letdown to LGBT Catholics.* Retrieved from https://www.advocate.com/religion/2016/4/08/pope-fra nciss-report-letdown-lgbt-catholics.

Roggemans, L., Spruyt, B., van Droogenbroeck, F., & Keppens, G. (2015). Religion and negative attitudes towards homosexuals: An analysis of urban young people and their attitudes towards homosexuality. *YOUNG, 23*(3), 254–276. https://doi.org/10.1177/1103308815586903.

Sokupa, V., & Majova, Z. (2006, September). Candidate of the left or the conservatives? *Mail & Guardian.*

Statistics South Africa. (2011a). *Census 2011: Census in brief*. Retrieved from https://www.statssa.gov.za/census/census_2011/census_products/Census_2011_Census_in_brief.pdf.

Statistics South Africa. (2011b). *Statistical release* (revised). Received from http://www.statssa.gov.za/publications/P03014/P030142011.pdf.

Statistics South Africa. (2014). *General household survey 2013.* Retrieved from https://www.gov.za/general-household-survey-ghs-2013.

Statistics South Africa. (2019). *SA population reaches 58.8 million.* Retrieved from https://www.statssa.gov.za/?p=12362.

Sutherland, C., Roberts, B., Gabriel, N., Struwig, J., & Gordon, S. (2016). *Progressive prudes: A survey of attitudes towards homosexuality & gender nonconformity in South Africa.* Saxonwold, South Africa: The Other Foundation.

Taylor, E., Guy-Walls, P., Wilkerson, P., & Addae, R. (2019). The historical perspectives of stereotypes on African-American males. *Journal of Human Rights and Social Work, 4*, 213–225. https://doi.org/10.1007/s41134-019-00096-y.

Tombolato, M. A., Maia, A. C. B., Uziel, A. P., & Santos, M. A. (2018). Prejudice and discrimination in the everyday life of same-sex couples raising children. *Estudos de Psicologia* (Campinas), *35*(1), 111–122. https://doi.org/10.1590/1982-02752018000100011.

Tung, V. W. S., King, B. E. M., & Tse, S. (2020). The tourist stereotype model: Positive and negative dimensions. *Journal of Travel Research, 59*(1), 37–51. https://doi.org/10.1177/0047287518821739.

UNESCO. (2016). *Out in the open.* Paris, France: UNESCO.

van Dijk, H., Meyer, B., van Engen, M., & Loyd, D. L. (2017). Microdynamics in diverse teams: A review and integration of the diversity and stereotyping literatures. *Academy of Management Annals, 11*(1), 517–557.

Vincent, L., & Howell, S. (2014). 'Unnatural', 'un-African' and 'ungodly': Homophobic discourse in democratic South Africa. *Sexualities, 17*(4), 472–483. https://doi.org/10.1177/1363460714524766.

Wike, R., Horowitz, J., Simmons, K., Poushter, J., Ponce, A., Barker, C., & Devlin, K. (2013). *The global divide on homosexuality.* New York, NY: Pew Research Centre.

CHAPTER 22

Unfinished Business: Advancing Workplace Gender Equity Through Complex Systems Strategies Supporting Work/Family Dynamics

Ester R. Shapiro and Emu Kato

PRELUDE: REFLECTIONS ON THE COVID-19 PANDEMIC AS CRISIS, CHALLENGE AND INSPIRATION TO PROMOTE TRANSFORMATIONAL GENDER INCLUSION

When COVID-19 hit greater Boston in Spring 2020 and closed our majority non-White urban commuter campus, we were in the midst of our Psychology Capstone course on Gender, Culture, and Health Equity. For Ester, this class embodies my educational and social activism as I teach women (and courageous men) how to transform intersecting experiences of gendered, racialized oppression into professional knowledge and leadership skills needed to develop impactful social change careers. For Emu, the class was part of an Organizational Studies research internship, Resources for Educational Success and Wellness for diverse students at UMASS Boston (Kato, Lee, Martin, & Shapiro, 2020; Shapiro

E. R. Shapiro (✉) · E. Kato
Department of Psychology, University of Massachusetts, Boston, MA, USA
e-mail: Ester.Shapiro@umb.edu

© The Author(s), under exclusive license to Springer Nature Switzerland AG 2021
J. Marques (ed.), *Exploring Gender at Work*,
https://doi.org/10.1007/978-3-030-64319-5_22

425

2020). We use Hurtado, Alvarez, Guillermo-Wann, Cuellar, and Arellano (2012) Multi-Contextual Model for Diverse Learning Environments, which maps characteristics of transformational Inclusive Educational Institutions supporting student capacity to both succeed in school and develop habits of mind and competencies toward living in a multicultural world. Together, we have learned to appreciate complex systems/social ecological models with multi-systemic "mappings" of factors contributing to outcomes of interest. These models help us identify individual factors, relationships, organizational factors, and public policies that can inadvertently conspire together to protect inequalities or can offer systemic leverage points for change. They are applied in many disciplines in addition to health equity, for example, as we review later, in assessing University institutional success in supporting women in medicine and science (Kalpazidou Schmidt, Ovseiko, Henderson, & Kiparoglou, 2020).

As a Cuban American immigrant woman, who has taken her share of hits for violating gendered cultural norms in both academic and family settings, Ester appreciates that our students have experienced both economic deprivation and educational inequalities "teaching" them to lower their aspirations and de-value their knowledge from hard-won experiences. For this reason, the course incorporates principles of Participatory Action Research supporting collaborative leadership development toward enhancing social change (Shapiro & Little, 2020). We begin class by sharing challenging experiences and affirming educational aspirations, valuing inclusive knowledge as "cultural wealth" (Yosso & Burciaga, 2016), celebrating the enormous diversity of backgrounds enriching our learning. Together, we confront the life and death consequences of health inequalities, working from the film "Unnatural Causes: Is Inequality Making us Sick" which immediately inspires appreciation for the Social Justice oriented multi-systemic theoretical frameworks and inclusive research methods needed to implement change. We study critical, multi-systemic theories and participatory action research methods generating knowledge designed for action addressing inequalities. We affirm the roles of Participatory Action Research and Cultural Humility as empowering strategies for life-long learning, methods valuing knowledge gained from lived experiences of the most excluded beginning with ourselves. We connect these values with methods in community-engaged participatory action research utilized in community economic development and organizing for equity (all course readings are described in Shapiro et al., 2018). Grounding our discussions in student lived experiences, we had critiqued the broken US health care system with its multiple, intersecting inequalities and destructive forces of poverty, gendered racism, individualization of responsibility for consequences of "poor choices" and "risky behaviors", and privatized responsibility for the care of the most vulnerable blighting the lives of so many of our students. We also celebrated the kinship and generosity allowing them to do so much with so little on behalf of those they love. Together, we challenged the unjust social conditions and unfair stereotypes that had dimmed visions of possible futures, and affirmed the power of inclusive dialogues as resources generating transformational knowledge.

Our Spring 2020 class convened a community of shared learning fortunate in our great range of voices representing Black, Latina/o/x, US immigrant (Haiti, Central and Latin America, Lebanon, Italy), and transnational/international (Morocco, Pakistan, China, Japan) men, women, and LGBTQ working students. Our course curriculum draws on multi-disciplinary, multi-systemic understandings of health equity as foundational to shared human development, working across Critical Organizational Studies, Health Psychology, transnational Feminist and US Women of Color Gender Equity Social Movements, inspiring and mobilizing students to translate their observations from lived experiences of social inequality into knowledge advancing their professional development while advocating for health equity (Shapiro, 2014, 2018; Shapiro et al., 2018).

Suddenly on March 12, 2020, our educational mission took on even greater urgency as pandemic precautions forced us into remote Zoom classrooms, exposing our inequalities. As the pandemic restructured workplace, family, and social ties we observed in real time how social determinants of health inequalities devastated the lives of our highly diverse working commuter students, responsible for extended kin in our most vulnerable communities. Together as teacher, students and partners in learning, we observed differential lived experiences of societal inequalities: who had access to broadband and computers required for remote learning? Who had to study, work, and contribute to caretaking of their own and extended kin's children, elders, the disabled, and vulnerable others, including those that fell ill from COVID-19, or died, or experienced long recoveries? Who lived in crowded housing in a COVID-19 "hot spot" as they scrambled to pay Boston's already unaffordable rents, now facing eviction? Who was considered an "essential worker", risking their lives for low-wage work in a city known for its many prestigious teaching hospitals but lacking access to needed testing or basic physical protective equipment including masks? Who had to increase their own work-shifts because everyone else in their household had lost their jobs during the shut-down? Who lived in mixed-status immigrant families who worried about deportations or barred entries? Who had to postpone life-saving counseling sessions because they lacked a private space in their home? Who was forced to endure unrelenting family censure due to their non-traditional gender choices and sexual preferences, without spaces of acceptance outside their homes?

Yet in this time of heightened crisis, our class diversity and course approach to global/comparative, complex systems/multi-systemic, social justice thinking on social determinants of health equity throughout shared development in intertwined lives offered an ideal "laboratory" for inclusive participatory inquiry. Appreciating these realities, we began to work individually and collectively on topics of shared interest while articulating educational hope, voicing professional aspirations, and identifying steps in working toward career goals. We identified students interested in working on the continuing class research project, "Resources for Educational Success and Wellness at UMASS Boston" (Kato et al., 2020). A team of students struggling with intensified mental health concerns studied effective holistic stress reduction approaches supported by research evidence and served as class consultants on stress reduction resources available on campus and in the community. Their work became even more meaningful as students experienced severe stresses when the pandemic struck. We also brought together a team of immigrant identified Women of Color with experiences and interests in addressing Maternal and Child Health inequalities through culturally sensitive, socio-politically contextualized approaches to Birth and Reproductive Justice.

By far everyone's favorite paper in this and all my classes is Public Health scholar/activist Camara Jones's accessible, influential analysis of "Levels of Racism" (2000; also see video of her Ted Talk at Emory University, 2014). Jones uses "A Gardner's Tale" as metaphor to identify three entangled levels at which societal institutions and organizations, relationships of unequal power, and our internalized beliefs regarding expressions and ethics of gendered lives, are mutually reinforcing, co-conspiring to protect the status quo. Students learned how sociopolitical contexts of inequality were protected by ideologies and institutional practices that taught us to blame ourselves and our families for our personal defects and bad choices resulting in ill health. They learned to use an ecological life course approach in mapping variables contributing to ill health or flourishing, and the value of participatory methods in identifying action steps and promoting community organizing for health equity with accountability in Abraham Wandersman's participatory community research model for "Getting to Outcomes". Through training in critical cultural competence and cultural humility, we connected student lived experiences of health inequalities to systematic observations and analysis of needed change. Our own, specific local expressions of the global COVID-19 pandemic highlighted both our differences due to gendered, racialized, and economic inequalities and our human interdependence and shared fates. We recognized our intensified reliance on webs of support connecting family, neighborhood, workplace, schools and government as employment, access to health care, and safe affordable housing became matters of life and death.

The COVID-19 pandemic with its interruption of "business as usual" has exposed enormous gaps in supports offered to families for care of the most vulnerable (Power, 2020) and the ways these fall disproportionately on women. Yet this moment of crisis also offers an opportunity to better understand forces contributing to current dilemmas in work/family dynamics, while pointing the way toward potential re-design (Mlambo-Ngcuka & Dalli, 2020).

Re-visioning Work Family Dynamics as Complex Systems: Achieving Valued Goals of Gender Inclusion with Undivided Equity

In the United States, Europe, and around the world, most people of all nationalities, genders, racial and religious backgrounds endorse gender equity as a valued personal and societal goal across multiple domains of their lives and work (Pew Global, 2020; Thébaud & Halcomb, 2019). Yet while most may endorse gender equity as a social value, we deeply disagree about effective actions implementing its actualization. We have witnessed over a century of successes promoting gender equity through laws eliminating barriers to women's social participation while enhancing protections and rights including securing women's rights to vote, to own property, to decide if and when to have children, to achieve equal opportunities in employment, and to be protected from Gender Based Violence in its many forms. The United Nations Millenial Development and Sustainable Development Goals have made Gender Equity central to poverty reduction, with some significant successes (United Nations Women, 2020).

Meanwhile gender equity remains elusive, what some call an unfinished revolution (Swinth, 2019). Why does workplace gender inclusion remain "Unfinished Business" (Slaughter, 2015) and a "stalled revolution" (England, Levine, & Mishel, 2020)? Many of us who fought personally and politically for societal gender equity during what's termed feminism's Second Wave, now elders, have celebrated the growing societal recognition of gender complexity, expanding visibility and inclusion of beautiful varieties of personhood. At the same time, we are shocked at the enduring effects of narrow, imposed gender roles and accompanying stereotypes and biases, especially as these are manifested at the intersection of the workplace and gendered family life course demands. Changed demographics at the heart of family lives—how we make a living, the timing and number of our children, how we share care for children and elders—have challenged societies to re-vision gender at work. Workplace gender inclusion has been shown to contribute to business effectiveness and profitability (Moen, 2017; Williams, Berdahl, & Vandello, 2016), with traditionally male dominated industries paying a "masculinity penalty" (Foreign Policy Analytics, 2020). Evidence on gender and workplace equity in the United States and internationally consistently finds that women enduringly experience greater workplace inequality, as characterized by lower wages and fewer positions of leadership.

Analysis of global economic and demographic changes from a workplace gender equity perspective (Catalyst, 2020; Cooper, 2017; Power, 2020; Williams et al., 2016) suggests that women all over the world have found it necessary to increase their contributions to the economic survival needs of their most vulnerable kin. These effects have been greatly intensified by the COVID-19 pandemic, suggesting that workplace gender inclusion and women's economic participation may be set back significantly by the pandemic unless strategic actions are taken (Williams, 2020). Sociologist Arlie Hochschild's influential study *The Second Shift* (1989) was the first to document the "stalled" gender equity revolution as resulting from societal failure to support women in their homemaking and child caretaking responsibilities. Her ethnographic study and interviews exposed the ingenious lies men and women, husbands and wives, told themselves and each other to hide these contradictions between their hoped-for egalitarianism and the realities of sexist roles at work and home. She also uncovered significant strains in marital intimacy and in burdened child behavior as societal level inequalities, women's high levels of caretaking burden and role strain, eroded family well-being.

Blair-Loy, Hochschild, Pugh, Williams, and Hartmann (2015) convened Hochschild and experts in work family dynamics and gender equity to review "stability and transformation", identifying impactful factors preserving the status quo and contributing to possibilities of change. Following the failure to change gender polarized and stereo-typed work/family dynamics in the decades since the book's publication, they review the multiple levels at which gender roles are implemented and experienced. They argue for a multi-systemic approach that examines macro-level policies prescribing roles for government, organizations, non-profits, and educational systems. The authors also note that work all over the world has become more globalized as well as more precarious, creating maximum flexibility for capital flows and just-in-time manufacturing at the lowest costs but detrimental to workers and their dependents. Others warn that these models of economic development are environmentally unsustainable, requiring a more critical perspective on societal values and how to plan for changes more consistent with these values.

Bell Meriläinen, Taylor, and Tienari (2019) edited a special issue of the journal *Human Relations*, titled "Time's up! Feminist theory and activism meets organization studies", suggesting that a feminist analysis can contribute positively to our shared desire for improving lives all over the world through workplace gender inclusion. Contributing to the special issue, Tyler (2019) warns that gender inclusion in management needs to be accompanied by a critical perspective which reconsiders ethics broadly in light of what we value, alongside a revisioning of aims and practices of gender inclusion. Tyler suggests that a focus on embodied ethics has implications for the workplace as a space for "assembly" or the performance of alternative ways of expressing gender complexity and diversity. She argues that Organizational Inclusion consistent with feminist and social justice social movements can begin to counteract the powerful stabilizing effects of polarized gender roles maintaining stability in practices that are neither desirable in terms of ethics, employee well-being, nor even profitable. Without these insights, management strategies for gender inclusion may instead contribute to backlash and hardening of stereotyped gender roles. These may translate into workplace "masculinity contests" (Berdahl, Cooper, Glick, Livingston, & Williams,

2018), environments encouraging gender polarized ideologies about men and women's work/life roles (Leslie, King, & Clair, 2019), and discriminatory Human Resource practices reinforcing stereotypes (Stamarski & Son Hing, 2015).

Historically, during this period of stalled progress toward workplace gender inclusion, global capitalism has intensified values and practices that reinforce workplace gender inequalities. These economic ideologies promised that if governments focus on providing the greatest freedom for profit-making, while privatizing responsibility for family survival needs, the rising tide will lift all boats, allowing women, children, and families to benefit. However, the individualization and privatization of caretaking responsibilities have resulted in intensified polarization regarding the proper roles of men and women, punishing women who work (Brandth, Halrynjo, & Kvande, 2017). In the United States and Europe, where these trends began, White, educated women from the highest economic strata were encouraged to enter the workplace and to view this as an emancipatory "choice", with the expectation that low-wage caretakers could be hired to fulfill family responsibilities. However, we are seeing the collapse of these agreements about how women can "lean in" or "have it all". In Europe, we first saw the tensions in the "choices" made by executive working women Italy and Spain, where choosing to remain childless was the only way to reconcile childbearing responsibilities and child care expectations in their strongly Catholic nations. We are now seeing these trends in China, where a reversal of the one-child law and the growing aging of the population are creating heightened expectations for women's caretaking roles as a private family responsibility (Ji, Wu, Sun, & He, 2017). Le, Newman, Menzies, Zheng and Fermelis (2020) review the limited literature on work-life balance in Asia, arguing that advancing this work requires a specific focus on regional economics and culture.

In Japan, a masculinized culture of "overwork" requires the "good worker" to prove their devotion through unsustainable, ultimately unbearable hours resulting in high suicide rates. Emu was inspired to work in Organizational Studies by observing the impacts on both women and men of the rigid gender stereotyping of workplace roles and effects on mental health distress. In countries with the greatest gaps between gendered family expectations and workplace failure to support family and kinship responsibilities, women are "choosing" to remain single, forego childbearing, or abandon challenging careers in favor of more flexible employment with lower expectations for putting in long hours. *Emu observes:* The reason why I am interested specifically in work environments is because people spend so much of their lives there, especially in Japan. I have always wanted to help Japanese people in some way and I think combining Organizational and Psychological perspectives on the expectations of overwork are especially valuable. Japan seemed always problematic regard on workplace environment including work-life balance and gender issues. A culture of overwork pressure for men has a huge impact on illness and suicide, so much so that there is a word for karoshi or "death from overwork" (Doner, 2019; Takahashi, 2019).

Although data shows that the official worktime in Japan is shorter than the United States, the problem is people also work while they are off the clock which can be forced or "voluntary" in keeping with presumed values of women who prioritize family and men who prioritize work obligations. Many companies expect their employees to work unpaid overtime. Also, despite Japan having more days of paid vacation than the United States, many employees refuse to use these. As we will discuss later, these same gender ideologies apply to men's limited use of parental leave unless public/private policies and partnerships provide incentives while also addressing stereotypes. Often times, Japanese men feel pressure from their boss or coworkers not to take any time off. Some companies force them to use paid vacation for sick time. Many of them go out to drink after work, as this is considered as their job to have some drinks and associate with workers and entertain their boss. Most workplaces are male dominated because of the deeply rooted beliefs viewing men exclusively as breadwinners and women as housewives. Also, data shows that harassment toward women remains a serious unsolved issue in the Japanese workplace, as in many other countries. Marriage and pregnancy disadvantage women despite the law, in Japan as in the United States. With different sources, but similar effects, women's biological role in childbearing becomes a barrier as they "choose" part-time work that is more flexible instead of full time pursuing their more ambitious careers. The whole social fabric conspires with these roles: Japanese elementary schools have parent teacher associations (PTA) where parents most of whom are mothers are expected to volunteer for school activities. Despite the fact they are called "volunteers", it is pressured and forced by school and other mothers to participate, so it is hard to balance for working mothers. Although the government is trying to encourage women to work by implementing family friendly policies supporting work-life balance, and these policies have been helpful, I and others observe these gendered expectations create severe burdens for office workers and penalize women as they try to balance work and family responsibilities. Women need to pick either job or having children, and those who pick their job are perceived as "losers" in the "feminity contest" that complements the "masculinity contests" we discuss later in this paper. This communicates an underlying message in Japanese society that women's goal is to have a happy family. Although younger people both men and women would prefer greater equality in work roles and in family responsibilities, it is harder for younger Japanese workers to bring change because most of the companies are based on a seniority system so that the companies' policies reflect older workers ideas. This contributes to continuation of power in organizations, as I never seen or heard any boycott by workers to bring change or anything, which I am not sure if they are allowed to do so on the first place. But younger people definitely have very little power in the companies. On top of that, women have less power than men. The research we reviewed and articles specific to Japan showed me that the work environment issues in Japan are deeply enrooted in our cultures. I do want to bring changes into the Japanese work environment, and appreciate that understanding gender within culture, appreciating stereotypes, biases, and discrimination people face, consciously or unconsciously, is crucial to accomplishing impactful change. Ester reflects that gender inequalities reflect both culturally grounded gendered stereotypes and social differences in national policies for what Amartya Sen terms the capabilities approach in Human Development. How we invest society's money to achieve valued outcomes in health, education, and income? The capability approach argues that we can't be educated without schools, we can't be healthy without both health care and access to health social determinants (i.e., safe and secure housing, affordable healthy food), and we can't earn a living wage without shared social responsibility for care of the vulnerable, especially during critical life course transitions of childbirth, care of infants and young children, care of the disabled and the elderly. The United Nations and Measure of America have developed tracking for these components of the Human Development Index, in the United States for each state and around the world, arguing that "We can't change what we don't measure". We also recognize: we can't fix what we don't value.

Re-visioning Tensions Between Work and Caretaking Responsibilities: A Matter of Values

Williams et al. (2016) review extensive social psychological research to identify reasons for the enormous mismatch between changing realities of employment and what we term "work/family" or "work/life" conflict, integration, or balance. Williams argues that the workplace serves an important societal function in defining highly valued and personally cherished identities around highly stereotyped masculine and feminine roles. A masculinized, class-based "work devotion schema" associates male success with long work hours unimpeded by family demands. In contrast, for women, this "work devotion schema" is considered a moral hazard, interfering with the family caretaking focus associated with being a "good woman". Drawing on extensive research, Williams suggests that generational preferences by young men toward re-defining masculinity to include meaningful family and fathering roles may contribute to shifting these workplace norms (Madhusoodanan, 2018). However, stated gender equity preferences at an individual or family level continue to confront barriers at the level of both organizational and governmental policies, leading to constrained decision making by individuals and families. Additionally, narrow psychological approaches focused on personal identities, gender stereotyping reinforcing inequalities by individual managers, and individual preferences or choices have interfered with implementing what Williams et al. (2016) term the "clear business case" supporting positive impacts of work/family flexibility for all employees, for customer experience, and for company profitability.

Brandth et al. (2017) suggest that disentangling forces contributing to change and stability in work family life require a change in frameworks and methods toward understanding dynamics as emerging from competing logics regarding regulation, economies, and ethics as these guide what we value as societies. Taking a comparative approach, they explore assumptions and consequences of societal beliefs and state roles regarding the individualization and privatization of family centered economic and caretaking responsibilities. As a gender and work equity legal and policy scholar, Williams (2020) has written important reviews assessing facilitators and barriers to women's workplace inclusion by attending to practices and policies promoting work/life balance. In a recent essay on how COVID-19 has exposed gender inequalities at work, Williams notes that in the US policies and legal protections for workers who also care for vulnerable family members are limited, uneven, varying by workplace and by patchwork of state and federal laws and policies, leaving many workers and their loved ones unprotected with limited recourses (Williams, Work-Life Policy Center, 2020). As we will discuss in the following review, single theme attempts to manage change often defeat our best efforts due to the entangled complexity of what some have described as "Wicked Problems" in Complex Systems.

Disrupting Stability of Wicked Problems in Work Life Dynamics with Complexity and Developmental Systems Thinking

Multiple disciplines in sociology, public health, environmental sciences, organizational management and leadership, and economics among many others have turned to complexity sciences to better understand the multiple forces that contribute to outcomes. Replacing cause and effect thinking, these approaches recognize the interdependence of factors and the unpredictability of interactive effects and unexpected contributions of even seemingly small factors leading to emergent outcomes (Capra & Luisi, 2016; Walby, 2007). Psychologist Enns (2008) focused on stereo-typed masculinity as a complex systems problem interfering with women's societal equality. Bringing Complexity Sciences to Business Management toward understanding Large Scale Change supporting sustainable business practices, Waddock, Meszoely, Waddell, and Dentoni (2015) argue that highly specialized knowledge will be of limited value in confronting real-world "wicked" problems requiring large-scale, transformational rather than incremental change.

"Wicked Problems" are so described because of their multi-systemic entanglements and seemingly inexhaustible capacity to defeat our supposedly effective, well-meaning but narrowly conceptualized solutions. Donella Meadows' influential work (see Meadows, 1999 and the Meadows online archive) on systems sciences, economic growth, and sustainability challenged us to re-consider "growth" in economic theory through systems thinking. With many detractors during years advancing economic neoliberalism seeking to eliminate regulations on industry protecting employees or the planet, Meadows' ideas are finding new relevance. Meadows and other systems thinkers in Organizational, Economic

Development, and Sustainability Studies propose that the most impactful ways to intervene in a complex system is to identify leverage points facilitating change, and those contributing to systems stability and interfering with desired change. Listing 12 points of intervention, in reverse order from least to most effective, Meadows lists number one as The Power to Transcend Paradigms (Meadows, 1999). Although Meadows' work did not directly address work/family dynamics, her call to consider values, goals, and consequences echoes in much of the current work marshalling the power of business in creating partnerships that support gender inclusion as part of societally supported economic inclusion promoting human rights and environmental sustainability.

Writing for applied organizational and policy studies, visionary business writers committed to gender equity in re-imagining possible futures agree that the work must begin with the ideologies and assumptions that prioritize what we value and how our beliefs and practices proceed from these values. A global comparative perspective is especially valuable in illuminating some of the assumptions and practices that have so limited progress toward gender inclusion. Comparative systems thinking helps workers, managers, and policy makers assess the consequences of varied approaches by identifying agreed upon valued outcomes and insisting on accountability in measuring progress toward change. In their recent work Brandth, B., Halrynjo, S., & Kvande, E. (Eds.). (2017). *Work-family dynamics: Competing logics of regulation, economy and morals*, the volume Editors argue that changing economies emphasizing profit and reducing worker flexibility and protections are changing the logics of gender, work, and care world wide but with different effects depending on the values or ethics guiding national policies. In the United States, with one of the starkest systems designed to maximize profit and privatize family responsibilities, Gerson (2017) studied how couples seeking to establish gender equitable families confronted barriers and achieved compromises supporting possible alternatives. These and other authors argue that the process of change must begin with examining the language we use to describe "work/family conflict" as we begin to re-vision possibilities for change.

Starting from their earlier paper on Complexity, Wicked Problems, and Large Scale Change, in that article focused on the electricity grids, Waddock (2018) takes up questions of values in envisioning possible futures supporting more favorable outcomes. Taking up critical work on the ethics of economic growth in facing challenges of justice and sustainability, Waddock (2018) follows Meadows and other systems thinkers in suggesting that incremental and reformist approaches to Large Scale Change often defeat us due to multiple, interwoven strategies protecting systemic continuity and stability. She argues that transformational change requires "Shamanic Leadership", or the ability to "shape the shift" in envisioning new directions for organizations toward a sustainable enterprise economies in which businesses and jobs join with governments and other institutions in supporting families and communities in harmony with the natural environment and social justice needs. Waddock suggests that "memes" or inspiring images tapping core cultural values are needed for visionary leadership supporting transformational change. While we agree with the importance of systems thinking and ethics in re-visioning change, we believe, following the work of Robert Chambers in Participatory Rural Development and Meredith Minkler in Community Organizing for Health Equity (Minkler, 2012) that collaborative leadership informed by Participatory Research can best inspire and mobilize the shared work of identifying challenges and working toward agreed upon solutions required for large-scale change (George, Baker, Tracey, & Joshi, 2019; Shapiro & Little, 2020).

Complexity, Transdisciplinarity and the Gendered Life Course: Highlighting Work Family Dynamics as Leverage Points Promoting Change

In the United States the integration of women into paid work during the feminist "second wave" of the 1960s to 1970s, coincided with changing economies eroding the male breadwinner's earning of a "family wage". At the same time, these changes in work were accompanied by enduring social ideologies and public policies insisting that caretaking of children and elders along with homemaking remained the private responsibility of individuals and families, falling predominantly on the shoulders of women. Men who seek to increase family time and require workplace flexibility also experience penalties in evaluation and advancement. A growing United States and global comparative literature explores how variations in social policies such as opportunities for flexible scheduling, paid parental leave, convenient affordable child care, and protection of family time from after-hours workplace demands, produce a win–win combination of increased corporate profits and innovation while also enhancing organizational and societal gender equity and family well-being.

Ester reflects on gender complexity and its relevance/impact in time (historical and personal) and space (national and geographic): Born in Cuba during revolutionary times and immigrating as a child to racially segregated South Florida, I have remained inspired by social contracts that help us actualize equality in all spheres of life. In the United States during adolescence, I welcomed feminist and civil rights movements as offering guideposts to a valued life. I began my Clinical Psychology Doctoral studies, in 1974, I was 21 years old and my same-age women cousins were marrying and having children. Like many women of my generation initiating long preparation toward careers, I planned to postpone childbearing for at least a decade. Interested in studying how gender equity could be achieved at the interface of our changing work opportunities and family lives, I was fortunate to study with pioneering feminist sociologist Alice Rossi, who had turned to narrative study of lives to better understand how women and men were negotiating these changing spaces. Alice believed that the biology of reproduction made women vulnerable to remaining fully responsible for the care of infants and young children and wrote a then groundbreaking paper on the biosocial interface of sex roles. She insisted that awareness of these biological realities would allow employers, policy makers, and women with their families to make intentional decisions on behalf of gender equity. Alice's advice in changing gender roles: mothers need to leave babies with their fathers early and often. At the time she was accused of biological reductionism and rejected by feminist academics. Yet her visionary perspective recognizing the impacts of biology on gendered shared development, requiring targeted practices and policy solutions, has been supported by multi-disciplinary analysis. We find in 2020 that radically transformed demographic change resulting in smaller, more isolated seemingly autonomous families with two working adults remain tethered to gendered ideals of women as essential, unpaid caretakers of the vulnerable which includes infants and young children, the disabled, and increasingly the elderly. My own teaching, writing, and practice continue to study how we co-create knowledge toward shared accountability during important shared life course transitions (birth, death, coming of age, education, and workplace) that best sustains conditions allowing collective growth and thriving while supporting wellness as fairness across generational time in the settings where we live and work.

Connecting Personal, Organizational, and Economic Development: Complex Systems Principles Connecting Our Relationships, Environments, and Shared Fates

In better understanding progress and barriers toward achieving gender inclusion and equity in the workplace, we join others in many fields concerned with knowledge for socially accountable, sustainable change. Ester first began to appreciate the importance of Participatory Approaches to Community Economic Development through her work supporting Massachusetts Latinx communities who are the poorest Latinx in the entire United States when compared to White population incomes. Working in Latina/Latin American women's health and rights, she began to read transdisciplinary Organizational Studies connecting individuals to social movements in achieving change, especially in women's health and in education (Shapiro, 2014, 2018). Reading on multi-systemic approaches to workplace gender equity for this chapter, she discovered critical engaged Organizational research emphasizing holistic systems thinking consistent with integrative life course health equity, in publications as varied as the *Journal of Supply Chain Management* (Touboulic, McCarthy, & Matthews, 2020) and *Global Sustainability* (Waddock, 2020). Whatever our own lines of work, we have learned how "just in time" manufacturing driven solely by policies enhancing profit without considering other valued outcomes has become highly, tragically visible during the COVID-19 pandemic. We have witnessed self-amplifying intersections of failed access to Personal Protective Equipment, precarious often underpaid and now dangerous employment for "essential workers" in factories and health care settings alike, and the continuing problem of unpaid caretaking for vulnerable family members falling on the shoulders of women who must work for wages, a second shift of child care and household responsibilities, and a third shift of care for the ill, elderly or disabled that societies fail to support. With Touboulic et al. and many others, we find that complexity science as a tool contributing to valued outcomes must begin with examination of values embedded in our assumptions, toward new imaginaries or collective visions articulating "how the world ought to be". We appreciate that racial, gender, and economic inequalities are interconnected, mutually reinforcing, and specific to the spaces where we live and work, to historical time, and to an evolving life course where we care for each other and sustain shared lives through births, maturation and aging, periods where the vulnerable are cared for and all contribute to an evolving future.

A complex systems approach to social change as it impacts multiple ecologies of the gendered life course identifies gender equity as a "wicked problem" requiring a targeted multi-systemic approach through partnerships identifying valued outcomes, selecting impactful leverage points sensitive to contexts, and accountable to measurable outcomes. This work recognizes the complexity and diversity of our changing ideals as well as changing realities of employment, public policies regarding social, corporate, and individual responsibility, alongside changes in household organizations, intergenerational relationships, and kinship ties. Further, as in adrienne maree brown's text on *Emergent Strategies* in organizing for change toward possible futures (brown, 2017), complex systems teach us that we must practice at the smallest scale the ethics of mutual respect and shared leadership we want to bring into the world on a larger scale. Writing about her work as a community organizer, and now teaching this work in communities and organizations, she describes the transformation of organizations from White heterosexual male dominant to Black Queer women of color organizing highlighting collaboration and co-creation of knowledge and shared actions with accountability in achieving social change.

Striving toward a paradigm shift grounded in complexity sciences we contribute to the conversation on complexity sciences and systems thinking an integrative cultural/developmental life course approach (also see Shapiro & Little, 2020) with the following features:

- **A historically informed, culturally grounded gendered life course perspective** recognizing connections between embodied experiences, societal processes, and health and well-being outcomes without insisting on biological determinism yet recognizing our human desire to care for vulnerable others. We appreciate the universality of interdependence throughout shared human development, even as cultures shape our thinking about these realities differently. We recognize myths of decontextualized individualism as failing to protect the health, well-being, and economic success of our own lives, our families and communities, and our environment. Alongside the Women of Color coalitonal Birth Justice/Reproductive Justice movement, we affirm our human interdependence while recognizing women as people with rights and not as Vessels destined to matter only when contributing to a child's development (Ross & Solinger, 2017).

- **A transdisciplinary approach to frameworks, methods, practices, and outcomes** that begins by questioning binaries and shifting frames to prioritize human complexity, interdependence, consequences, and accountability. Examples: social determinants approaches require that we re-define "growth" and "development" while examining the underlying values as well as what responsibilities are excluded and fall on the shoulders of the most vulnerable.

- **Multi-systemic mapping of barriers and resources** in multiple systems facilitating positive outcomes, and impacts of multifaceted, site specific (i.e., workplace, educational setting, neighborhood) intersecting power inequalities on opportunities, decision making, and outcomes (Pugh, 2017).

- **A global comparative perspective appreciating how work and family roles and responsibilities are defined** and gender equitable flexibility is supported or impeded through cultural beliefs as well as organizational practices and governmental public policies (Ji et al., 2017; Kaufman, 2020).

As suggested by Capra and Luisi (2016), a systems frame of mind and contributions of complexity sciences allow us to ask new questions in new ways, identifying the web of mutually reinforcing vicious circles impeding desired change while identifying the most impactful leverage points disentangling these stabilizing forces and supporting innovative possibilities for increased gender inclusion. This approach allows us to identify solutions affirming the varieties and complexities of gender in work, family, and community life around the world and highlighting shared social and organizational responsibility for collective well-being.

Where to Start Working Toward Gender Inclusion: Leverage Points Identified in the Literature on Workplace Gender Equity

Complexity Sciences allow us to view outcomes as emerging from unexpected, often unpredictable interactions and at times unexpected consequences of interventions. Yet working from these perspectives paradoxically allows us to connect interventions with identified, desired, measurable outcomes, permitting much greater accountability that in turn helps us invest in interventions that make a difference. These approaches help map multi-systemic factors offering impactful leverage points catalyzing measurable change. *Global comparative literatures identify three transformative leverage points:* (1) *Gender-neutral paid family/kinship care leave* when meeting life course challenges of childbearing/adoption and infant care; (2) *Public/private partnerships* providing flexible, predictable employment and institutional supports for early childhood care, schooling, and dependent caretaking needs for workers at all income levels (Thébaud & Halcomb, 2019); (3) *Systems-minded organizational interventions addressing gender stereotyping of work/family decisions* in Human Resources administration and in leadership training for both managers and workers (Chang & Milkman, 2020).

Disentangling Levels of Gendered Work-Place Inequality: Beginning with Institutional and Societal Policies and Responsibilities

Research on workplace gender inequalities as they impact career choices, salaries, promotions, and leadership positions, suggests a primary turning-point can be found in what some term a "motherhood penalty". This penalty is charged to those contributing to childbearing, adoption, early infant care, and organizing the daily needs of a household and its dependent members. Men and women's hopes for gender equitable work for wages and fair caretaking and homemaking responsibilities consistently confront realities of social contracts regarding the individualization and privatization of responsibility for family lives, which are highly variable by country and region. Although societal gender stereotyping imposes workplace expectations tied to traditional masculine and feminine roles, their power is institutionalized by practices of gendered role enactment.

Consistently, women are more likely to be called on to bring coffee, order lunch, or take meeting notes, and more likely penalized for failing to put workplace first by being too involved with their household/family demands. These beliefs and practices translate to fewer promotions and limited advancement into leadership positions. Further, research shows that racialized gender stereotypes are imposed on women in the workplace, where implicit White male norms often label their leadership as too aggressive. These gendered expectations and penalties are intensified for women and men from economically vulnerable, racially targeted, and other marginalized groups, impeding workplace gender equity.

Recent transdisciplinary work on workplace gender inclusion has focused on workplace idealization of specific ideologies regarding masculinity, a culture of overwork, and "masculinity competitions" requiring extreme demonstrations of workplace devotion. Both men and women in the workplace experience these demands that contradict stated values regarding work/family balance. Focusing on parental leave, Kaufman (2020) titled her recent book *Fixing Parental Leave: The Six Month Solution*. Reviewing approaches to parental leave, she argues that offering six months of gender-neutral leave for parents of all genders and backgrounds; requiring that men take parental leave by having it expire if not used so that utilization is equalized; and protecting income and employment for workers who take parental leave, is associated with the best employment and family outcomes. Comparing the United States, United Kingdom, and European Union policies, Kauman finds that the United States offers the worst possible conditions for working families, as no paid parental leave is offered, workers experience minimal protections of their employment if they do not return immediately to work, and health care is offered primarily through employers and will be lost if the worker extends parental leave. Finally, the United States privatizes early child care and child schooling, assuming that workers who need child care will pay for it out of pocket. These are the conditions in the United States that have created a perfect storm in the wake of COVID-19, exposing the burdens on working families and especially on women working precarious jobs with little flexibility that place their own health and that of their families at risk.

FROM TEACHING WOMEN WORKERS COPING SKILLS TO ORGANIZING SYSTEMIC CHANGE TOWARD WORKPLACE GENDER INCLUSION

Gendered stereotyping has been identified as a critical leverage point that can greatly contribute to workplace gender inclusion, when it is thought about from a complex systems perspective. In his compelling book presenting extensive research on his concept of stereotype threat, Whistling Vivaldi, African American Social Psychologist Claude Steele demonstrates how even seemingly slight invocations of widely held negative societal stereotypes (Women fail at math; Black students do poorly on standardized tests; White men can't play basketball) measurably burden on-site performance for those targeted. "Whistling Vivaldi" is among Steele's repertoire of self-presentations (along with wearing a suit) designed as active, performative solutions to the problem of gendered racism in public life. Joan Williams and colleagues at the Center for Work and Family Law similarly describe "savvy" for women in positions of business leadership as requiring careful strategic navigation of multiple, contradictory stereotypes. They recommend carefully designed interventions in the workplace that anticipate and counteract gendered expectations. While unjust assumptions and conditions in the workplace may make these strategic readings of stereotypes necessary for equity and inclusion, Williams, Steele, and others following from this work argue for structural and systemic solutions to the societal conditions within which "stereotype threat" is only among many societal strategies enforcing workplace intersectional/gendered exclusion.

Research on increasing inclusion of women and underrepresented groups in Science and Technology (STEM) studies and careers finds that targeted single-dimension attempts to increase the flow of students and workers through affirmative action, individual self-affirmation, or teacher and employer training to counter implicit bias, are undermined by persistent impacts of gender stereotyping reinforcing multi-systemic practices of exclusion. Schmidt, Ovseiko, Henderson, and Kiparoglou (2020) conducted a systematic evaluation of gender equity strategies used by European University and Medical School programs, whose ability to apply for research funds required demonstrated progress toward specified gender inclusion and leadership outcomes. Successful program strategies operated at the interface of Organizational Culture changes (i.e., workload allocation, scheduling, zero-tolerance for gendered bullying),

Career Development (i.e., mentoring & support with attention to key transitions and to changing needs for work/family flexibility), and Organizational self-monitoring and outcomes analysis. Complexity sciences require interventions grounded in the specific, unique characteristics of local organizations and institutions (i.e., Universities or Medical Schools as compared to Health Care Delivery Systems; European & Canadian context of public minded services rather than US individualization and privatization), at the same time that they appreciate how strategies operate across systems to produce emergent outcomes both intended and unanticipated. Consistent with a gender-sensitive life course approach, they mapped successful interventions in multiple domains that considered the caretaking responsibilities women carry at critical moments in science careers, cultivating role models, and training faculty and administrators in the effects of gender stereotypes. Emu noted that in Japan gender stereotypes continue to be advanced in the media by showing only males as doctors or executives. She appreciates the way models with "mapping" allow both strategic and comprehensive interventions. Ester noted that in the European Union and United Kingdom/Commonwealth nations that are part of the Award and its agreements, application for certain kinds of funding requires certification in achieving a "Silver Award" denoting significant progress toward gender inclusion, requiring not only good intentions but also accountability to successful outcomes. They also noted that in the qualitative interviews, women faculty complained that they conducted the majority of administrative service work required to submit reviews toward the Award. Their meticulous analysis documents how a complex systems framework accounting for dynamics of change and stability helps illuminate and mobilize impactful interventions. However, it is no surprise to readers of this chapter that this study also found women scientists were more likely to carry the heavier administrative burdens required by the laudatory, effective, and time-consuming monitoring and evaluation process. At the University of Massachusetts, at Boston, we have a similar documentation that Women faculty, especially Women of Color, carry higher administrative and mentoring responsibilities (Steele, 2011; Williams & Dempsey, 2018).

The Path Ahead: Education for Possible Futures

As the global pandemic continues, it has precipitated worldwide recognition of our interdependent ailments while identifying opportunities for transformation centered on gender justice and the crucial role of business organizations in contributing to transformative change. Intersectional approaches working from within complexity sciences/complex adaptive systems help us recognize how racism, poverty, and barriers in access to educational and economic opportunities dynamically co-occur with sexism and heterosexism, effects that pile up for both individuals and targeted groups over time. We suggest that complexity sciences, socio-politically informed ecological models that contextualize how we create systems in which some thrive and many suffer, and gender-sensitive life course approaches centered on shared responsibility for the care of the most vulnerable among us, help us appreciate how best to support evolving choreographies of gendered selves in life course time and specific spaces where we live and work. Yet as we show in this chapter, just because a problem is complex, that is, persistent and "wickedly" entangled in ways that protect its enduring stability, seemingly resisting well-intentioned change, does not mean it is insurmountable. We dedicate this chapter to the truly essential work of increasing workplace gender inclusion, as we witnessed a global pandemic of gendered, generational, economic inequalities. We appreciate that seemingly good intentions are easily subverted by barriers and contradictions across multiple systems and no longer good enough. Turning to Complex Systems models for transformational gender inclusion, we renew our commitment to workplace gender equity recognizing our complexities as foundational to sustaining our interdependent lives, dedicating this chapter to knowledge promoting inclusion with accountability to shared values.

Chapter Key Takeaways

- The COVID-19 pandemic with its interruption of "business as usual" has exposed enormous gaps in supports offered to families for care of the most vulnerable and the ways these fall disproportionately on women.
- In the United States, Europe, and around the world, most people of all nationalities, genders, racial and religious backgrounds endorse gender equity as a valued personal and societal goal across multiple domains of their lives and work. Yet while most may endorse gender equity as a social value, we deeply disagree about effective actions implementing its actualization.

- Gender equity remains elusive, what some call an unfinished revolution. Evidence on gender and workplace equity in the United States and internationally consistently finds that women enduringly experience greater workplace inequality, as characterized by lower wages and fewer positions of leadership.
- Global capitalism has intensified values and practices that reinforce workplace gender inequalities.
- The work-place serves an important societal function in defining highly valued and personally cherished identities around highly stereotyped masculine and feminine roles. A masculinized, class-based "work devotion schema" associates male success with long work hours unimpeded by family demands. In contrast, for women, this "work devotion schema" is considered a moral hazard, interfering with the family caretaking focus associated with being a "good woman".
- Multiple disciplines in sociology, public health, environmental sciences, organizational management and leadership, and economics among many others have turned to complexity sciences to better understand the multiple forces that contribute to outcomes. These approaches recognize the interdependence of factors and the unpredictability of interactive effects and unexpected contributions of even seemingly small factors leading to emergent outcomes.
- Research on workplace gender inequalities as they impact career choices, salaries, promotions, and leadership positions, suggests a primary turning-point can be found in what some term a "motherhood penalty". This penalty is charged to those contributing to childbearing, adoption, early infant care, and organizing the daily needs of a household and its dependent members.

REFERENCES

Bell, E., Meriläinen, S., Taylor, S., & Tienari, J. (2019). Time's up! Feminist theory and activism meets organization studies. *Human Relations, 72*(1), 4–22.

Berdahl, J. L., Cooper, M., Glick, P., Livingston, R. W., & Williams, J. C. (2018). Work as a masculinity contest. *Journal of Social Issues, 74*(3), 422–448.

Blair-Loy, M., Hochschild, A., Pugh, A., Williams, J., & Hartmann, H. (2015). Stability and transformation in gender, work, and family: Insights from the second shift for the next quarter century. *Community, Work & Family, 18*(4), 435–454.

Brandth, B., Halrynjo, S., & Kvande, E. (Eds.). (2017). *Work-family dynamics: Competing logics of regulation, economy and morals.* New York: Taylor & Francis.

brown, a. m. (2017). *Emergent strategy: Shaping change, changing worlds.* Chico, CA: AK Press.

Capra, F., & Luisi, P. (2016). *The systems way of life: A unifying vision.* Cambridge: Cambridge University Press.

Catalyst. (2020). *COVID-19: Women, equity and inclusion in the future of work.* Report retrieved from https://www.catalyst.org/wp-content/uploads/2020/05/Covid_19_Women_Equity_Inclusion_Future_of_Work.pdf.

Chang, E. H., & Milkman, K. L. (2020). Improving decisions that affect gender equality in the workplace. *Organizational Dynamics, 49*(1), 100709.

Cooper, M. (2017). *Family values: Between neoliberalism and the new social conservatism.* Cambridge: MIT Press.

Doner, M. (2019). Calling for a gender-sensitive approach to karoshi and overwork disorders in Japan. *Global Health: Annual Review, 1*(4).

England, P., Levine, A., & Mishel, E. (2020). Progress toward gender equality in the United States has slowed or stalled. *Proceedings of the National Academy of Sciences, 117*(13), 6990–6997.

Enns, C. Z. (2008). Toward a complexity paradigm for understanding gender role conflict. *The Counseling Psychologist, 36*(3), 446–454.

Foreign Policy Analytics. (2020). *Women as levers of change: Unleashing the power of women to transform male-dominated industries.* Foreign Policy Analytics, Special Report.

George, G., Baker, T., Tracey, P., & Joshi, H. (2019). Inclusion and innovation: A call to action. In *Handbook of inclusive innovation.* Cheltenham: Edward Elgar Publishing.

Gerson, K. (2017). The logics of work, care and gender change in the new economy. In B. Brandth et al. (Eds.), *Work–family dynamics: Competing logics of regulation, economy and morals* (Vol. 2). Abingdon: Routledge.

Hurtado, S., Alvarez, C. L., Guillermo-Wann, C., Cuellar, M., & Arellano, L. (2012). A model for diverse learning environments. In *Higher education: Handbook of theory and research* (pp. 41–122). Cham: Springer.

Ji, Y., Wu, X., Sun, S., & He, G. (2017). Unequal care, unequal work: Toward a more comprehensive understanding of gender inequality in post-reform urban China. *Sex Roles, 77*(11–12), 765–778.

Jones, C. P. (2000). Levels of racism: A theoretic framework and a gardener's tale. *American Journal of Public Health, 90*(8), 1212–1217.

Jones, C. P. (2014). *Levels of racism: A ted talk at Emory University.* Retrieved from You Tube: https://www.youtube.com/watch?v=GNhcY6fTyBM.

Kalpazidou Schmidt, E., Ovseiko, P. V., Henderson, L. R., & Kiparoglou, V. (2020). Understanding the Athena SWAN award scheme for gender equality as a complex social intervention in a complex system: Analysis of Silver award action plans in a comparative European perspective. *Health Research Policy and Systems, 18*(1), 1–21.

Kato, E., Lee, C., Martin, T., & Shapiro, E. (2020). *Resources for student educational success and wellness on an urban commuter college campus: Organizational and student-centered perspectives.* Poster presented at the Undergraduate Research Conference, College of Liberal Arts, University of Massachusetts, Boston. Manuscript in preparation.

Kaufman, G. (2020). *Fixing parental leave: The six month solution.* New York: NYU Press.

Le, H., Newman, A., Menzies, J., Zheng, C., & Fermelis, J. (2020). Work–life balance in Asia: A systematic review. *Human Resource Management Review, 30*, 100766.

Leslie, L. M., King, E. B., & Clair, J. A. (2019). Work-life ideologies: The contextual basis and consequences of beliefs about work and life. *Academy of Management Review, 44*(1), 72–98.

Madhusoodanan, J. (2018). What will it take to fix work-life balance? *Knowable Magazine (From Annual Reviews).* https://www.knowablemagazine.org/art icle/society/2018/what-will-it-take-fix-work-life-balance.

Meadows, D. H. (1999). *Leverage points: Places to intervene in a system.* The Donella Meadows Archive, Academy for Systems Change. Retrieved from: https://donellameadows.org/archives/leverage-points-places-to-interv ene-in-a-system/.

Minkler, M. (Ed.). (2012). *Community organizing and community building for health and welfare.* Rutgers University Press.

Mlambo-Ngcuka, P., & Dalli, H. (2020). *Op-ed: How COVID-19 can bring gender justice.* United Nations Women. Retrieved from: https://www.unw omen.org/en/news/stories/2020/7/op-ed-joint-how-covid-19-can-bring-gender-justice.

Moen, P. (Ed.). (2017). Redesigning careers and care for the twenty-first century. Special Issue, *Community, Work & Family, 20*(5), 497–499 (Introduction).

Pew Global. (2020). *Worldwide optimism about future of gender equality, even as many see advantages for men.* Retrieved online: https://www.pewresearch. org/global/2020/04/30/worldwide-optimism-about-future-of-genderequ ality-even-as-many-see-advantages-for-men/.

Power, K. (2020). The COVID-19 pandemic has increased the care burden of women and families. *Sustainability: Science, Practice and Policy, 16*(1), 67–73.

Pugh, A. (Ed.). (2017). *Beyond the cubicle: Job insecurity, intimacy and the flexible self.* Oxford: Oxford University Press.

Ross, L., & Solinger, R. (2017). *Reproductive justice: An introduction* (Vol. 1). Oakland: University of California Press.

Schmidt, E. K., Ovseiko, P. V., Henderson, L. R., & Kiparoglou, V. (2020). Understanding the Athena SWAN award scheme for gender equality as a complex social intervention in a complex system: Analysis of Silver award action plans in a comparative European perspective. *Health Research Policy and Systems, 18*(1), 1–21.

Shapiro, E. (2018). Transforming development through just communities: A life-long journey of inquiry. In L. Comas-Diaz & C. Vasquez (Eds.), *Latina psychologists: Thriving in the cultural borderlands*. New York: Routledge.

Shapiro, E. (2020). Liberation psychology, creativity, and arts-based activism and artivism: Culturally meaningful methods connecting personal development and social change. In E. Torres Rivera & L. Comas-Diaz (Eds.), *Liberation psychology: Theory, method, practice, and social justice*. Washington, DC: American Psychological Association Press.

Shapiro, E. R. (2014). Translating Latin American/US Latina frameworks and methods in gender and health equity: Linking women's health education and participatory social change. *International Quarterly of Community Health Education, 34,* 19–36.

Shapiro, E., Andino Valdez, F., Bailey, Y., Furtado, G., Lamothe, D., Mohammad, K., & Wood, N. (2018). Teaching health and human rights in a psychology capstone: Cultivating connections between rights, personal wellness, and social justice. In E. Choudhury & R. Srikanth (Eds.), *Interdisciplinary approaches to human rights* (pp. 312–330). New York, NY: Routledge.

Shapiro, E. R., & Little, T. V. (2020). Inclusive leadership development through Participatory Inquiry: Cultivating Cultural Humility. In J. Margues (Ed.), *The Routledge companion to inclusive leadership*. Routledge.

Slaughter, A. M. (2015). *Unfinished business: Women men work family*. New York: Simon and Schuster.

Stamarski, C. S., & Son Hing, L. S. (2015). Gender inequalities in the workplace: The effects of organizational structures, processes, practices, and decision makers' sexism. *Frontiers in Psychology, 6,* 1400.

Steele, C. M. (2011). *Whistling Vivaldi: And other clues to how stereotypes affect us (issues of our time)*. New York: W. W. Norton.

Swinth, K. (2019). *Feminism's forgotten fight: The unfinished struggle for work and family*. Cambridge: Harvard University Press.

Takahashi, M. (2019). Sociomedical problems of overwork-related deaths and disorders in Japan. *Journal of Occupational Health, 61*(4), 269–277.

Thébaud, S., & Halcomb, L. (2019). One step forward? Advances and setbacks on the path toward gender equality in families and work. *Sociology Compass, 13*(6), e12700.

Touboulic, A., McCarthy, L., & Matthews, L. (2020). Re-imagining supply chain challenges through critical engaged research. *Journal of Supply Chain Management, 56*(2), 36–51.

Tyler, M. (2019). Reassembling difference? Rethinking inclusion through/as embodied ethics. *Human Relations, 72*(1), 48–68.

Waddock, S. (2020). Achieving sustainability requires systemic business transformation. *Global Sustainability, 3*(e12), 1–12.

Waddock, S. (2018). Shaping the shift: Shamanic leadership, memes, and transformation. *Journal of Business Ethics, 155*(4), 931–939.

Waddock, S., Meszoely, G. M., Waddell, S., & Dentoni, D. (2015). The complexity of wicked problems in large scale change. *Journal of Organizational Change Management, 28*, 993–1012.

Walby, S. (2007). Complexity theory, systems theory, and multiple intersecting social inequalities. *Philosophy of the Social Sciences, 37*(4), 449–470.

Williams, J. C. (2020). *Reports and editorials on worklife flexibility, business outcomes and worker well-being.* Center for WorkLife Law. https://worklifelaw.org/.

Williams, J. C., Berdahl, J. L., & Vandello, J. A. (2016). Beyond work-life "integration". *Annual Review of Psychology, 67*, 515–539.

Williams, J. C., & Dempsey, R. (2018). *What works for women at work: Four patterns working women need to know.* New York: NYU Press.

Yosso, T. J., & Burciaga, R. (2016). *Reclaiming our histories, recovering community cultural wealth.* Center for Critical Race Studies at UCLA Research Brief, 5.

CHAPTER 23

Men, Women, and Work–Life Balance: Then, Now, and in the Future

Candy Williams

WORK–LIFE BALANCE VS. WORK–LIFE INTEGRATION

What do you think of when you hear the term work–life balance? Do you think of scales equally balanced, or do you think of equal time at work and equal time at home? What do you think of when you hear the term work–life integration? Do you think about blending work time with personal time, or do you think of alternate work schedules?

Work–life balance and work–life integration are defined differently by different people.

Work–life balance is defined as the amount of time you spend doing your job compared to the amount of time you spend with your family and doing things that you enjoy (Cambridge Dictionary). Work–life integration is defined as harmonizing work experiences with other areas of life.

Work–life balance and work–life integration are terms often used in today's workplace. Work–life integration occurs when a leader merges personal activities with work during the workday (Barootes, 2015). In an

C. Williams (✉)
Williams Executive Leadership Development LLC, Los Angels, CA, USA

© The Author(s), under exclusive license to Springer Nature Switzerland AG 2021
J. Marques (ed.), *Exploring Gender at Work*,
https://doi.org/10.1007/978-3-030-64319-5_23

453

INC article, Jacob Morgan suggests that as the business moves forward, there is a movement toward work–life integration and away from work–life balance. These two topics affect men and women in the working world. While there are many articles about women and how they balance home and work life very often men are forgotten. In more traditional roles, men went out for work, and women stayed home to care for the home and children. In today's culture, there are both men and women are in the workplace, and in some households, men are more involved in caring for children and others in the home (Williams, 2019). In many U.S. cities, it is an economic necessity for both men and women to work.

In the Past

Over the years, the world of work has evolved and developed. During the industrial revolution, many people worked long hours in locations where there were poor working conditions. Men, women, and children worked at that time. The long hours took a toll on workers' health and family life. During the 1940s reform workers advocated for fewer work hours. During the 1940s to 1960s, the working generations were exposed to many hardships at a young age. For many, it was hard to make a living. Fair labor practices allowed for more flexibility with work hours and established the 40-h workweek. This allowed workers more time off for workers to rest and have healthier lifestyles. Work–life balance was introduced as a way to allow more flexibility for working women. During the women's liberation movement, women advocated for flexibility in work schedules and for maternity leave. The children of baby boomers, Gen Xers (born around 1961 to 1980), grew up seeing parents work long hours. As a result of this generation, many put more emphasis on creating work–life balance in their own lives. Many take advantage of leave flexibility programs. Millennials (Born between 1981 and 2000) move toward employers that will help their career development support the lifestyle that they have created (Gambles, Lewis, & Rapoport, 2006).

Work–life balance has emerged as a way of talking about the challenges of combining paid work and other parts of life. The language originated in the U.S. and the U.K. In the past; there was a clearer division between work and home life. And employee would go to work and a set time and leave at a set time. Once the work shift was over, it was time to focus on family or other activities. There was a clear distinction. In today's work world, the lines are more blurred. Today there are telework options, and some companies offer flexibility with schedules.

Work–Life Balance Today

Today telework, working offsite, hoteling, and flexible work schedules allow workers more time to take care of personal needs and family needs. Teleworking is good for the environment in that it cuts down on traffic. As employers recruit, many are offering hiring incentives, which include options to promote health and wellness long with work–life balance/integration options. Work–life balance helps contribute to a healthy work environment. Maintaining a work–life balance helps to reduce stress and helps prevent burnout at work. Chronic stress is one of the most common health issues in the workplace. Stress can lead to depression, anxiety, insomnia, and other health issues (Kohll 2018). If stress continues for an extended period of time, it may lead to burnout.

In today's workplace, work–life balance is often managed by managing time. With some employers, staff can make adjustments in their work schedules, for example, instead of working 8 to 5 instead work 7 to 4 or 9 to 6. Having this flexibility is a plus for many employees (Joyner, 2012). However, some don't find the shifting of time as beneficial if the employee is still not setting boundaries around work hours. They are continuing to check emails and other work tasks instead of focusing on the family while at home can lead to other stress or health issues. Even with flex schedules, the lines may be blurred without a clear boundary between work and home life. Others in today's workplace find that work–life integration is a more realistic option as it allows employees to integrate work with the home in a more seamless way. The employee has to be mindful of turning off and setting boundaries as needed at home. At the end of the day, the employee's ability to maintain energy levels and control time and workflow is what is important.

Work–Life Balance for Men

With more dual-income families, men are called upon to be more involved in day-to-day care for children. Men have to take children to school, cook meals, and attend parent meetings. They have to stay home with sick children and, in some cases, take off work for kid's medical appointments. There has been limited research on men and work–life balance.

Men are seen as the primary income earner, and there is a stigma when men take off for children. Men were traditionally seen as the primary income earners, and women have seen more as caregivers (Weber & Cissna-Heath, 2016). There was a time in the past when it was the norm for a man to expect that his wife would give up her career to take care of children (Kolhatar, 2013). In today's world, many men marry women who have careers. Men have traditionally had more flexibility for working outside of the home while their wives cared for children.

Today many men are more involved. In some cases, men are the primary person in the household for picking children up from school or other caregiving activities. Men sometime face stigma from their peers when they function in caregiving roles. Men have traditionally had more flexibility to advance in their careers because they have the flexibility of time to work long hours or travel as needed while their wife or partner cared for children. There are some employers who may have a stigma about men or women with children because there is an assumption that they may not be as available as a single person. In the past and even in some cases today, men and women are passed over for promotions or career advancement opportunities because their employer assumes they are not going to be fully engaged and present for work or work-related travel. Some working fathers were not able to attend their children's sports activities, and school plays and later took back at this time with regret.

Men in certain fields experience extra challenges. In some leadership roles, men are expected to allow their wives or partners to help with children and household help. In a Pew study from 2013 about how mothers and fathers spend their time, it was noted that 50% of working fathers and 56% of working mothers found it difficult to balance work and family while working. Both men and women preferred to be home with children but needed to work for income. It's noted that men spend more time with their children now than they did in prior generations, but most employers have not adjusted to the shift (Kolhatkar, 2013). Many men in today's workforce want to be more involved as fathers. Some men are working toward changing the work culture in companies around work–life balance and work–life integration. A group of men at Deloitte consulting group started a support group for men, which aims to help working fathers. They help each other to navigate balancing family life and work. It is important to note the men need work–life balance too.

Work–Life Balance for Women

In prior generations, men were expected to provide things for the family, such as food, clothing, shelter, and education. The expectation was that he be a good provider. He was the leader of the family (Green, 2016). For the woman, the expectation was more complicated. She was expected to manage and make the best of her husband's salary, prepare the meals, the washing, making, and the mending of the clothes, furnishing and cleaning the house, counsel the children as well as make some sort of entertainment available for the family (Chinn, 1991). Women were expected to be home and do housework. As the domestic industry changed, more opportunities became available for women to work outside of the home, specifically at the turn of the century with the advent of World War I. As the workforce changed during the nineteenth and twentieth centuries, so did women's involvement in the workforce. Women began working outside of the home as well as taking leadership roles. This trend continued to increase as more women opted to work outside of the home during the 1950s. Although the increase in women's employment slowed in the 1990s, women now constitute 46% of all full-time and part-time workers, somewhat short of the 51% share of the population (Eagly & Carli, 2007). Women have begun to outpace men in educational attainment. Women now have a substantial advantage over men earning more degrees and pursuing advanced degrees.

According to the U.S. Census Bureau (Bauman, 2016), women were more likely to complete their education than their mother's grandmothers and are more educated than men in general. Women's share of Bachelor degrees increased in the twentieth century until the immediate post-world war II period when large numbers of war veterans entered the universities. After 1950, women's share of bachelor degrees rose rapidly and passed the 50% mark in 1981–1982, according to the census bureau (Eagly & Carli, 2007). In the 1950s, there was an increase in the number of working mothers in the workforce (Collins, 2009). Today almost half of the workforce are dual-earning couples. Increases in the cost of living often require that both people work.

Over the years, women who traditionally may have been focused on matters related to taking care of family and home now have to care for the home while also performing well at work. The term working mother came about during the 1970s. The term work–life balance came about during the 1960s. It was during this time that studies around women changing roles at home and in the workplace were initiated. Many women had to find child care or take children to school so they could work outside of the house. At the workday, women faced helping children with homework, preparing meals, and household duties. Work–life balance involves managing both, work and life.

Work–Life Balance in the Future

Many employers are just starting to explore more flexible workplace. Work–life balance is more commonly known; however, work–life integration is started to be a more accepted term. Work–life integration allows for more of an individual approach to work and life satisfaction. While much progress has been made in the area, many employers still have room for growth in this area. Job satisfaction today is often tied to flexibility in the workplace. Satisfaction and happiness in the workplace may vary from person to person. Technology has opened more opportunities for working remotely. Having the ability to work anywhere is seen as a plus by many workers. Many employers are offering telework programs in the private and public sectors. Other employers are offering flexibility in work schedules. Alternate work schedules allow employees more time to take care of personal and family needs. Companies that are open and committed to supporting staff with work–life balance can cut down on absenteeism and help save on other costs.

Work–life balance is not about dividing your hours evenly throughout the day but more about having the flexibility to get things done in your personal and professional life while still having the energy to enjoy a personal life (Sanfilippo 2020). In today's mobile workforce, more professionals are turning from the concept of work–life balance to the concepts of work–life integration, where work and life are paired together, thanks to technology. It is to the advantage of employers to support flexible work locations as it can contribute to more productivity and greater personal satisfaction (Douglas, 2014). Being in a standard office does not indicate productivity. Workers can be most creative and productive while working in a different setting or on a conference call anywhere around the world.

While some employers may see a strong work ethic as coming in early or working late, it very often leads to problems. Work fatigue very often leads to being less effective and efficient. Work fatigue often leads back to being less productive and efficient (Douglas). Younger generations are demanding more flexibility in the workplace. They may be more concerned with having projects work around their schedules and may request more flexibility with their time. Flexible work settings have been showing decreased stress and higher levels of job satisfaction. When employees are more comfortable, they are more productive. There are still different theories about work–life balance and work–life integration. When creating policies, employers must be mindful and fair to coworkers who need work–life balance but don't have family obligations. Staff who are not married with children also need to be included in work–life balance-related policies.

Key Takeaways

As one sector of the workforce gets older and the amount of younger workers increases, business leaders should consider being more open to employees who have roles as caregivers as well as a primary income earner. A business leader should learn to find the value in what employees do. Just because someone works 80 hours per week does not make them a better employee. A man or woman who is striving for a happier and more balanced life may be more comfortable and productive if they are allowed the flexibility to attend their child's school play or drive their child to school. Leaders in business should judge employees on results and not just how many hours they work as long as they perform well. As a society, we need to move away from the stigma of asking for flexibility in work hours. Both caregiver roles and income earner roles are important, and the components and functions of those roles help to make a good leader (Baldelomar, 2016).

As dual family income earners increase and younger workers enter the workforce, more flexibility in work–life balance and work–life integration may be expected.

As this chapter is being written, the world is dealing with the COVID-19 Pandemic. Daily life and work have been affected. Suddenly Jobs have been lost, schools are closed and due to shelter in place orders school children are now home with parents who are off work or who are teleworking. Many families are dealing with online school requirements and zoom meetings for work. This requires careful time management and coordination for work and family.

Real change won't happen until there is a cultural change that involves values that prioritize family, health, and well-being. Employers can help with this by offering flexible schedules and allowing telework in any location. Employers can also help by providing resources to employees who may need help managing work tasks. It should be noted that there continues to be disagreement among professions and among scholars about work–life balance and work–life integration. As a society, policy, technology, work, and life in general advance, work–life balance, and work–life integration will continue to change.

COVID-19 and Work–Life Balance/Work–Life Integration

At the time of writing this chapter, we are experiencing the pandemic of COVID-19. As a result, there have been many changes around the world. There have been a large number of deaths, business closures, job losses, school closures, and overall changes in our way of life. There are new expectations, such as wearing masks and practicing social distancing. In an effort to stop the spread of a virus, governments required that people stay home and shelter in place. Only essential workers are allowed to work. There has been a great effect on employees who have families to care for. During this time, children are out of school. Many K-12 and University students have now been forced to take their classes online. As a result, parents have to help children with school work and home-work. They have to make sure that their children are taking care of classes online and completing their assignments. They have to balance this while doing their own work at home. Essential workers have to make other arrangements for child care while their children are out of school. This has had a significant effect on many families. Some parents have the flexibility to work from home, while others do not. Some parents are essential workers, and some have lost their jobs due to COVID-19 related business closures. The situations mentioned above are examples of work–life integration. The events around COVID-19 have lead many organizations revamp or to move forward with their telework options to be more flexible with staff work schedules. Moving forward, as the work slowly starts to reopen, work–life integration is being considered in many companies. When employees feel that they have more control over their time in work and in-home life, they tend to feel they have more control over their stress levels and feel more motivated and productive at work. There are still different theories about work–life balance and work–life integration. Employees who telework also need to be aware of monitoring time on virtual meetings and phone calls. It is important to take breaks and get up from the desk to move around.

23 MEN, WOMEN, AND WORK–LIFE BALANCE: THEN ...   461

TIPS FOR WORK–LIFE BALANCE AND WORK–LIFE INTEGRATION

Don't Aim for Perfection

Instead, work on what is realistic for your situation. This may take time to develop and to see what will work. This may require different approaches and assessing what works for you. Sometimes you may have to work late, or you may not stick to the exact schedule. It's ok. Just make adjustments as needed. As life happens, you may need to go in early or work late. Workaround what is needed at the moment and move forward.

Limit Time on Social Media

Employees need downtime to help recharge and reset. Downtime is needed to help with productivity. Breaks are needed away from work and checking emails. Social media can be very time consuming and maybe a distraction from rest and family time. Set the alarm and limit your time. Only check emails and return phone calls at a certain time of the day. Try to minimize activities that waste your time and limit them to the end of your day.

Vacations or Time off Are Important for Health

Long hours may ultimately lead to burnout or affect health in a negative way. It's important for your body and mind to unplug from work. This allows your body to reenergize so that you have more energy and work or at home. Vacations are good for your health, your heart health, and your overall wellness and well-being. Whether you take time off alone or with the family taking the mental break helps. If you are working on a budget, there are a number of creative things that can be done at home to create a relaxing atmosphere at home. The key is just taking the time to relax.

Self-Care for Leaders

In a recent study about self-care for leaders, some suggestions were noted that are part of work–life balance. Self-care is an important step to advance productivity, improve psychological health, and decrease exhaustion among business owners. Effective suggestions are integrating rest, relaxation, and restorative practices that promote self-care, remain fundamental for leaders. These are tools that could assist small-business owners with work–life balance, enhanced professional performance, and positive work outcomes. Self-care helps decrease stress and anxiety. Small-business owners and others in leadership roles should make time for physical exercise, meditating before critical decisions, unwinding from stressful encounters, and even turning their cell phones and email notifications off for even thirty minutes. This would be a progressive step in decreasing the stress in order to recharge the mind (Ryce & Harrell, 2018).

Plan Ahead

Set goals for projects that motivate or are a priority for you. Arrange your workday so that it may be as productive as possible. Block off certain times for checking email and phone messages. Checking email can waste time affect productivity.

Taking time to make a plan ahead of time and setting a plan that includes a time cushion can be helpful. Gage the time of day that you have the most energy and do tasks that require more energy at that time.

Take the Phone Out of the Bedroom at Night

Turning off the cell phone at night can help contribute to more restful sleep. Use a standard alarm clock rather than a cell phone alarm. Use the first hour of the morning for reflection, exercise, or other activities to start the morning before turning on the cell phone. Take time to think about your day and how well you want the day to go. Taking this step helps to set boundaries so that you can rest.

Wake Up and Start the Day Early

Waking up and starting the day early allows you to start the day in a more productive way. Though it may be tempting, don't just lay there, get up and start moving. Getting up and getting the day started can put you on the path to be more productive and make the best use of your time and energy. Starting the day an hour earlier can allow you extra uninterrupted time to focus on self-care.

Rest

Many people take sleep and rest for granted. A good night's sleep is very important and good for your health. Rest reduces stress. Rest breaks and lunch breaks are required by labor laws and needed during the workday and support employees' health. Good quality sleep can help to boost your immune system and improve your energy levels. Good quality sleep can help with mental health, and it even helps with weight management. Take breaks. Don't work through your breaks. Take time to relax and decompress.

Be Present with the Activities You Are Doing

Focus your time and attention on one task at a time. Thoroughly enjoy and engage in the moment and focus on the experience. Being present allows you to be at peace and to acknowledge your feelings. It gives you time to reflect and honor how you feel. This can help with focus and clarify in life overall.

Communicate with the Employer

Open communication with employers about individual needs for family or medical matters is important. The human resources department staff may be able to provide information about leave options and schedules. There may be some differences in flexibility between public and private sector employers and what is allowed. Check resources for the employee assistance program and see what options are available.

Employers can help with work–life balance by initiating policies and procedures that allow employees flexibility.

Exercise, Proper Health, and Nutrition

As part of a work–life balance routine, it is important to incorporate proper exercise and nutrition. Some prefer to exercise before work, and some prefer after work. Taking a walk during lunchtime is also an option. The key is making sure to get up and move around. Proper nutrition is good for overall health and helps to maintain needed energy levels. Planning and preparing meals in advance can be helpful when it comes to making healthier food choices if you pack your lunch, you are less tempted to stop at the hamburger place.

Prepare the Night Before for Work the Next Day

Pick out clothes for work the night before. Making these choices the night before saves time in the morning. Take care of laundry or ironing ahead of time so that clothes are ready to go when needed. If you have children or a partner in caring for and you need help, make it a family activity and ask for help.

Maintain a Clean, Clutter-Free Workspace and Home

If your space and environment are clear, it helps to clear your mind. When you are working on a project and feeling stuck, try taking a 10 minutes break and just clean up and toss items that are no longer needed. When you return work, the energy may feel lighter and more able to focus.

Manage Your Time and Make a Plan

Develop a list and add time slots to help with task organization for the day. Don't get discouraged if you don't meet each item exactly on time. Allow a time cushion in between tasks as needed. Getting tasks and thoughts organized can help you to complete the task during the day. Having a written plan allows you to check off a task that is completed.

Consider Working with a Personal Development or Life Coach

Coaches help with achievement of goals. Personal development coaches provide training guidance on goal development and steps needed to achieve goals. As the client it would be up to you to follow up on what the coach recommends. There are also coaches available for the workplace to help leaders and teams to reach their goals within a company.

Employers Can Offer Access to Exercise

Some employers have exercise facilities onsite while others help pay for gym membership—yoga, meditation classes, and other health and wellness programs. Team exercise and fitness challenges are some activities that are being used by some companies to help encourage staff to stay with their company.

Employers and Childcare Options

Some larger companies offer childcare facilities onsite. If your employer offers, child care considers exploring this option or other options that are close to your employer. Talk with the human resources representative at your company to see what options are available to alternate work schedules or family leave as needed.

Telework Options

Today's technology allows telework and other remote work opportunities. If teleworking, it is important to make sure your equipment is up to date and that you have access to phones and video conferencing if needed. If you need a quiet workspace, make arrangements in advance to prepare. Telework may be done in different locations as long as the internet is available. The use of cell phones is also an option that many employers are using.

Employers Can Ask Employees What They Needed/engage Employees

Employers can check in with staff for ideas on what they need to increase more productivity or what they need to thrive in their work setting. Employees can share their ideas for morale-building events or activities. Employers can incorporate healthy habits into daily activities. Physical and mental health are needed for a healthy life at home and at work. It is important to have regular health checkups as well to help maintain good health.

Avoid Toxic Work Environments

Do work that you love. Doing a job that you don't like can be stressful. Work should not be draining. You need to feel motivated to come to work. Being unhappy at work can lead to unhappiness at home and personal life as well. While we may all have moments at work that we dislike, it is essential to find aspects of the job that you do like and focus on that. Whatever task it is that you perform, try to prepare for it mentally and make the workflow for you. If it's a job that you just feel you can no longer do, then start seeking employment in a setting that works better for you. In order to make a change in this area, you must start submitting resumes and job applications.

Make Time for Friends and Family

Set boundaries for the time that work is done at home. Let coworkers know to call or not to expect a response to calls or emails after a particular time. Ensure your team is aware of time boundaries so that you can have a separation between work and home life when needed. Don't beat yourself up if sometimes you have to work late to complete a project. Just make sure that you don't have to work late every day.

CONCLUSION

Work–life balance and work–life integration are useful tools for maintaining a healthy life experience in the workplace and at home. At the end of the day, each individual has to select the path that is best for them. It may mean using both strategies. As time moves forward and technology and work cultures change, there may be other options in the future. With Covid-19 our way of working is being challenges. It is essential to make the best of and enjoy the time and space you are in right now. Seek resources and tools that work for you and your family. As men and women, you have the power to choose the approach that works best for you to have a well balanced or well-integrated life. Take the time to reflect and take action on the path that works best for you.

CHAPTER TAKEAWAYS

- Work–life balance and work–life integration are terms often used in today's workplace. These two topics affect men and women in the working world.
- With more dual-income families, men are called upon to be more involved in day-to-day care for children. Today many men are more involved. Men sometime face stigma from their peers when they function in caregiving roles.

- Over the years, women who traditionally may have been focused on matters related to taking care of family and home now have to care for the home while also performing well at work.
- Many employers are just starting to explore more flexible workplace. Work–life balance is more commonly known; however, work–life integration is started to be a more accepted term. Work–life integration allows for more of an individual approach to work and life satisfaction.
- Real change won't happen until there is a cultural change that involves values that prioritize family, health, and well-being. Employers can help with this by offering flexible schedules and allowing telework in any location.

REFERENCES

Baldelomar, R. (2016, October). How men, business leaders and government can make work-life balance a reality. *Forbes.* https://www.forbes.com/sites/raquelbaldelomar/2016/10/30/how-men-business-leaders-and-government-can-make-work-life-balance-a-reality/#3198f9c844b6.

Barootes, B. (2015). *Ted talk: Switched: Work-life balance to work-life integration.*

Bauman, K. (2016). Shift toward greater educational attainment for women began 20 years ago. *United State Census Bureau Blogs.* Retrieved from https://www.census.gov/newsroom/blogs/random-samplings/2016/03/shift-toward-greater-educational-attainment-for-women-began-20-years-ago.html.

Chinn, C. (1991). A hidden matriarchy among urban poor of England 1880–1939. *Labor History Review, 56*(3), 9–10. Retrieved from https://connection.ebscohost.com/c/articles/5838061/hidden-matriarchy-among-urban-poor-england-1880-1939.

Collins, G. (2009). *When everything changed: The amazing journey of American women from 1960 to the present* (1 st ed.) New York, NY: Little, Brown.

Douglas, D. (2014). Why work-life integration Trumps work-life integration. https://www.fastcompany.com/3030120/why-work-life-integration-trumps-work-life-balance.

Eagly, A., & Carli, L. (2007). *Through the labyrinth: The truth about how women become leaders.* Boston, MA: Harvard Business Review Press.

Gambles, R., Lewis, S., & Rapoport, R. (2006). *The myth of work-life balance: The challenge of our time for men, women, and societies* (p. 34). Wiley. https://doi.org/10.1002/9780470713266.

Green, A. (2016). *Women in nonprofit leadership: Strategies for work-life balance.* New Castle: New Cambridge Scholars Publishing.

https://dictionary.cambridge.org/us/dictionary/english/work-life-balance.

Joyner, J. (2012, June 26). Why men can't have it all. *The Atlantic.*

Kohll, A. (2018, March 27). The evolving definition of work-life balance. *Forbes.* https://www.forbes.com/sites/alankohll/2018/03/27/the-evolving-definition-of-work-life-balance/#37f53af29ed3.

Kolhatar, S. (2013, May). Men are people too .... *Bloomberg.*

Morgan, J. Inc, https://www.inc.com/jacob-morgan/work-life-balance-is-becoming-work-life-integration.html.

Pew Research Center. (2013, March). *How mothers and fathers spend their time.* https://www.pewsocialtrends.org/2013/03/14/chapter-4-how-mothers-and-fathers-spend-their-time/.

Ryce, S., & Harrell, S. P. (2018). *Self-care for leaders: Cultivating extraordinary functioning & psychological well-being; a quantitative study examining burnout and self-care practices of small-business owners.* Pepperdine University.

Sanfilippo, M. (2020, March 3). *How to improve your work-life balance today.* https://www.businessnewsdaily.com/5244-improve-work-life-balance-today.html.

Weber, M. J., & Cissna-Heath, K. (Eds.). (2016). *Women in leadership and work-family integration.*

https://www.kumanu.com/defining-work-life-balance-its-history-and-future/

Williams, C. (2019). *Best practices of women leaders in the public sector.* Pepperdine University. https://digitalcommons.pepperdine.edu/etd/1118.

INDEX